[redacted]

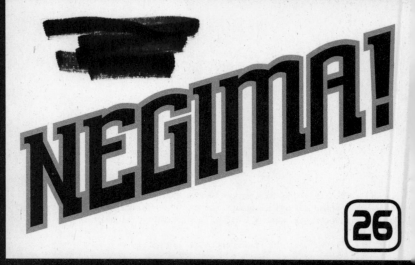

NEGIMA!

26

Ken Akamatsu

TRANSLATED AND ADAPTED BY
Alethea Nibley and Athena Nibley

LETTERING AND RETOUCH BY
Steve Palmer

[redacted]

DEL REY

BALLANTINE BOOKS • NEW YORK

A Del Rey Manga/Kodansha Trade Paperback Original

Negima! volume 26 copyright © 2009 Ken Akamatsu
English translation copyright © 2010 Ken Akamatsu

Published in the United States by Del Rey, an imprint of The Random House Publishing Group, a division of Random House, Inc., New York.

DEL REY is a registered trademark and the Del Rey colophon is a trademark of Random House, Inc.

Publication rights arranged through Kodansha Ltd.

First published in Japan in 2009 by Kodansha Ltd., Tokyo

ISBN 978-0-345-52111-8

Printed in the United States of America

www.delreymanga.com

9 8 7 6 5 4 3 2 1

Translators/adapters: Alethea Nibley and Athena Nibley
Lettering and retouch: Steve Palmer

Honorifics Explained

Throughout the Del Rey Manga books, you will find Japanese honorifics left intact in the translations. For those not familiar with how the Japanese use honorifics and, more important, how they differ from American honorifics, we present this brief overview.

Politeness has always been a critical facet of Japanese culture. Ever since the feudal era, when Japan was a highly stratified society, use of honorifics—which can be defined as polite speech that indicates relationship or status—has played an essential role in the Japanese language. When addressing someone in Japanese, an honorific usually takes the form of a suffix attached to one's name (example: "Asuna-san"), is used as a title at the end of one's name, or appears in place of the name itself (example: "Negi-sensei," or simply "Sensei!").

Honorifics can be expressions of respect or endearment. In the context of manga and anime, honorifics give insight into the nature of the relationship between characters. Many English translations leave out these important honorifics and therefore distort the feel of the original Japanese. Because Japanese honorifics contain nuances that English honorifics lack, it is our policy at Del Rey not to translate them. Here, instead, is a guide to some of the honorifics you may encounter in Del Rey Manga.

-san: This is the most common honorific and is equivalent to Mr., Miss, Ms., or Mrs. It is the all-purpose honorific and can be used in any situation where politeness is required.

-sama: This is one level higher than "-san" and is used to confer great respect.

-dono: This comes from the word "tono," which means "lord." It is an even higher level than "-sama" and confers utmost respect.

-kun: This suffix is used at the end of boys' names to express familiarity or endearment. It is also sometimes used by men

among friends, or when addressing someone younger or of a lower station.

-chan: This is used to express endearment, mostly toward girls. It is also used for little boys, pets, and even among lovers. It gives a sense of childish cuteness.

Bōzu: This is an informal way to refer to a boy, similar to the English terms "kid" and "squirt."

Sempai/Senpai: This title suggests that the addressee is one's senior in a group or organization. It is most often used in a school setting, where underclassmen refer to their upperclassmen as "sempai." It can also be used in the workplace, such as when a newer employee addresses an employee who has seniority in the company.

Kohai: This is the opposite of "sempai" and is used toward underclassmen in school or newcomers in the workplace. It connotes that the addressee is of a lower station.

Sensei: Literally meaning "one who has come before," this title is used for teachers, doctors, or masters of any profession or art.

Anesan (or *nesan*): A generic term for a girl, usually older, that means "sister."

Ojōsama: A way of referring to the daughter or sister of someone with high political or social status.

-[blank]: This is usually forgotten in these lists, but it is perhaps the most significant difference between Japanese and English. The lack of honorific means that the speaker has permission to address the person in a very intimate way. Usually, only family, spouses, or very close friends have this kind of permission. Known as *yobisute,* it can be gratifying when someone who has earned the intimacy starts to call one by one's name without an honorific. But when that intimacy hasn't been earned, it can be very insulting.

A Word from the Author

Presenting *Negima!* volume 26!

In the last volume, Fate defeated Negi yet again, but, provoked by Rakan's movie, Negi starts his training from hell. And on the last page of this volume, something shocking appears!...You'll just have to wait and see what it is. (^^)

Now then, starting with the limited edition of volume 27, the second OAD series will begin. The Magical World arc has gotten more intense and more interesting, so please watch the anime DVD!

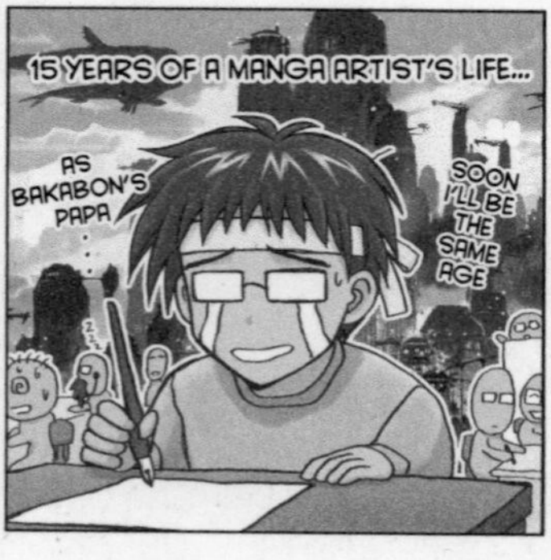
15 YEARS OF A MANGA ARTIST'S LIFE...
SOON I'LL BE THE SAME AGE
AS BAKABON'S PAPA . . .

As in the past, they'll all be sold through preorders. For details, check the official site or the flyer inside this book (in the Japanese version only).

Ken Akamatsu
www.ailove.net

26

魔法先生ネギま!

MAGISTER NEGI MAGI

赤松健

Ken Akamatsu

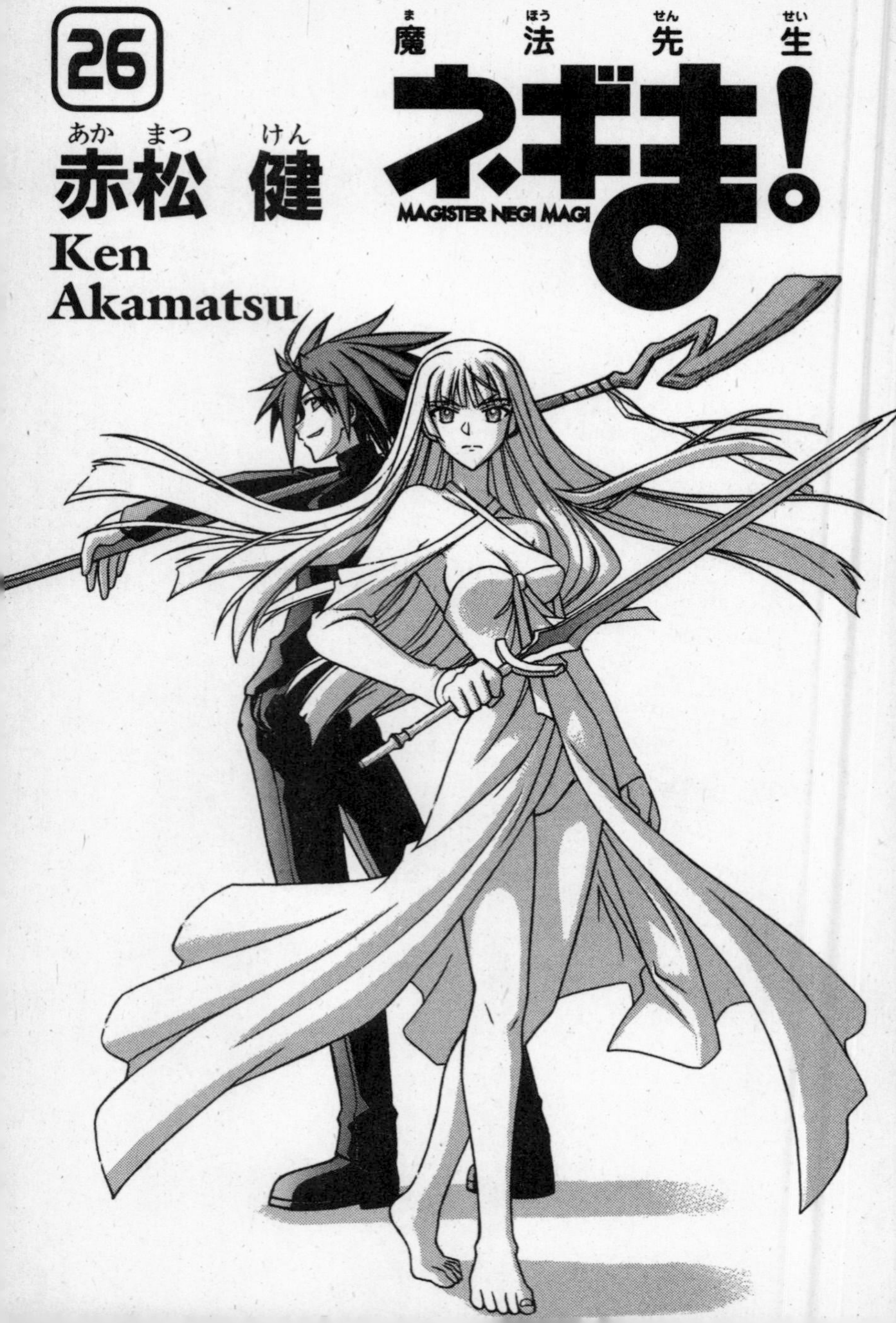

CONTENTS

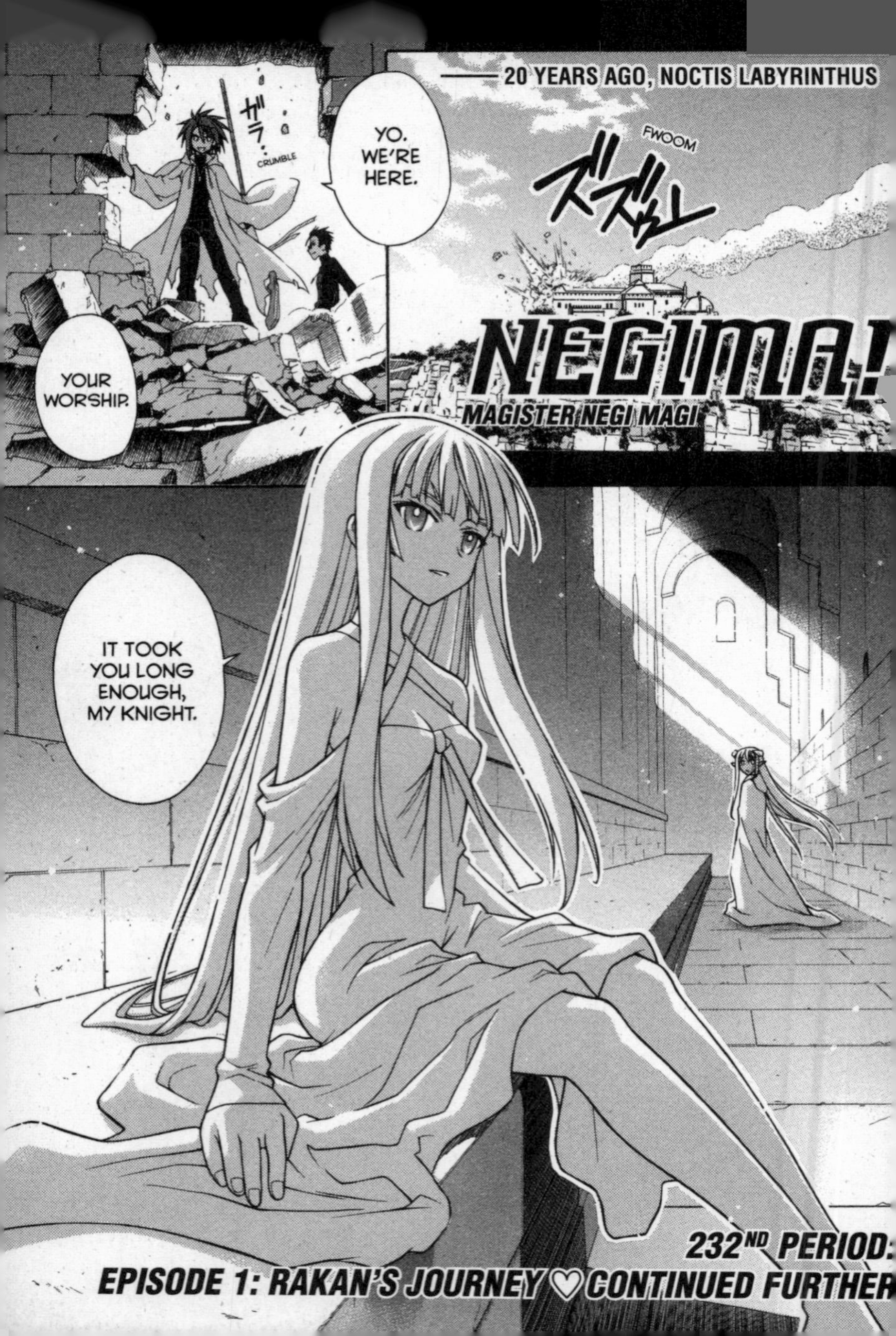
——20 YEARS AGO, NOCTIS LABYRINTHUS
FWOOM
NEGIMA!
MAGISTER NEGI MAGI
ガラ
CRUMBLE
YO. WE'RE HERE.
YOUR WORSHIP.
IT TOOK YOU LONG ENOUGH, MY KNIGHT.
232ND PERIOD:
EPISODE 1: RAKAN'S JOURNEY ♡ CONTINUED FURTHER

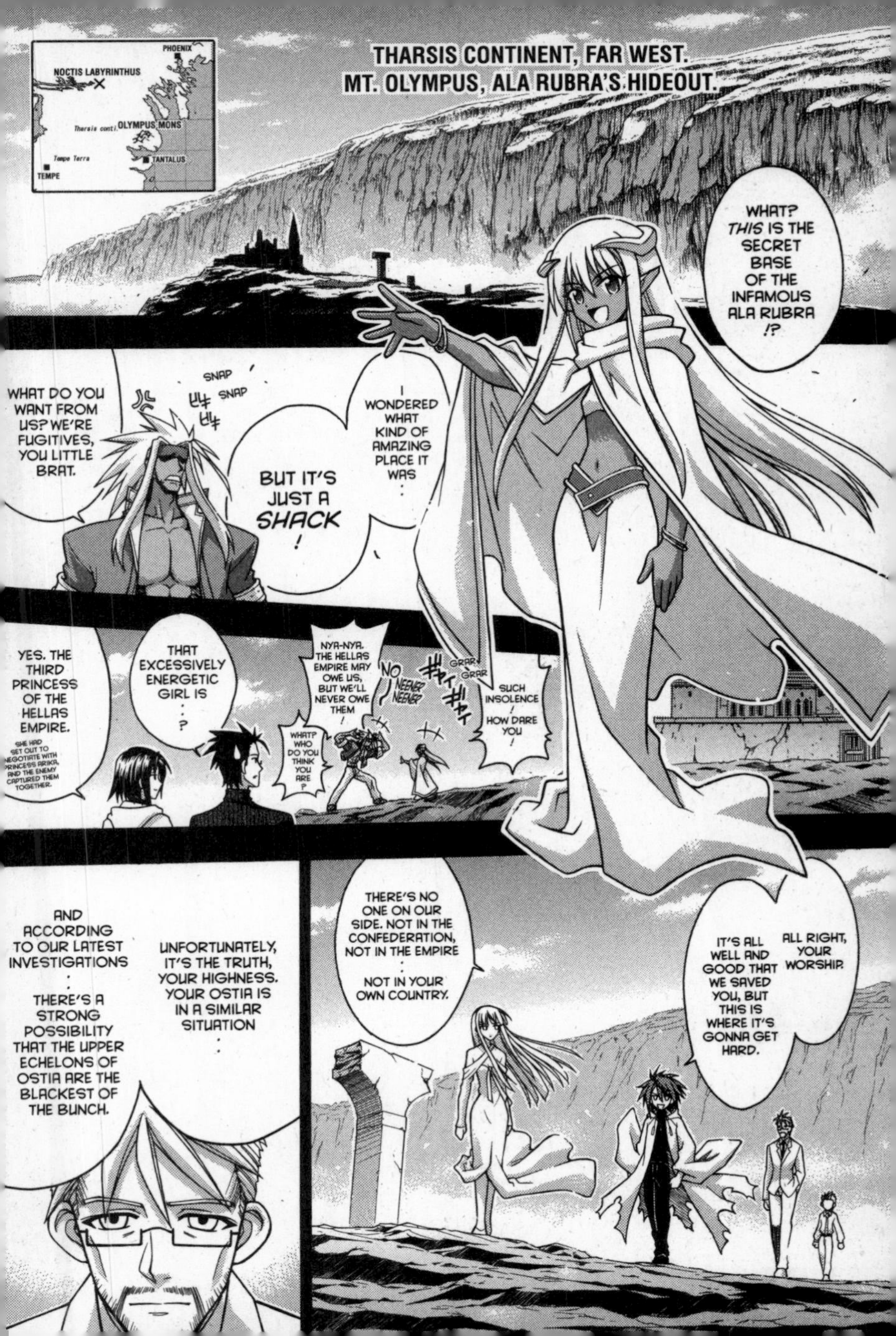
THARSIS CONTINENT, FAR WEST.
MT. OLYMPUS, ALA RUBRA'S HIDEOUT.
PHOENIX
NOCTIS LABYRINTHUS
Tharsis conti.
OLYMPUS MONS
Tempe Terra
TANTALUS
TEMPE
WHAT? THIS IS THE SECRET BASE OF THE INFAMOUS ALA RUBRA !?
I WONDERED WHAT KIND OF AMAZING PLACE IT WAS . .
BUT IT'S JUST A SHACK !
SNAP SNAP
WHAT DO YOU WANT FROM US? WE'RE FUGITIVES, YOU LITTLE BRAT.
SUCH INSOLENCE ! HOW DARE YOU !
GRAR GRAR
NO ! NEENER NEENER
NYA-NYA. THE HELLAS EMPIRE MAY OWE US, BUT WE'LL NEVER OWE THEM !
WHAT? WHO DO YOU THINK YOU ARE ?
THAT EXCESSIVELY ENERGETIC GIRL IS . . . ?
YES. THE THIRD PRINCESS OF THE HELLAS EMPIRE.
SHE HAD SET OUT TO NEGOTIATE WITH PRINCESS ARIKA, AND THE ENEMY CAPTURED THEM TOGETHER.
ALL RIGHT, YOUR WORSHIP.
IT'S ALL WELL AND GOOD THAT WE SAVED YOU, BUT THIS IS WHERE IT'S GONNA GET HARD.
THERE'S NO ONE ON OUR SIDE. NOT IN THE CONFEDERATION, NOT IN THE EMPIRE . . . NOT IN YOUR OWN COUNTRY.
UNFORTUNATELY, IT'S THE TRUTH, YOUR HIGHNESS. YOUR OSTIA IS IN A SIMILAR SITUATION . . .
AND ACCORDING TO OUR LATEST INVESTIGATIONS . . . THERE'S A STRONG POSSIBILITY THAT THE UPPER ECHELONS OF OSTIA ARE THE BLACKEST OF THE BUNCH.

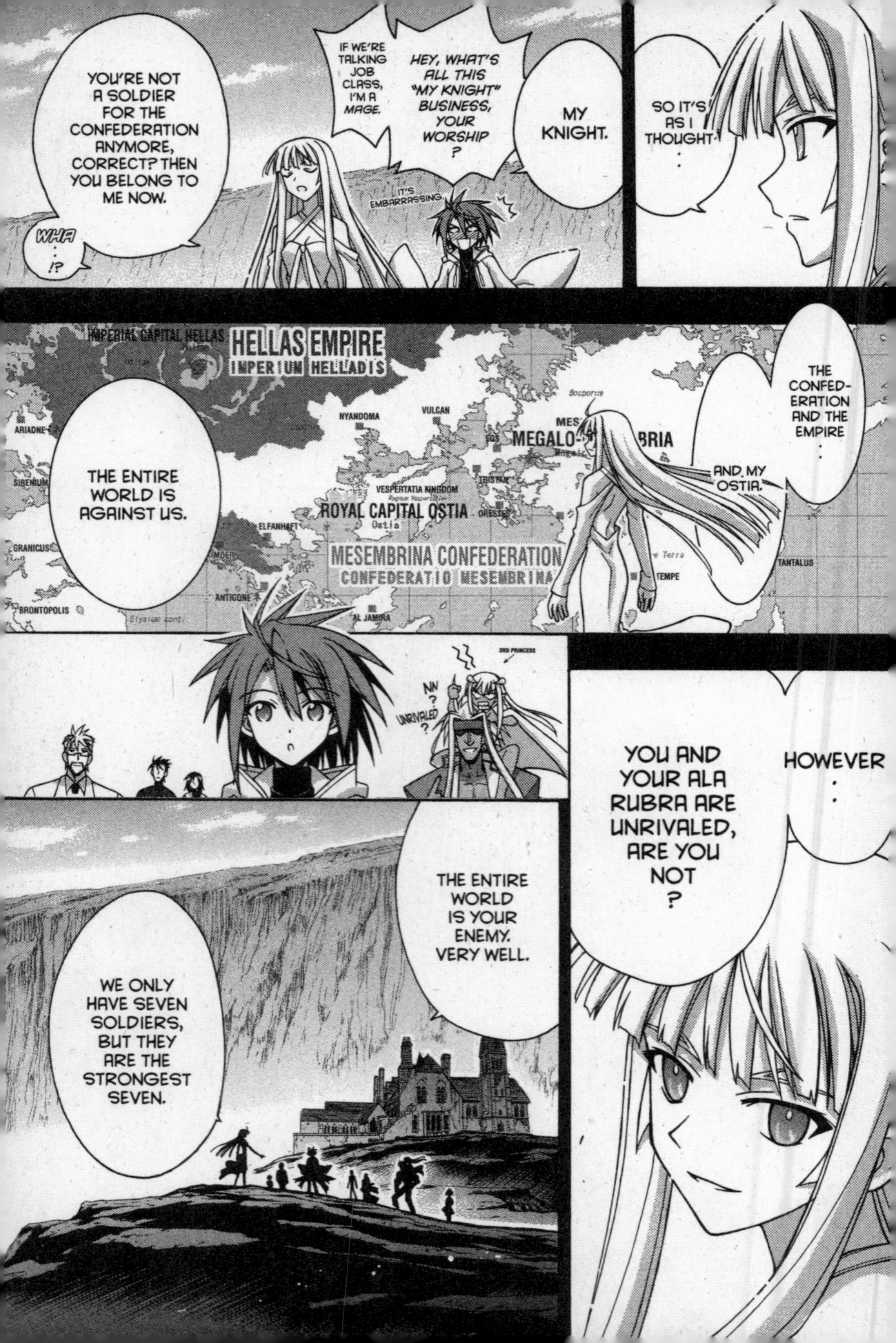
SO IT'S AS I THOUGHT...
MY KNIGHT.
HEY, WHAT'S ALL THIS "MY KNIGHT" BUSINESS, YOUR WORSHIP?
IF WE'RE TALKING JOB CLASS, I'M A MAGE.
IT'S EMBARRASSING.
YOU'RE NOT A SOLDIER FOR THE CONFEDERATION ANYMORE, CORRECT? THEN YOU BELONG TO ME NOW.
WHA...!?
THE CONFEDERATION AND THE EMPIRE...
AND MY OSTIA.
IMPERIAL CAPITAL HELLAS
HELLAS EMPIRE
IMPERIUM HELLADIS
NYANDOMA
VULCAN
MEGALO-
BRIA
ARIADNE
SIBENIUM
VESPERTATIA KINGDOM
TRISTAN
ROYAL CAPITAL OSTIA
Ostia
ORESTES
ELFANHAFT
GRANICUS
MESEMBRINA CONFEDERATION
CONFEDERATIO MESEMBRINA
TANTALUS
TEMPE
ANTIGONE
BRONTOPOLIS
AL JAMIRA
THE ENTIRE WORLD IS AGAINST US.
HOWEVER...
YOU AND YOUR ALA RUBRA ARE UNRIVALED, ARE YOU NOT?
3RD PRINCESS
NN?
UNRIVALED?
THE ENTIRE WORLD IS YOUR ENEMY. VERY WELL.
WE ONLY HAVE SEVEN SOLDIERS, BUT THEY ARE THE STRONGEST SEVEN.

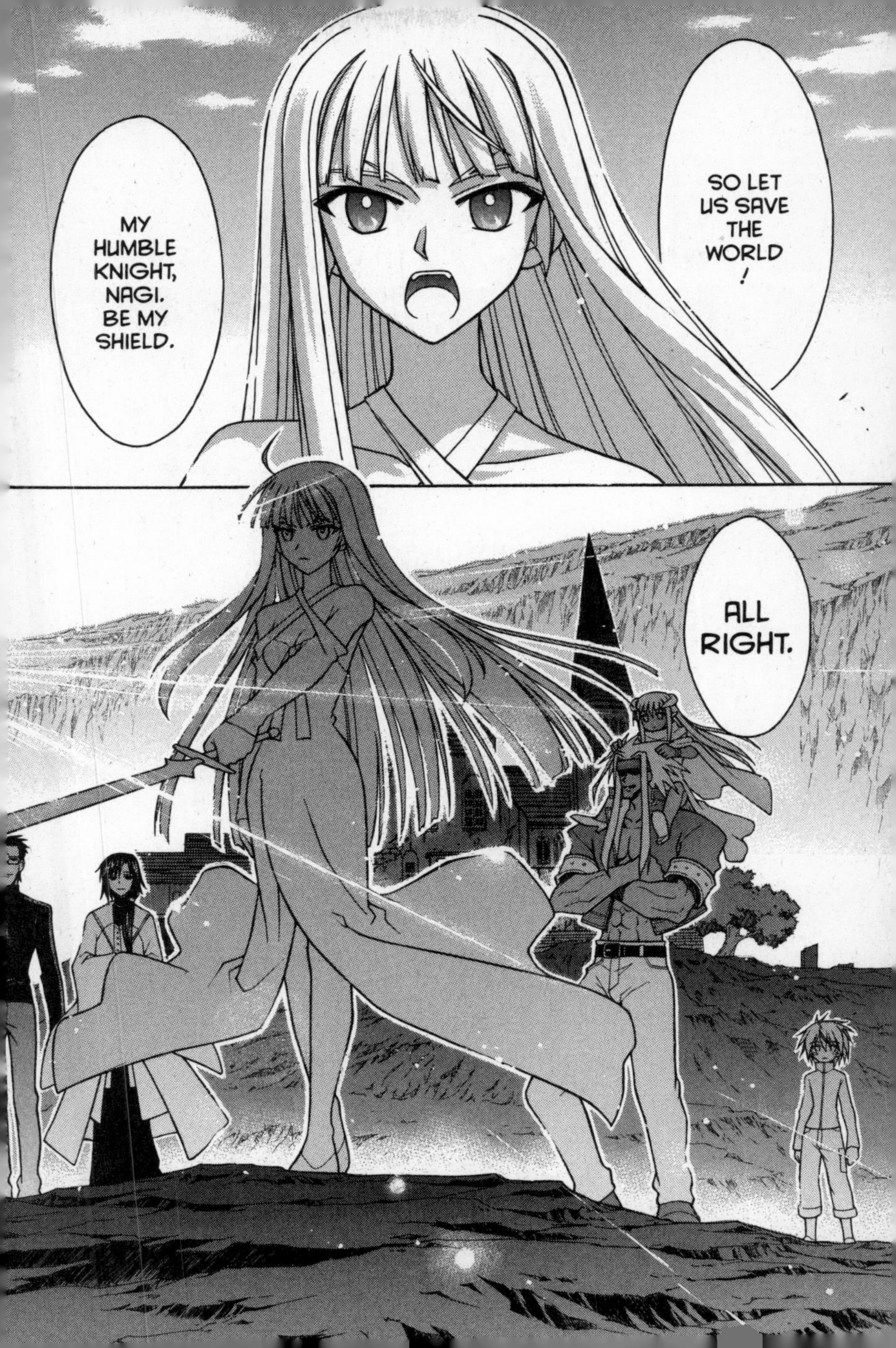
SO LET US SAVE THE WORLD!
MY HUMBLE KNIGHT, NAGI. BE MY SHIELD.
ALL RIGHT.

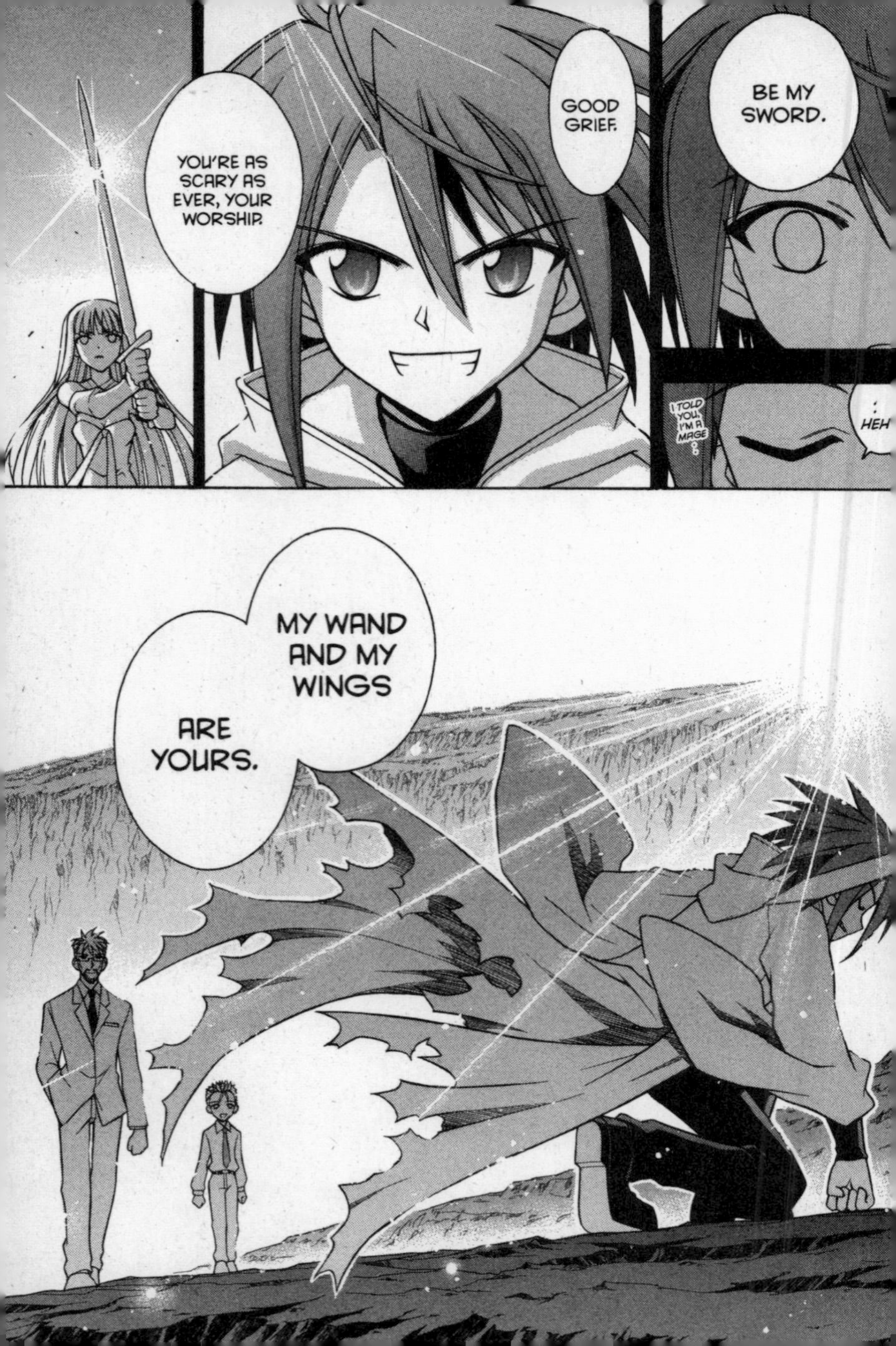
BE MY SWORD.
: HEH
I TOLD YOU, I'M A MAGE?
GOOD GRIEF.
YOU'RE AS SCARY AS EVER, YOUR WORSHIP.
MY WAND AND MY WINGS ARE YOURS.

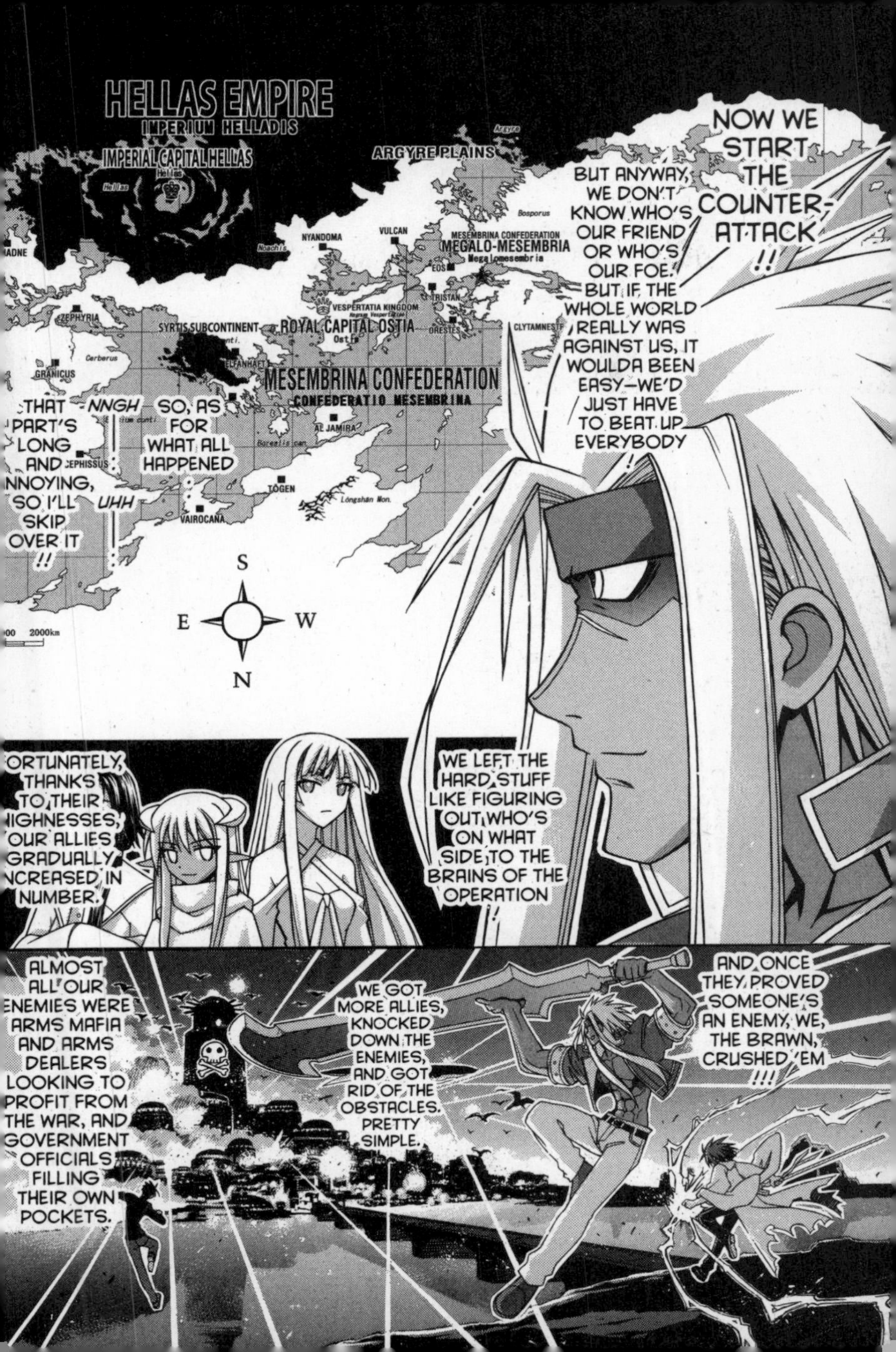
NOW WE START THE COUNTER-ATTACK!!
BUT ANYWAY, WE DON'T KNOW WHO'S OUR FRIEND OR WHO'S OUR FOE. BUT IF THE WHOLE WORLD REALLY WAS AGAINST US, IT WOULDA BEEN EASY—WE'D JUST HAVE TO BEAT UP EVERYBODY!
HELLAS EMPIRE
IMPERIUM HELLADIS
IMPERIAL CAPITAL HELLAS
Hellas
ARGYRE PLAINS
Argyra
Bosporus
NYANDOMA
VULCAN
MESEMBRINA CONFEDERATION
MEGALO-MESEMBRIA
Megalomesembria
Noachis
EOS
TRISTAN
VESPERTATIA KINGDOM
ZEPHYRIA
SYRTIS SUBCONTINENT
ROYAL CAPITAL OSTIA
Ostia
ORESTES
CLYTAMNESTR
Cerberus
GRANICUS
ELFANHAFT
MESEMBRINA CONFEDERATION
CONFEDERATIO MESEMBRINA
AL JAMIRA
CEPHISSUS
TŌGEN
Longshān Mon.
VAIROCANA
S
E
W
N
2000km
SO, AS FOR WHAT ALL HAPPENED
NNGH... UHH...
THAT PART'S LONG AND NNOYING, SO I'LL SKIP OVER IT!!
WE LEFT THE HARD STUFF LIKE FIGURING OUT WHO'S ON WHAT SIDE TO THE BRAINS OF THE OPERATION!
ORTUNATELY, THANKS TO THEIR IGHNESSES, OUR ALLIES GRADUALLY NCREASED IN NUMBER.
AND ONCE THEY PROVED SOMEONE'S AN ENEMY, WE, THE BRAWN, CRUSHED 'EM!!!
WE GOT MORE ALLIES, KNOCKED DOWN THE ENEMIES, AND GOT RID OF THE OBSTACLES. PRETTY SIMPLE.
ALMOST ALL OUR ENEMIES WERE ARMS MAFIA AND ARMS DEALERS LOOKING TO PROFIT FROM THE WAR, AND GOVERNMENT OFFICIALS FILLING THEIR OWN POCKETS.

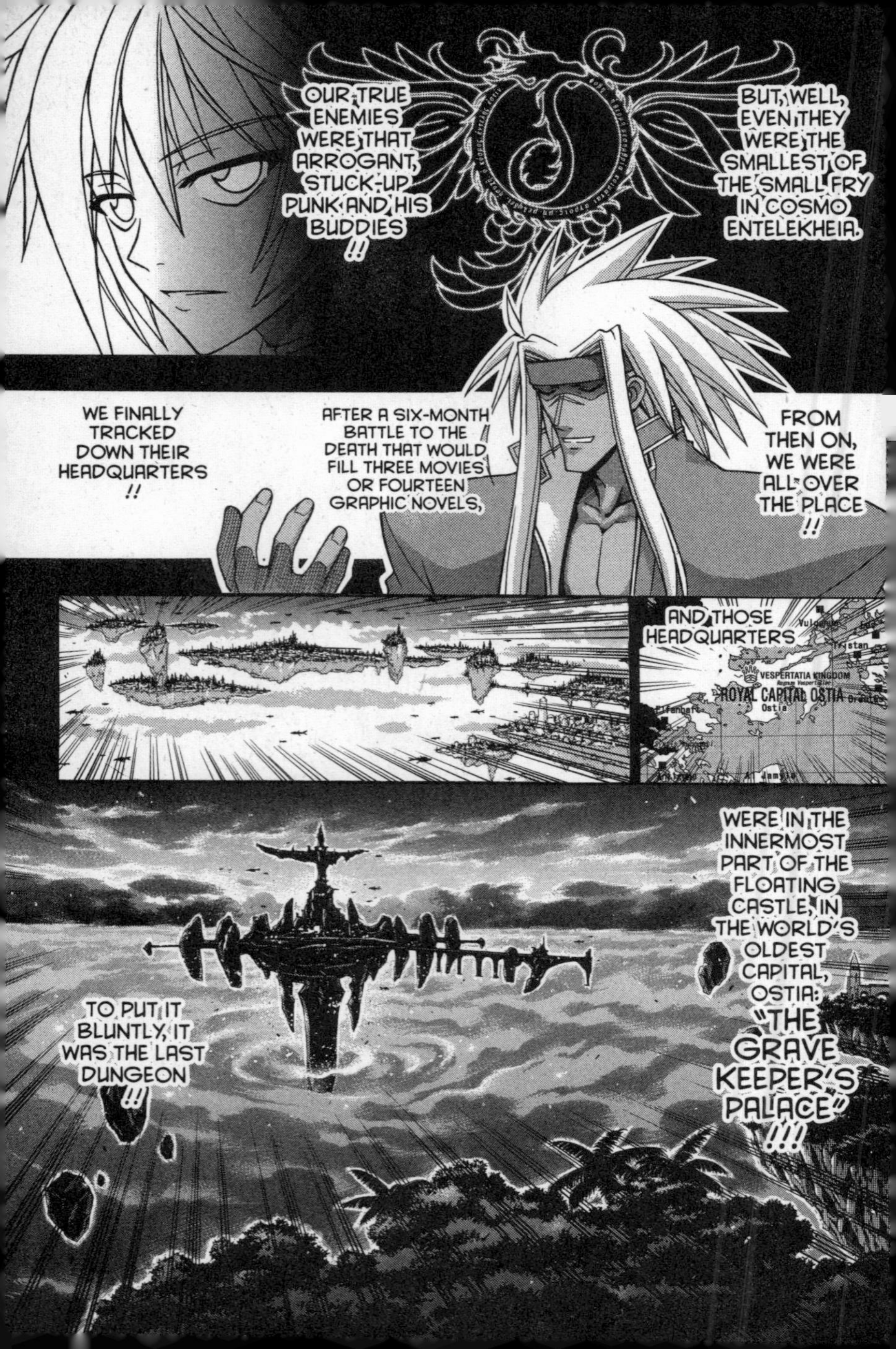
OUR TRUE ENEMIES WERE THAT ARROGANT, STUCK-UP PUNK AND HIS BUDDIES!!
BUT, WELL, EVEN THEY WERE THE SMALLEST OF THE SMALL FRY IN COSMO ENTELEKHEIA.
FROM THEN ON, WE WERE ALL OVER THE PLACE!!
AFTER A SIX-MONTH BATTLE TO THE DEATH THAT WOULD FILL THREE MOVIES OR FOURTEEN GRAPHIC NOVELS,
WE FINALLY TRACKED DOWN THEIR HEADQUARTERS!!
AND THOSE HEADQUARTERS
VESPERTATIA KINGDOM
ROYAL CAPITAL OSTIA
Ostia
Tristan
WERE IN THE INNERMOST PART OF THE FLOATING CASTLE, IN THE WORLD'S OLDEST CAPITAL, OSTIA: "THE GRAVE KEEPER'S PALACE"!!!
TO PUT IT BLUNTLY, IT WAS THE LAST DUNGEON!!

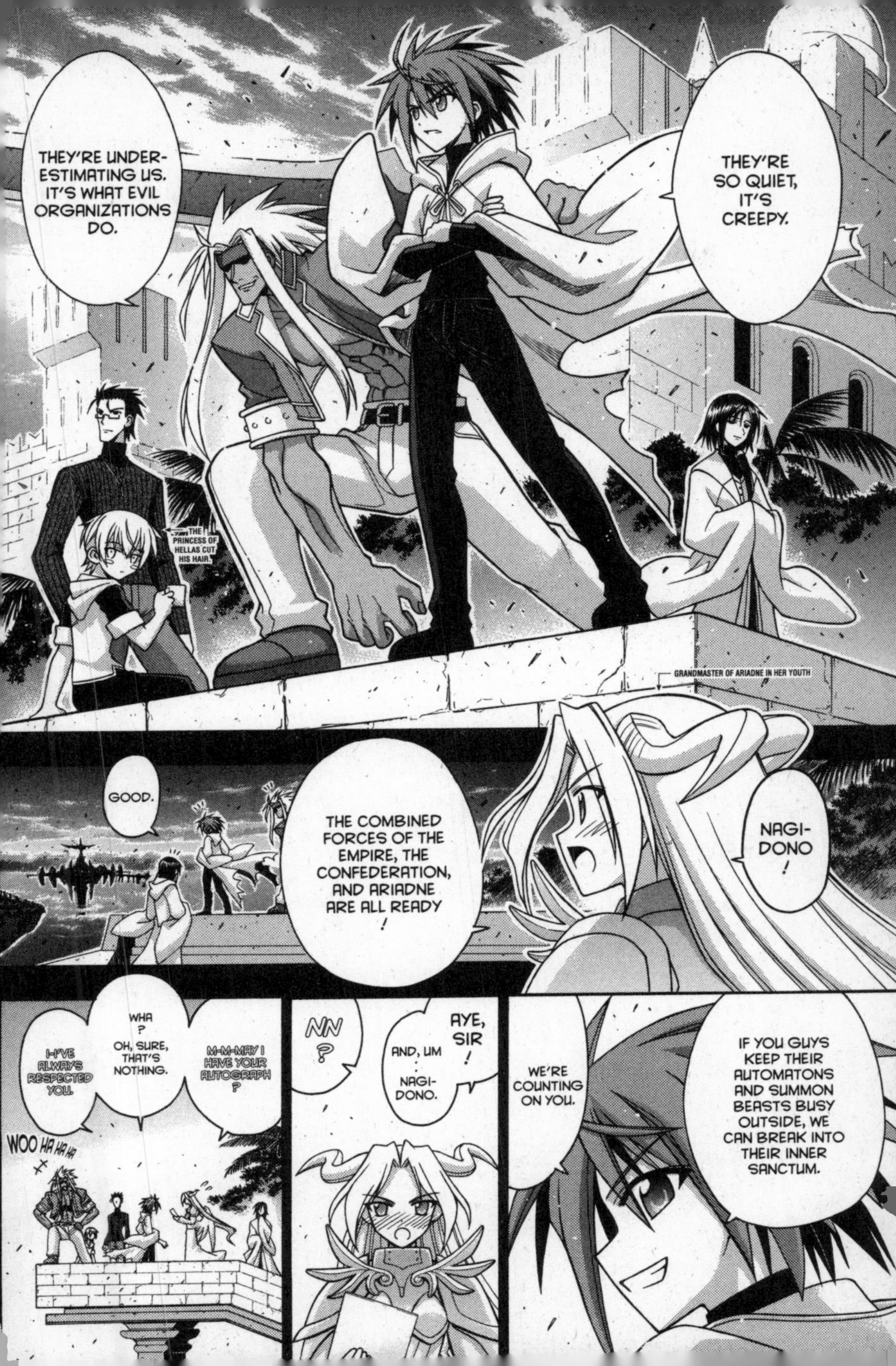
THEY'RE SO QUIET, IT'S CREEPY.
THEY'RE UNDER-ESTIMATING US. IT'S WHAT EVIL ORGANIZATIONS DO.
THE PRINCESS OF HELLAS CUT HIS HAIR.
GRANDMASTER OF ARIADNE IN HER YOUTH
NAGI-DONO!
THE COMBINED FORCES OF THE EMPIRE, THE CONFEDERATION, AND ARIADNE ARE ALL READY!
GOOD.
IF YOU GUYS KEEP THEIR AUTOMATONS AND SUMMON BEASTS BUSY OUTSIDE, WE CAN BREAK INTO THEIR INNER SANCTUM.
WE'RE COUNTING ON YOU.
AYE, SIR!
AND, UM... NAGI-DONO.
NN?
M-M-MAY I HAVE YOUR AUTOGRAPH?
WHA? OH, SURE, THAT'S NOTHING.
I-I'VE ALWAYS RESPECTED YOU.
WOO HA HA HA

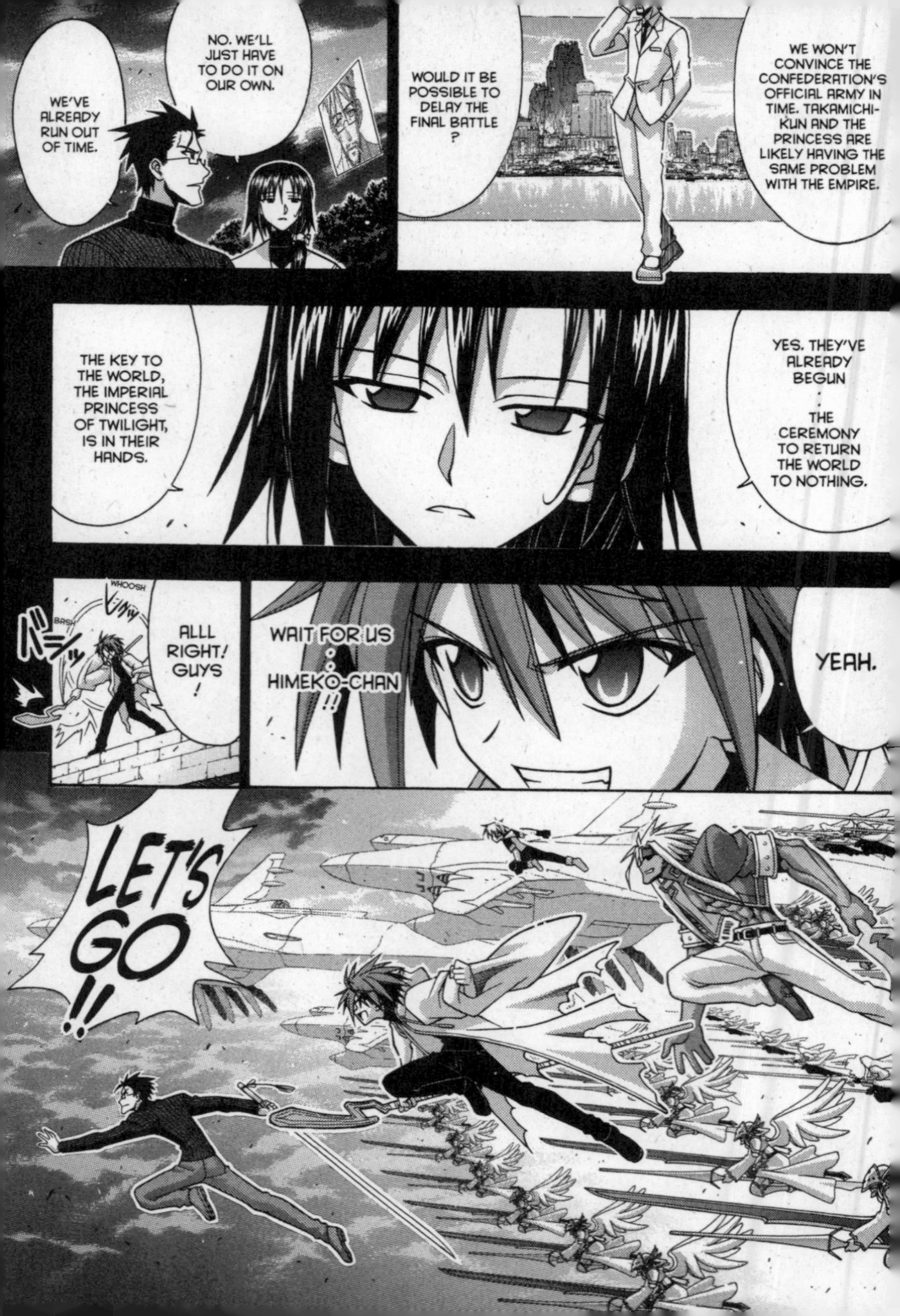
WE WON'T CONVINCE THE CONFEDERATION'S OFFICIAL ARMY IN TIME. TAKAMICHI-KUN AND THE PRINCESS ARE LIKELY HAVING THE SAME PROBLEM WITH THE EMPIRE.
WOULD IT BE POSSIBLE TO DELAY THE FINAL BATTLE ?
NO. WE'LL JUST HAVE TO DO IT ON OUR OWN.
WE'VE ALREADY RUN OUT OF TIME.
YES. THEY'VE ALREADY BEGUN : THE CEREMONY TO RETURN THE WORLD TO NOTHING.
THE KEY TO THE WORLD, THE IMPERIAL PRINCESS OF TWILIGHT, IS IN THEIR HANDS.
YEAH.
WAIT FOR US : . . HIMEKO-CHAN !!
ALLL RIGHT! GUYS !
WHOOSH
BASH
LET'S GO !!

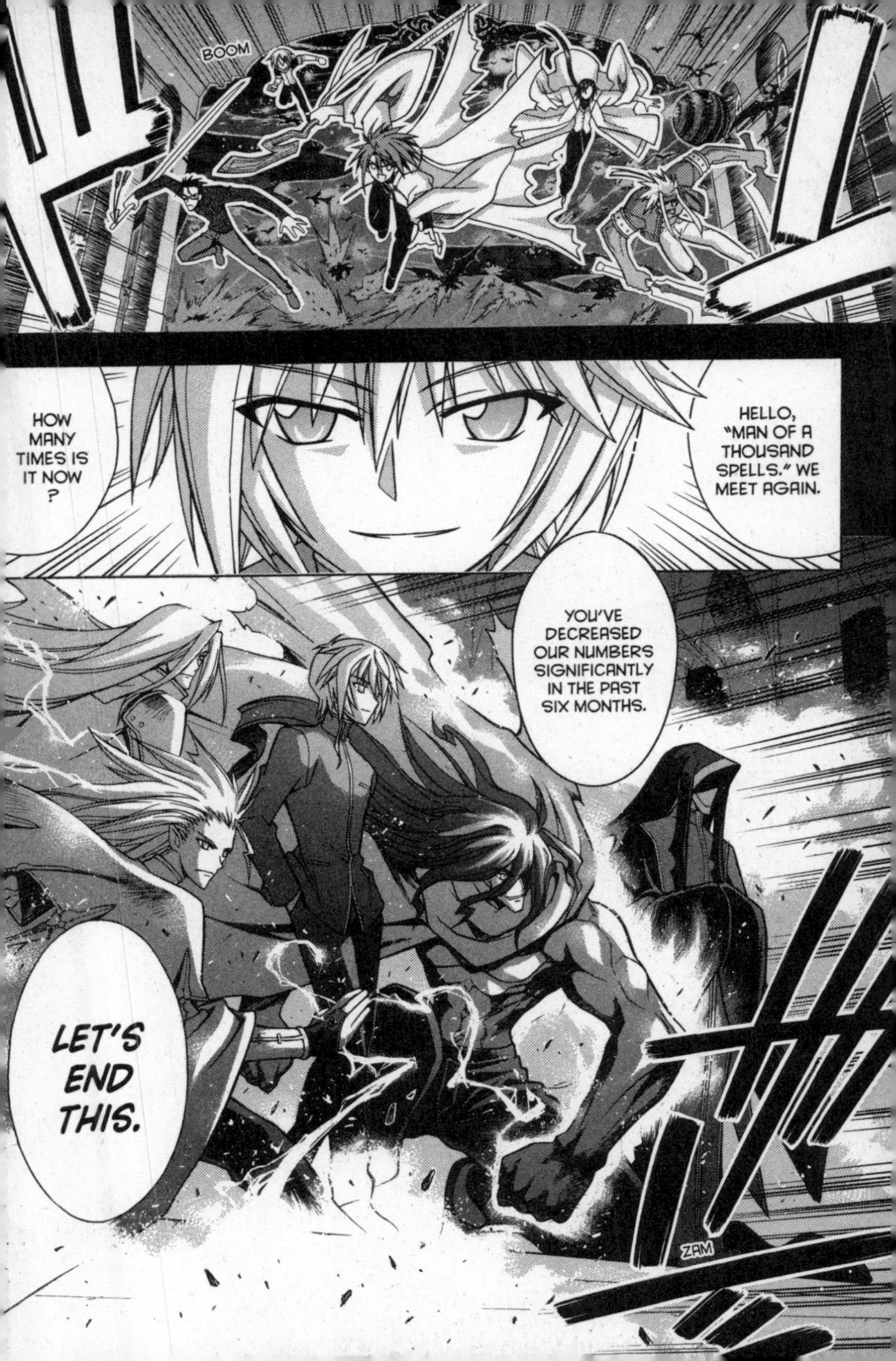
BOOM
HELLO, "MAN OF A THOUSAND SPELLS." WE MEET AGAIN.
HOW MANY TIMES IS IT NOW?
YOU'VE DECREASED OUR NUMBERS SIGNIFICANTLY IN THE PAST SIX MONTHS.
ZAM
LET'S END THIS.

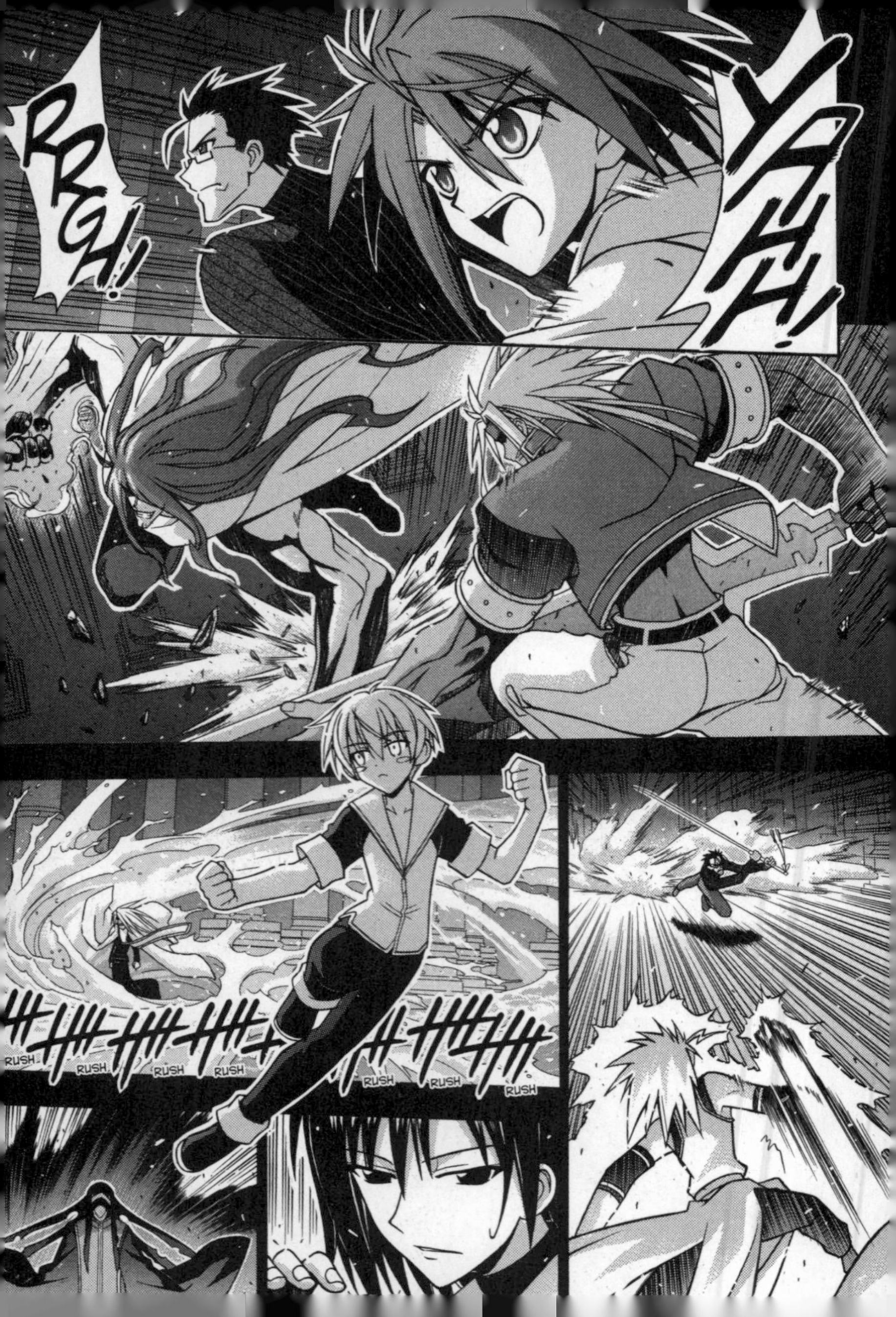
YAHH!
RRGH!
RUSH RUSH RUSH RUSH RUSH RUSH RUSH

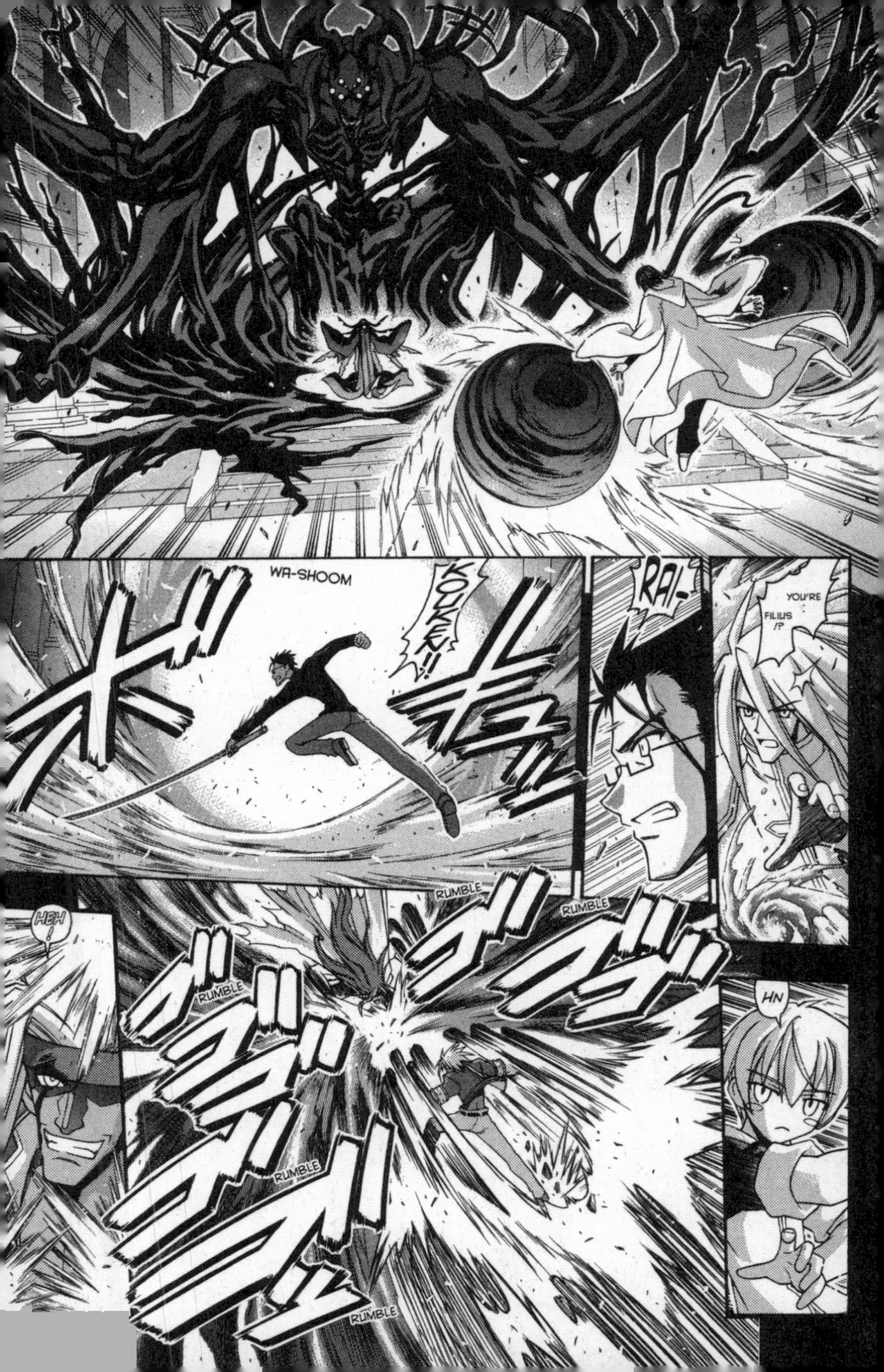
YOU'RE FILIUS !?
RAI-
WA-SHOOM
KOUKEN!!
HN
RUMBLE
RUMBLE
RUMBLE
RUMBLE
RUMBLE
HEH !

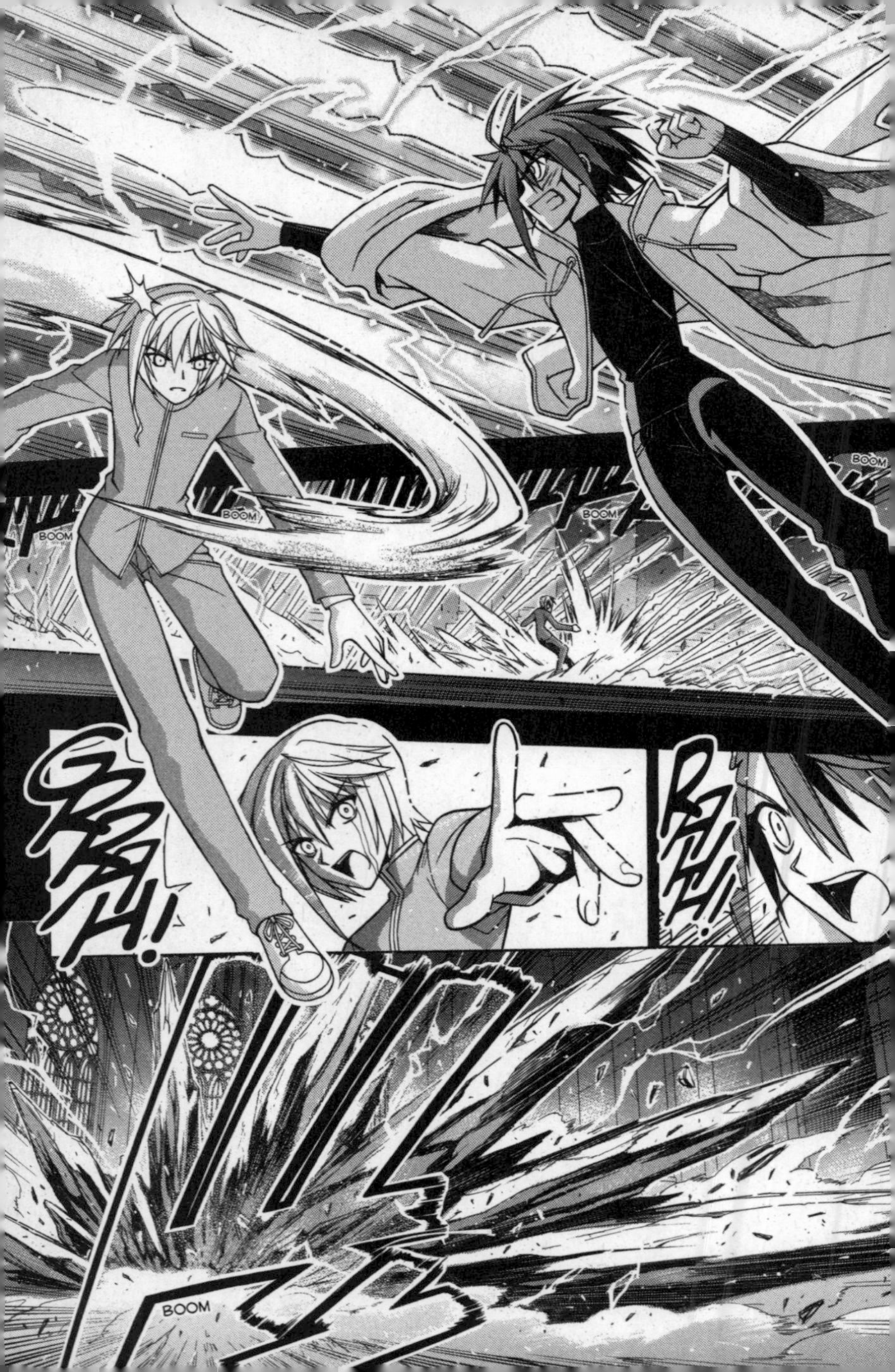
BOOM
BOOM
BOOM
BOOM
RAAH!
GRAAH!
BOOM

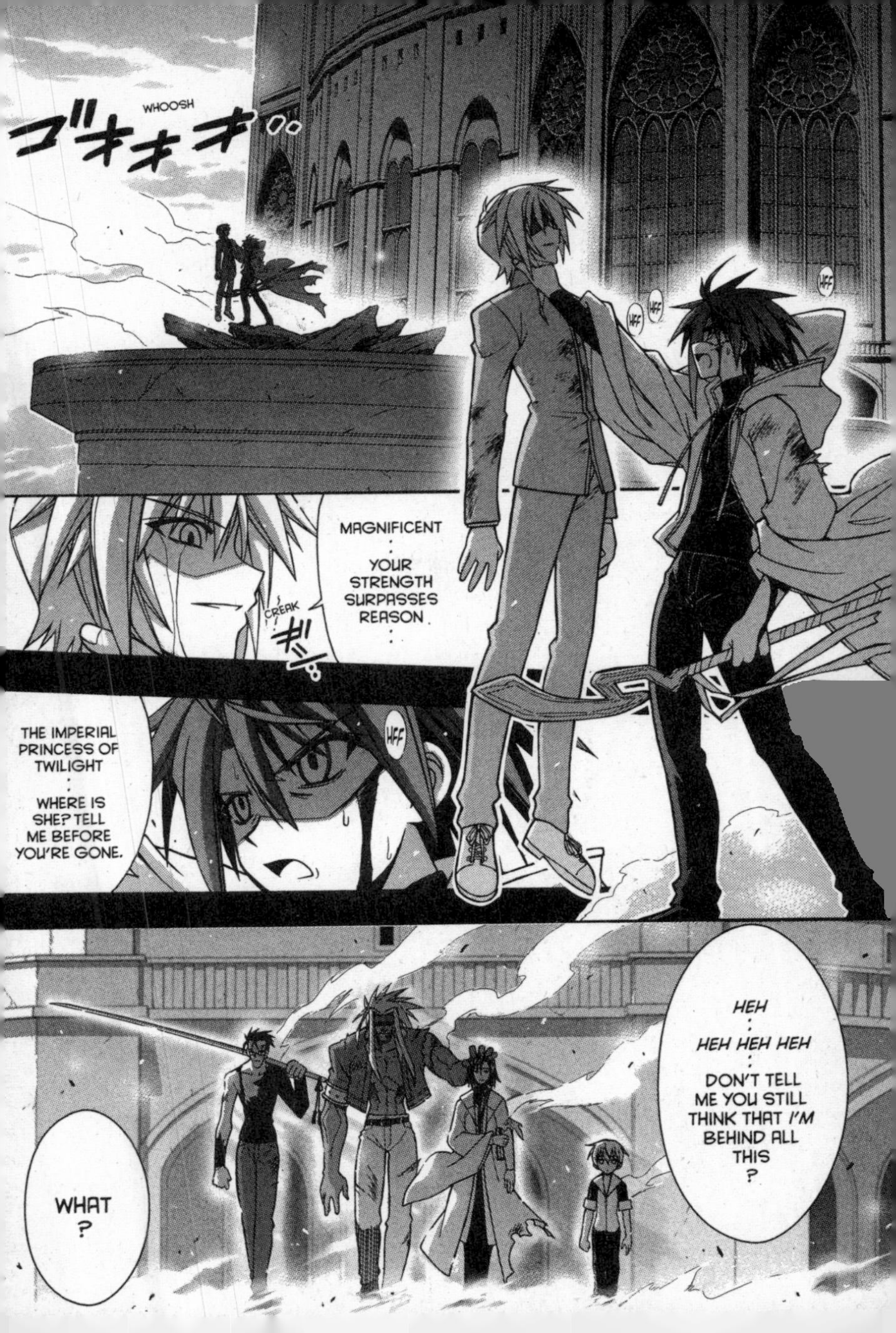
HFF
HFF
HFF
WHOOSH
MAGNIFICENT
:
YOUR STRENGTH SURPASSES REASON
:
CREAK
THE IMPERIAL PRINCESS OF TWILIGHT
:
WHERE IS SHE? TELL ME BEFORE YOU'RE GONE.
HFF
HEH
:
HEH HEH HEH
:
DON'T TELL ME YOU STILL THINK THAT *I'M* BEHIND ALL THIS
?
WHAT
?

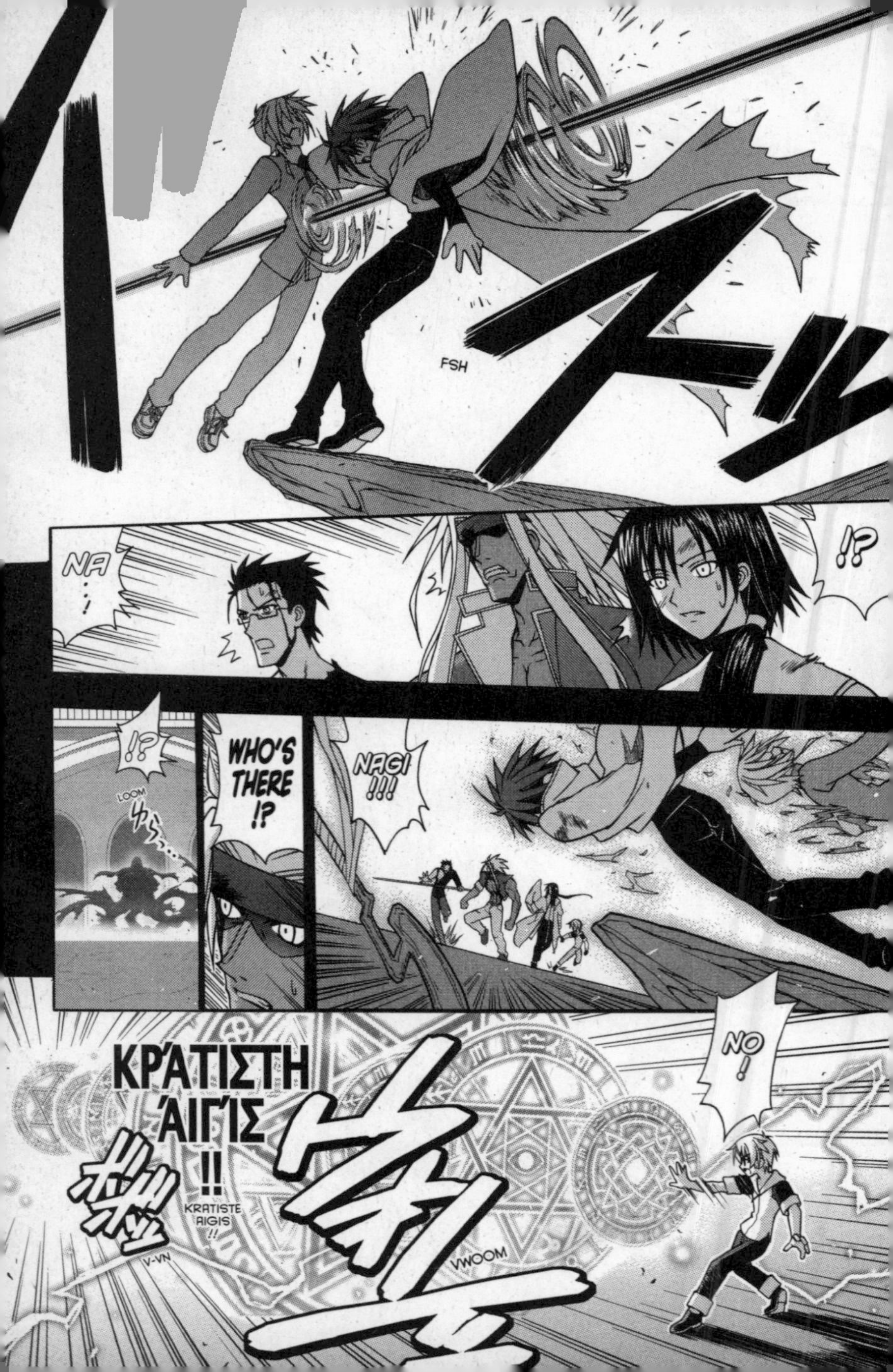
FSH
!?
NA...!
NAGI!!!
WHO'S THERE !?
!?
LOOM
NO!
ΚΡΆΤΙΣΤΗ ΆΙΓΊΣ!!
KRATISTE AIGIS!!
VWOOM
V-VN

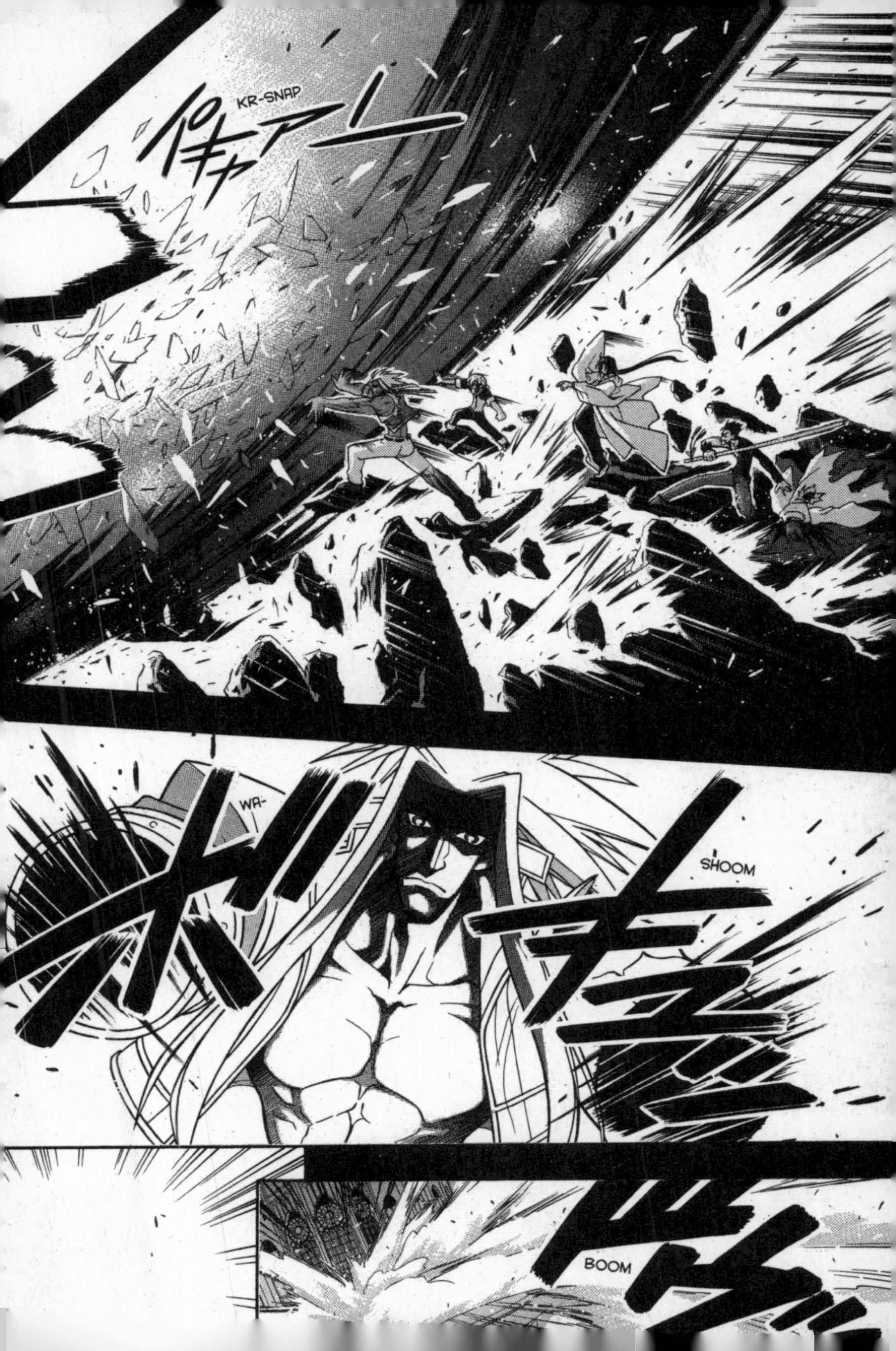
KR-SNAP
SHOOM
WA-
BOOM

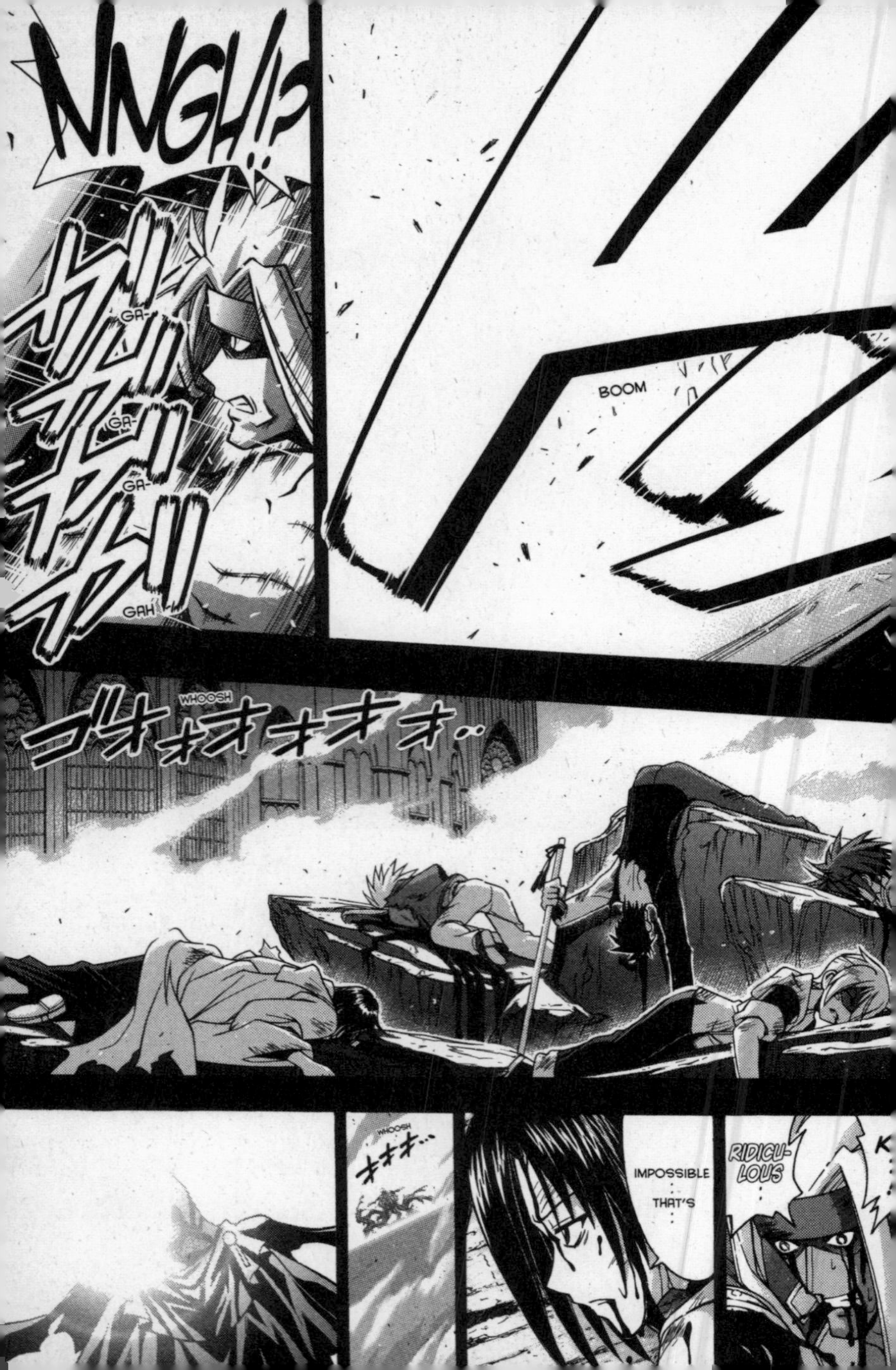
BOOM
NNGH!?
GA-
GA-
GA-
GAH
WHOOSH
K...
RIDICU-LOUS...
IMPOSSIBLE
THAT'S...
WHOOSH

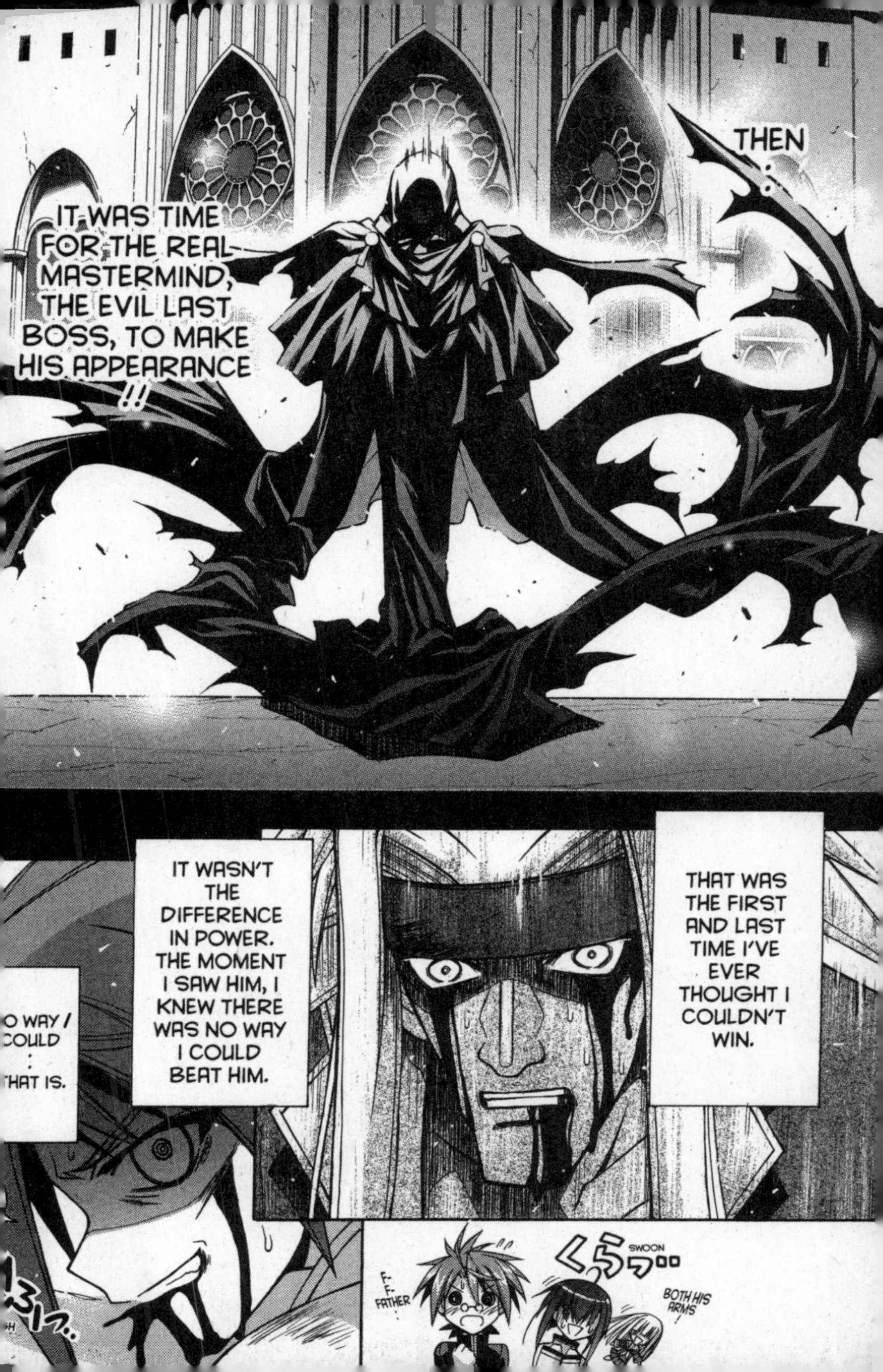
THEN
:
IT WAS TIME FOR THE REAL MASTERMIND, THE EVIL LAST BOSS, TO MAKE HIS APPEARANCE !!
THAT WAS THE FIRST AND LAST TIME I'VE EVER THOUGHT I COULDN'T WIN.
IT WASN'T THE DIFFERENCE IN POWER. THE MOMENT I SAW HIM, I KNEW THERE WAS NO WAY I COULD BEAT HIM.
SWOON
BOTH HIS ARMS !
F-F-FATHER
O WAY / COULD
:
THAT IS.

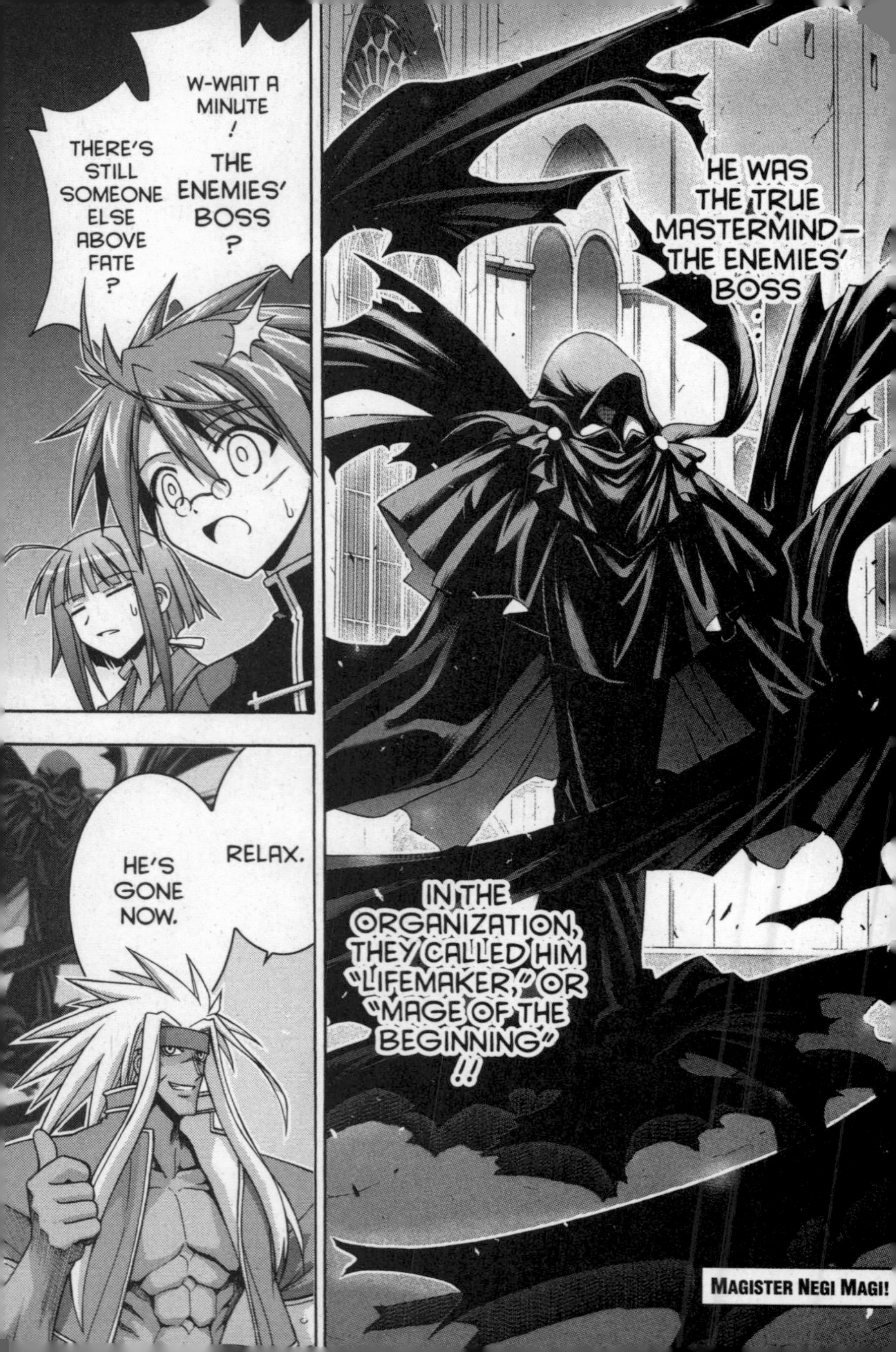
HE WAS THE TRUE MASTERMIND— THE ENEMIES' BOSS...
IN THE ORGANIZATION, THEY CALLED HIM "LIFEMAKER," OR "MAGE OF THE BEGINNING"!!
MAGISTER NEGI MAGI!
W-WAIT A MINUTE! THE ENEMIES' BOSS?
THERE'S STILL SOMEONE ELSE ABOVE FATE?
RELAX.
HE'S GONE NOW.

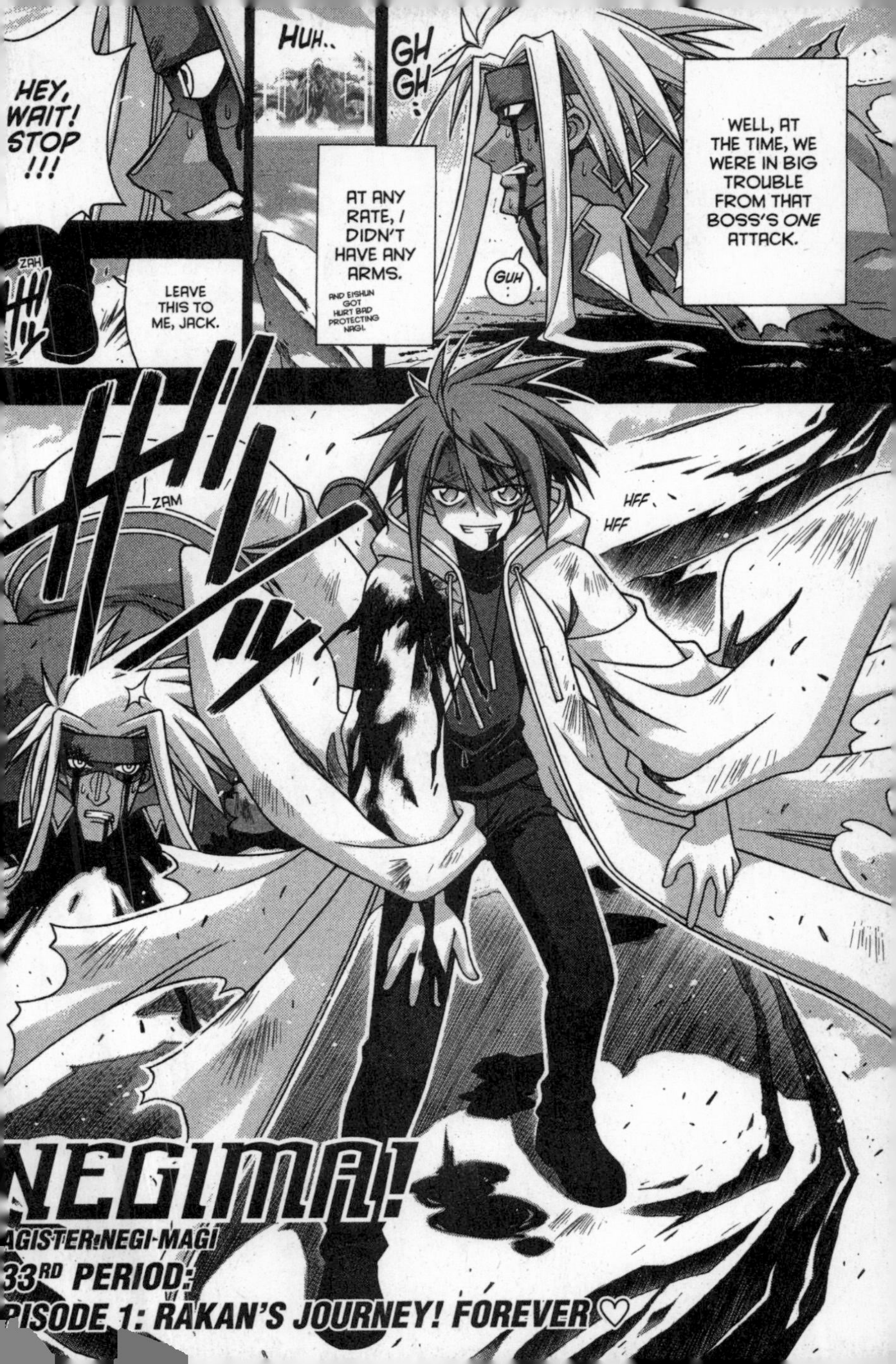
WELL, AT THE TIME, WE WERE IN BIG TROUBLE FROM THAT BOSS'S *ONE* ATTACK.
GH GH
GUH
AT ANY RATE, I DIDN'T HAVE ANY ARMS.
AND EISHUN GOT HURT BAD PROTECTING NAGI.
HUH..
HEY, WAIT! STOP!!!
LEAVE THIS TO ME, JACK.
ZAH
HFF HFF
ZAM
NEGIMA!
AGISTER NEGI-MAGI
33RD PERIOD:
PISODE 1: RAKAN'S JOURNEY! FOREVER ♡

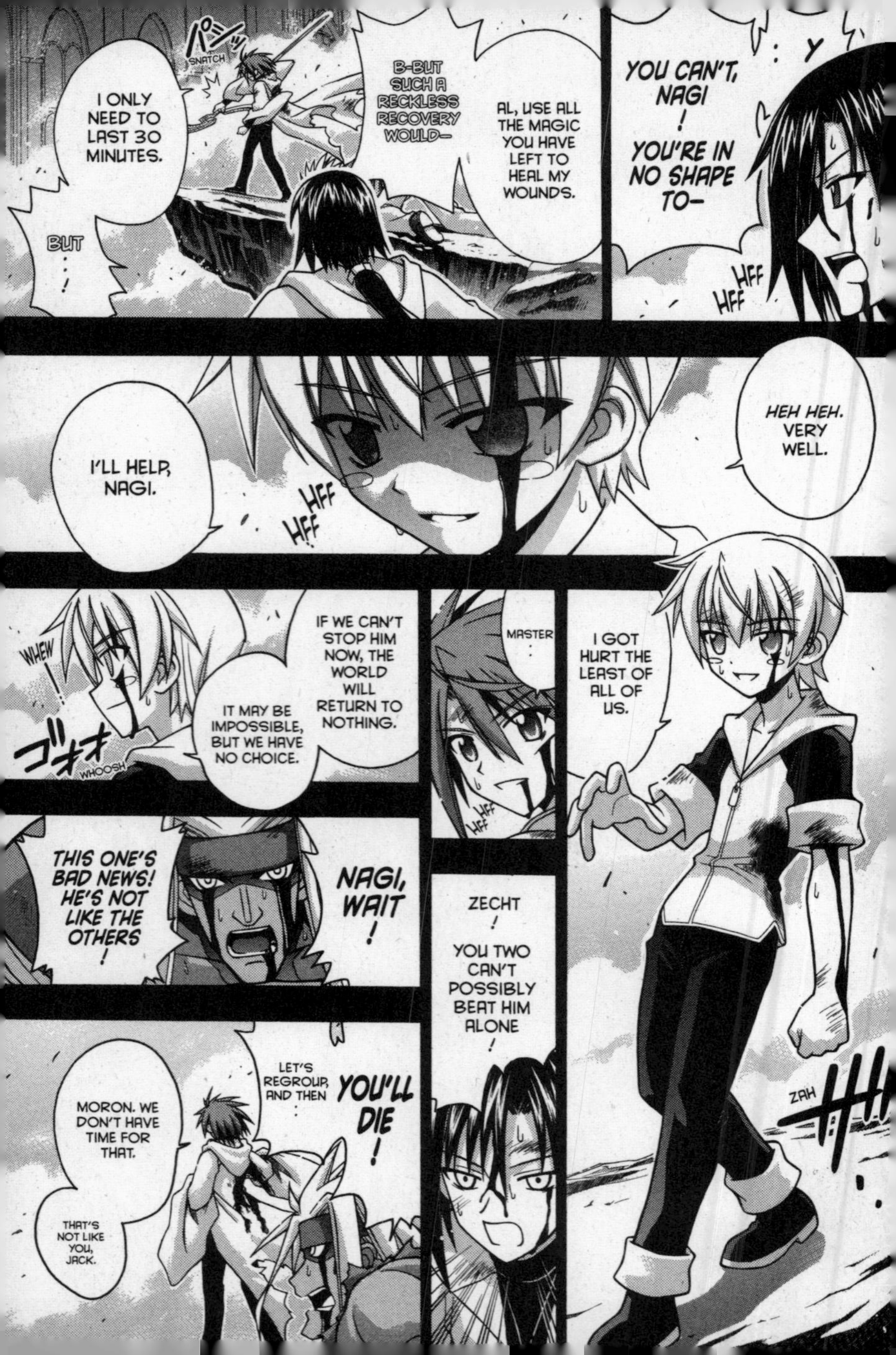
YOU CAN'T, NAGI! YOU'RE IN NO SHAPE TO—
HFF HFF
AL, USE ALL THE MAGIC YOU HAVE LEFT TO HEAL MY WOUNDS.
B-BUT SUCH A RECKLESS RECOVERY WOULD—
パシッ
SNATCH
I ONLY NEED TO LAST 30 MINUTES.
BUT...!
HEH HEH. VERY WELL.
I'LL HELP, NAGI.
HFF HFF
I GOT HURT THE LEAST OF ALL OF US.
MASTER...
HFF HFF
IF WE CAN'T STOP HIM NOW, THE WORLD WILL RETURN TO NOTHING.
IT MAY BE IMPOSSIBLE, BUT WE HAVE NO CHOICE.
WHEW
ゴオオ
WHOOSH
ZECHT! YOU TWO CAN'T POSSIBLY BEAT HIM ALONE!
NAGI, WAIT!
THIS ONE'S BAD NEWS! HE'S NOT LIKE THE OTHERS!
ZAH
YOU'LL DIE!
LET'S REGROUP, AND THEN...
MORON. WE DON'T HAVE TIME FOR THAT.
THAT'S NOT LIKE YOU, JACK.

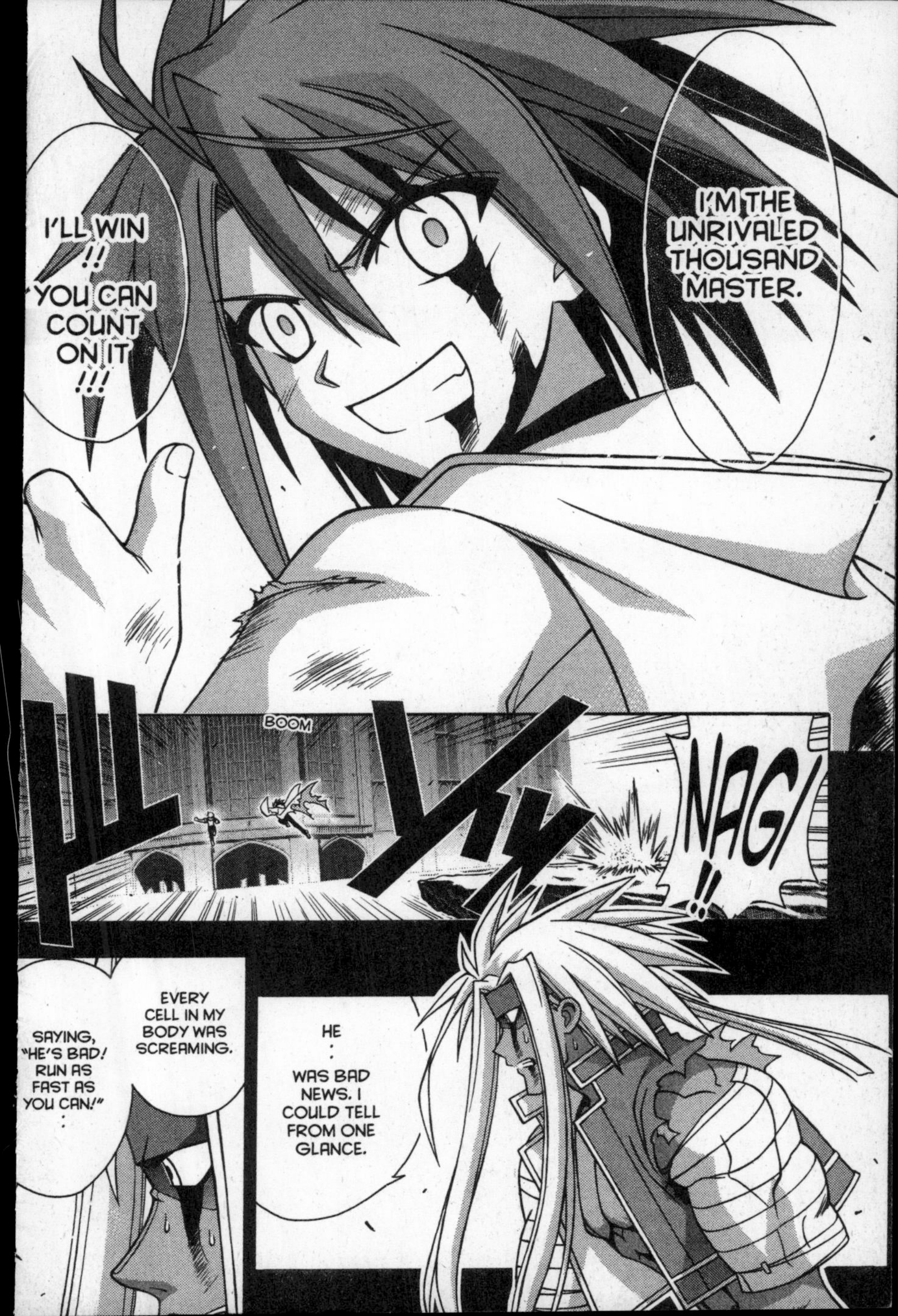
I'M THE UNRIVALED THOUSAND MASTER.
I'LL WIN !! YOU CAN COUNT ON IT !!!
NAGI !!
BOOM
HE : WAS BAD NEWS. I COULD TELL FROM ONE GLANCE.
EVERY CELL IN MY BODY WAS SCREAMING.
SAYING, "HE'S BAD! RUN AS FAST AS YOU CAN!" :

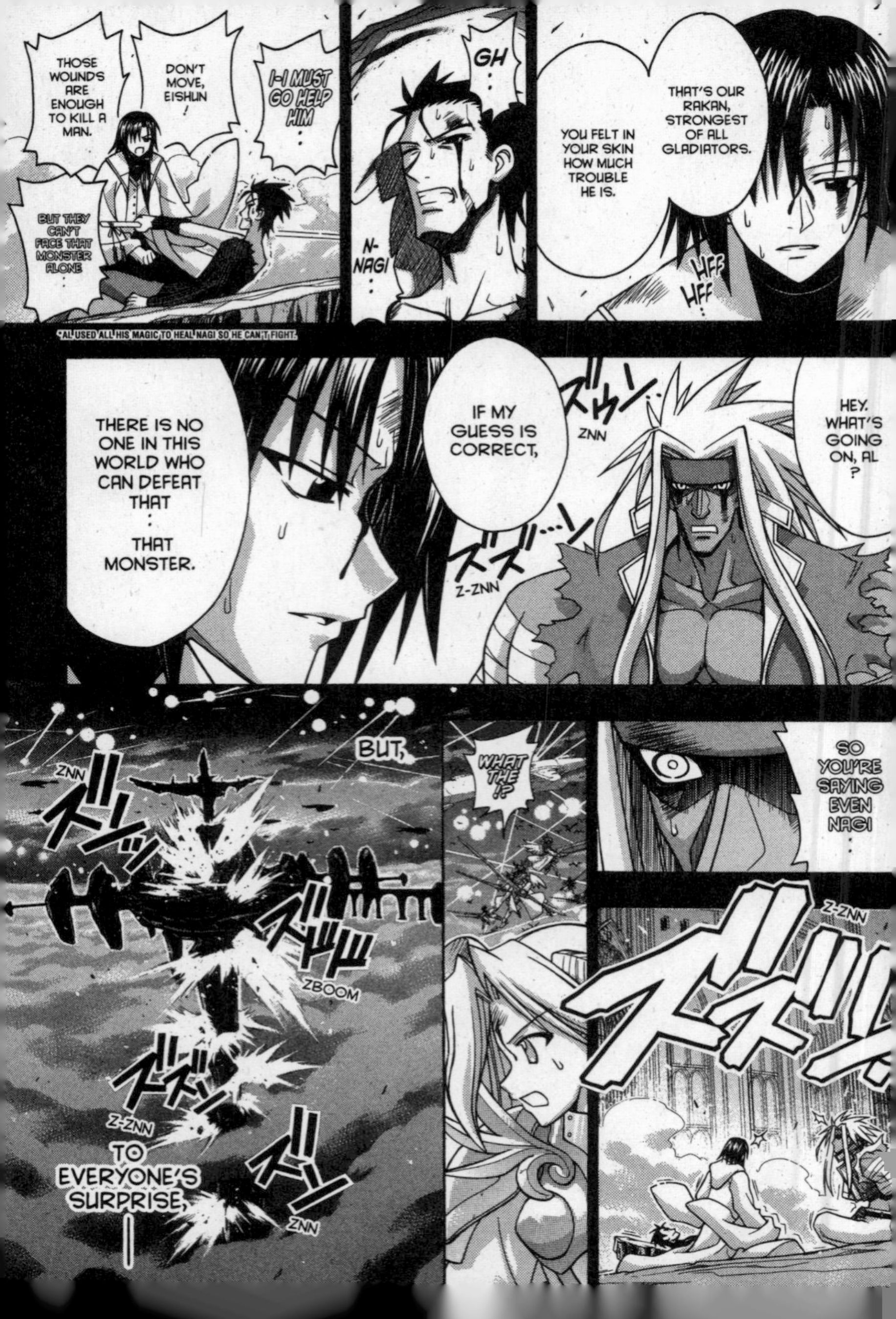
THAT'S OUR RAKAN, STRONGEST OF ALL GLADIATORS.
YOU FELT IN YOUR SKIN HOW MUCH TROUBLE HE IS.
HFF HFF
GH...
N-NAGI...
I-I MUST GO HELP HIM...
DON'T MOVE, EISHUN!
THOSE WOUNDS ARE ENOUGH TO KILL A MAN.
BUT THEY CAN'T FACE THAT MONSTER ALONE...
*AL USED ALL HIS MAGIC TO HEAL NAGI SO HE CAN'T FIGHT.
HEY. WHAT'S GOING ON, AL?
ZNN
IF MY GUESS IS CORRECT,
Z-ZNN
THERE IS NO ONE IN THIS WORLD WHO CAN DEFEAT THAT...
THAT MONSTER.
SO YOU'RE SAYING EVEN NAGI...
Z-ZNN
WHAT THE !?
BUT,
ZNN
ZBOOM
Z-ZNN
TO EVERYONE'S SURPRISE, —
ZNN

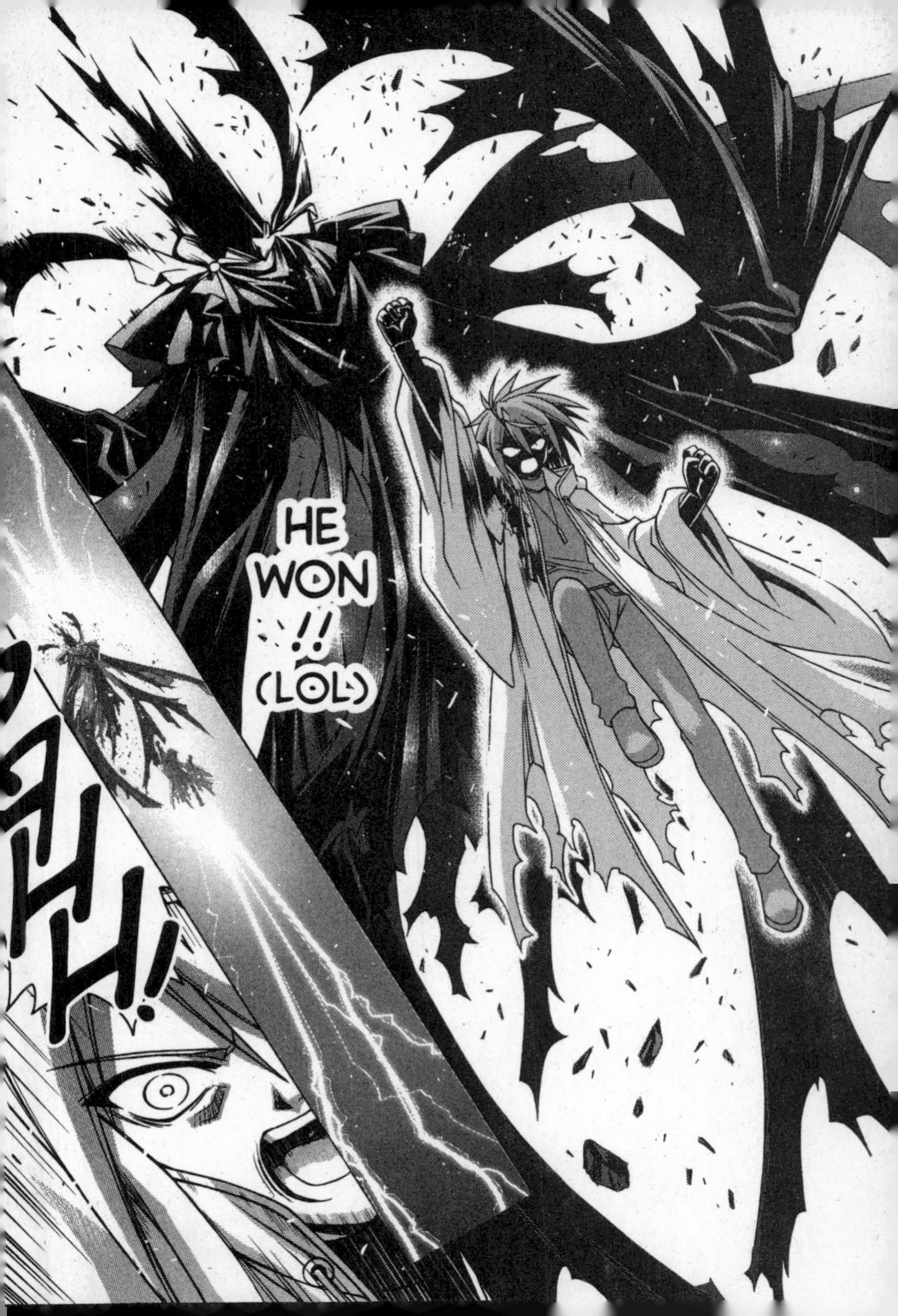
HE WON !! (LOLS)

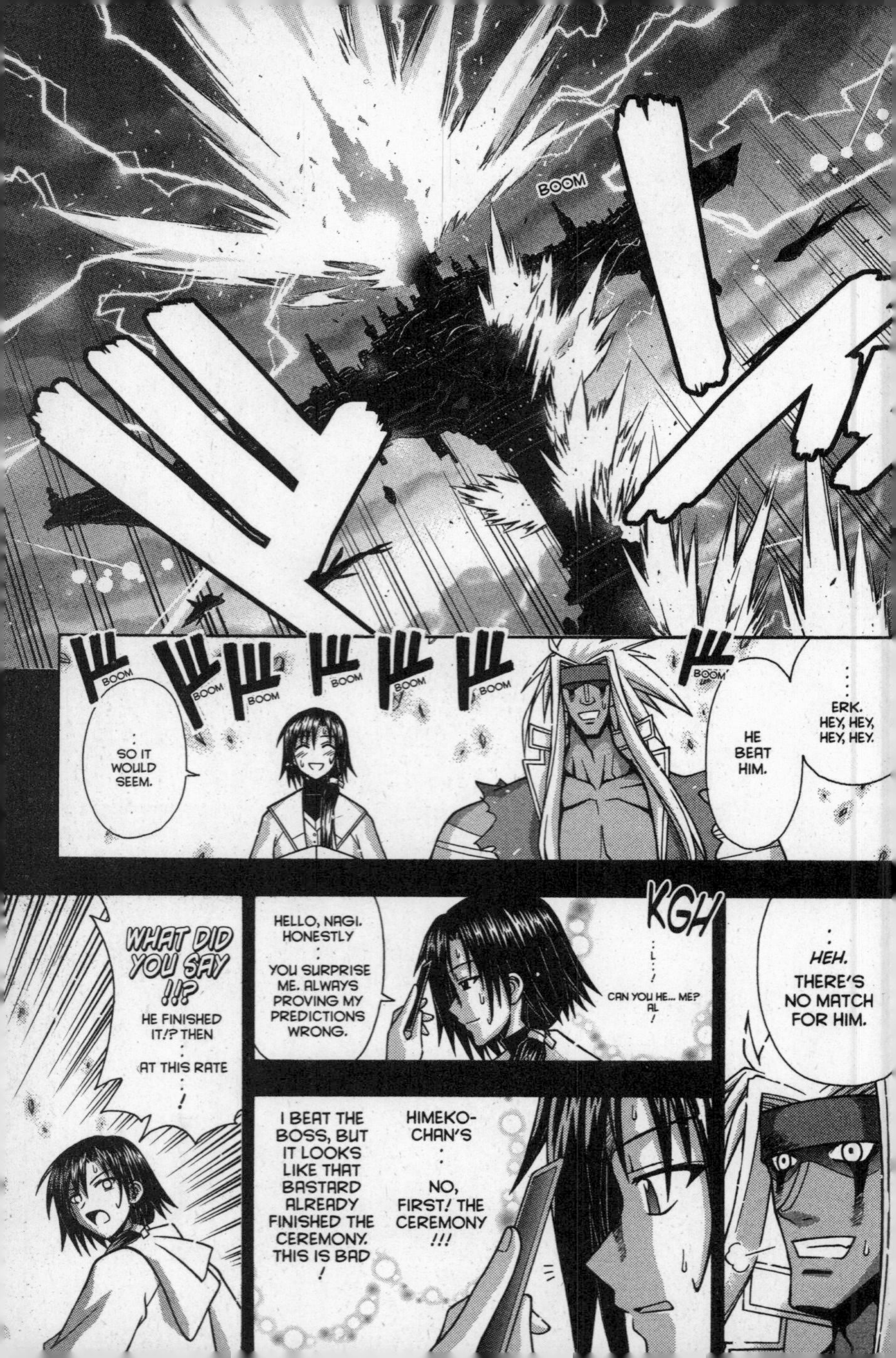
BOOM
ERK. HEY, HEY, HEY, HEY.
HE BEAT HIM.
BOOM BOOM BOOM BOOM BOOM BOOM BOOM
...SO IT WOULD SEEM.
...HEH. THERE'S NO MATCH FOR HIM.
KGH
...L...!
CAN YOU HE... ME? AL!
HELLO, NAGI. HONESTLY... YOU SURPRISE ME. ALWAYS PROVING MY PREDICTIONS WRONG.
HIMEKO-CHAN'S... NO, FIRST! THE CEREMONY!!!
I BEAT THE BOSS, BUT IT LOOKS LIKE THAT BASTARD ALREADY FINISHED THE CEREMONY. THIS IS BAD!
WHAT DID YOU SAY!!?
HE FINISHED IT!? THEN... AT THIS RATE...!

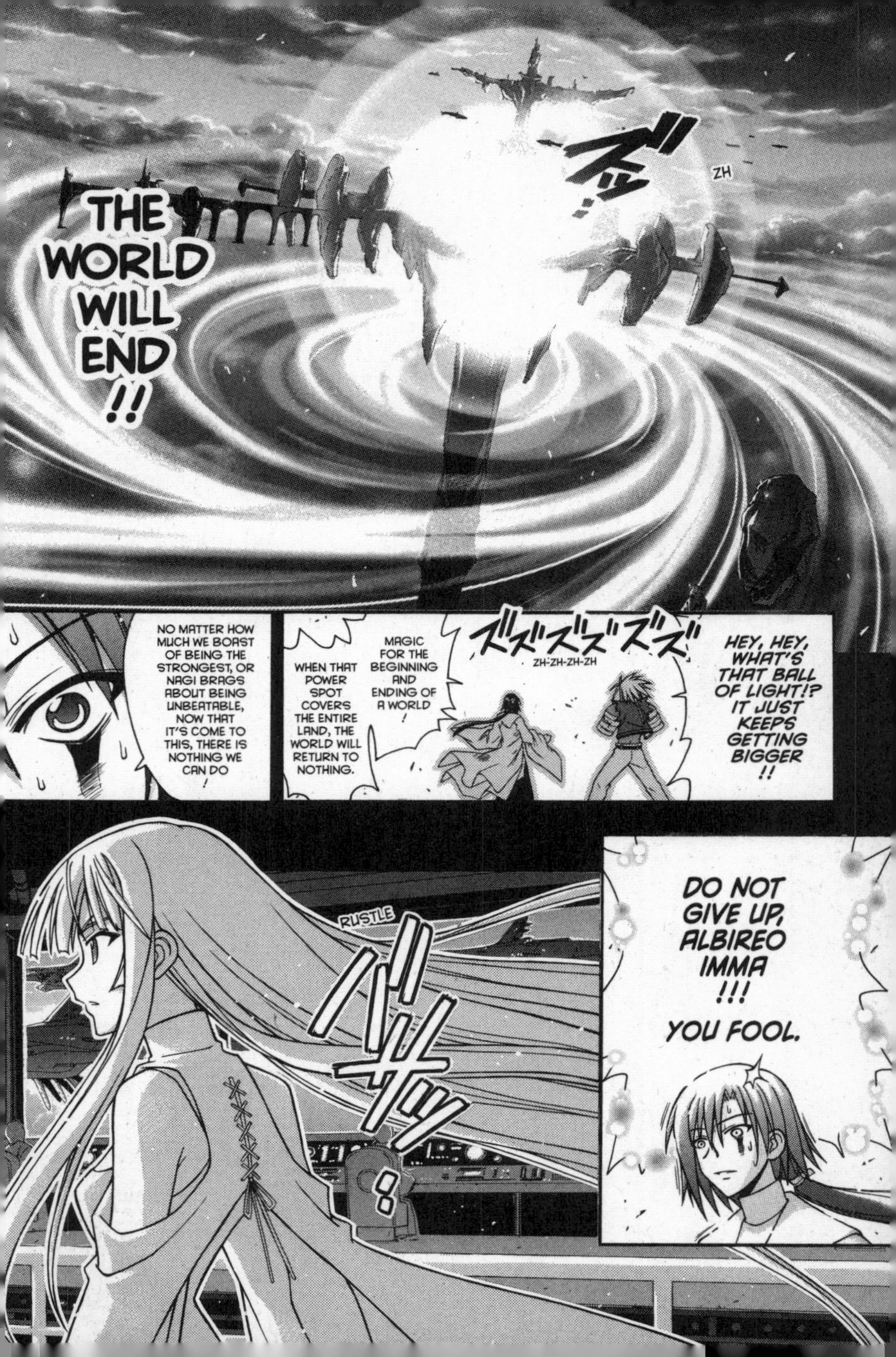
ZH
THE WORLD WILL END!!
ZH-ZH-ZH-ZH
HEY, HEY, WHAT'S THAT BALL OF LIGHT!? IT JUST KEEPS GETTING BIGGER!!
MAGIC FOR THE BEGINNING AND ENDING OF A WORLD!
WHEN THAT POWER SPOT COVERS THE ENTIRE LAND, THE WORLD WILL RETURN TO NOTHING.
NO MATTER HOW MUCH WE BOAST OF BEING THE STRONGEST, OR NAGI BRAGS ABOUT BEING UNBEATABLE, NOW THAT IT'S COME TO THIS, THERE IS NOTHING WE CAN DO!
DO NOT GIVE UP, ALBIREO IMMA!!!
YOU FOOL.
RUSTLE

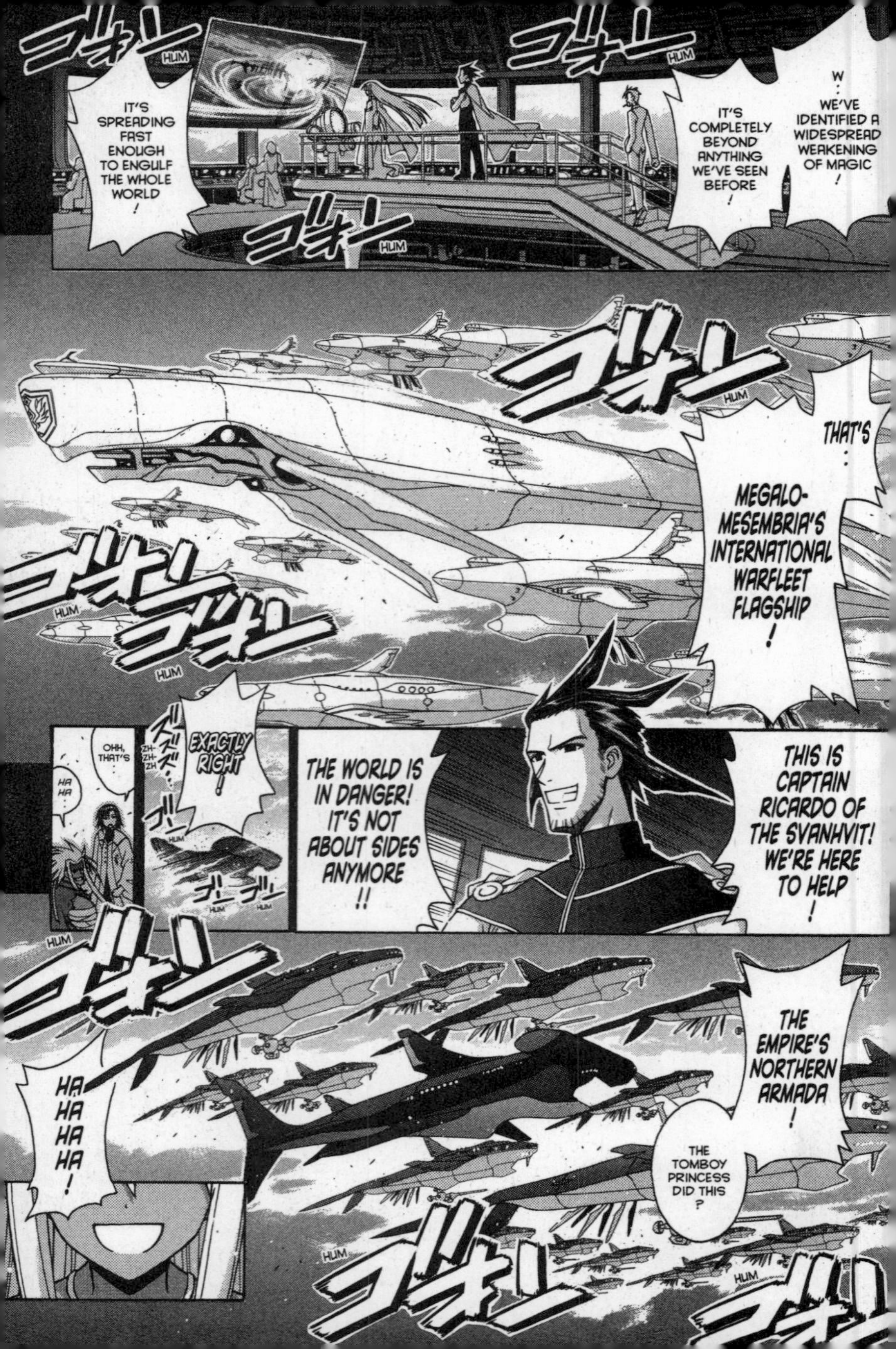

HUM
W... WE'VE IDENTIFIED A WIDESPREAD WEAKENING OF MAGIC!
IT'S COMPLETELY BEYOND ANYTHING WE'VE SEEN BEFORE!
HUM
IT'S SPREADING FAST ENOUGH TO ENGULF THE WHOLE WORLD!
HUM
HUM
THAT'S... MEGALO-MESEMBRIA'S INTERNATIONAL WARFLEET FLAGSHIP!
HUM
HUM
THIS IS CAPTAIN RICARDO OF THE SVANHVIT! WE'RE HERE TO HELP!
THE WORLD IS IN DANGER! IT'S NOT ABOUT SIDES ANYMORE!!
EXACTLY RIGHT!
ZH-ZH-ZH
HUM
HUM HUM
OHH, THAT'S...
HA HA...
HUM
THE EMPIRE'S NORTHERN ARMADA!
THE TOMBOY PRINCESS DID THIS?
HA HA HA HA HA!
HUM
HUM

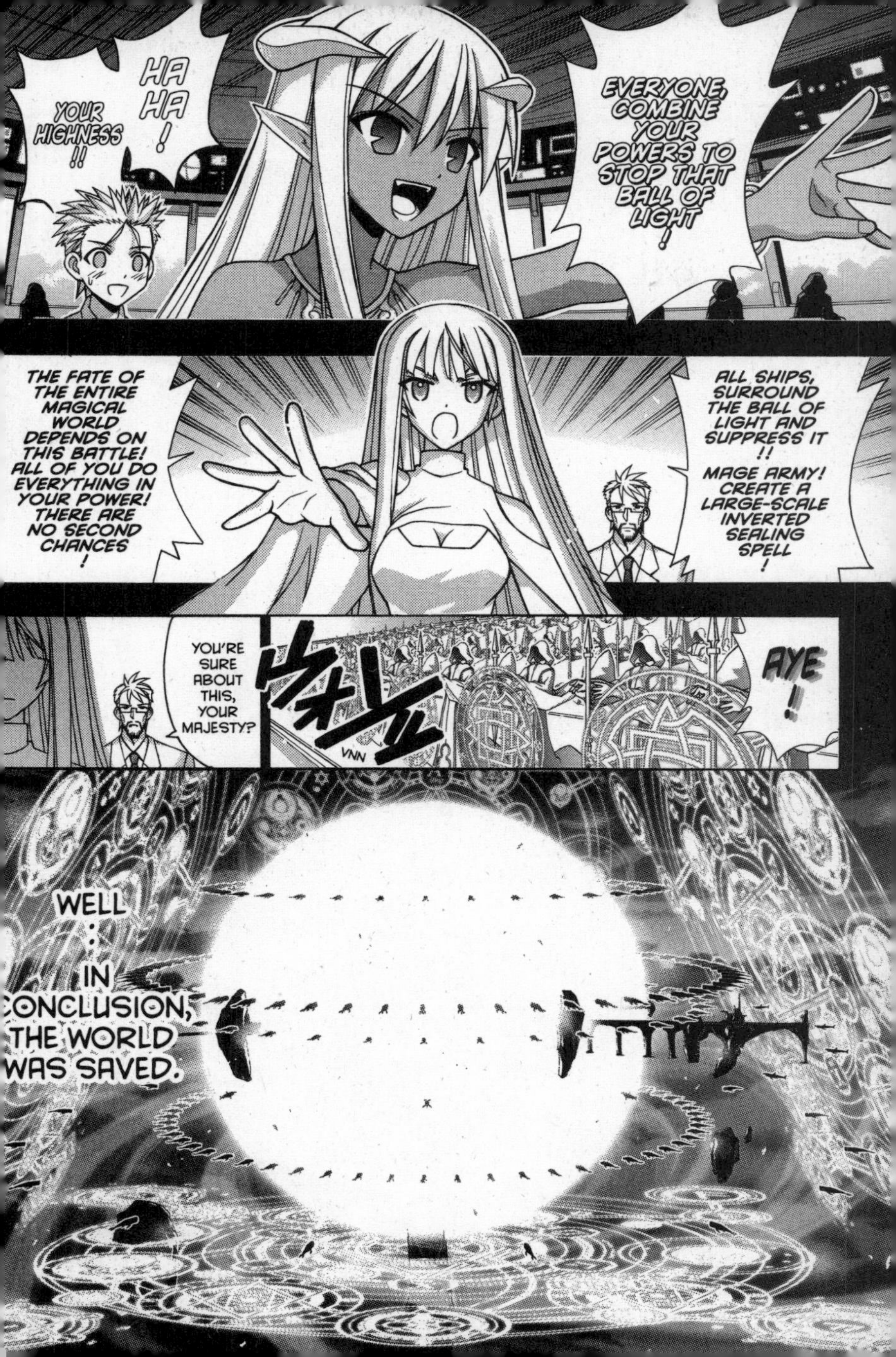
EVERYONE, COMBINE YOUR POWERS TO STOP THAT BALL OF LIGHT!
HA HA!
YOUR HIGHNESS!!
ALL SHIPS, SURROUND THE BALL OF LIGHT AND SUPPRESS IT!! MAGE ARMY! CREATE A LARGE-SCALE INVERTED SEALING SPELL!
THE FATE OF THE ENTIRE MAGICAL WORLD DEPENDS ON THIS BATTLE! ALL OF YOU DO EVERYTHING IN YOUR POWER! THERE ARE NO SECOND CHANCES!
AYE!!
VNN
YOU'RE SURE ABOUT THIS, YOUR MAJESTY?
WELL... IN CONCLUSION, THE WORLD WAS SAVED.

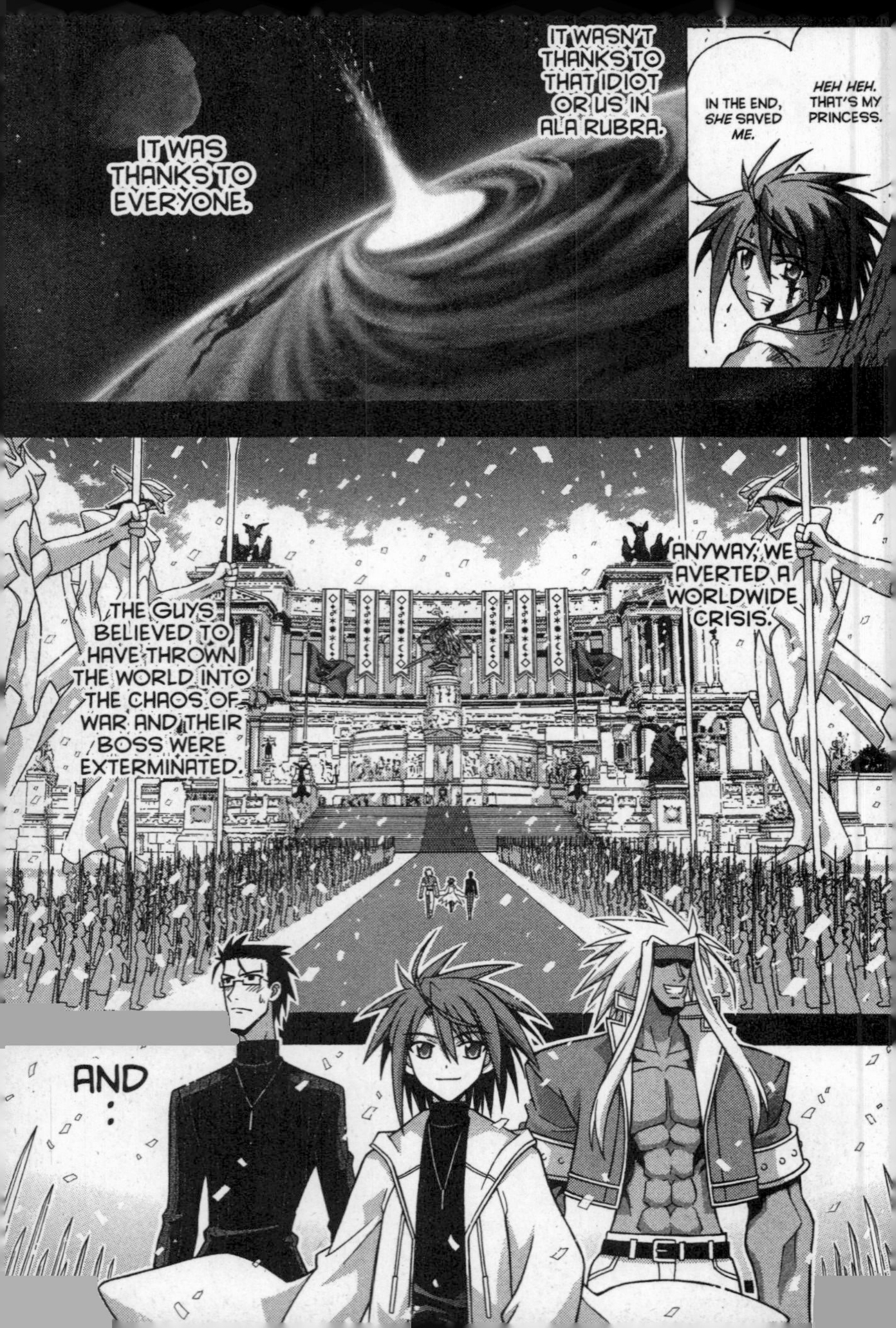
HEH HEH. THAT'S MY PRINCESS.
IN THE END, *SHE* SAVED ME.
IT WASN'T THANKS TO THAT IDIOT OR US IN ALA RUBRA.
IT WAS THANKS TO EVERYONE.
ANYWAY, WE AVERTED A WORLDWIDE CRISIS.
THE GUYS BELIEVED TO HAVE THROWN THE WORLD INTO THE CHAOS OF WAR AND THEIR BOSS WERE EXTERMINATED.
AND :

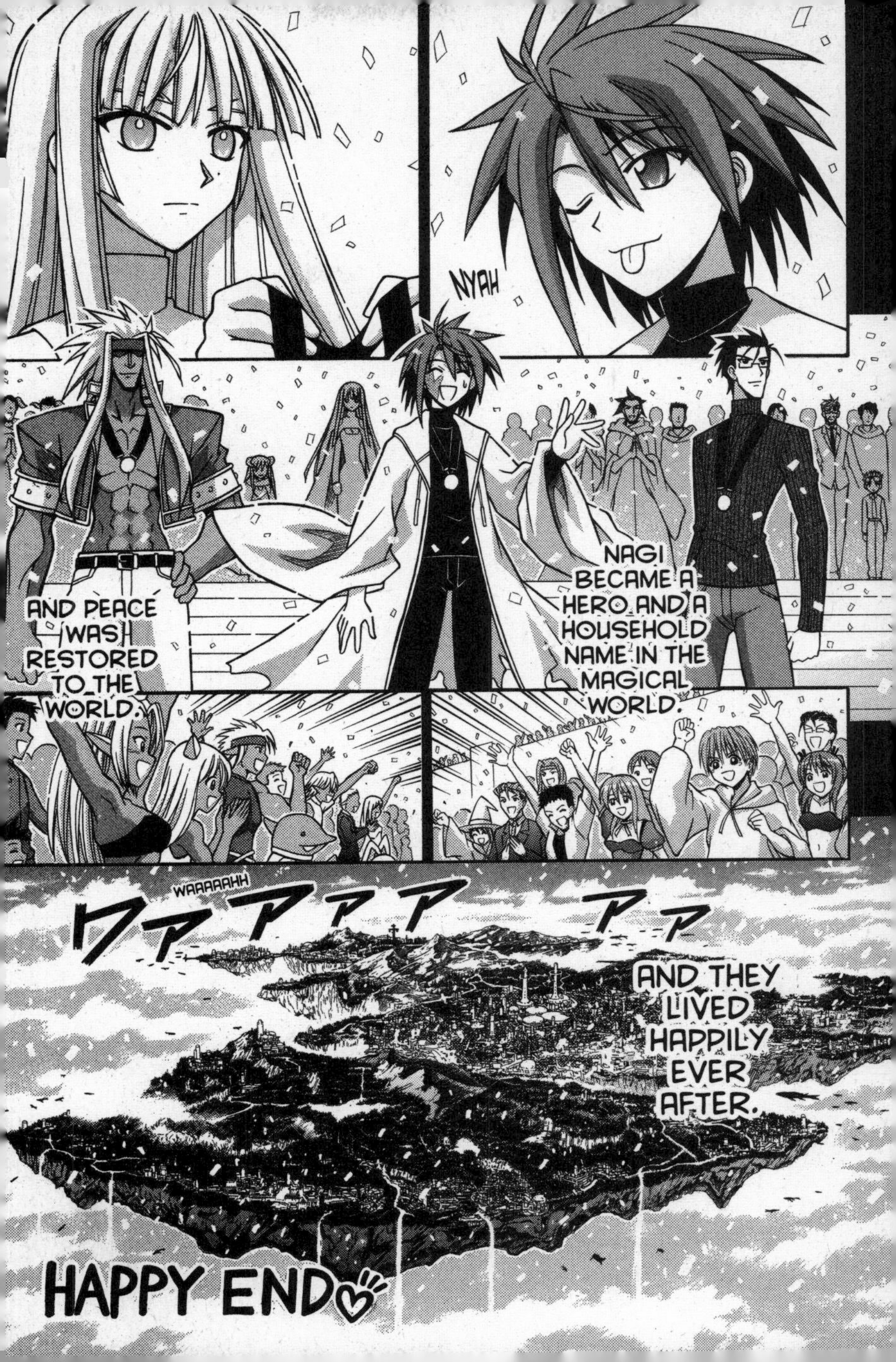
NYAH
NAGI BECAME A HERO AND A HOUSEHOLD NAME IN THE MAGICAL WORLD.
AND PEACE WAS RESTORED TO THE WORLD.
WAAAAAHH
ワアアア アア
AND THEY LIVED HAPPILY EVER AFTER.
HAPPY END♡

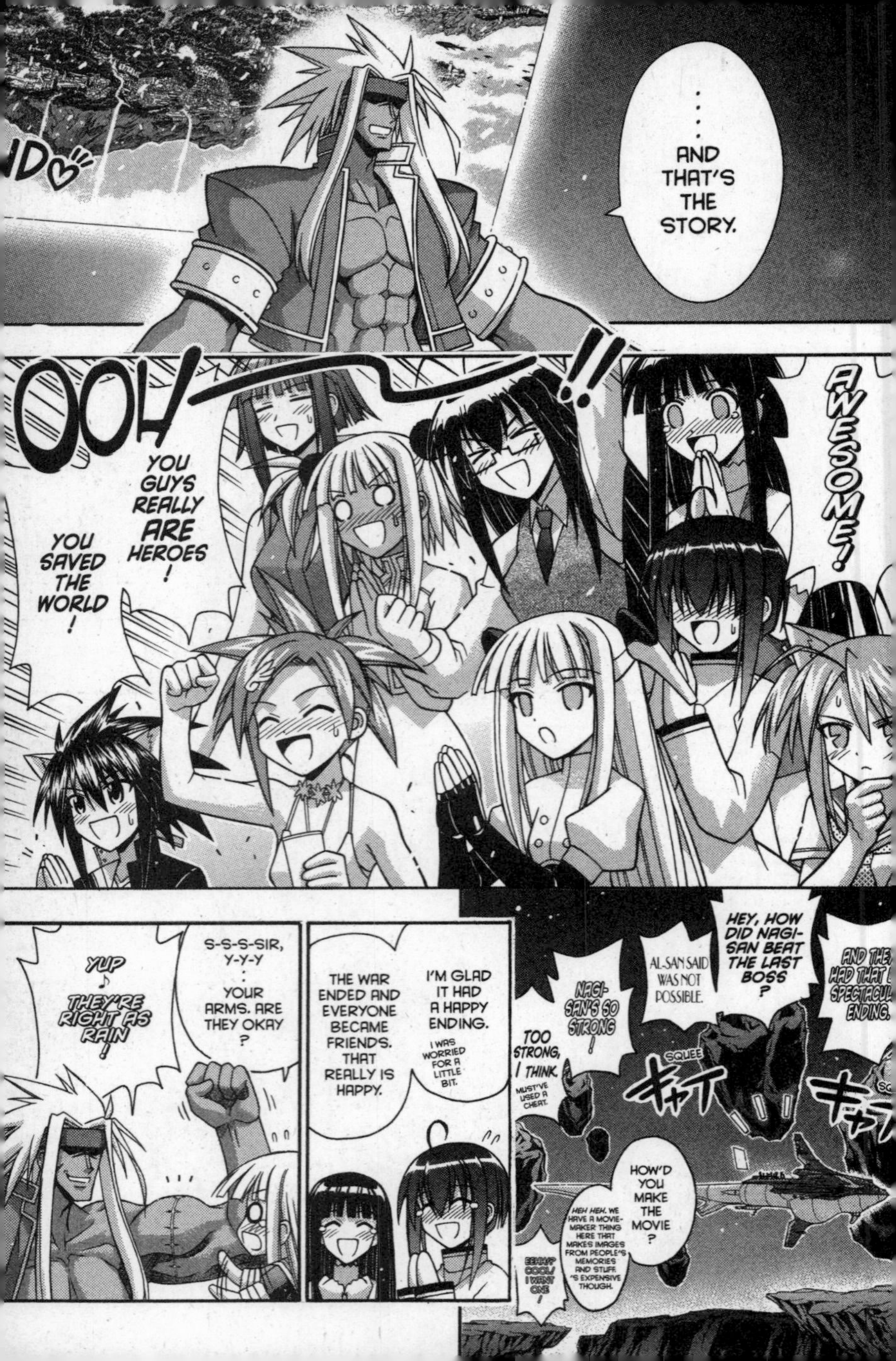
. . . . AND THAT'S THE STORY.
AWESOME!
OOH—!!
YOU GUYS REALLY ARE HEROES!
YOU SAVED THE WORLD!
HEY, HOW DID NAGI-SAN BEAT THE LAST BOSS?
AL-SAN SAID WAS NOT POSSIBLE.
NAGI-SAN'S SO STRONG!
TOO STRONG, I THINK.
MUST'VE USED A CHEAT.
SQUEE
キャイ
HOW'D YOU MAKE THE MOVIE?
HEH HEH. WE HAVE A MOVIE-MAKER THING HERE THAT MAKES IMAGES FROM PEOPLE'S MEMORIES AND STUFF. 'S EXPENSIVE THOUGH.
EEHH? COOL! I WANT ONE!
I'M GLAD IT HAD A HAPPY ENDING.
I WAS WORRIED FOR A LITTLE BIT.
THE WAR ENDED AND EVERYONE BECAME FRIENDS. THAT REALLY IS HAPPY.
S-S-S-SIR, Y-Y-Y : YOUR ARMS. ARE THEY OKAY?
YUP ♪ THEY'RE RIGHT AS RAIN!

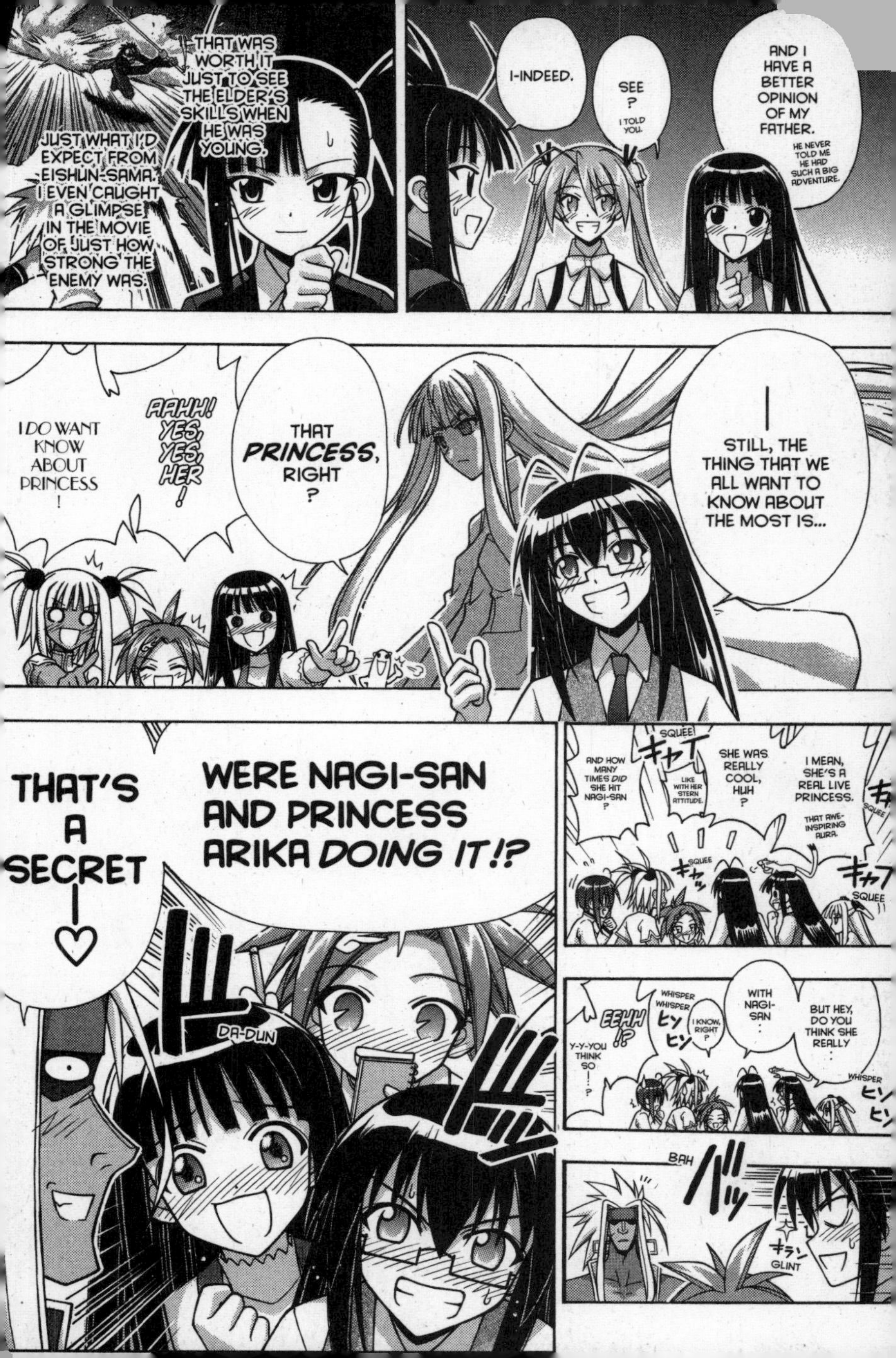
AND I HAVE A BETTER OPINION OF MY FATHER.
HE NEVER TOLD ME HE HAD SUCH A BIG ADVENTURE.
SEE? I TOLD YOU.
I-INDEED.
THAT WAS WORTH IT JUST TO SEE THE ELDER'S SKILLS WHEN HE WAS YOUNG.
JUST WHAT I'D EXPECT FROM EISHUN-SAMA. I EVEN CAUGHT A GLIMPSE IN THE MOVIE OF JUST HOW STRONG THE ENEMY WAS.
STILL, THE THING THAT WE ALL WANT TO KNOW ABOUT THE MOST IS...
THAT PRINCESS, RIGHT?
AAHH! YES, YES, HER!
I DO WANT KNOW ABOUT PRINCESS!
I MEAN, SHE'S A REAL LIVE PRINCESS.
THAT AWE-INSPIRING AURA.
SHE WAS REALLY COOL, HUH?
LIKE WITH HER STERN ATTITUDE.
AND HOW MANY TIMES DID SHE HIT NAGI-SAN?
SQUEE
SQUEE
SQUEE
SQUEE
BUT HEY, DO YOU THINK SHE REALLY...
WITH NAGI-SAN...
I KNOW, RIGHT?
WHISPER WHISPER
EEHH!?
Y-Y-YOU THINK SO...!?
WHISPER
BAH
GLINT
WERE NAGI-SAN AND PRINCESS ARIKA DOING IT!?
THAT'S A SECRET ♡
DA-DUN

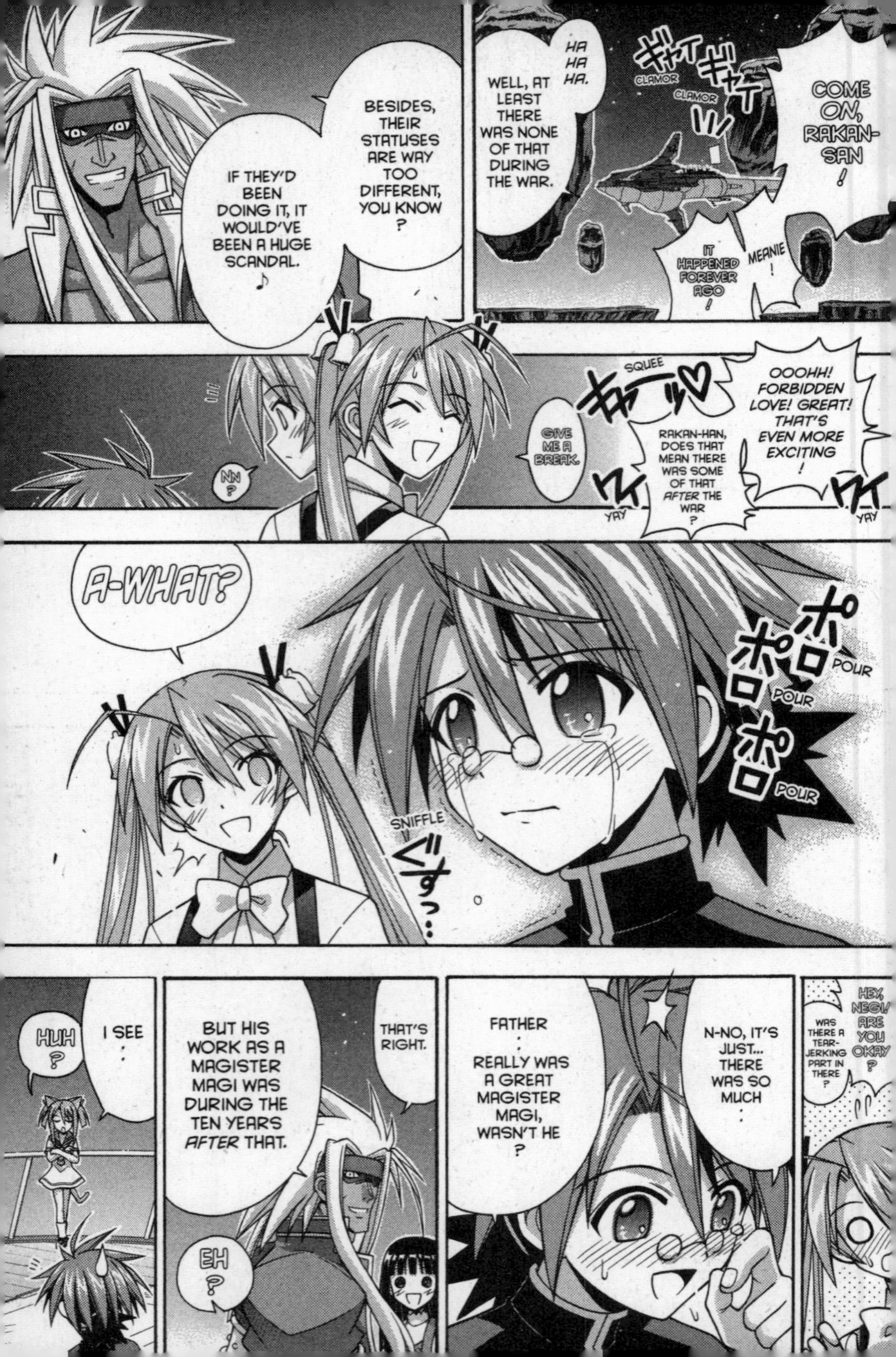

COME ON, RAKAN-SAN!
CLAMOR
CLAMOR
MEANIE!
IT HAPPENED FOREVER AGO!
HA HA HA.
WELL, AT LEAST THERE WAS NONE OF THAT DURING THE WAR.
BESIDES, THEIR STATUSES ARE WAY TOO DIFFERENT, YOU KNOW?
IF THEY'D BEEN DOING IT, IT WOULD'VE BEEN A HUGE SCANDAL. ♪
OOOHH! FORBIDDEN LOVE! GREAT! THAT'S EVEN MORE EXCITING!
YAY
SQUEE
RAKAN-HAN, DOES THAT MEAN THERE WAS SOME OF THAT *AFTER* THE WAR?
YAY
GIVE ME A BREAK.
NN?
POUR
POUR
POUR
SNIFFLE
A-WHAT?
HEY, NEGI! ARE YOU OKAY?
WAS THERE A TEAR-JERKING PART IN THERE?
N-NO, IT'S JUST... THERE WAS SO MUCH:
FATHER: REALLY WAS A GREAT MAGISTER MAGI, WASN'T HE?
THAT'S RIGHT.
BUT HIS WORK AS A MAGISTER MAGI WAS DURING THE TEN YEARS *AFTER* THAT.
EH?
I SEE:
HUH?

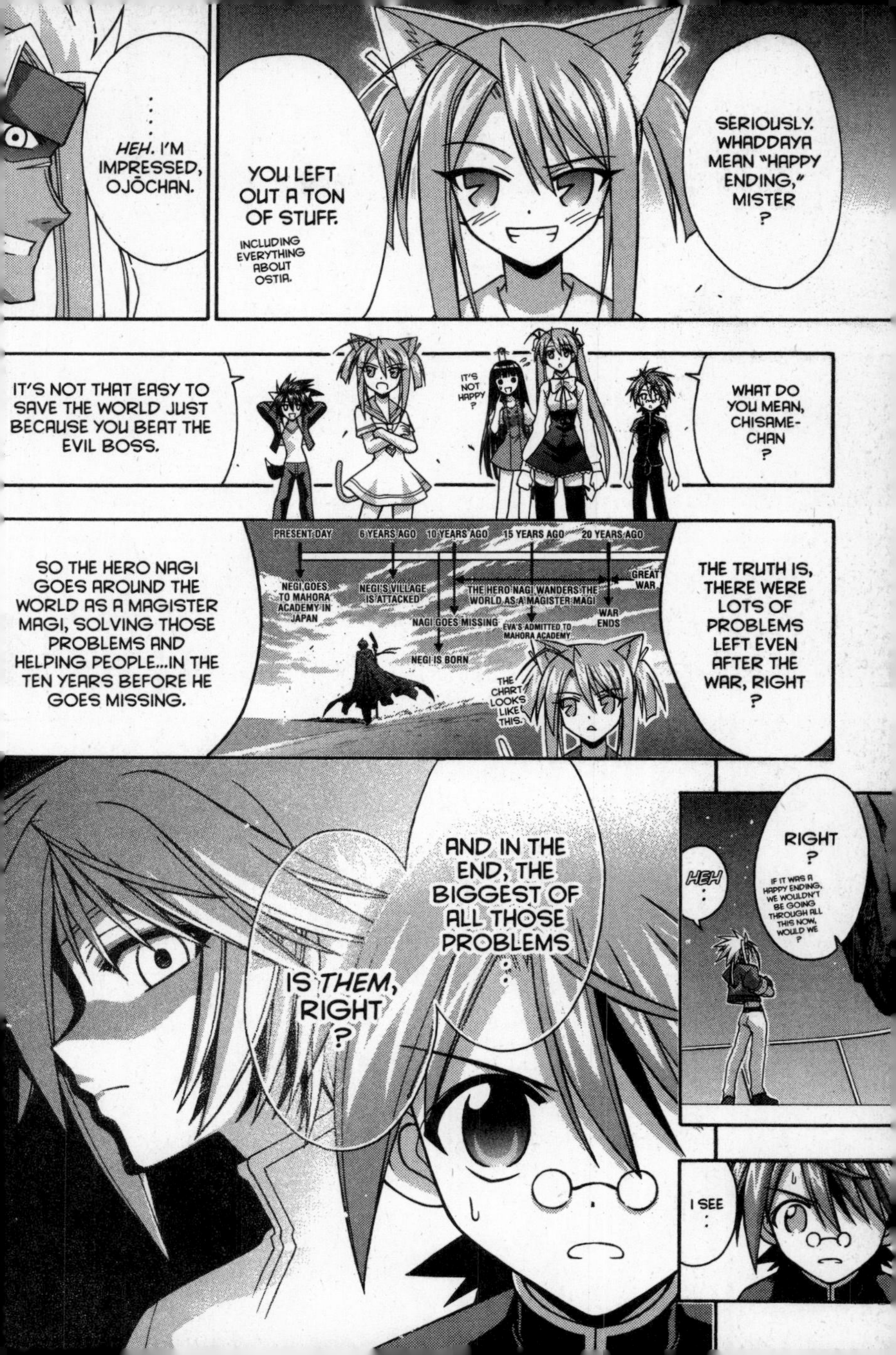
SERIOUSLY. WHADDAYA MEAN "HAPPY ENDING," MISTER?
YOU LEFT OUT A TON OF STUFF.
INCLUDING EVERYTHING ABOUT OSTIA.
...*HEH*. I'M IMPRESSED, OJŌCHAN.
WHAT DO YOU MEAN, CHISAME-CHAN?
IT'S NOT HAPPY?
IT'S NOT THAT EASY TO SAVE THE WORLD JUST BECAUSE YOU BEAT THE EVIL BOSS.
THE TRUTH IS, THERE WERE LOTS OF PROBLEMS LEFT EVEN AFTER THE WAR, RIGHT?
PRESENT DAY
6 YEARS AGO
10 YEARS AGO
15 YEARS AGO
20 YEARS AGO
GREAT WAR
WAR ENDS
THE HERO NAGI WANDERS THE WORLD AS A MAGISTER MAGI
EVA'S ADMITTED TO MAHORA ACADEMY
NAGI GOES MISSING
NEGI IS BORN
NEGI'S VILLAGE IS ATTACKED
NEGI GOES TO MAHORA ACADEMY IN JAPAN
THE CHART LOOKS LIKE THIS.
SO THE HERO NAGI GOES AROUND THE WORLD AS A MAGISTER MAGI, SOLVING THOSE PROBLEMS AND HELPING PEOPLE...IN THE TEN YEARS BEFORE HE GOES MISSING.
AND IN THE END, THE BIGGEST OF ALL THOSE PROBLEMS...
IS *THEM*, RIGHT?
RIGHT?
IF IT WAS A HAPPY ENDING, WE WOULDN'T BE GOING THROUGH ALL THIS NOW, WOULD WE?
HEH...
I SEE...

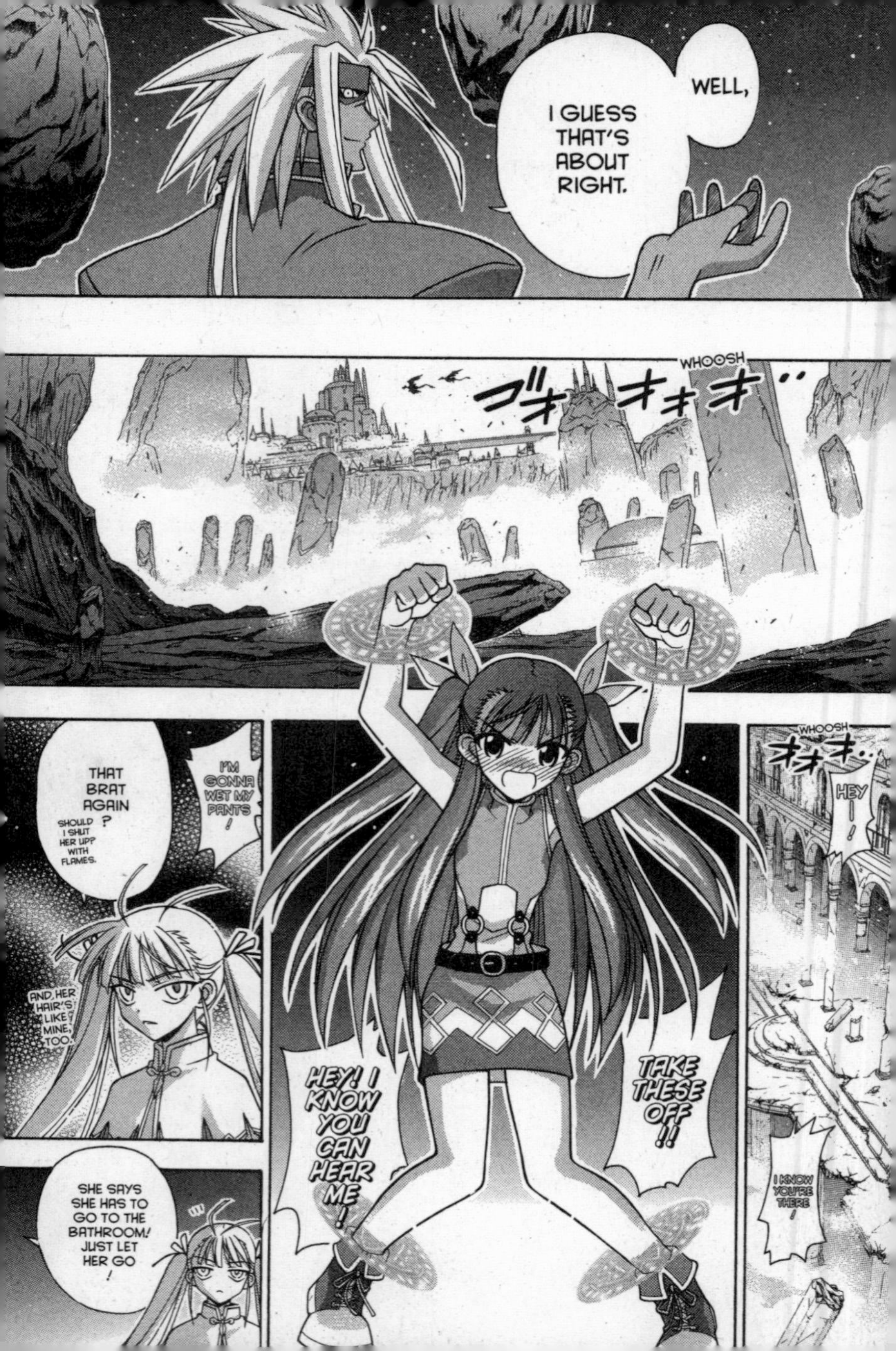
WELL, I GUESS THAT'S ABOUT RIGHT.
WHOOSH
ゴオオオ
WHOOSH
オォォ…
HEY!
I KNOW YOU'RE THERE!
HEY! I KNOW YOU CAN HEAR ME!
TAKE THESE OFF!!
I'M GONNA WET MY PANTS!
THAT BRAT AGAIN?
SHOULD I SHUT HER UP? WITH FLAMES.
AND, HER HAIR'S LIKE MINE, TOO.
SHE SAYS SHE HAS TO GO TO THE BATHROOM! JUST LET HER GO!

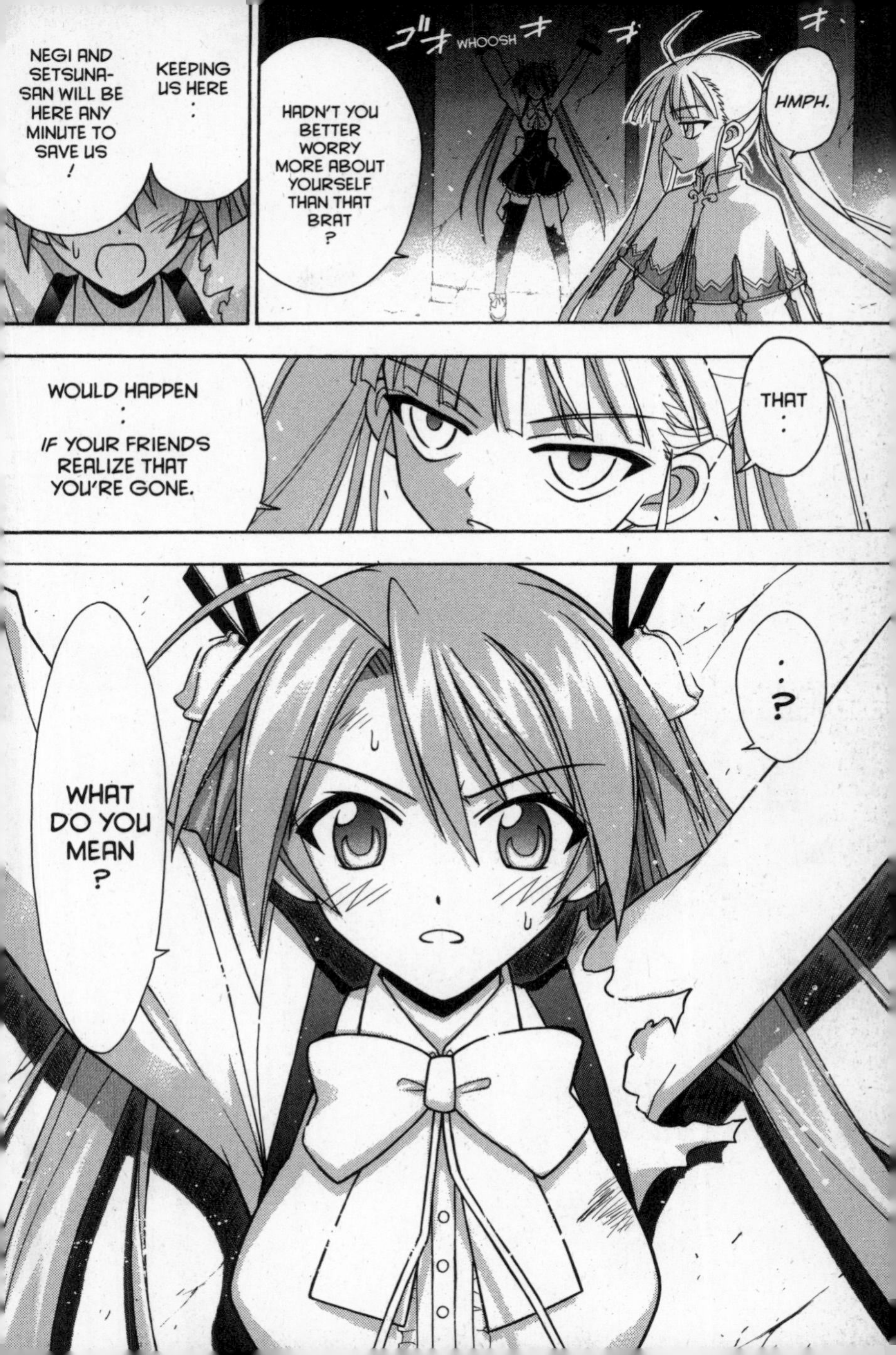
ゴオ WHOOSH オ オ オ
HMPH.
HADN'T YOU BETTER WORRY MORE ABOUT YOURSELF THAN THAT BRAT?
KEEPING US HERE :
NEGI AND SETSUNA-SAN WILL BE HERE ANY MINUTE TO SAVE US!
THAT :
WOULD HAPPEN :
IF YOUR FRIENDS REALIZE THAT YOU'RE GONE.
..?
WHAT DO YOU MEAN?

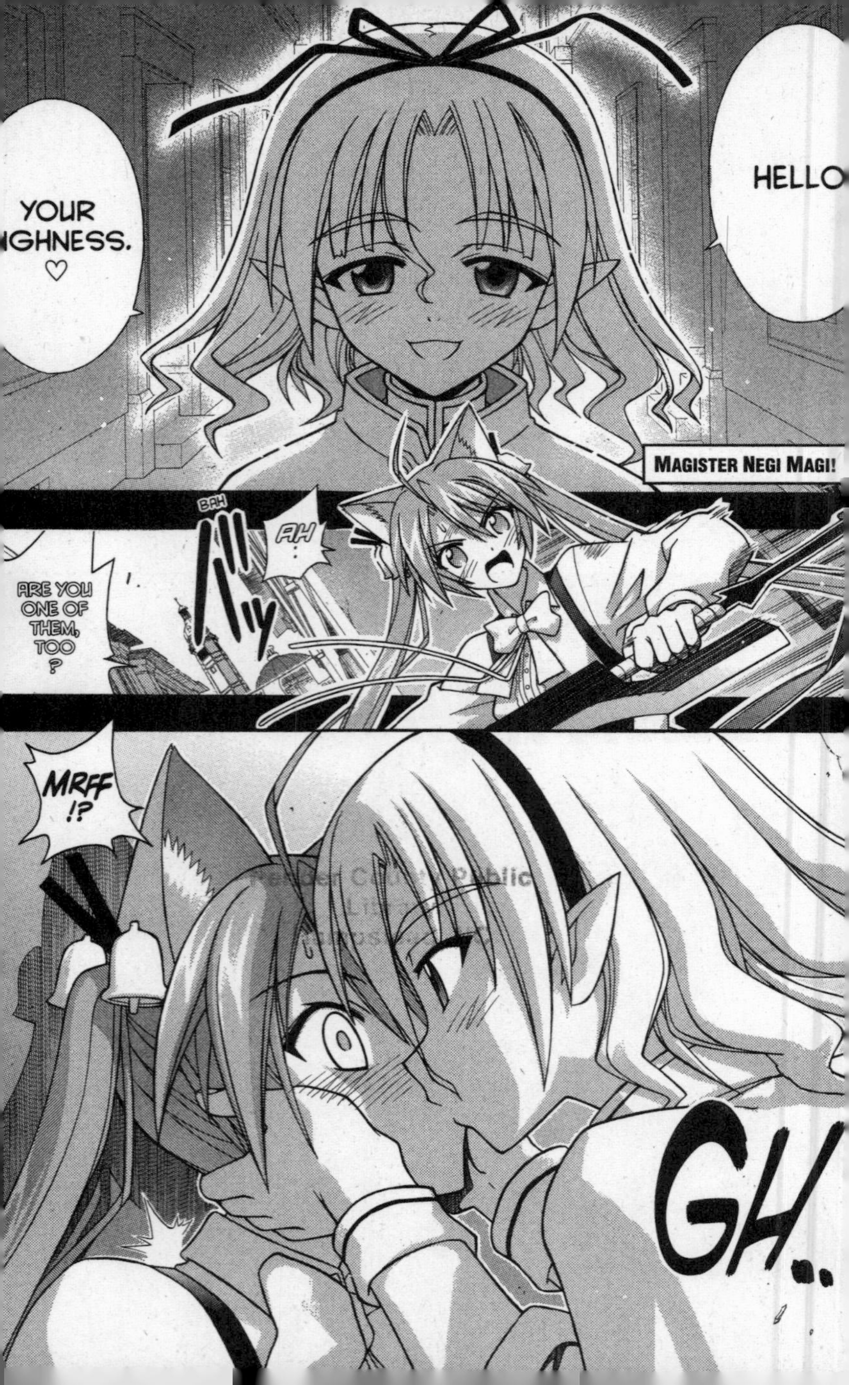
HELLO
YOUR
IGHNESS. ♡
MAGISTER NEGI MAGI!
BAH
AH
ARE YOU ONE OF THEM, TOO?
MRFF !?
GH..

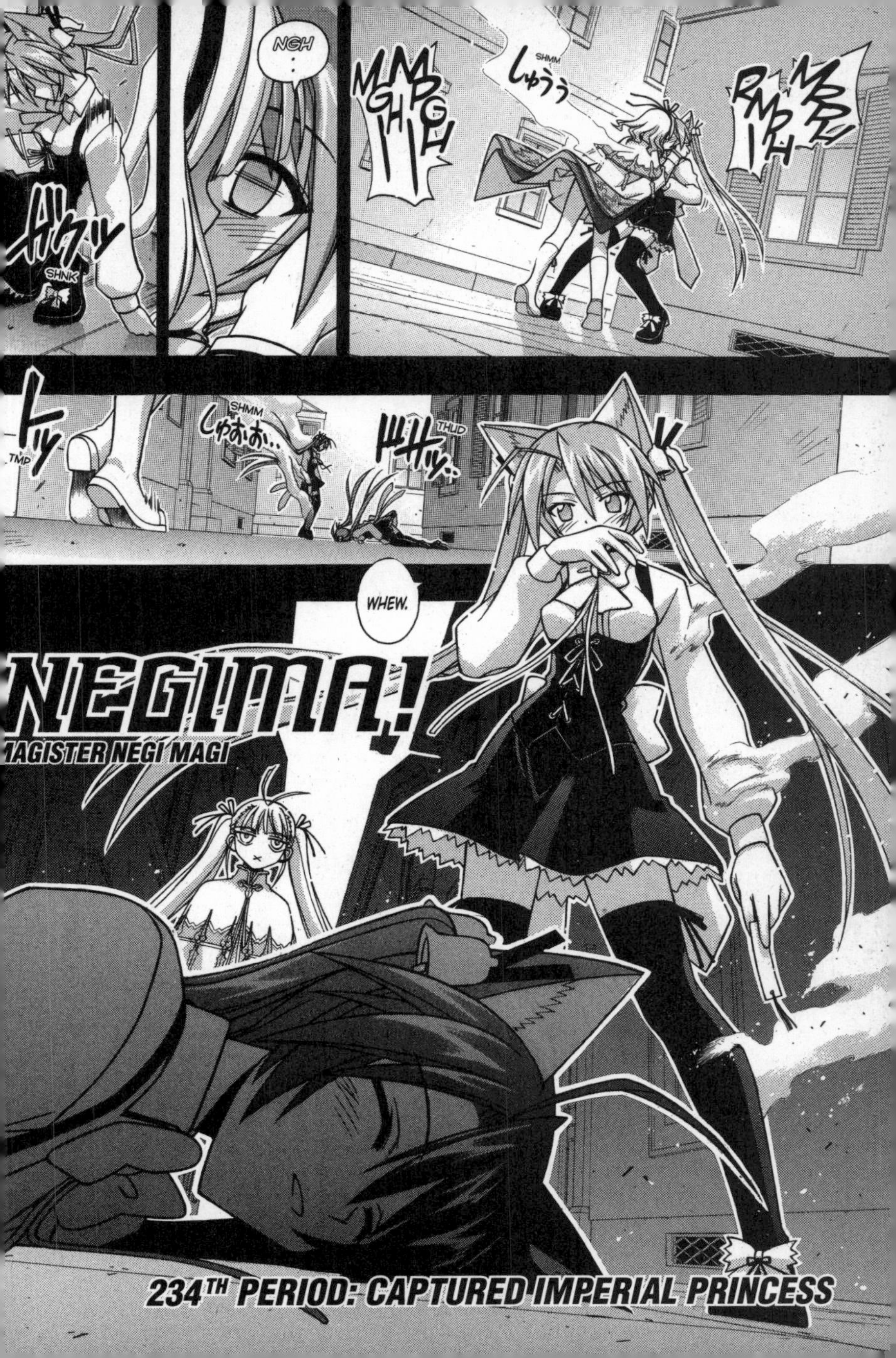

MRPH!
RMPH!
しゅううう
SHMM
MMGHH!
MPGHH!
NGH
. . .
ガクッ
SHNK
ザザッ
THUD
しゅおぉ…
SHMM
トッ
TMP
WHEW.
NEGIMA!
MAGISTER NEGI MAGI
234TH PERIOD: CAPTURED IMPERIAL PRINCESS

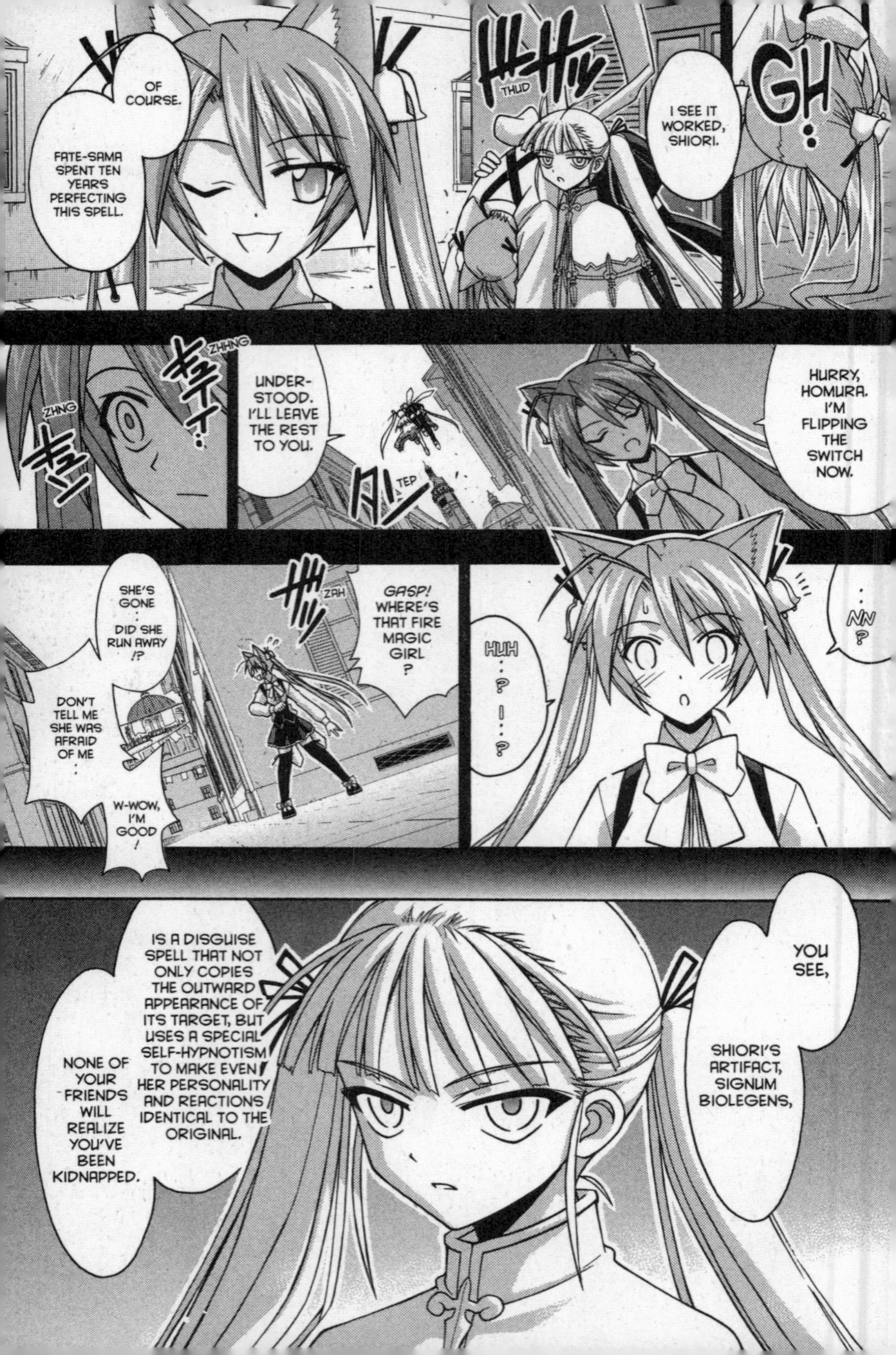
GH
I SEE IT WORKED, SHIORI.
THUD
OF COURSE.
FATE-SAMA SPENT TEN YEARS PERFECTING THIS SPELL.
HURRY, HOMURA. I'M FLIPPING THE SWITCH NOW.
UNDER-STOOD. I'LL LEAVE THE REST TO YOU.
TEP
ZHNG
ZHNG
...NN?
HUH...? I...?
GASP! WHERE'S THAT FIRE MAGIC GIRL?
ZAH
SHE'S GONE... DID SHE RUN AWAY!?
DON'T TELL ME SHE WAS AFRAID OF ME...
W-WOW, I'M GOOD!
YOU SEE,
SHIORI'S ARTIFACT, SIGNUM BIOLEGENS,
IS A DISGUISE SPELL THAT NOT ONLY COPIES THE OUTWARD APPEARANCE OF ITS TARGET, BUT USES A SPECIAL SELF-HYPNOTISM TO MAKE EVEN HER PERSONALITY AND REACTIONS IDENTICAL TO THE ORIGINAL.
NONE OF YOUR FRIENDS WILL REALIZE YOU'VE BEEN KIDNAPPED.

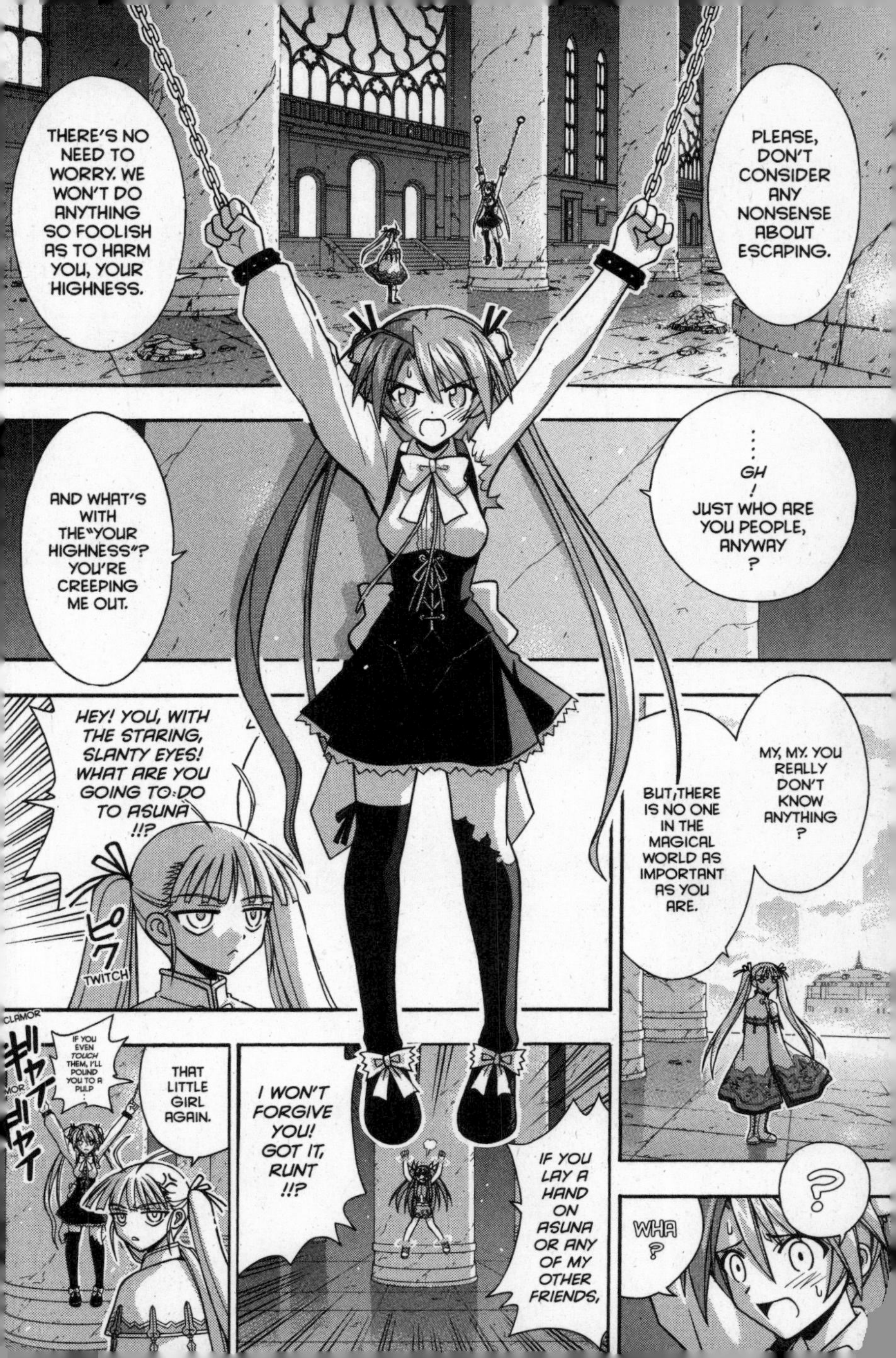
PLEASE, DON'T CONSIDER ANY NONSENSE ABOUT ESCAPING.
THERE'S NO NEED TO WORRY. WE WON'T DO ANYTHING SO FOOLISH AS TO HARM YOU, YOUR HIGHNESS.
...GH! JUST WHO ARE YOU PEOPLE, ANYWAY?
AND WHAT'S WITH THE "YOUR HIGHNESS"? YOU'RE CREEPING ME OUT.
MY, MY. YOU REALLY DON'T KNOW ANYTHING?
BUT, THERE IS NO ONE IN THE MAGICAL WORLD AS IMPORTANT AS YOU ARE.
HEY! YOU, WITH THE STARING, SLANTY EYES! WHAT ARE YOU GOING TO DO TO ASUNA!!?
ピク
TWITCH
?
WHA?
IF YOU LAY A HAND ON ASUNA OR ANY OF MY OTHER FRIENDS,
I WON'T FORGIVE YOU! GOT IT, RUNT!!?
THAT LITTLE GIRL AGAIN.
IF YOU EVEN TOUCH THEM, I'LL POUND YOU TO A PULP...
CLAMOR
ギャイギャイ

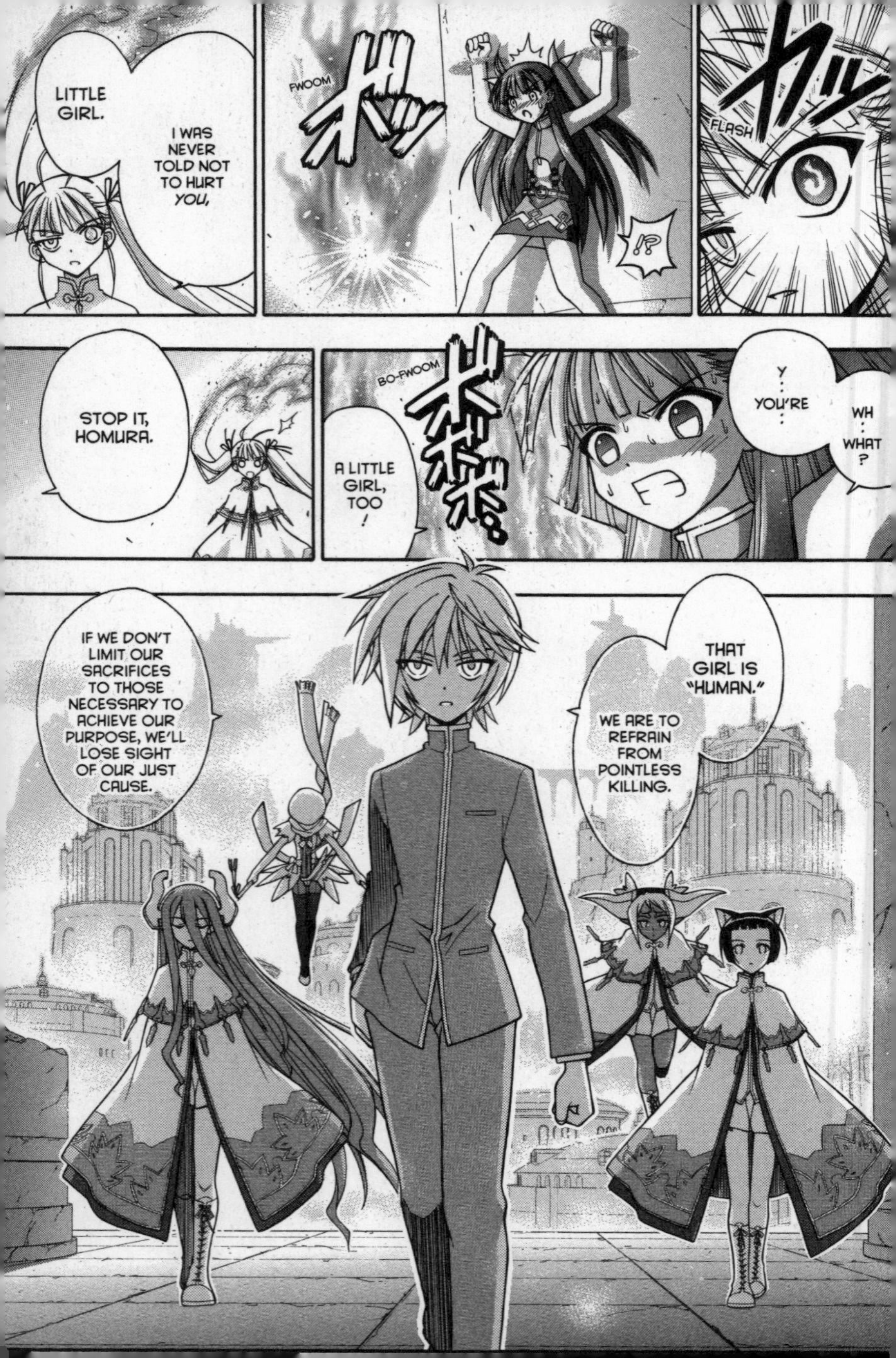
FLASH
FWOOM
!?
LITTLE GIRL.
I WAS NEVER TOLD NOT TO HURT *YOU*,
WH... WHAT?
Y... YOU'RE...
BO-FWOOM
A LITTLE GIRL, TOO!
STOP IT, HOMURA.
THAT GIRL IS "HUMAN."
WE ARE TO REFRAIN FROM POINTLESS KILLING.
IF WE DON'T LIMIT OUR SACRIFICES TO THOSE NECESSARY TO ACHIEVE OUR PURPOSE, WE'LL LOSE SIGHT OF OUR JUST CAUSE.

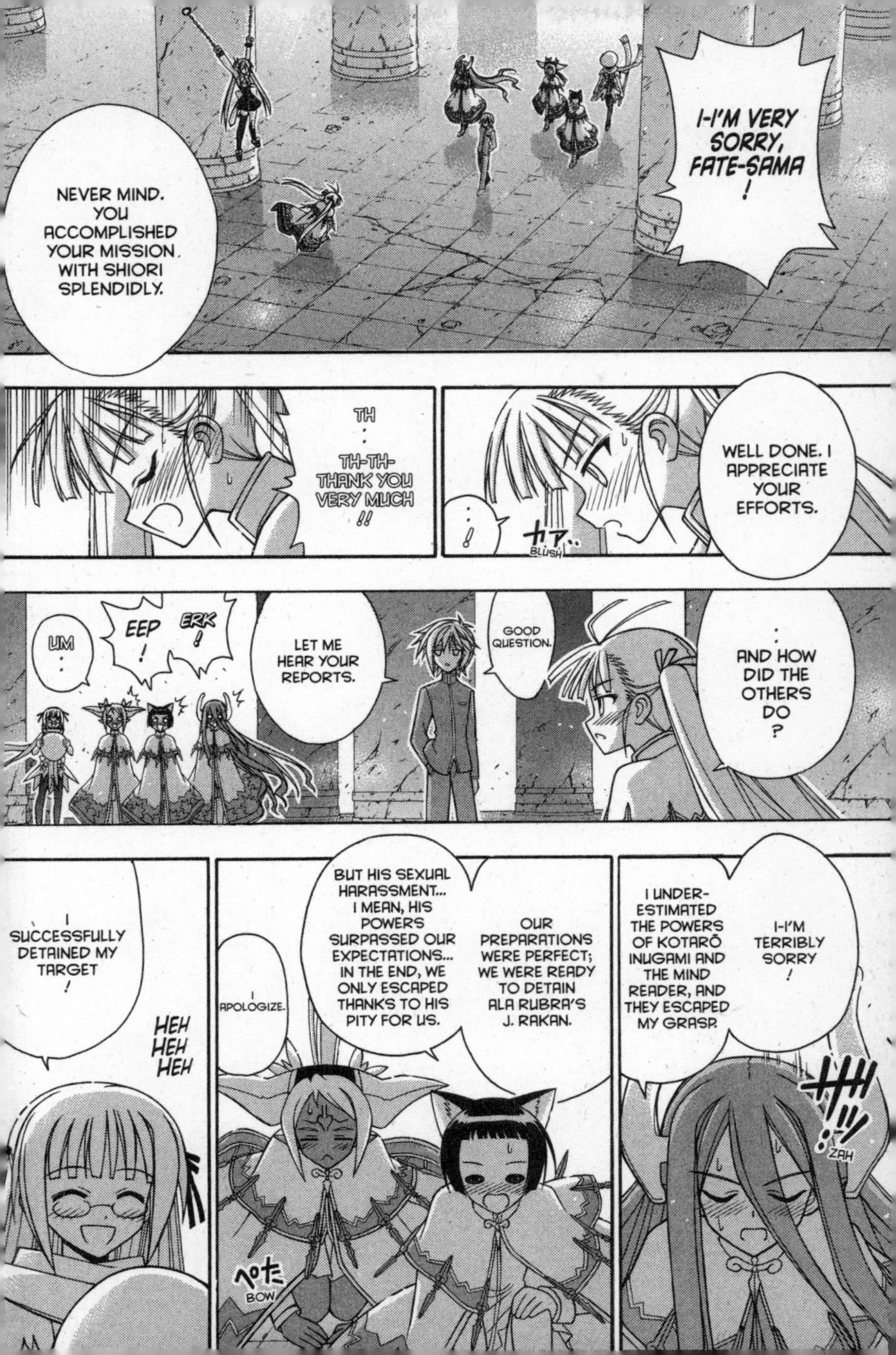
I-I'M VERY SORRY, FATE-SAMA!
NEVER MIND. YOU ACCOMPLISHED YOUR MISSION WITH SHIORI SPLENDIDLY.
WELL DONE. I APPRECIATE YOUR EFFORTS.
...!
BLUSH
TH... TH-TH-THANK YOU VERY MUCH!!
...AND HOW DID THE OTHERS DO?
GOOD QUESTION.
LET ME HEAR YOUR REPORTS.
ERK!
EEP!
UM...
I-I'M TERRIBLY SORRY!
I UNDER-ESTIMATED THE POWERS OF KOTARŌ INUGAMI AND THE MIND READER, AND THEY ESCAPED MY GRASP.
ZAH
OUR PREPARATIONS WERE PERFECT; WE WERE READY TO DETAIN ALA RUBRA'S J. RAKAN.
BUT HIS SEXUAL HARASSMENT... I MEAN, HIS POWERS SURPASSED OUR EXPECTATIONS... IN THE END, WE ONLY ESCAPED THANKS TO HIS PITY FOR US.
I APOLOGIZE.
BOW
I SUCCESSFULLY DETAINED MY TARGET!
HEH HEH HEH

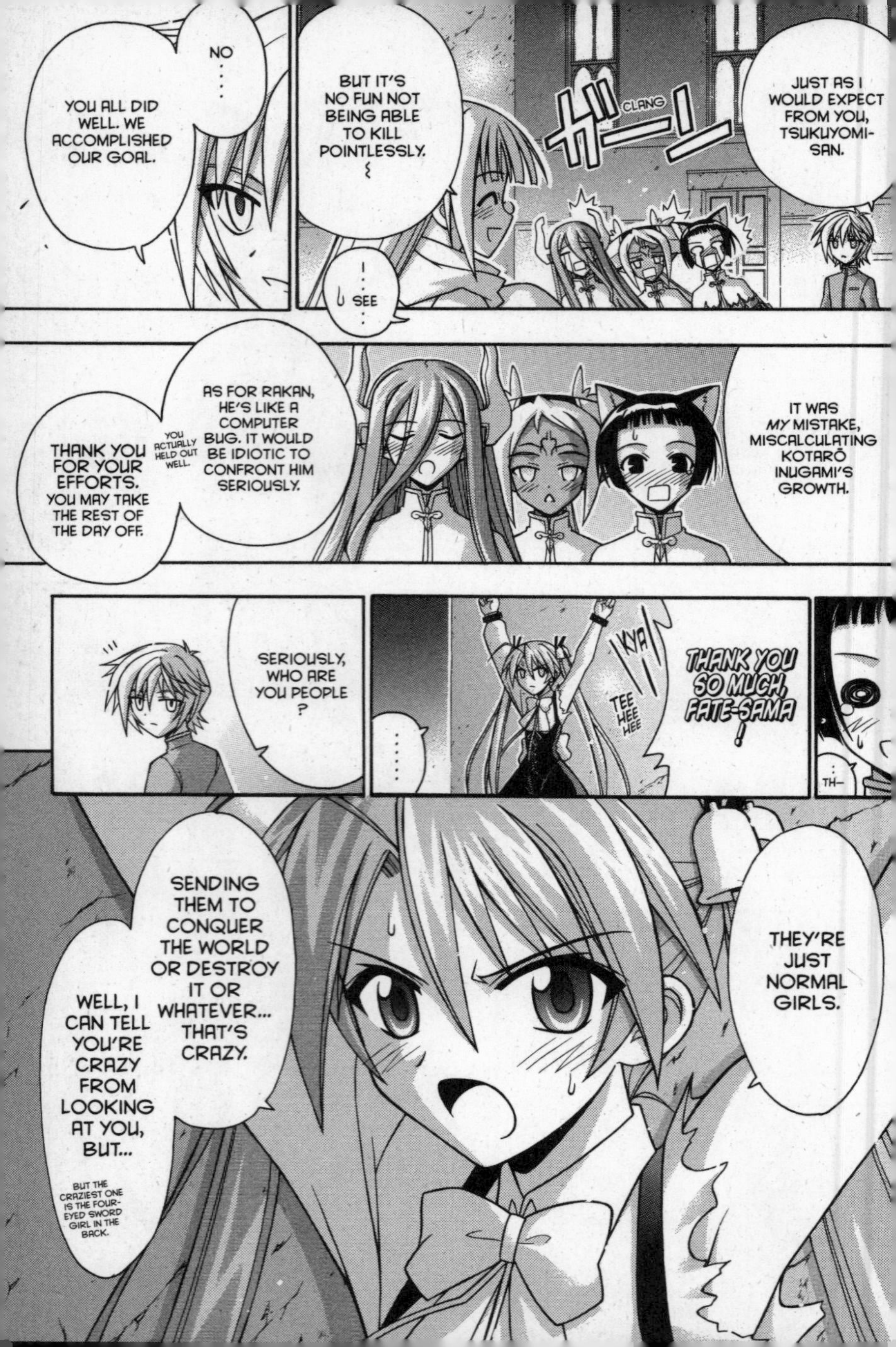
JUST AS I WOULD EXPECT FROM YOU, TSUKUYOMI-SAN.
CLANG
BUT IT'S NO FUN NOT BEING ABLE TO KILL POINTLESSLY.
I... SEE...
NO......
YOU ALL DID WELL. WE ACCOMPLISHED OUR GOAL.
IT WAS MY MISTAKE, MISCALCULATING KOTARŌ INUGAMI'S GROWTH.
AS FOR RAKAN, HE'S LIKE A COMPUTER BUG. IT WOULD BE IDIOTIC TO CONFRONT HIM SERIOUSLY.
YOU ACTUALLY HELD OUT WELL.
THANK YOU FOR YOUR EFFORTS. YOU MAY TAKE THE REST OF THE DAY OFF.
...TH—
THANK YOU SO MUCH, FATE-SAMA!
KYA!
TEE HEE HEE
......
SERIOUSLY, WHO ARE YOU PEOPLE?
THEY'RE JUST NORMAL GIRLS.
SENDING THEM TO CONQUER THE WORLD OR DESTROY IT OR WHATEVER... THAT'S CRAZY.
WELL, I CAN TELL YOU'RE CRAZY FROM LOOKING AT YOU, BUT...
BUT THE CRAZIEST ONE IS THE FOUR-EYED SWORD GIRL IN THE BACK.

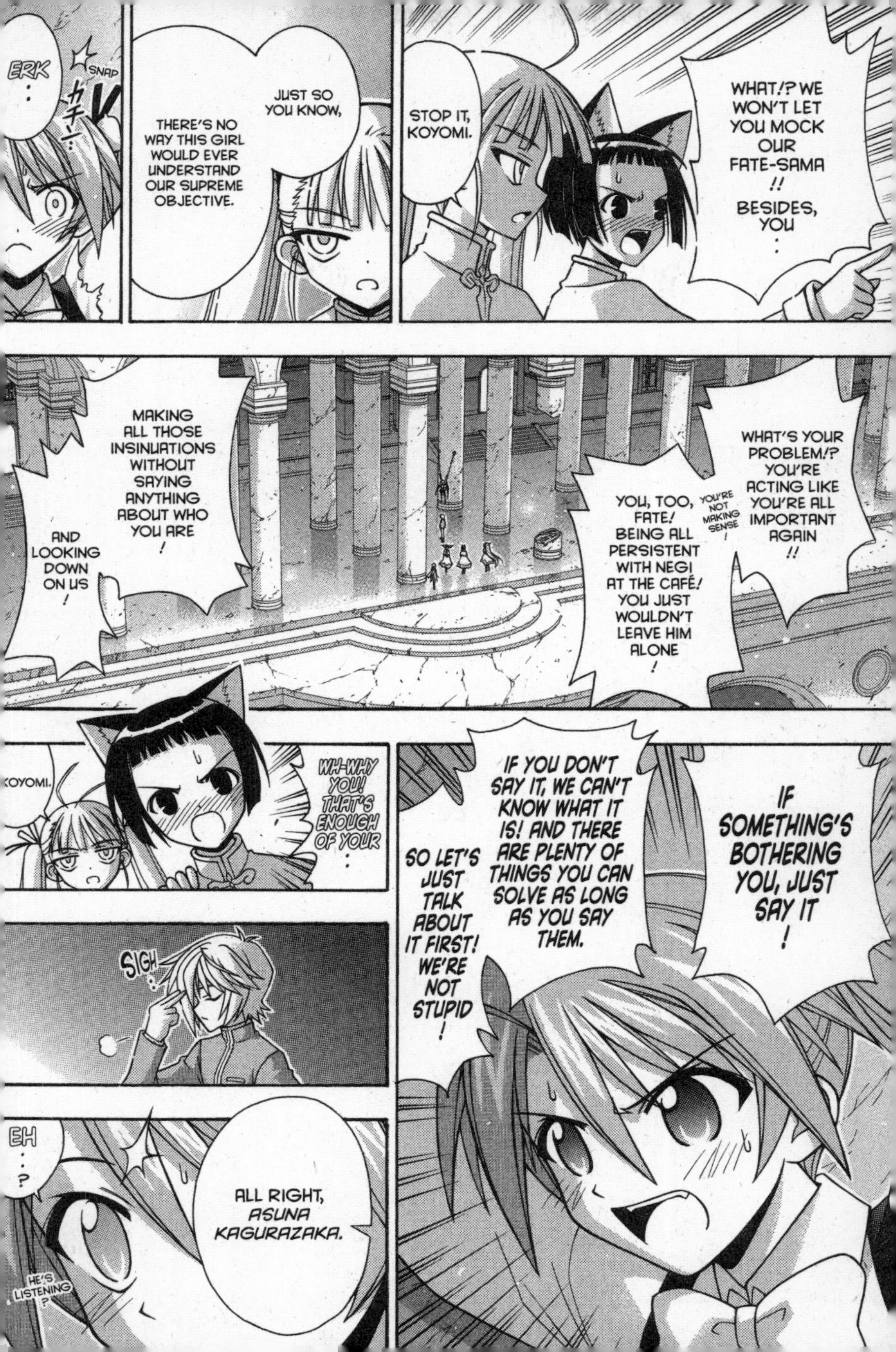
WHAT!? WE WON'T LET YOU MOCK OUR FATE-SAMA!! BESIDES, YOU...
STOP IT, KOYOMI.
JUST SO YOU KNOW,
THERE'S NO WAY THIS GIRL WOULD EVER UNDERSTAND OUR SUPREME OBJECTIVE.
SNAP
ERK...
WHAT'S YOUR PROBLEM!? YOU'RE ACTING LIKE YOU'RE ALL IMPORTANT AGAIN!!
YOU'RE NOT MAKING SENSE!
YOU, TOO, FATE! BEING ALL PERSISTENT WITH NEGI AT THE CAFÉ! YOU JUST WOULDN'T LEAVE HIM ALONE!
MAKING ALL THOSE INSINUATIONS WITHOUT SAYING ANYTHING ABOUT WHO YOU ARE!
AND LOOKING DOWN ON US!
IF SOMETHING'S BOTHERING YOU, JUST SAY IT!
IF YOU DON'T SAY IT, WE CAN'T KNOW WHAT IT IS! AND THERE ARE PLENTY OF THINGS YOU CAN SOLVE AS LONG AS YOU SAY THEM.
SO LET'S JUST TALK ABOUT IT FIRST! WE'RE NOT STUPID!
WH-WHY YOU! THAT'S ENOUGH OF YOUR...
KOYOMI.
SIGH...
ALL RIGHT, ASUNA KAGURAZAKA.
EH...?
HE'S LISTENING?

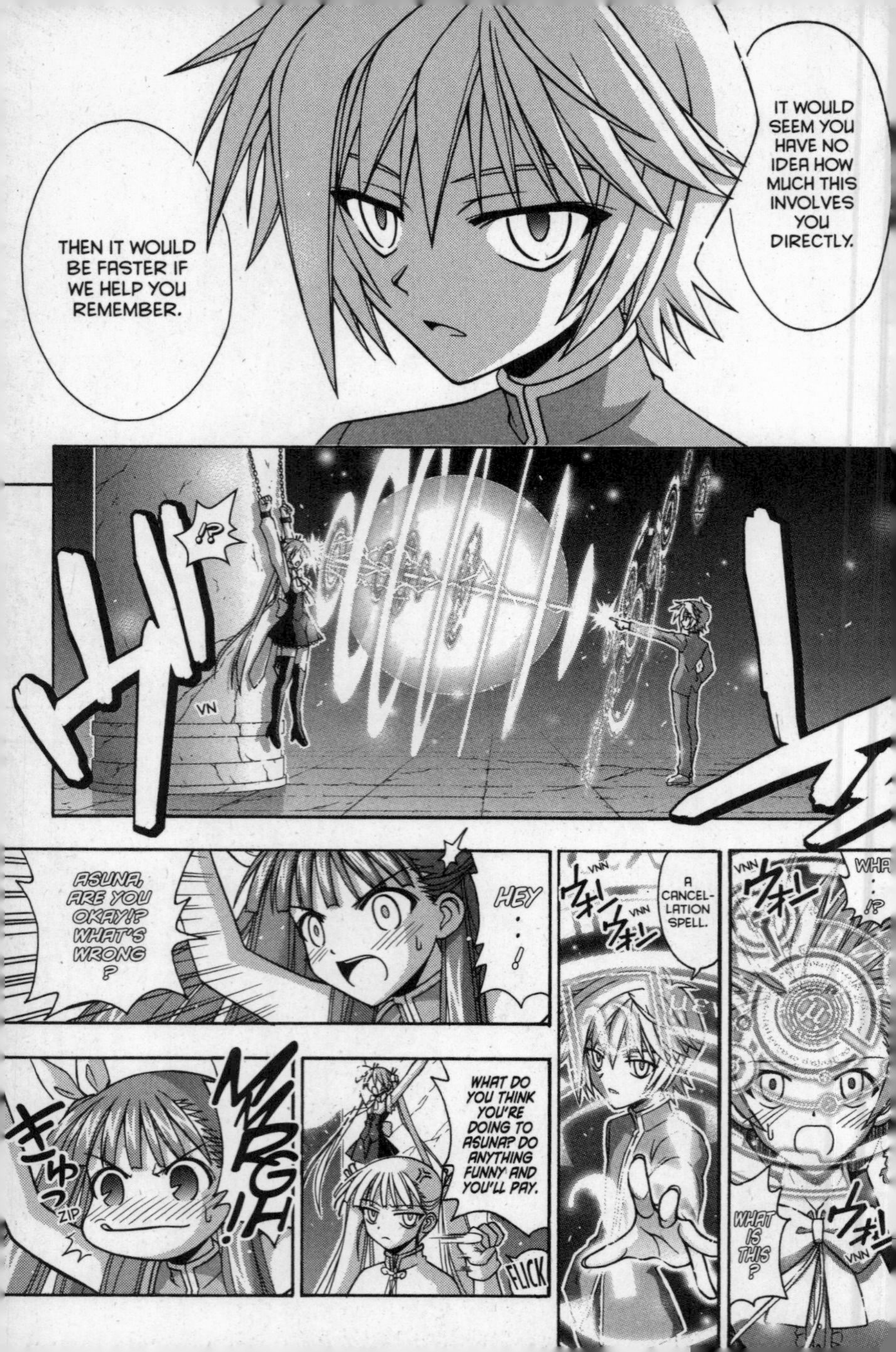
IT WOULD SEEM YOU HAVE NO IDEA HOW MUCH THIS INVOLVES YOU DIRECTLY.
THEN IT WOULD BE FASTER IF WE HELP YOU REMEMBER.
!?
VN
WHA . . . !?
VNN
WHAT IS THIS?
VNN
A CANCEL-LATION SPELL.
VNN
VNN
HEY . . . !
ASUNA, ARE YOU OKAY!? WHAT'S WRONG?
WHAT DO YOU THINK YOU'RE DOING TO ASUNA? DO ANYTHING FUNNY AND YOU'LL PAY.
FLICK
MMRGH!!
ZIP

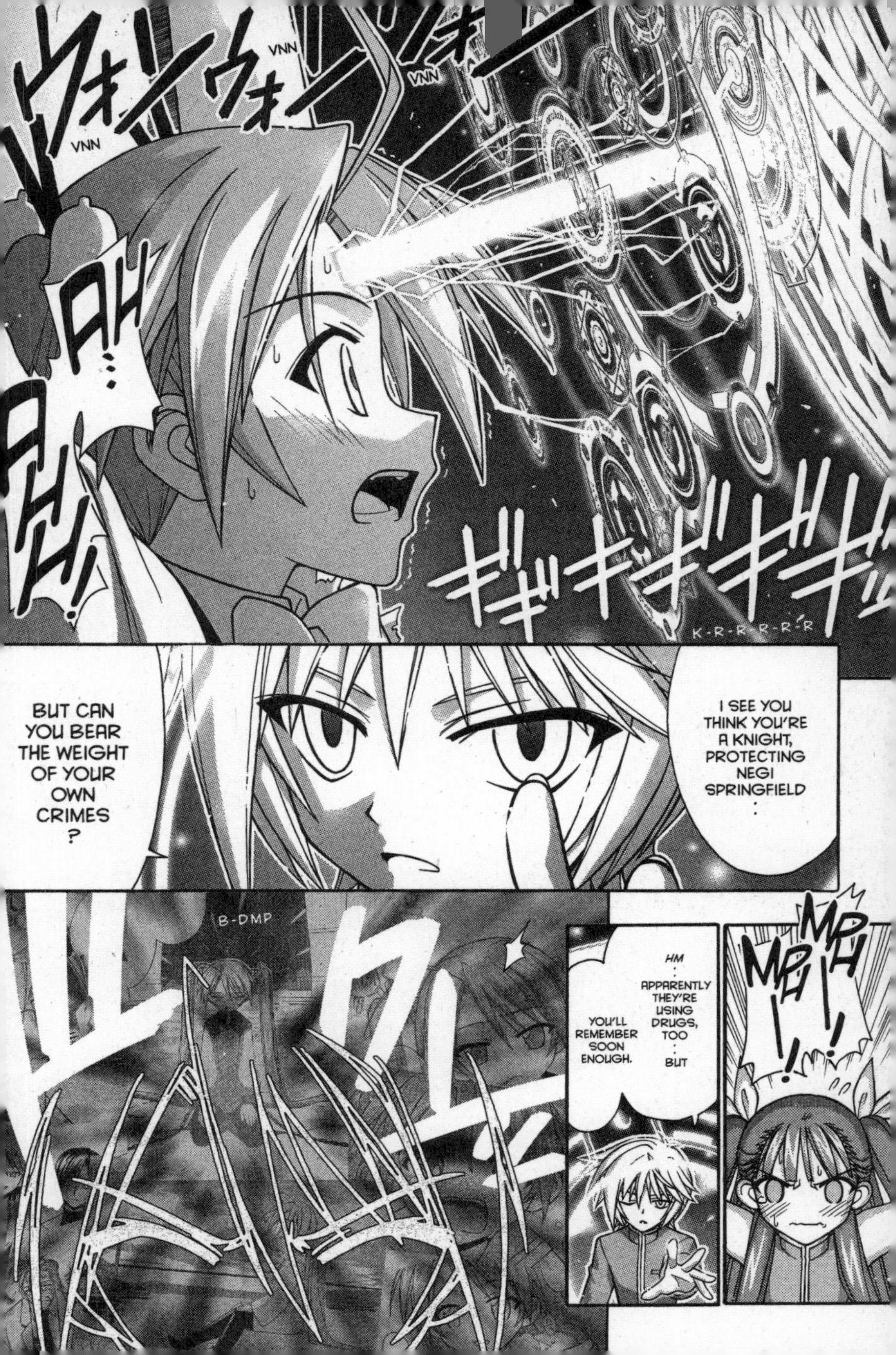
VNN
VNN
VNN
AH...!
K-R-R-R-R-R
I SEE YOU THINK YOU'RE A KNIGHT, PROTECTING NEGI SPRINGFIELD...
BUT CAN YOU BEAR THE WEIGHT OF YOUR OWN CRIMES?
MPH MPH!!
HM... APPARENTLY THEY'RE USING DRUGS, TOO... BUT
YOU'LL REMEMBER SOON ENOUGH.
B-DMP

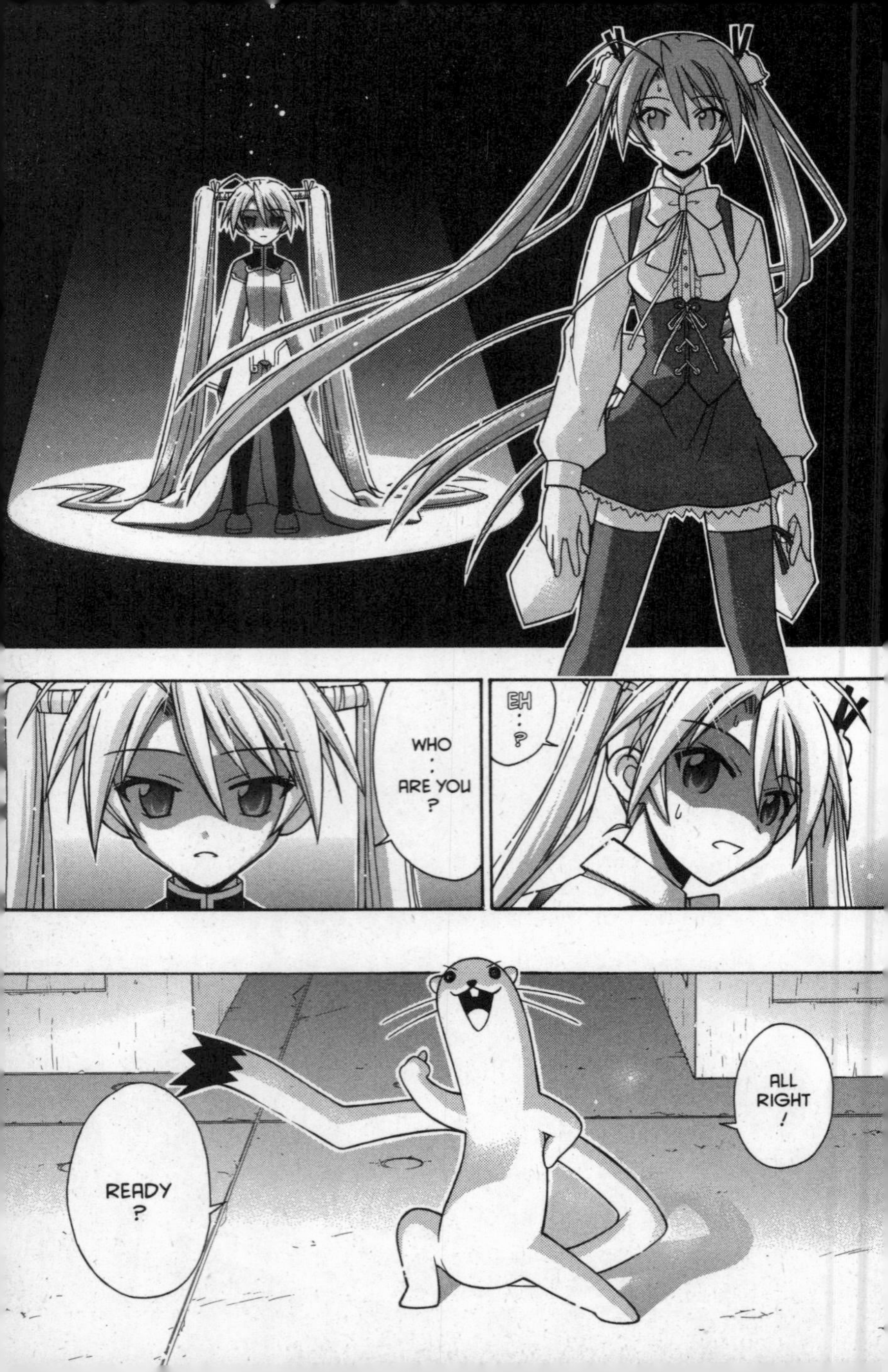
EH . . ?
WHO . . ARE YOU ?
ALL RIGHT !
READY ?

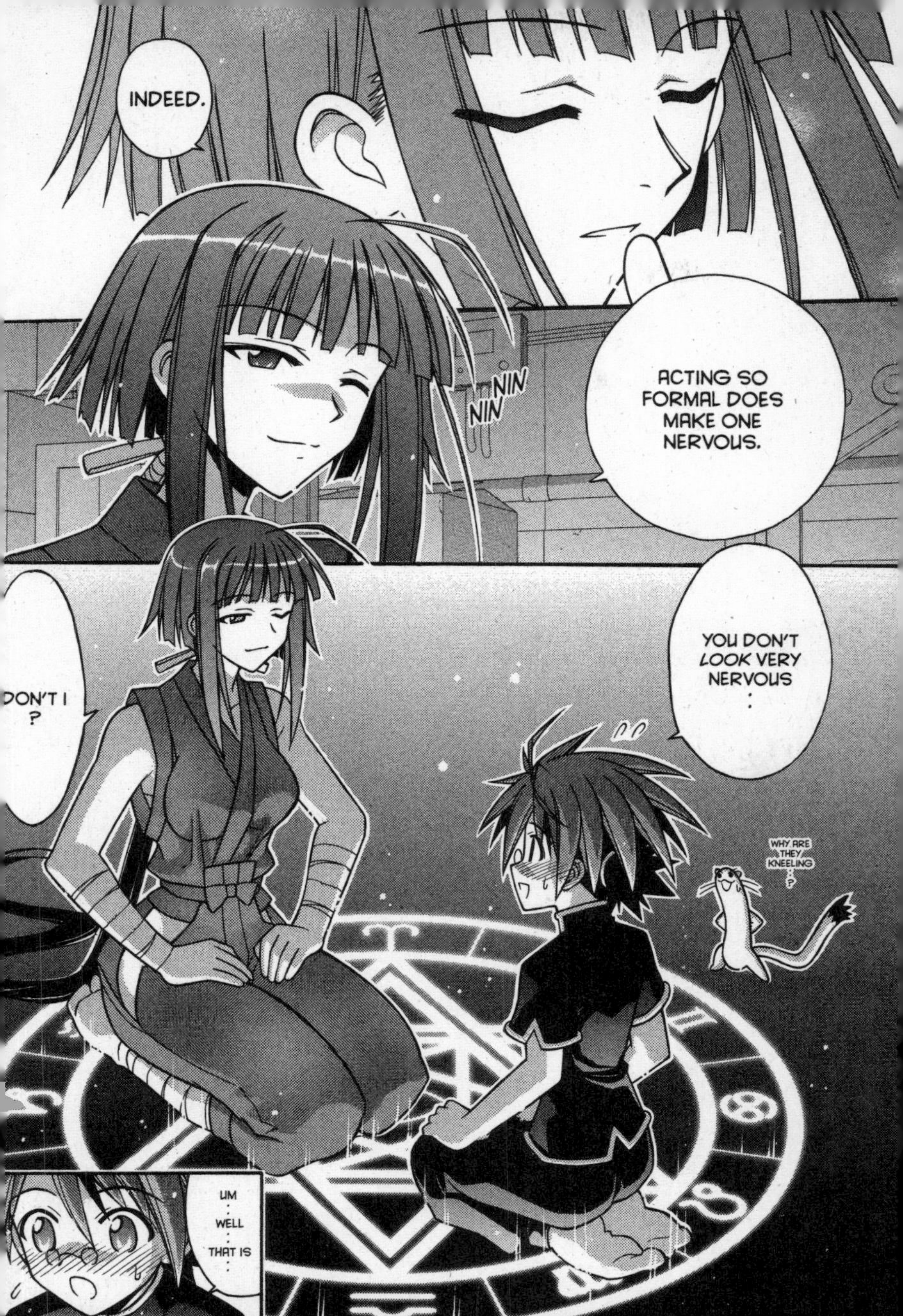
INDEED.
ACTING SO FORMAL DOES MAKE ONE NERVOUS.
NIN NIN
YOU DON'T *LOOK* VERY NERVOUS . .
WHY ARE THEY KNEELING . . ?
DON'T I ?
UM . . . WELL . . . THAT IS . . .

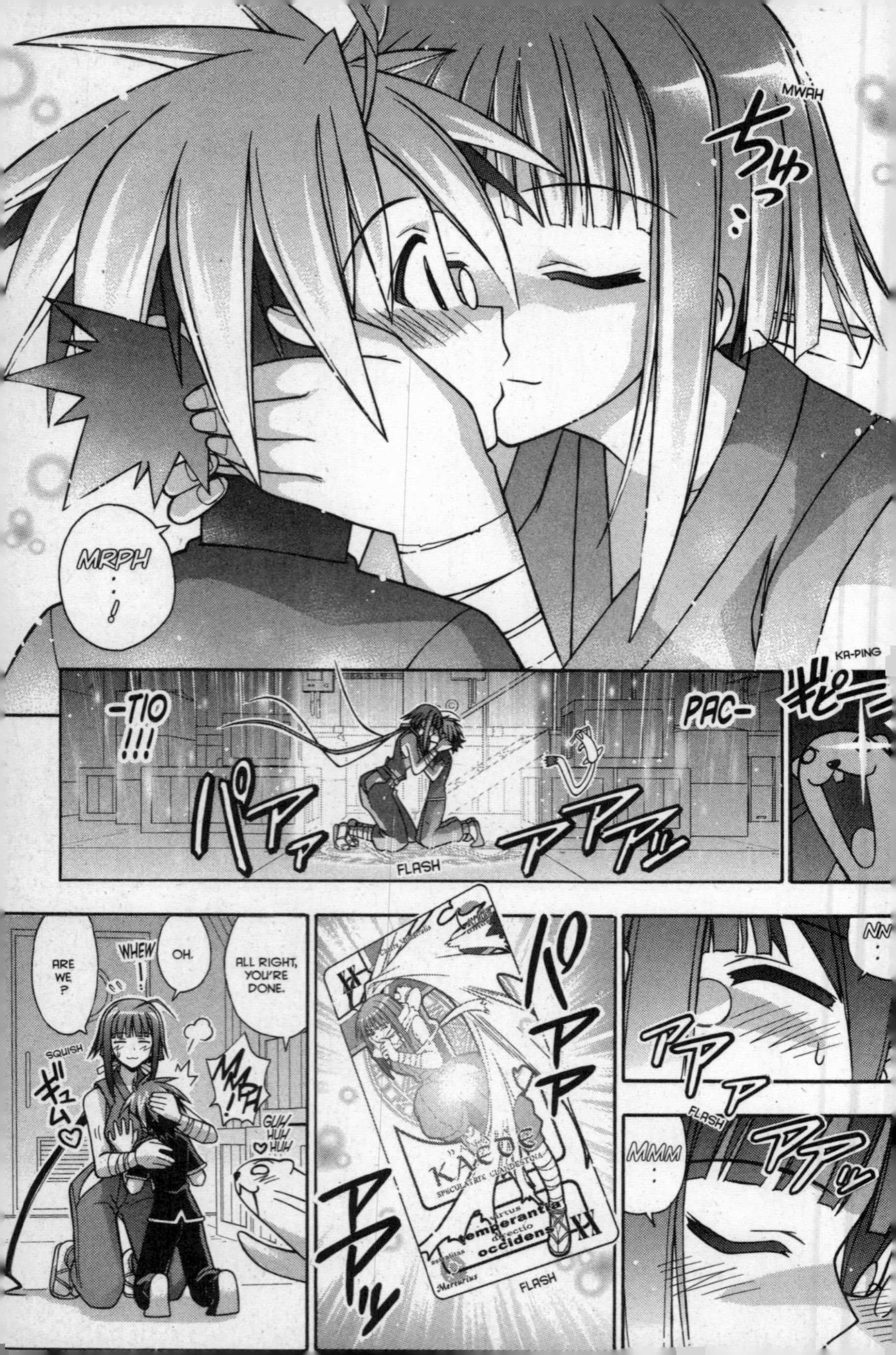

MWAH
ちゅっ
MRPH...!
KA-PING
PAC-
-TIO!!!
FLASH
NN...
MMM...
FLASH
KAEDE
SPECULATRIX CLANDESTINA
virtus
temperantia
directio
occidens
Mercurius
XX
FLASH
ALL RIGHT, YOU'RE DONE.
OH.
WHEW!
ARE WE?
SQUISH
MAAH!
GUH HUH HUH

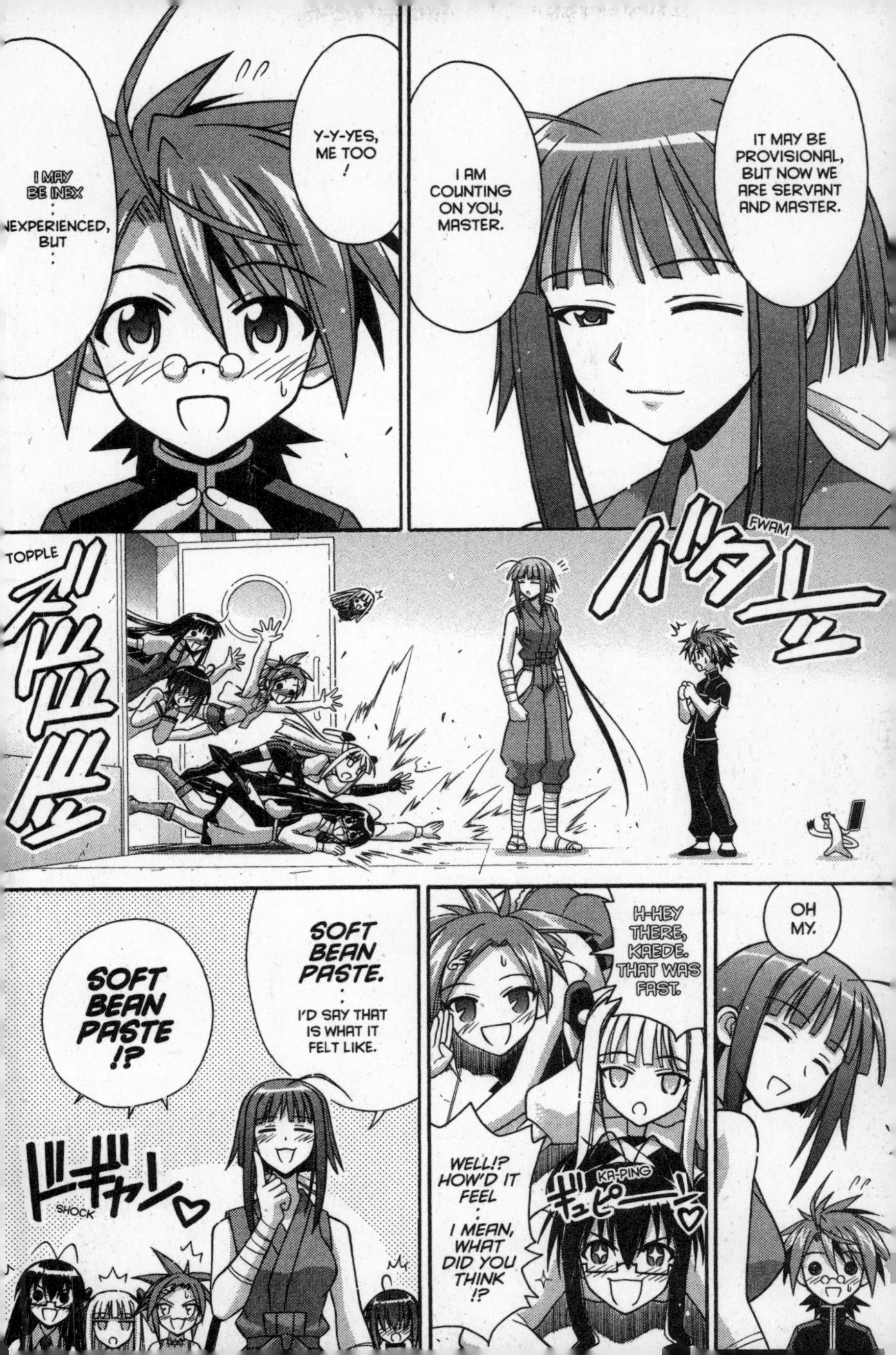
IT MAY BE PROVISIONAL, BUT NOW WE ARE SERVANT AND MASTER.
I AM COUNTING ON YOU, MASTER.
Y-Y-YES, ME TOO !
I MAY BE INEX : NEXPERIENCED, BUT :
FWAM
TOPPLE
OH MY.
H-HEY THERE, KAEDE. THAT WAS FAST.
WELL!? HOW'D IT FEEL : I MEAN, WHAT DID YOU THINK !?
KA-PING
SOFT BEAN PASTE. : I'D SAY THAT IS WHAT IT FELT LIKE.
SOFT BEAN PASTE !?
SHOCK

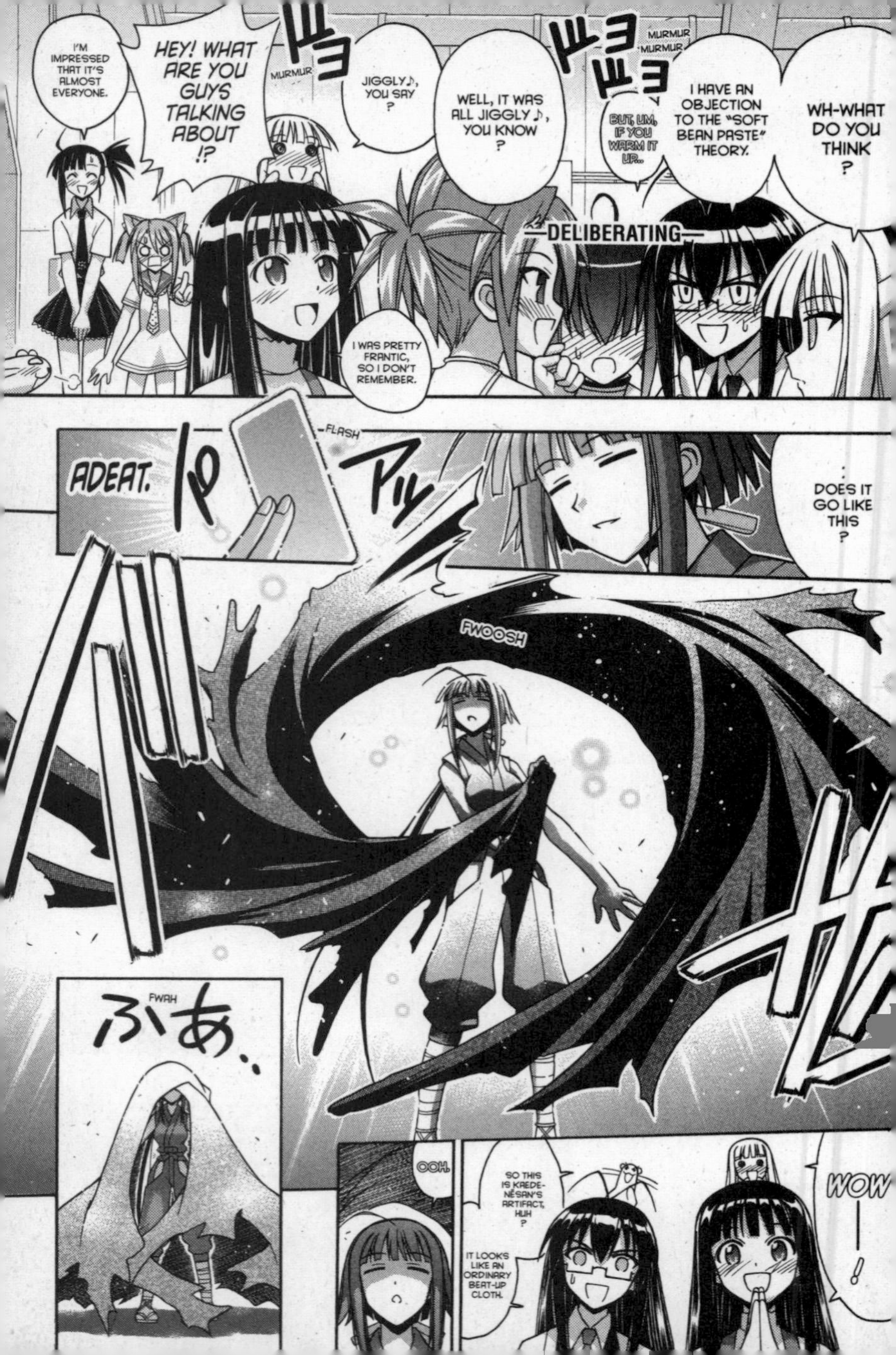
WH-WHAT DO YOU THINK?
I HAVE AN OBJECTION TO THE "SOFT BEAN PASTE" THEORY.
MURMUR MURMUR
BUT, UM, IF YOU WARM IT UP...
WELL, IT WAS ALL JIGGLY♪, YOU KNOW?
JIGGLY♪, YOU SAY?
MURMUR
HEY! WHAT ARE YOU GUYS TALKING ABOUT!?
I'M IMPRESSED THAT IT'S ALMOST EVERYONE.
—DELIBERATING—
I WAS PRETTY FRANTIC, SO I DON'T REMEMBER.
DOES IT GO LIKE THIS?
FLASH
ADEAT.
FWOOSH
WOW—!
SO THIS IS KAEDE-NÉSAN'S ARTIFACT, HUH?
IT LOOKS LIKE AN ORDINARY BEAT-UP CLOTH.
OOH.
FWAH
ふあ‥

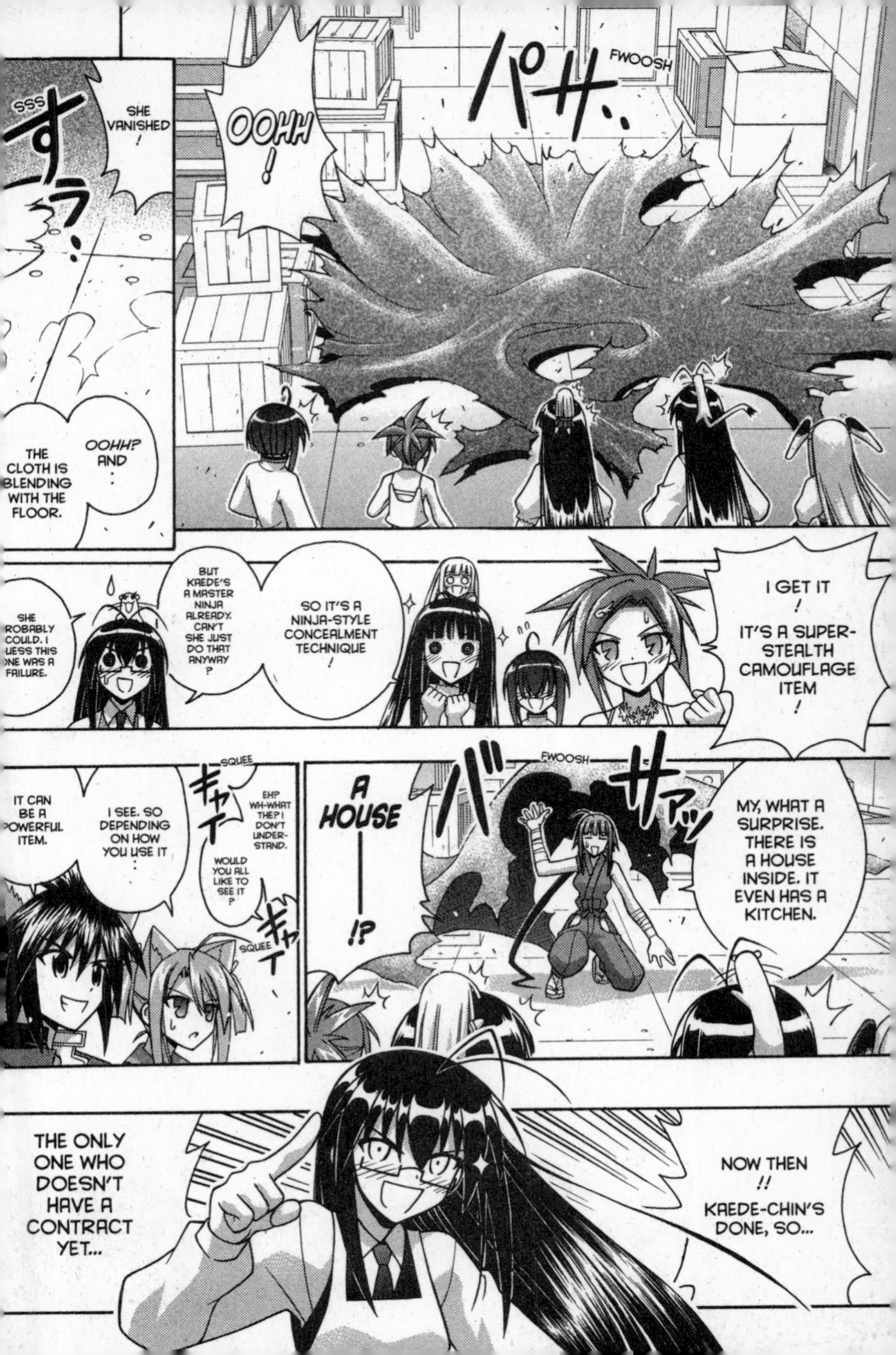
パサ
FWOOSH
OOHH!
SSS
すう
SHE VANISHED!
OOHH? AND...
THE CLOTH IS BLENDING WITH THE FLOOR.
I GET IT! IT'S A SUPER-STEALTH CAMOUFLAGE ITEM!
SO IT'S A NINJA-STYLE CONCEALMENT TECHNIQUE!
BUT KAEDE'S A MASTER NINJA ALREADY. CAN'T SHE JUST DO THAT ANYWAY?
SHE ROBABLY COULD. I UESS THIS NE WAS A FAILURE.
FWOOSH
バサァッ
MY, WHAT A SURPRISE. THERE IS A HOUSE INSIDE. IT EVEN HAS A KITCHEN.
A HOUSE——!?
SQUEE
ギャ
EH? WH-WHAT THE?! I DON'T UNDER-STAND.
WOULD YOU ALL LIKE TO SEE IT?
SQUEE
ギャ
I SEE. SO DEPENDING ON HOW YOU USE IT...
IT CAN BE A OWERFUL ITEM.
NOW THEN!! KAEDE-CHIN'S DONE, SO...
THE ONLY ONE WHO DOESN'T HAVE A CONTRACT YET...

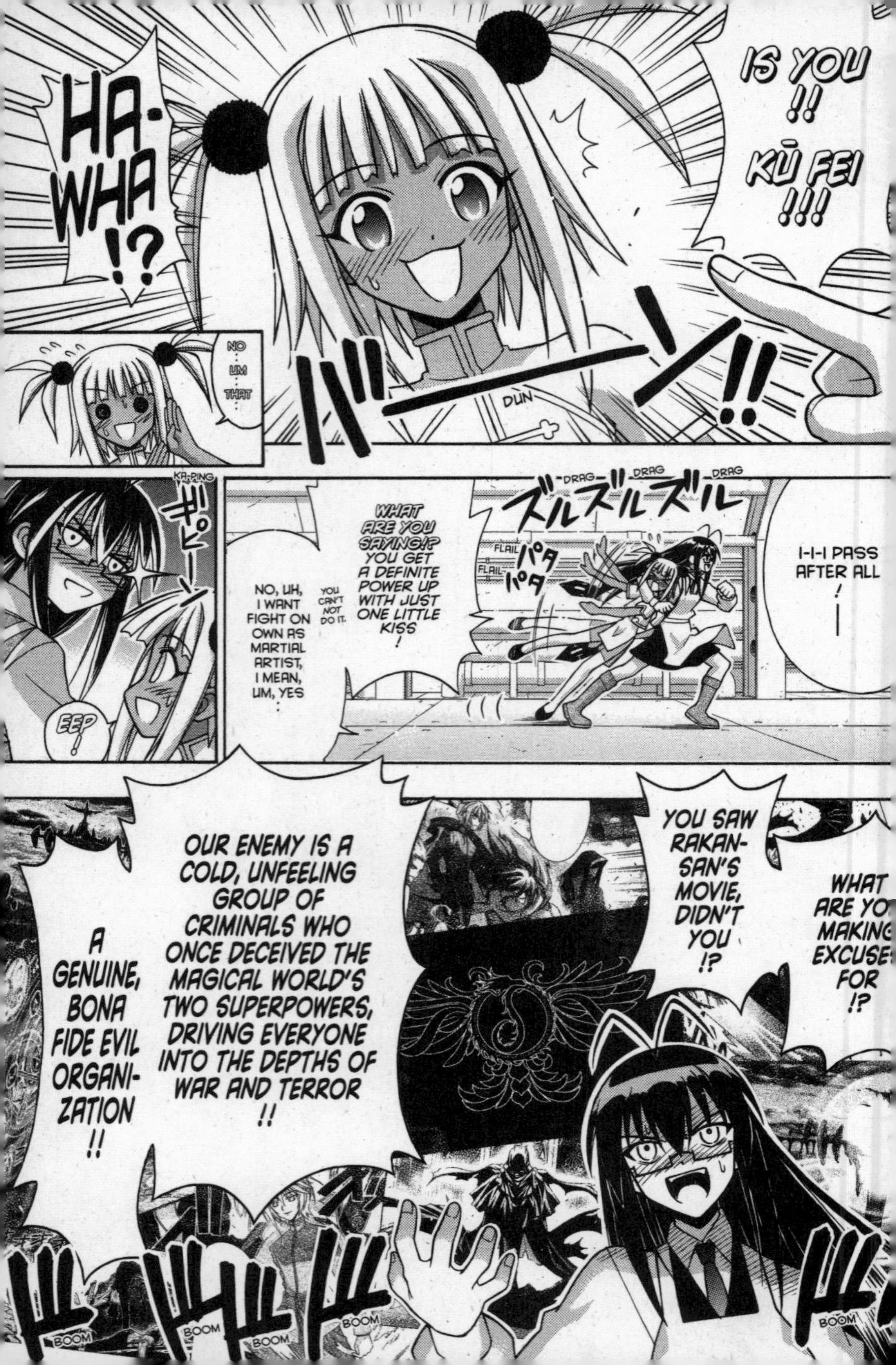
IS YOU !! KŪ FEI !!!
HA-WHA !?
バ——ン!!
DUN
NO... UM... THAT...
I-I-I PASS AFTER ALL !
ズルズルズル
DRAG DRAG DRAG
パタパタ
FLAIL FLAIL
WHAT ARE YOU SAYING!? YOU GET A DEFINITE POWER UP WITH JUST ONE LITTLE KISS !
YOU CAN'T NOT DO IT.
NO, UH, I WANT FIGHT ON OWN AS MARTIAL ARTIST, I MEAN, UM, YES...
KA-PING
EEP !
WHAT ARE YO MAKING EXCUSE FOR !?
YOU SAW RAKAN-SAN'S MOVIE, DIDN'T YOU !?
OUR ENEMY IS A COLD, UNFEELING GROUP OF CRIMINALS WHO ONCE DECEIVED THE MAGICAL WORLD'S TWO SUPERPOWERS, DRIVING EVERYONE INTO THE DEPTHS OF WAR AND TERROR !!
A GENUINE, BONA FIDE EVIL ORGANI-ZATION !!
BOOM
BOOM
BOOM
BOOM
BOOM

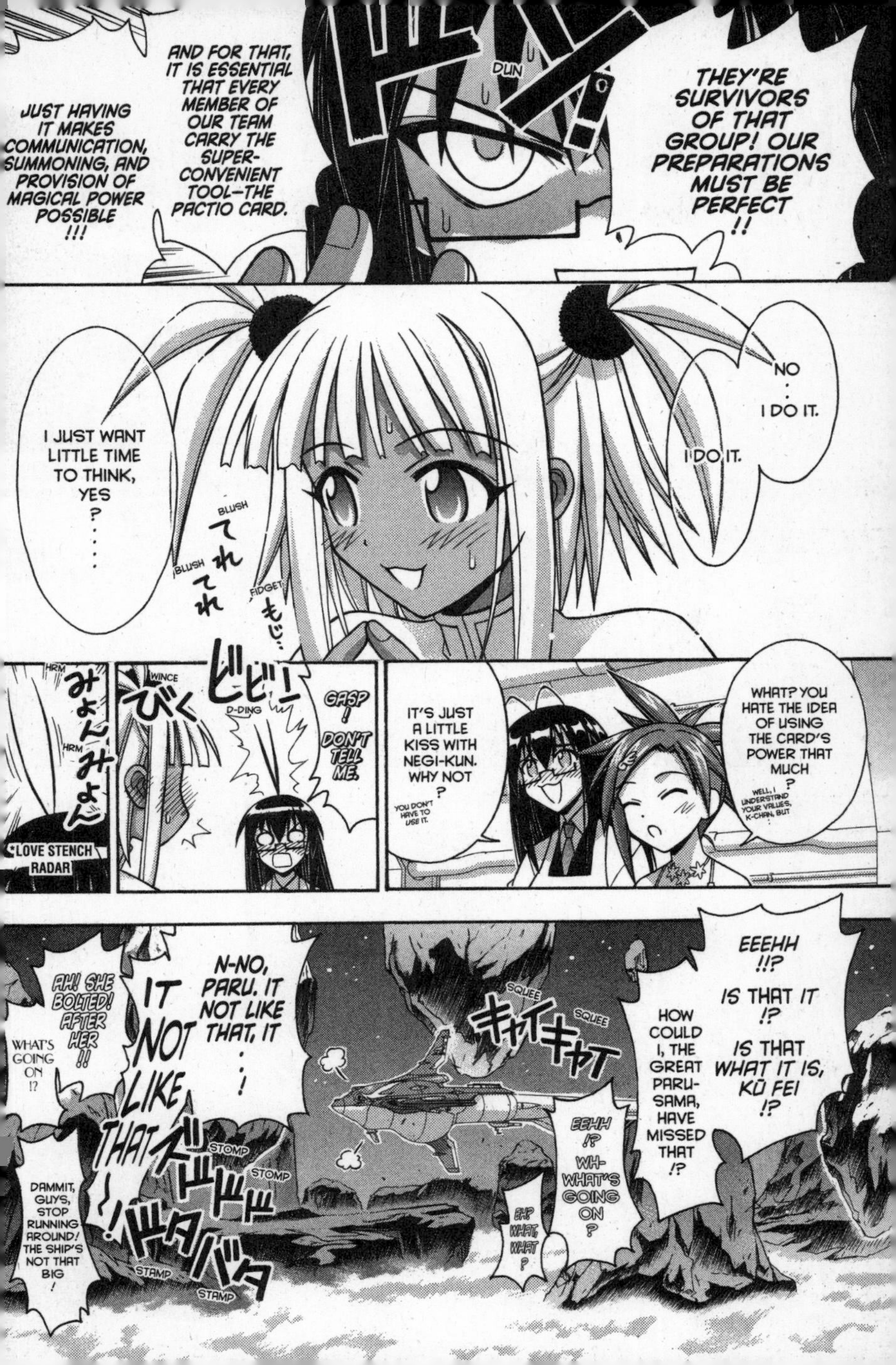

THEY'RE SURVIVORS OF THAT GROUP! OUR PREPARATIONS MUST BE PERFECT!!
DUN
AND FOR THAT, IT IS ESSENTIAL THAT EVERY MEMBER OF OUR TEAM CARRY THE SUPER-CONVENIENT TOOL—THE PACTIO CARD.
JUST HAVING IT MAKES COMMUNICATION, SUMMONING, AND PROVISION OF MAGICAL POWER POSSIBLE!!!
NO... I DO IT.
I DO IT.
BLUSH てれ BLUSH てれ
FIDGET もじ…
I JUST WANT LITTLE TIME TO THINK, YES?....
WHAT? YOU HATE THE IDEA OF USING THE CARD'S POWER THAT MUCH?
WELL, I UNDERSTAND YOUR VALUES, K-CHAN, BUT
IT'S JUST A LITTLE KISS WITH NEGI-KUN. WHY NOT?
YOU DON'T HAVE TO USE IT.
GASP! DON'T TELL ME.
D-DING ビビ！
WINCE びく
HRM みょん HRM みょん
*LOVE STENCH RADAR
EEEHH!!? IS THAT IT!? IS THAT WHAT IT IS, KŪ FEI!?
HOW COULD I, THE GREAT PARU-SAMA, HAVE MISSED THAT!?
EEHH!? WH-WHAT'S GOING ON?
EH? WHAT, WHAT?
SQUEE SQUEE
N-NO, PARU. IT NOT LIKE THAT, IT...!
IT NOT LIKE THAT~!
STOMP STOMP
AH! SHE BOLTED! AFTER HER!!
WHAT'S GOING ON!?
DAMMIT, GUYS, STOP RUNNING AROUND! THE SHIP'S NOT THAT BIG!
STAMP ドタバタ STAMP

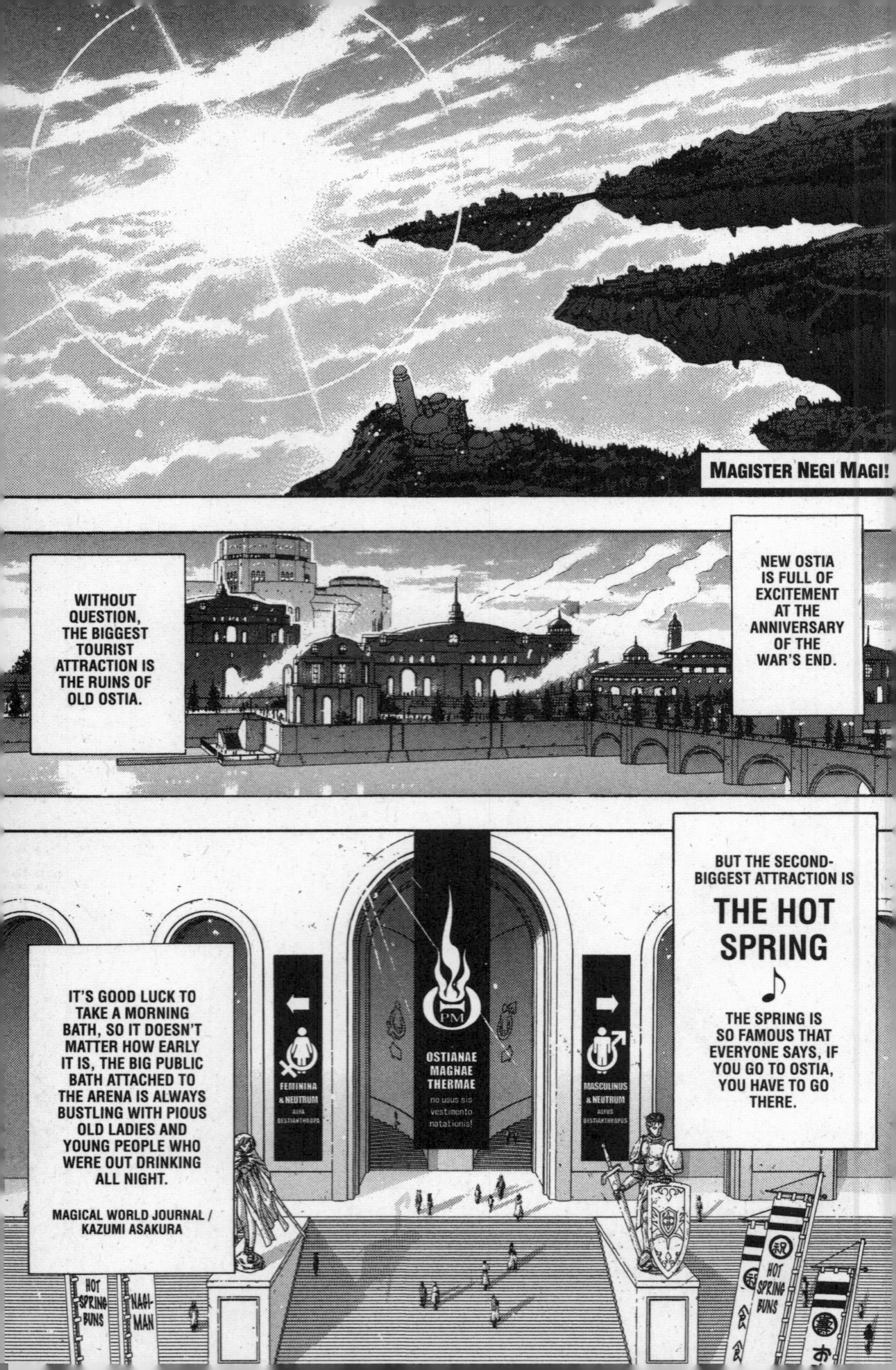
MAGISTER NEGI MAGI!
NEW OSTIA IS FULL OF EXCITEMENT AT THE ANNIVERSARY OF THE WAR'S END.
WITHOUT QUESTION, THE BIGGEST TOURIST ATTRACTION IS THE RUINS OF OLD OSTIA.
BUT THE SECOND-BIGGEST ATTRACTION IS
THE HOT SPRING ♪
THE SPRING IS SO FAMOUS THAT EVERYONE SAYS, IF YOU GO TO OSTIA, YOU HAVE TO GO THERE.
HOT SPRING BUNS
MASCULINUS & NEUTRUM
ALIUS BESTIANTHROPUS
OSTIANAE MAGNAE THERMAE
ne usus sis vestimento natationis!
FEMININA & NEUTRUM
ALIA BESTIANTHROPA
IT'S GOOD LUCK TO TAKE A MORNING BATH, SO IT DOESN'T MATTER HOW EARLY IT IS, THE BIG PUBLIC BATH ATTACHED TO THE ARENA IS ALWAYS BUSTLING WITH PIOUS OLD LADIES AND YOUNG PEOPLE WHO WERE OUT DRINKING ALL NIGHT.
MAGICAL WORLD JOURNAL / KAZUMI ASAKURA
NAGI-MAN
HOT SPRING BUNS

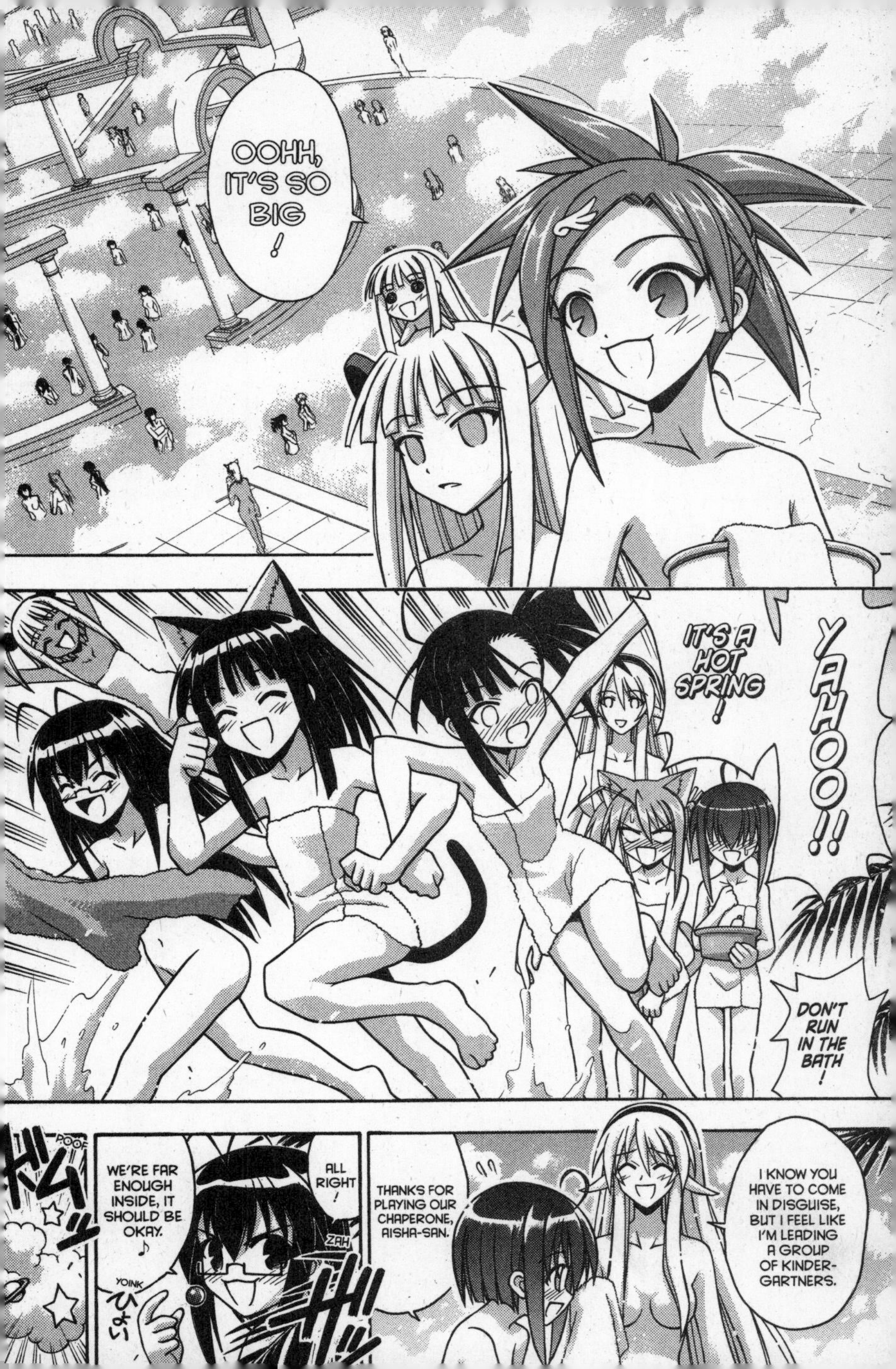

OOHH, IT'S SO BIG!
YAHOO!!
IT'S A HOT SPRING!
DON'T RUN IN THE BATH!
I KNOW YOU HAVE TO COME IN DISGUISE, BUT I FEEL LIKE I'M LEADING A GROUP OF KINDER-GARTNERS.
THANKS FOR PLAYING OUR CHAPERONE, AISHA-SAN.
ALL RIGHT!
WE'RE FAR ENOUGH INSIDE, IT SHOULD BE OKAY. ♪
ZAH
YOINK
ひょい
POOF

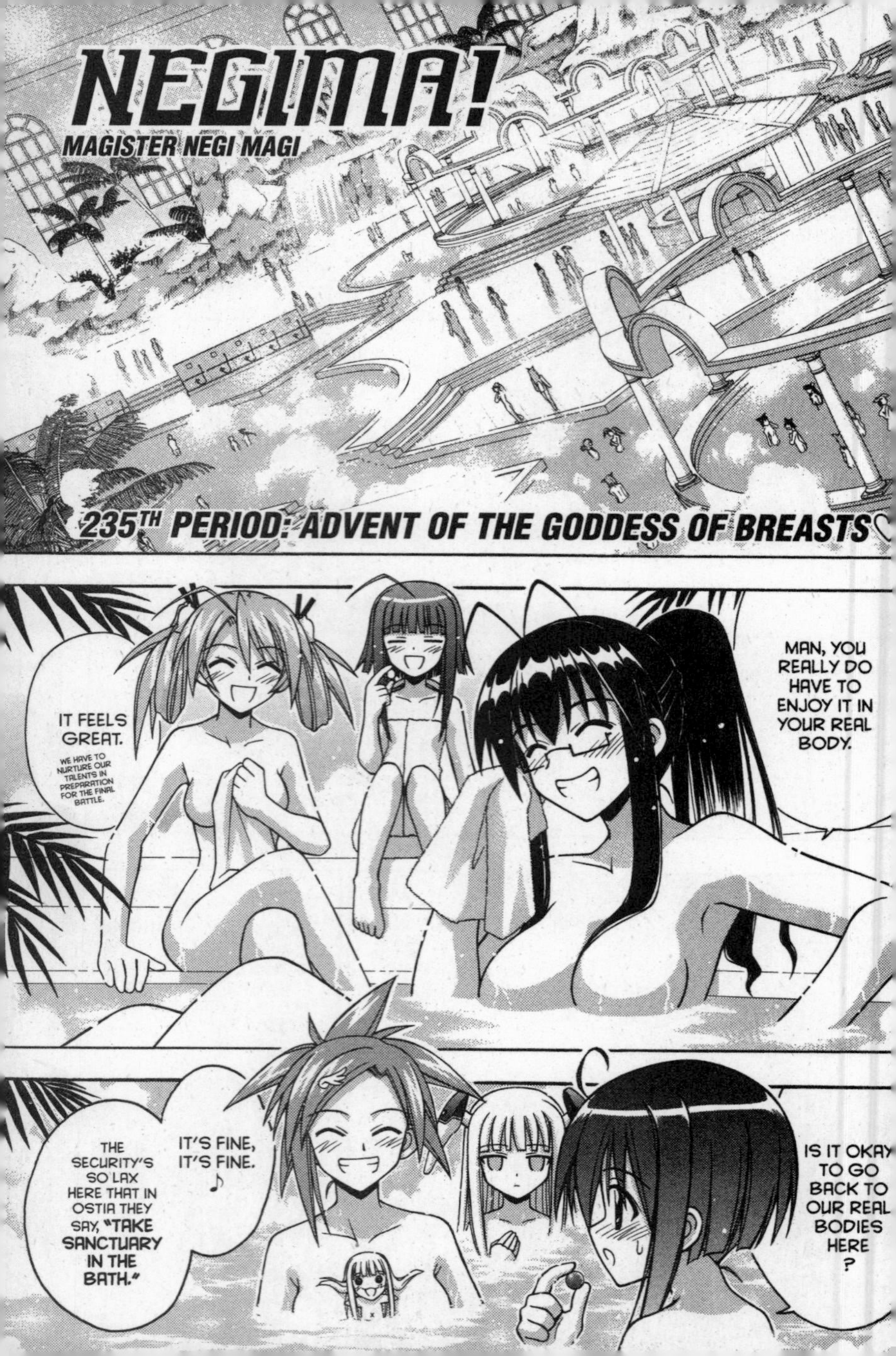
NEGIMA!
MAGISTER NEGI MAGI
235TH PERIOD: ADVENT OF THE GODDESS OF BREASTS♡
MAN, YOU REALLY DO HAVE TO ENJOY IT IN YOUR REAL BODY.
IT FEELS GREAT.
WE HAVE TO NURTURE OUR TALENTS IN PREPARATION FOR THE FINAL BATTLE.
IS IT OKAY TO GO BACK TO OUR REAL BODIES HERE?
IT'S FINE, IT'S FINE. ♪
THE SECURITY'S SO LAX HERE THAT IN OSTIA THEY SAY, "TAKE SANCTUARY IN THE BATH."

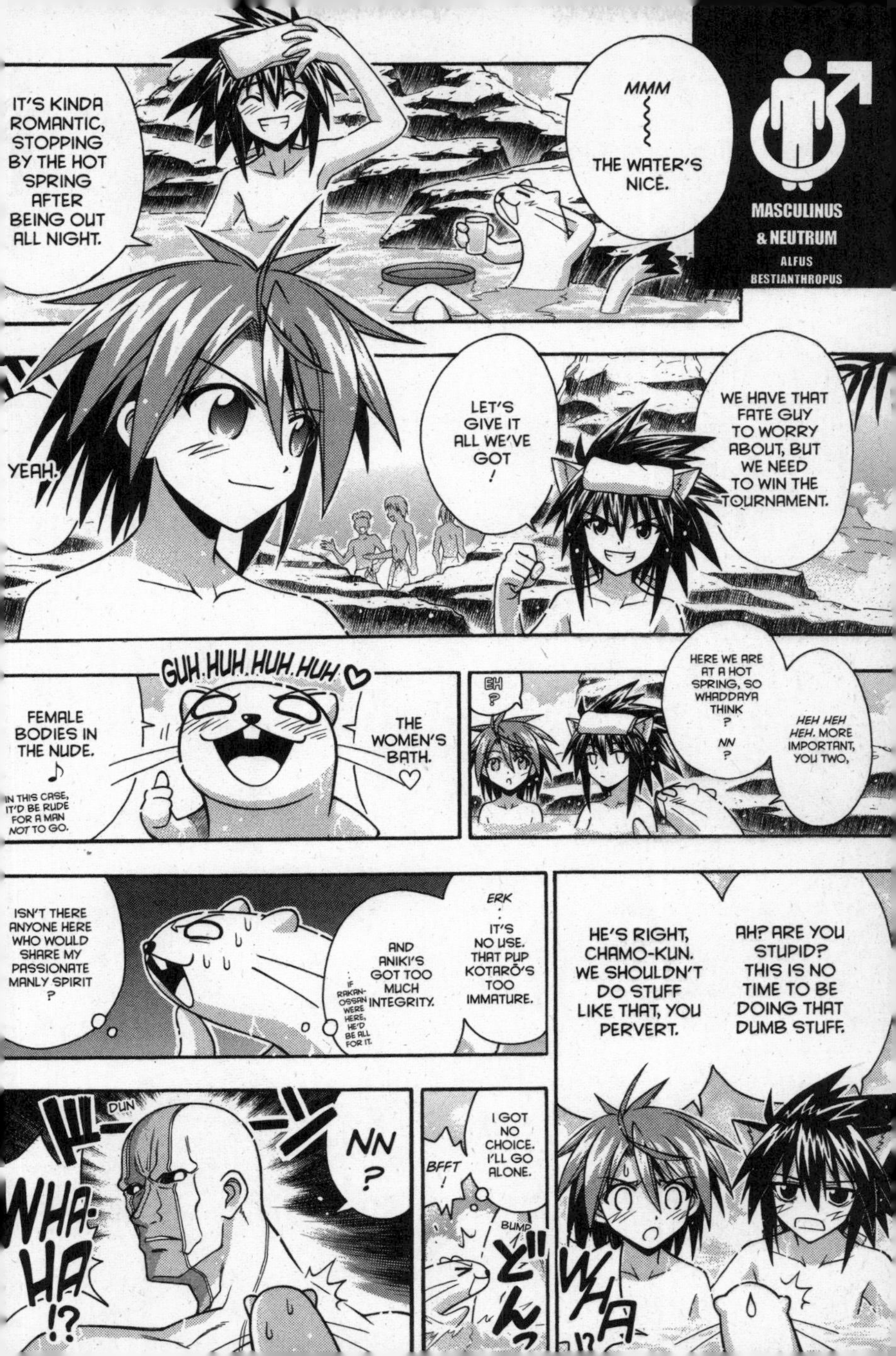

MASCULINUS & NEUTRUM
ALFUS
BESTIANTHROPUS
MMM THE WATER'S NICE.
IT'S KINDA ROMANTIC, STOPPING BY THE HOT SPRING AFTER BEING OUT ALL NIGHT.
WE HAVE THAT FATE GUY TO WORRY ABOUT, BUT WE NEED TO WIN THE TOURNAMENT.
LET'S GIVE IT ALL WE'VE GOT!
YEAH.
HEH HEH HEH. MORE IMPORTANT, YOU TWO,
HERE WE ARE AT A HOT SPRING, SO WHADDAYA THINK?
NN?
EH?
GUH HUH HUH HUH ♥
THE WOMEN'S BATH. ♡
FEMALE BODIES IN THE NUDE. ♪
IN THIS CASE, IT'D BE RUDE FOR A MAN *NOT* TO GO.
AH? ARE YOU STUPID? THIS IS NO TIME TO BE DOING THAT DUMB STUFF.
HE'S RIGHT, CHAMO-KUN. WE SHOULDN'T DO STUFF LIKE THAT, YOU PERVERT.
ERK...
IT'S NO USE. THAT PUP KOTARŌ'S TOO IMMATURE.
AND ANIKI'S GOT TOO MUCH INTEGRITY.
IF RAKAN-OSSAN WERE HERE, HE'D BE ALL FOR IT.
ISN'T THERE ANYONE HERE WHO WOULD SHARE MY PASSIONATE MANLY SPIRIT?
WHA-!?
I GOT NO CHOICE. I'LL GO ALONE.
BFFT!
BUMP
どん
NN?
DUN
WHA-HA-!?

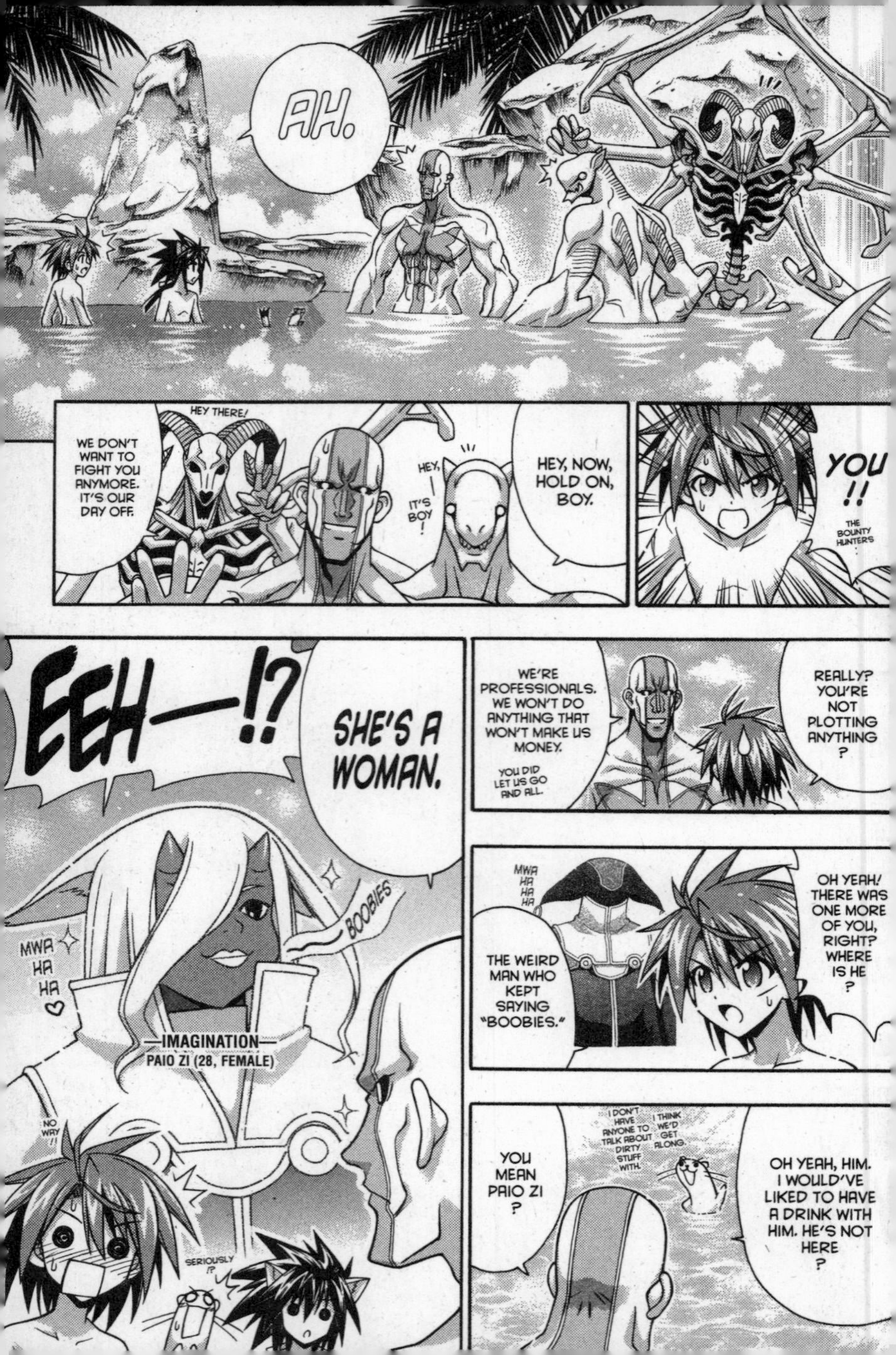
AH.
YOU !!
THE BOUNTY HUNTERS
HEY, NOW, HOLD ON, BOY.
HEY, IT'S BOY!
HEY THERE!
WE DON'T WANT TO FIGHT YOU ANYMORE. IT'S OUR DAY OFF.
REALLY? YOU'RE NOT PLOTTING ANYTHING?
WE'RE PROFESSIONALS. WE WON'T DO ANYTHING THAT WON'T MAKE US MONEY.
YOU DID LET US GO AND ALL.
OH YEAH! THERE WAS ONE MORE OF YOU, RIGHT? WHERE IS HE?
MWA HA HA HA
THE WEIRD MAN WHO KEPT SAYING "BOOBIES."
OH YEAH, HIM. I WOULD'VE LIKED TO HAVE A DRINK WITH HIM. HE'S NOT HERE?
I THINK WE'D GET ALONG.
I DON'T HAVE ANYONE TO TALK ABOUT DIRTY STUFF WITH.
YOU MEAN PAIO ZI?
SHE'S A WOMAN.
EEH—!?
BOOBIES
MWA HA HA ♡
—IMAGINATION—
PAIO ZI (28, FEMALE)
NO WAY!!
SERIOUSLY!?

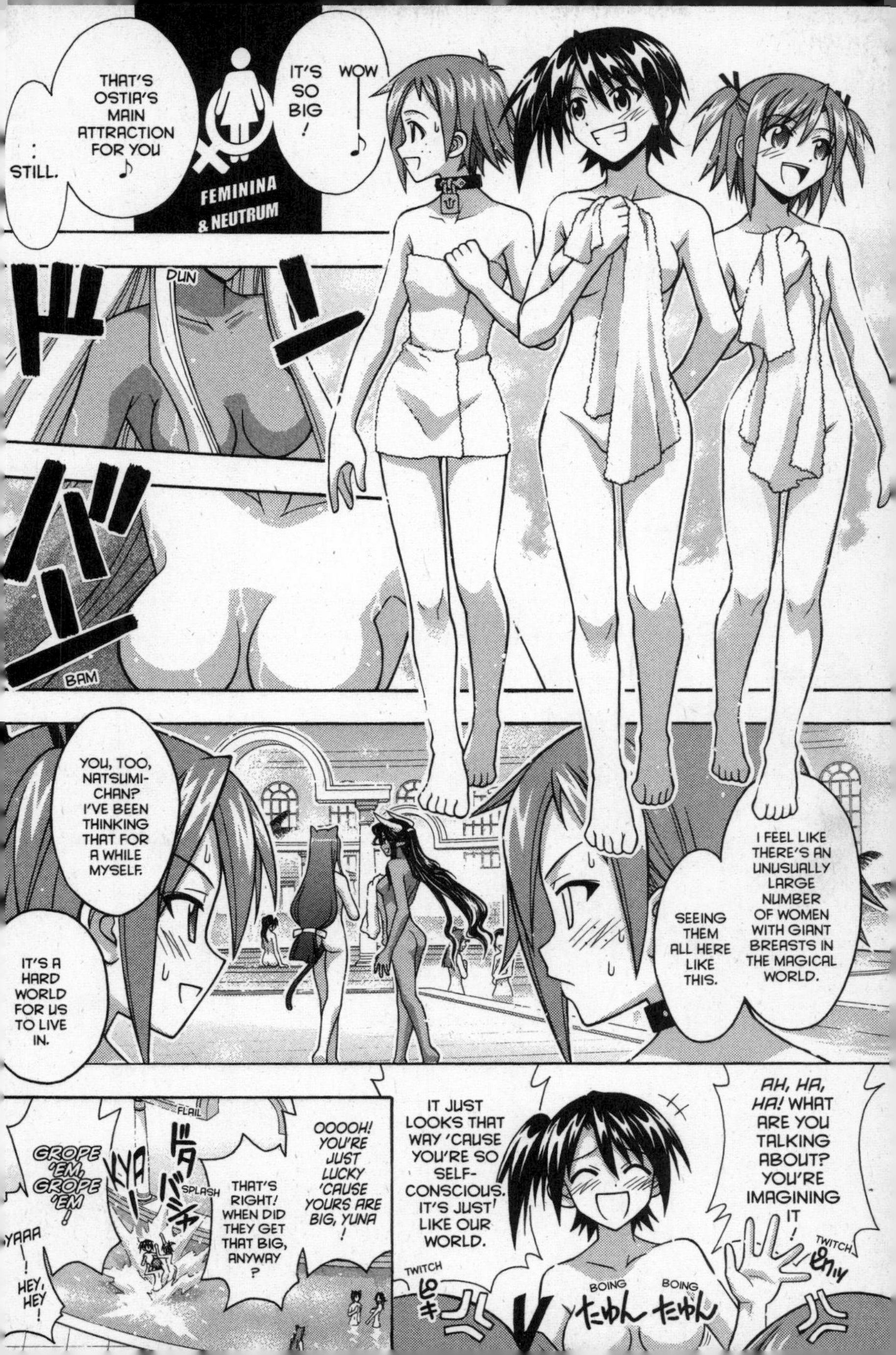
WOW ♪
IT'S SO BIG!
THAT'S OSTIA'S MAIN ATTRACTION FOR YOU ♪
: STILL.
FEMININA & NEUTRUM
DUN
BAM
I FEEL LIKE THERE'S AN UNUSUALLY LARGE NUMBER OF WOMEN WITH GIANT BREASTS IN THE MAGICAL WORLD.
SEEING THEM ALL HERE LIKE THIS.
YOU, TOO, NATSUMI-CHAN? I'VE BEEN THINKING THAT FOR A WHILE MYSELF.
IT'S A HARD WORLD FOR US TO LIVE IN.
AH, HA, HA! WHAT ARE YOU TALKING ABOUT? YOU'RE IMAGINING IT!
TWITCH
IT JUST LOOKS THAT WAY 'CAUSE YOU'RE SO SELF-CONSCIOUS. IT'S JUST LIKE OUR WORLD.
BOING たゆん
BOING たゆん
TWITCH
OOOOH! YOU'RE JUST LUCKY 'CAUSE YOURS ARE BIG, YUNA!
THAT'S RIGHT! WHEN DID THEY GET THAT BIG, ANYWAY?
FLAIL
SPLASH
GROPE 'EM, GROPE 'EM!
YAAA!
HEY, HEY!

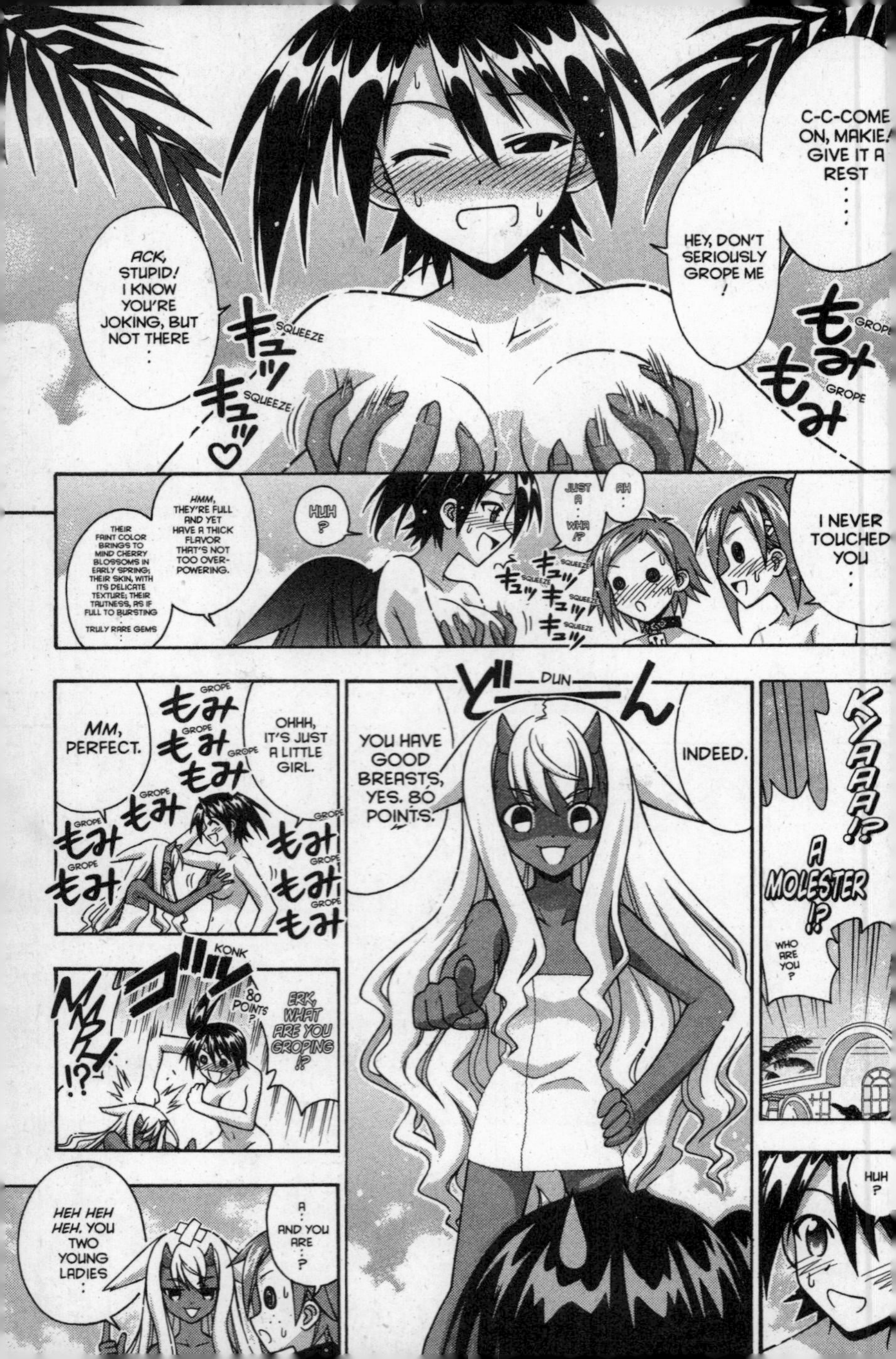
C-C-COME ON, MAKIE! GIVE IT A REST ...
HEY, DON'T SERIOUSLY GROPE ME!
もみ GROPE
もみ GROPE
キュッ SQUEEZE
キュッ SQUEEZE ♡
ACK, STUPID! I KNOW YOU'RE JOKING, BUT NOT THERE...
I NEVER TOUCHED YOU...
AH...
JUST A... WHA!?
キュッ SQUEEZE キュッ SQUEEZE キュッ SQUEEZE キュッ SQUEEZE キュッ SQUEEZE
HUH?
HMM, THEY'RE FULL AND YET HAVE A THICK FLAVOR THAT'S NOT TOO OVER-POWERING.
THEIR FAINT COLOR BRINGS TO MIND CHERRY BLOSSOMS IN EARLY SPRING; THEIR SKIN, WITH ITS DELICATE TEXTURE; THEIR TAUTNESS, AS IF FULL TO BURSTING
TRULY RARE GEMS...
KYAAA!?
A MOLESTER!?
WHO ARE YOU?
HUH?
どーん DUN
INDEED.
YOU HAVE GOOD BREASTS, YES. 80 POINTS.
OHHH, IT'S JUST A LITTLE GIRL.
MM, PERFECT.
もみ GROPE もみ GROPE もみ GROPE もみ GROPE もみ GROPE もみ GROPE もみ GROPE もみ GROPE もみ GROPE
ゴツ KONK
ERK, WHAT ARE YOU GROPING!?
80 POINTS?
A... AND YOU ARE...?
HEH HEH HEH. YOU TWO YOUNG LADIES...

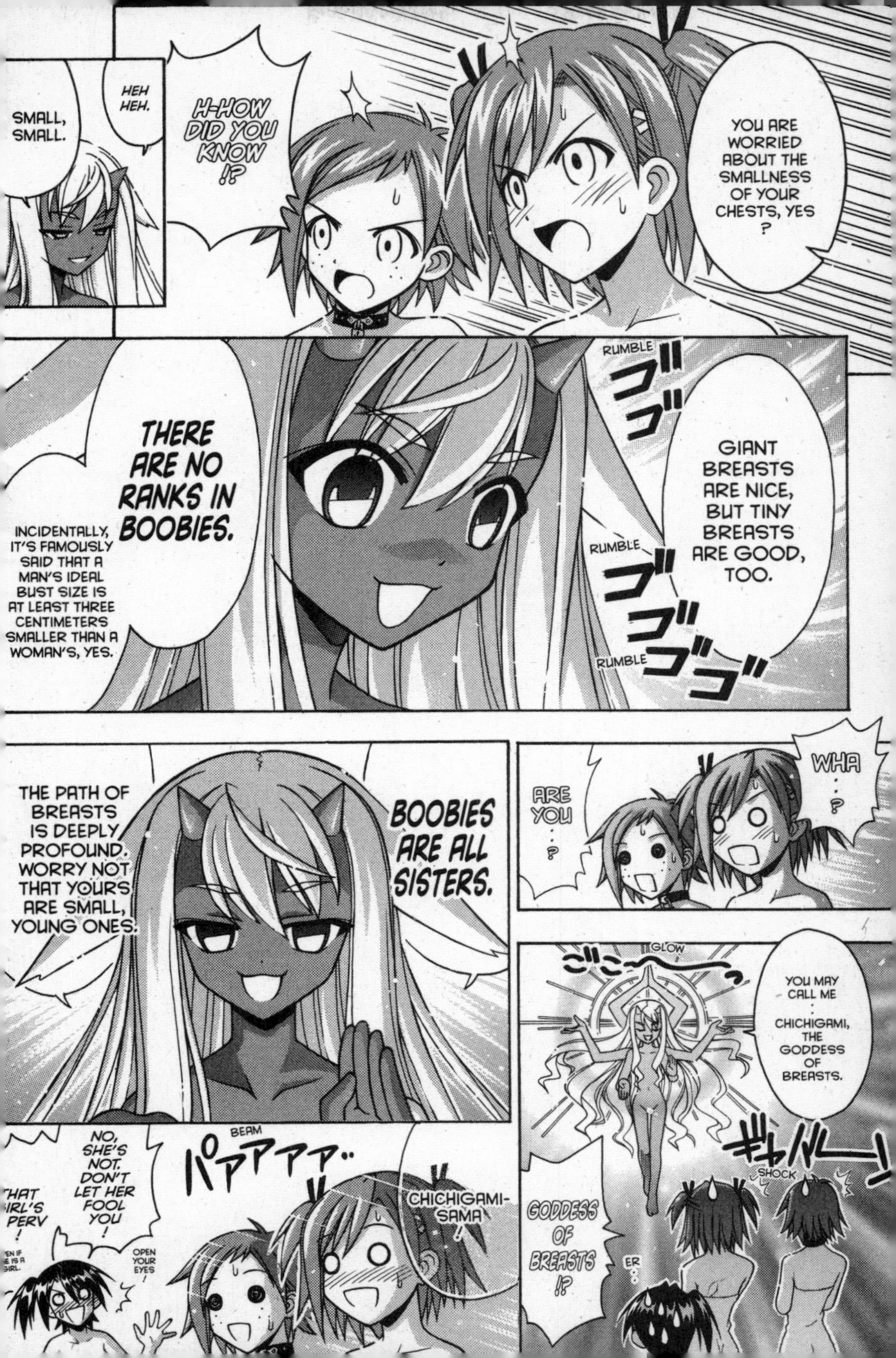
YOU ARE WORRIED ABOUT THE SMALLNESS OF YOUR CHESTS, YES ?
H-HOW DID YOU KNOW !?
HEH HEH.
SMALL, SMALL.
RUMBLE
GIANT BREASTS ARE NICE, BUT TINY BREASTS ARE GOOD, TOO.
RUMBLE
RUMBLE
THERE ARE NO RANKS IN BOOBIES.
INCIDENTALLY, IT'S FAMOUSLY SAID THAT A MAN'S IDEAL BUST SIZE IS AT LEAST THREE CENTIMETERS SMALLER THAN A WOMAN'S, YES.
WHA . . ?
ARE YOU . . ?
GLOW
YOU MAY CALL ME . . . CHICHIGAMI, THE GODDESS OF BREASTS.
SHOCK
GODDESS OF BREASTS !?
ER
BOOBIES ARE ALL SISTERS.
THE PATH OF BREASTS IS DEEPLY PROFOUND. WORRY NOT THAT YOURS ARE SMALL, YOUNG ONES.
BEAM
CHICHIGAMI-SAMA !
OPEN YOUR EYES !
NO, SHE'S NOT. DON'T LET HER FOOL YOU !

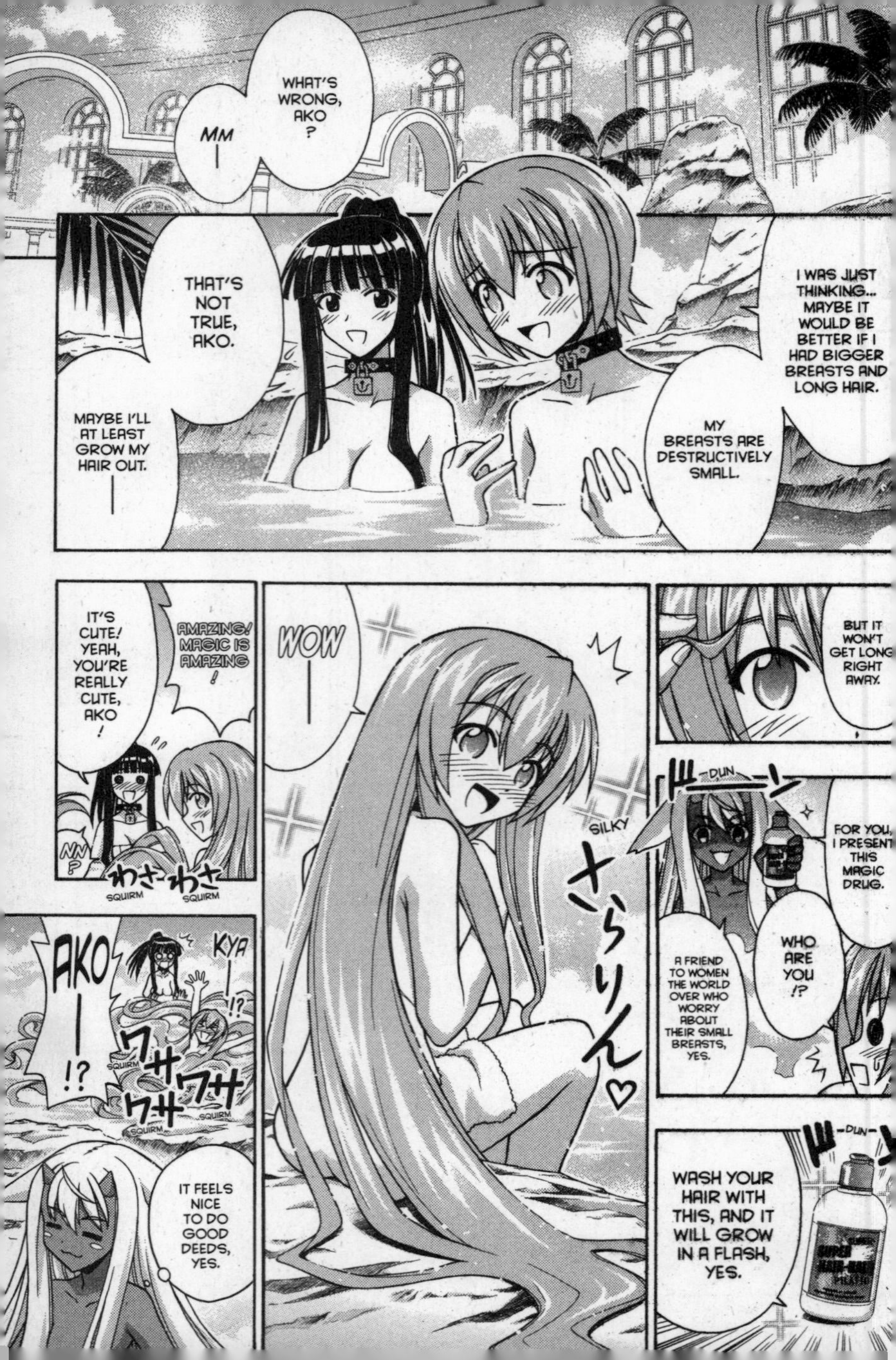

WHAT'S WRONG, AKO?
MM—
I WAS JUST THINKING... MAYBE IT WOULD BE BETTER IF I HAD BIGGER BREASTS AND LONG HAIR.
MY BREASTS ARE DESTRUCTIVELY SMALL.
THAT'S NOT TRUE, AKO.
MAYBE I'LL AT LEAST GROW MY HAIR OUT—
BUT IT WON'T GET LONG RIGHT AWAY.
DUN
FOR YOU, I PRESENT THIS MAGIC DRUG.
WHO ARE YOU!?
A FRIEND TO WOMEN THE WORLD OVER WHO WORRY ABOUT THEIR SMALL BREASTS, YES.
DUN
WASH YOUR HAIR WITH THIS, AND IT WILL GROW IN A FLASH, YES.
WOW—
さらりん♡
SILKY
IT'S CUTE! YEAH, YOU'RE REALLY CUTE, AKO!
AMAZING! MAGIC IS AMAZING!
NN?
わさ わさ
SQUIRM SQUIRM
AKO—!?
KYA—!?
ワサワサ ワサワサ
SQUIRM SQUIRM SQUIRM
IT FEELS NICE TO DO GOOD DEEDS, YES.

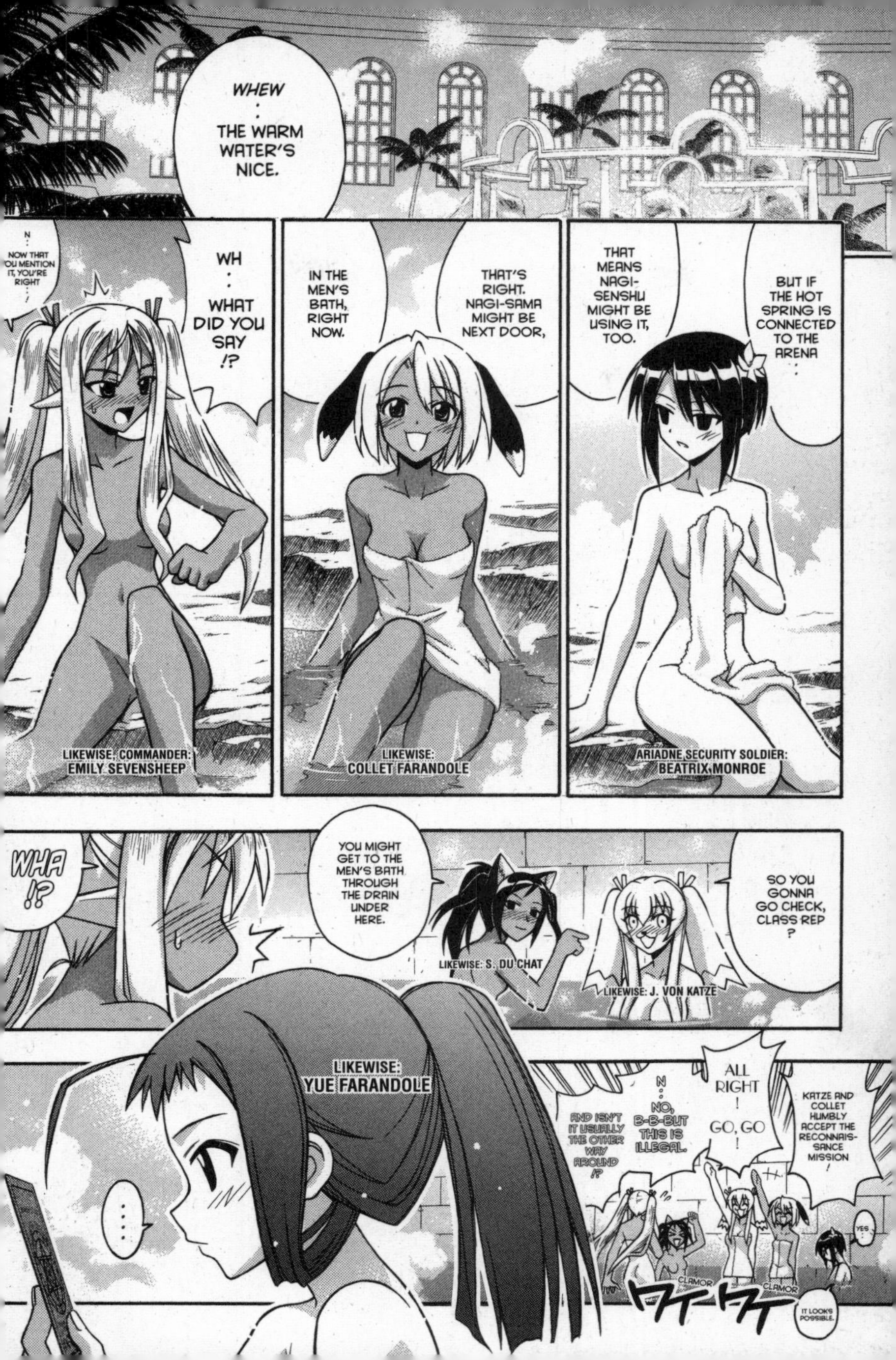
WHEW : THE WARM WATER'S NICE.
BUT IF THE HOT SPRING IS CONNECTED TO THE ARENA :
THAT MEANS NAGI-SENSHU MIGHT BE USING IT, TOO.
ARIADNE SECURITY SOLDIER: BEATRIX MONROE
THAT'S RIGHT. NAGI-SAMA MIGHT BE NEXT DOOR,
IN THE MEN'S BATH, RIGHT NOW.
LIKEWISE: COLLET FARANDOLE
WH : WHAT DID YOU SAY !?
N : NOW THAT OU MENTION IT, YOU'RE RIGHT :
LIKEWISE, COMMANDER: EMILY SEVENSHEEP
SO YOU GONNA GO CHECK, CLASS REP ?
LIKEWISE: J. VON KATZE
YOU MIGHT GET TO THE MEN'S BATH THROUGH THE DRAIN UNDER HERE.
LIKEWISE: S. DU CHAT
WHA !?
KATZE AND COLLET HUMBLY ACCEPT THE RECONNAIS-SANCE MISSION
YES
IT LOOKS POSSIBLE.
CLAMOR
CLAMOR
ALL RIGHT ! GO, GO !
N : NO, B-B-BUT THIS IS ILLEGAL.
AND ISN'T IT USUALLY THE OTHER WAY AROUND !?
LIKEWISE: YUE FARANDOLE
...

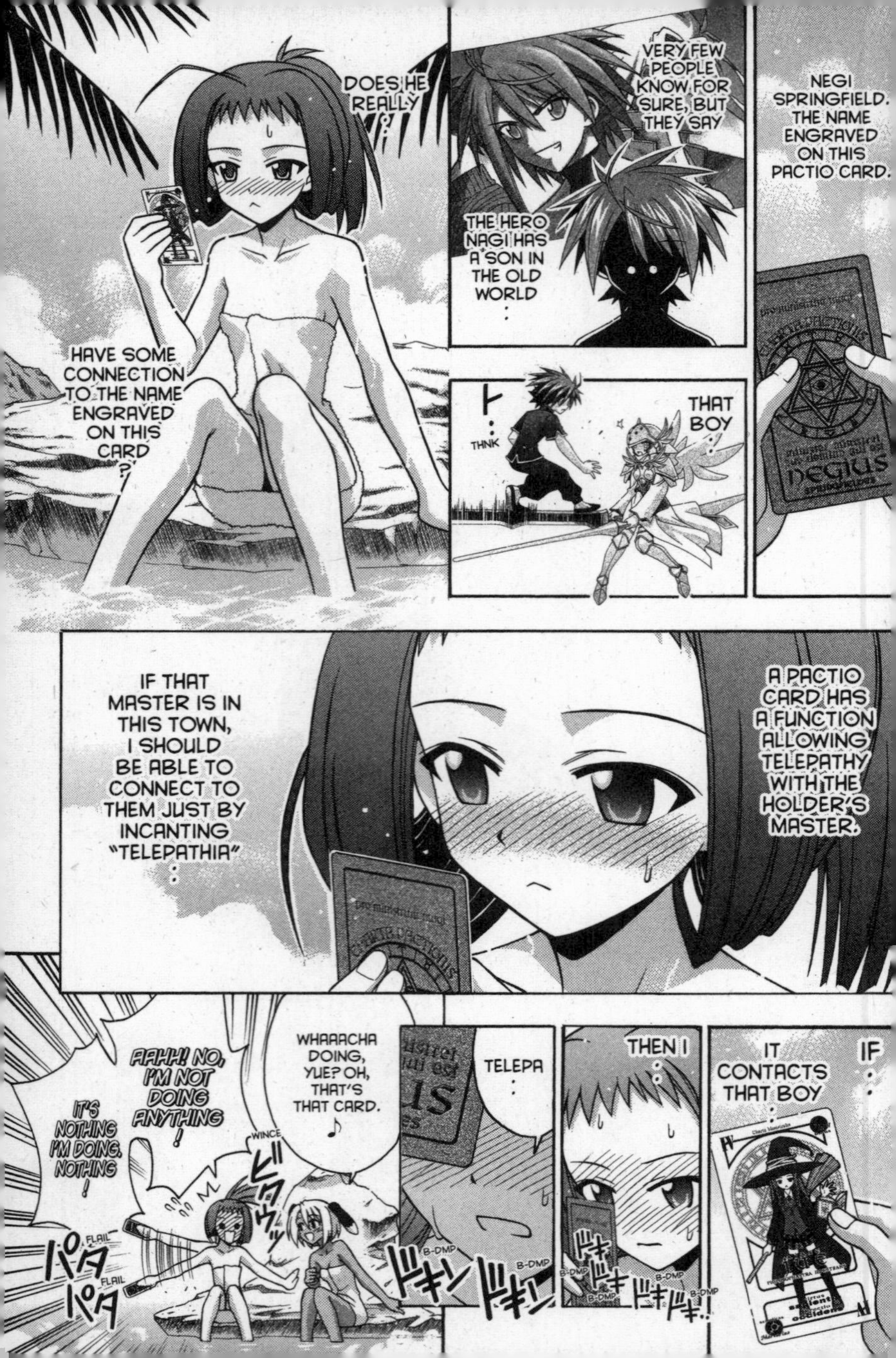
NEGI SPRINGFIELD. THE NAME ENGRAVED ON THIS PACTIO CARD.
VERY FEW PEOPLE KNOW FOR SURE, BUT THEY SAY
THE HERO NAGI HAS A SON IN THE OLD WORLD . . .
THAT BOY . . .
THNK
DOES HE REALLY . . .
HAVE SOME CONNECTION TO THE NAME ENGRAVED ON THIS CARD ?
A PACTIO CARD HAS A FUNCTION ALLOWING TELEPATHY WITH THE HOLDER'S MASTER.
IF THAT MASTER IS IN THIS TOWN, I SHOULD BE ABLE TO CONNECT TO THEM JUST BY INCANTING "TELEPATHIA" . . .
IF . . .
IT CONTACTS THAT BOY . . .
THEN I . . .
B-DMP
B-DMP
B-DMP
B-DMP
TELEPA . . .
B-DMP
B-DMP
WHAAACHA DOING, YUE? OH, THAT'S THAT CARD. ♪
WINCE
AAHH! NO, I'M NOT DOING ANYTHING!
IT'S NOTHING I'M DOING. NOTHING!
FLAIL
FLAIL

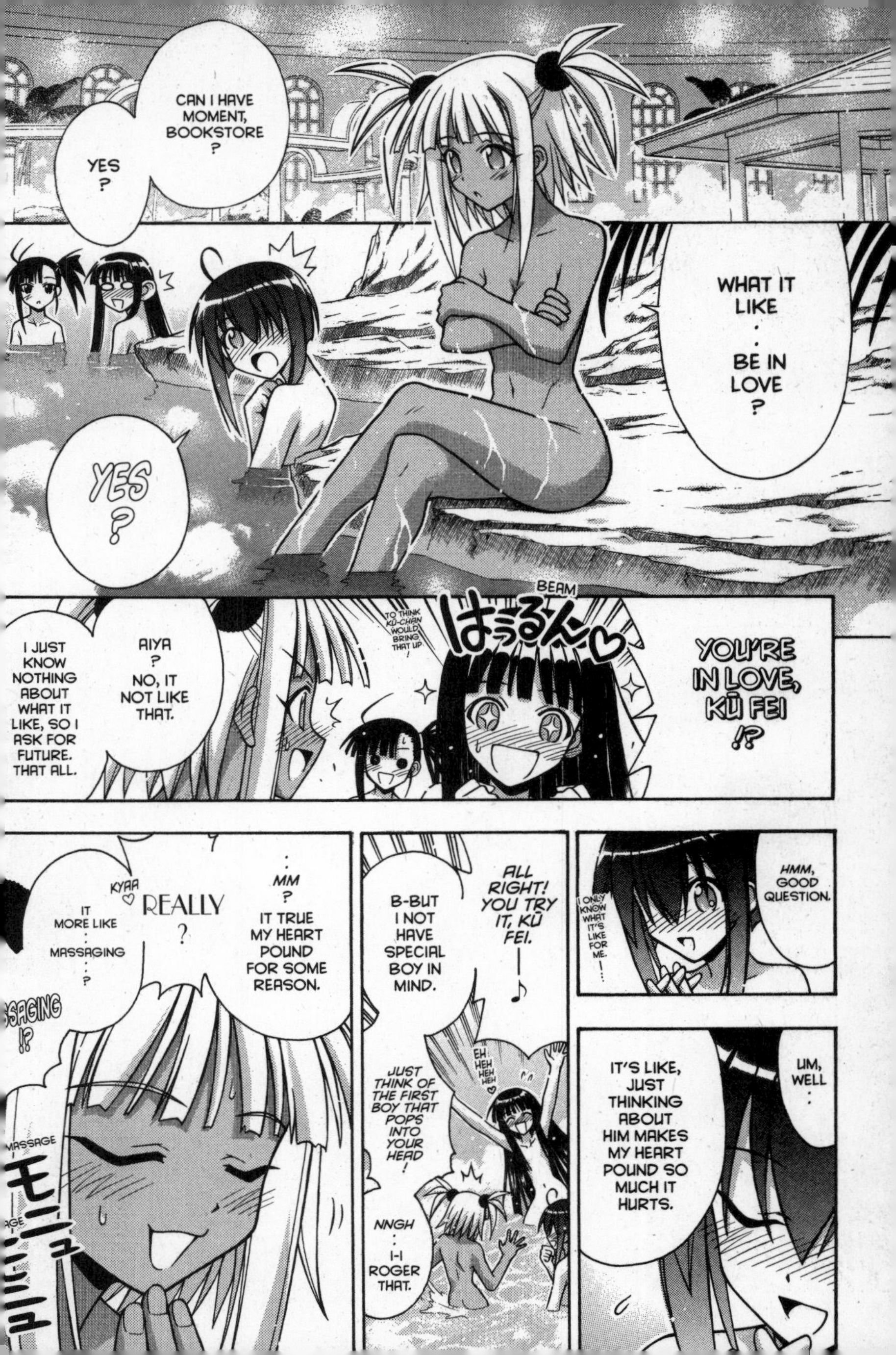

CAN I HAVE MOMENT, BOOKSTORE?
YES?
WHAT IT LIKE . . BE IN LOVE?
YES?
YOU'RE IN LOVE, KŪ FEI!?
BEAM
はぅるん♡
TO THINK KŪ-CHAN WOULD BRING THAT UP!
AIYA? NO, IT NOT LIKE THAT.
I JUST KNOW NOTHING ABOUT WHAT IT LIKE, SO I ASK FOR FUTURE. THAT ALL.
HMM, GOOD QUESTION.
I ONLY KNOW WHAT IT'S LIKE FOR ME...!
UM, WELL:
IT'S LIKE, JUST THINKING ABOUT HIM MAKES MY HEART POUND SO MUCH IT HURTS.
ALL RIGHT! YOU TRY IT, KŪ FEI!♪
B-BUT I NOT HAVE SPECIAL BOY IN MIND.
EH HEH HEH HEH♡
JUST THINK OF THE FIRST BOY THAT POPS INTO YOUR HEAD!
NNGH: I-I ROGER THAT.
MM? IT TRUE MY HEART POUND FOR SOME REASON.
KYAA♡
REALLY?
IT MORE LIKE... MASSAGING...?
SSAGING!?
MASSAGE
モニュ
AGE

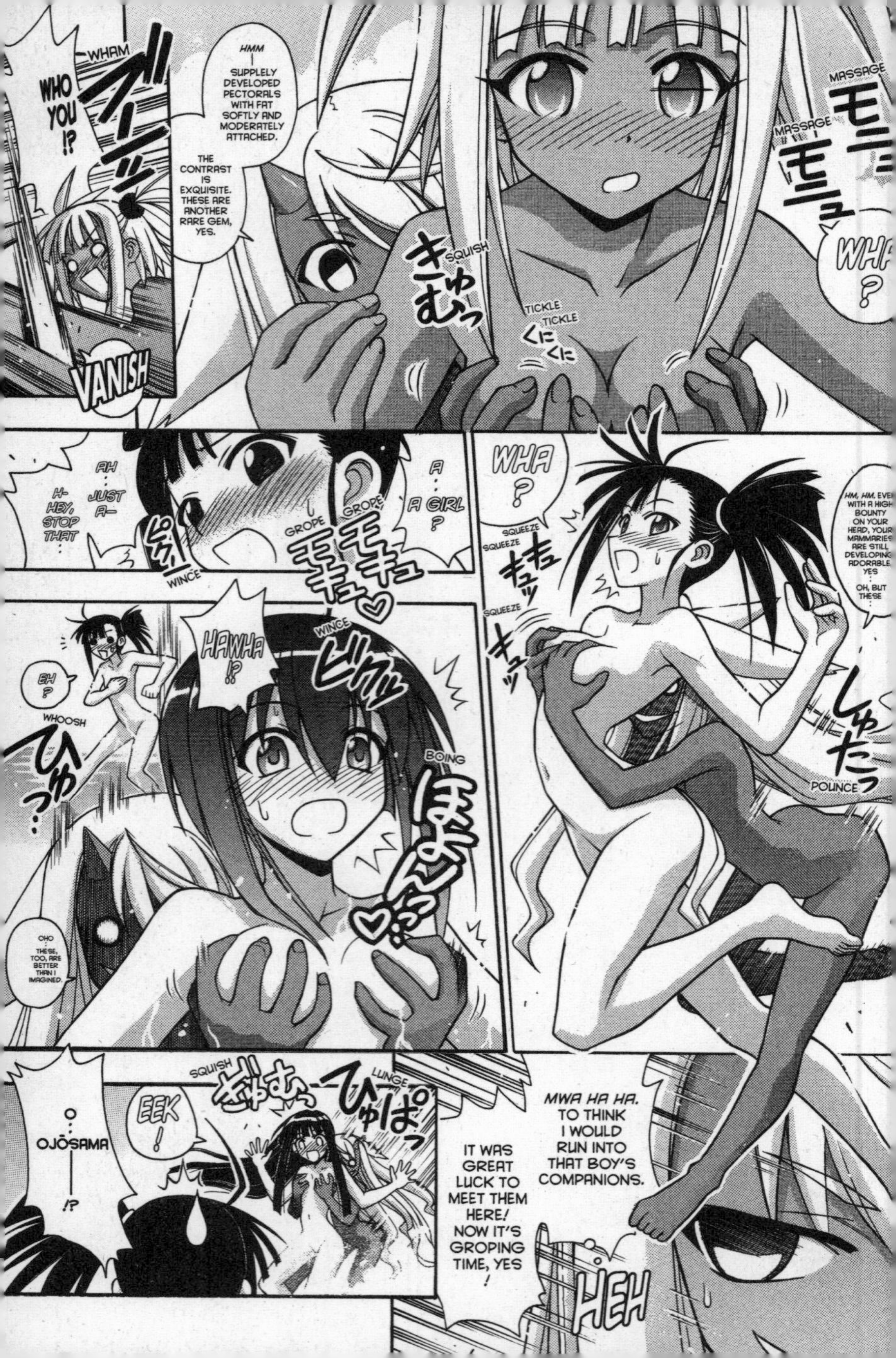
MASSAGE
MASSAGE
WHA ?
SQUISH
TICKLE
TICKLE
HMM I SUPPLELY DEVELOPED PECTORALS WITH FAT SOFTLY AND MODERATELY ATTACHED.
THE CONTRAST IS EXQUISITE. THESE ARE ANOTHER RARE GEM, YES.
WHAM
WHO YOU !?
VANISH
WHA ?
HM, HM. EVEN WITH A HIGH BOUNTY ON YOUR HEAD, YOUR MAMMARIES ARE STILL DEVELOPING ADORABLY, YES
OH, BUT THESE
SQUEEZE
SQUEEZE
SQUEEZE
POUNCE
A... A GIRL ?
AH... JUST A–
H-HEY, STOP THAT...
GROPE
GROPE
WINCE
HAWHA !?
WINCE
BOING
EH ?
WHOOSH
OHO THESE, TOO, ARE BETTER THAN I IMAGINED.
MWA HA HA. TO THINK I WOULD RUN INTO THAT BOY'S COMPANIONS.
IT WAS GREAT LUCK TO MEET THEM HERE! NOW IT'S GROPING TIME, YES !
HEH
SQUISH
LUNGE
EEK !
O... OJŌSAMA——!?

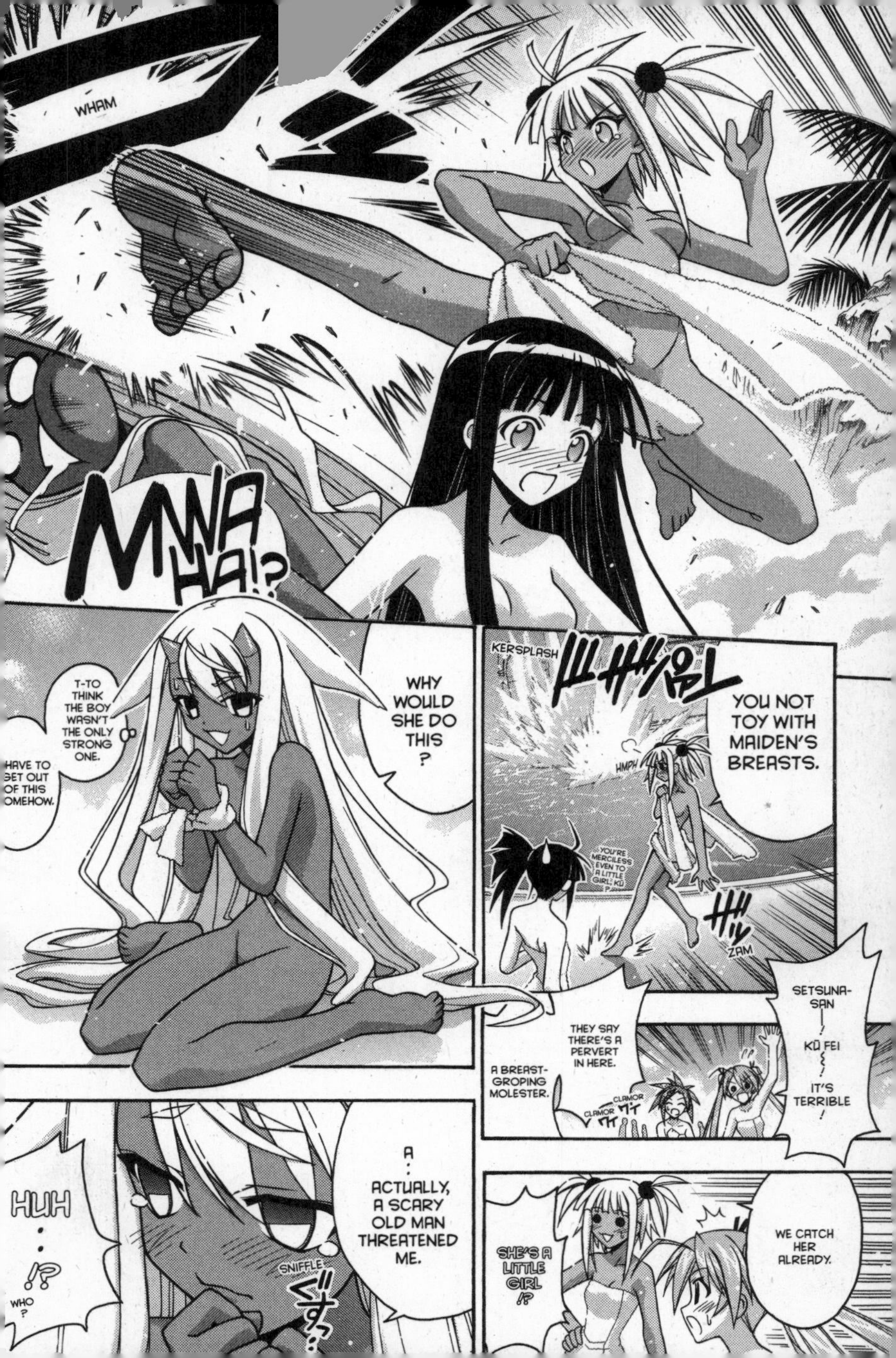
WHAM
MWA HA!?
KERSPLASH
YOU NOT TOY WITH MAIDEN'S BREASTS.
HMPH
YOU'RE MERCILESS EVEN TO A LITTLE GIRL, KŪ ?
ZAM
SETSUNA-SAN! KŪ FEI! IT'S TERRIBLE!
THEY SAY THERE'S A PERVERT IN HERE.
A BREAST-GROPING MOLESTER.
CLAMOR
CLAMOR
WHY WOULD SHE DO THIS?
T-TO THINK THE BOY WASN'T THE ONLY STRONG ONE.
HAVE TO GET OUT OF THIS OMEHOW.
WE CATCH HER ALREADY.
SHE'S A LITTLE GIRL!?
A... ACTUALLY, A SCARY OLD MAN THREATENED ME.
SNIFFLE
HUH...!?
WHO?

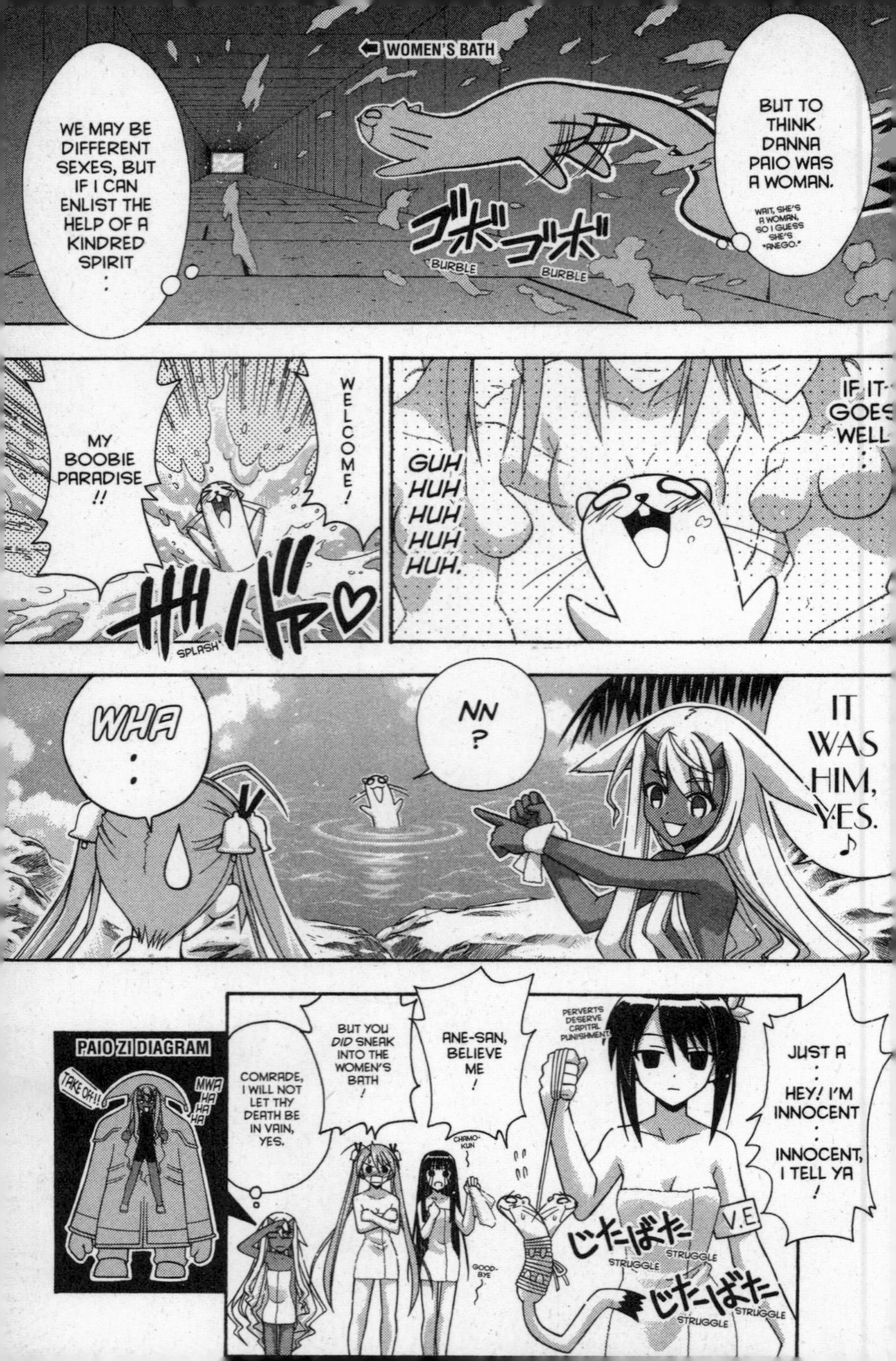

WOMEN'S BATH
BUT TO THINK DANNA PAIO WAS A WOMAN.
WAIT, SHE'S A WOMAN, SO I GUESS SHE'S "ANEGO."
ゴボゴボ
BURBLE BURBLE
WE MAY BE DIFFERENT SEXES, BUT IF I CAN ENLIST THE HELP OF A KINDRED SPIRIT...
IF IT GOES WELL...
GUH HUH HUH HUH HUH.
WELCOME!
MY BOOBIE PARADISE!!
ザバァ♡
SPLASH
IT WAS HIM, YES. ♪
NN?
WHA..
JUST A... HEY! I'M INNOCENT... INNOCENT, I TELL YA!
PERVERTS DESERVE CAPITAL PUNISHMENT!
ANE-SAN, BELIEVE ME!
BUT YOU *DID* SNEAK INTO THE WOMEN'S BATH!
COMRADE, I WILL NOT LET THY DEATH BE IN VAIN, YES.
CHAMO-KUN
GOOD-BYE
V.E.
じたばた
STRUGGLE STRUGGLE
じたーばた
STRUGGLE STRUGGLE
PAIO ZI DIAGRAM
TAKE OFF!!
MWA HA HA HA

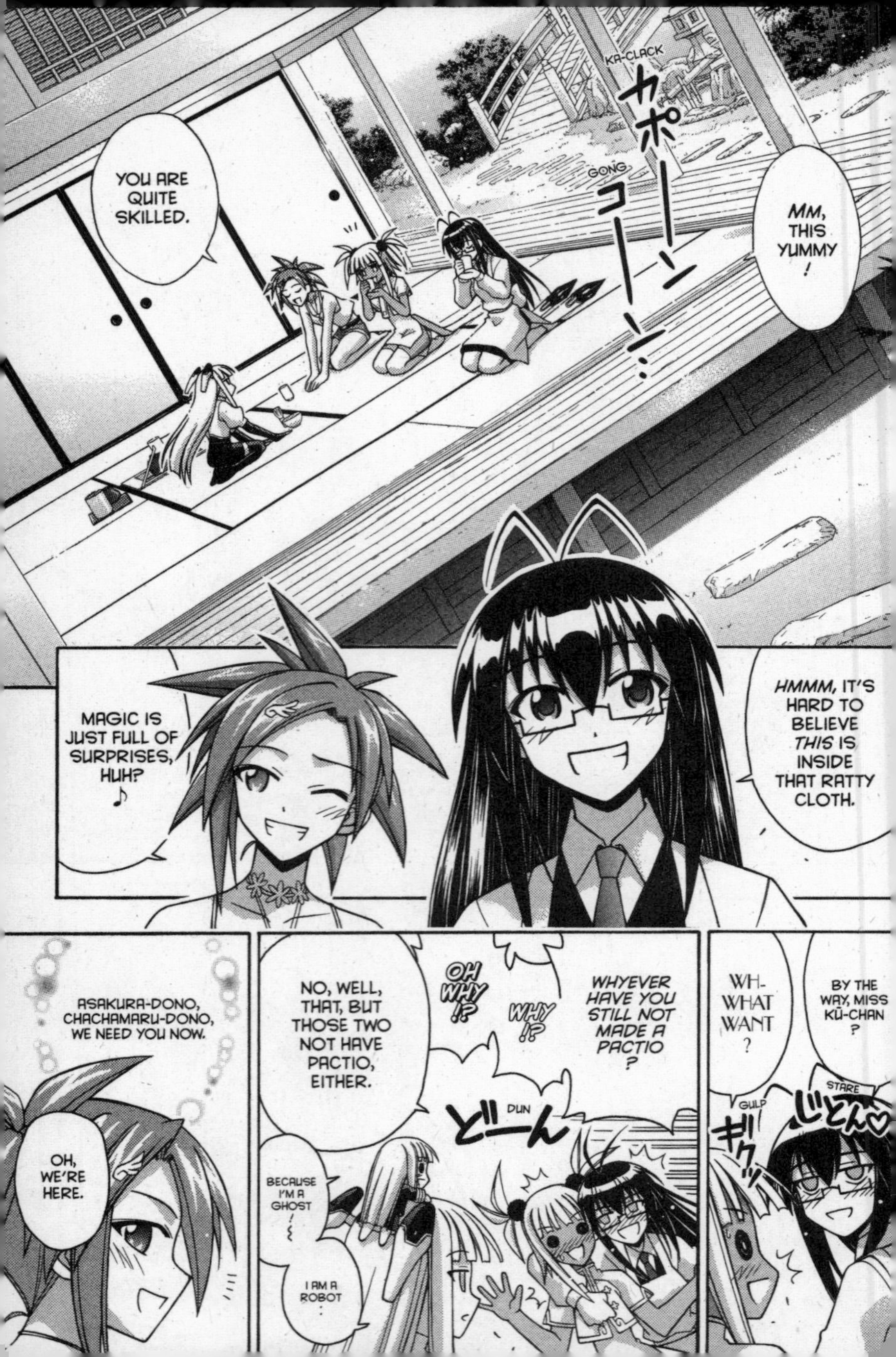

KA-CLACK
カポーーン
GONG
コーーン
MM, THIS YUMMY!
YOU ARE QUITE SKILLED.
HMMM, IT'S HARD TO BELIEVE THIS IS INSIDE THAT RATTY CLOTH.
MAGIC IS JUST FULL OF SURPRISES, HUH? ♪
BY THE WAY, MISS KŪ-CHAN?
WH-WHAT WANT?
STARE
じとん♡
GULP
ギクッ
WHYEVER HAVE YOU STILL NOT MADE A PACTIO?
WHY!?
OH WHY!?
DUN
どーん
NO, WELL, THAT, BUT THOSE TWO NOT HAVE PACTIO, EITHER.
BECAUSE I'M A GHOST!
I AM A ROBOT
ASAKURA-DONO, CHACHAMARU-DONO, WE NEED YOU NOW.
OH, WE'RE HERE.

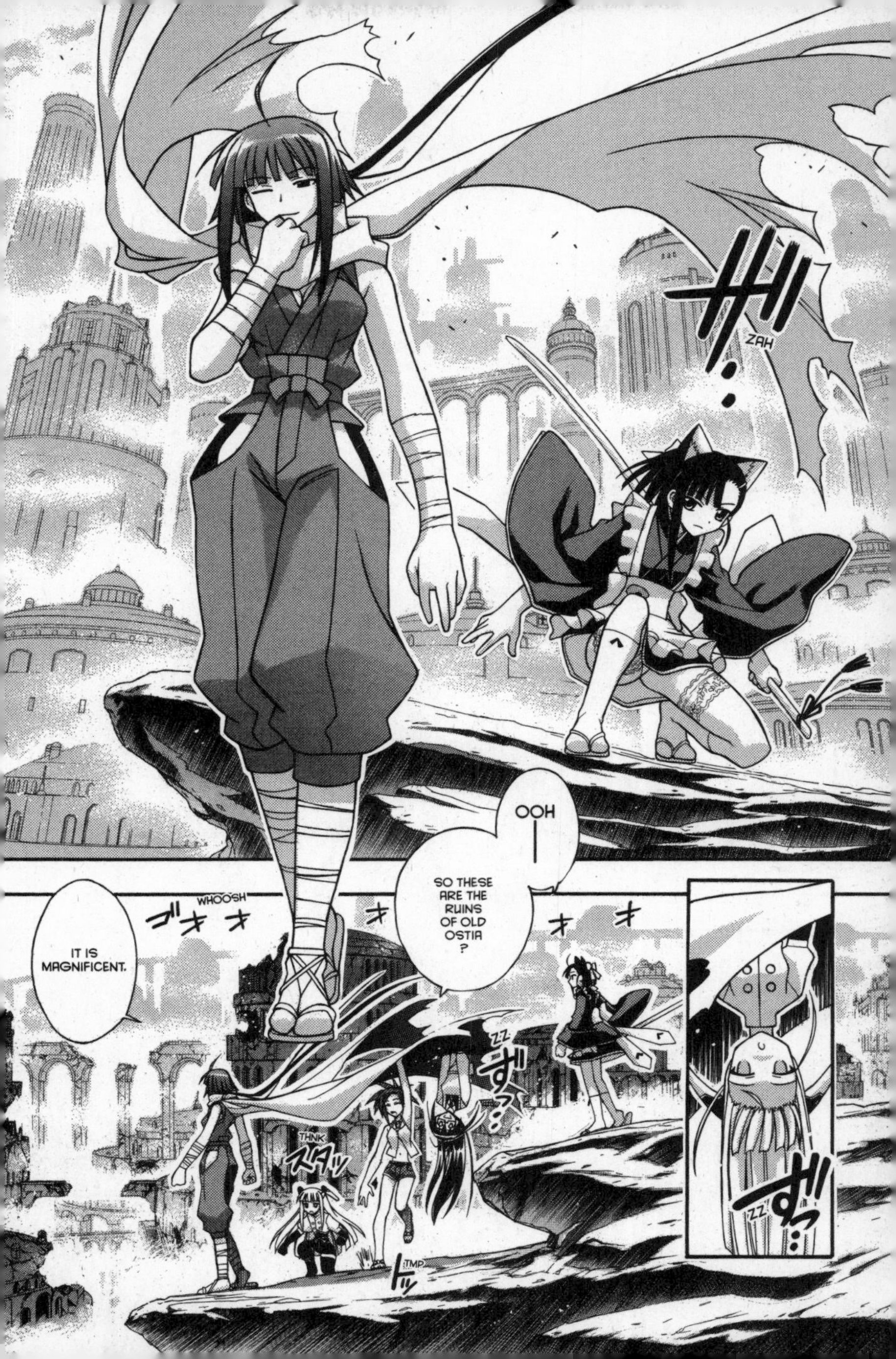

ZAH
OOH—
ZZ
SO THESE ARE THE RUINS OF OLD OSTIA?
IT IS MAGNIFICENT.
WHOOSH
ZZ
THNK
TMP

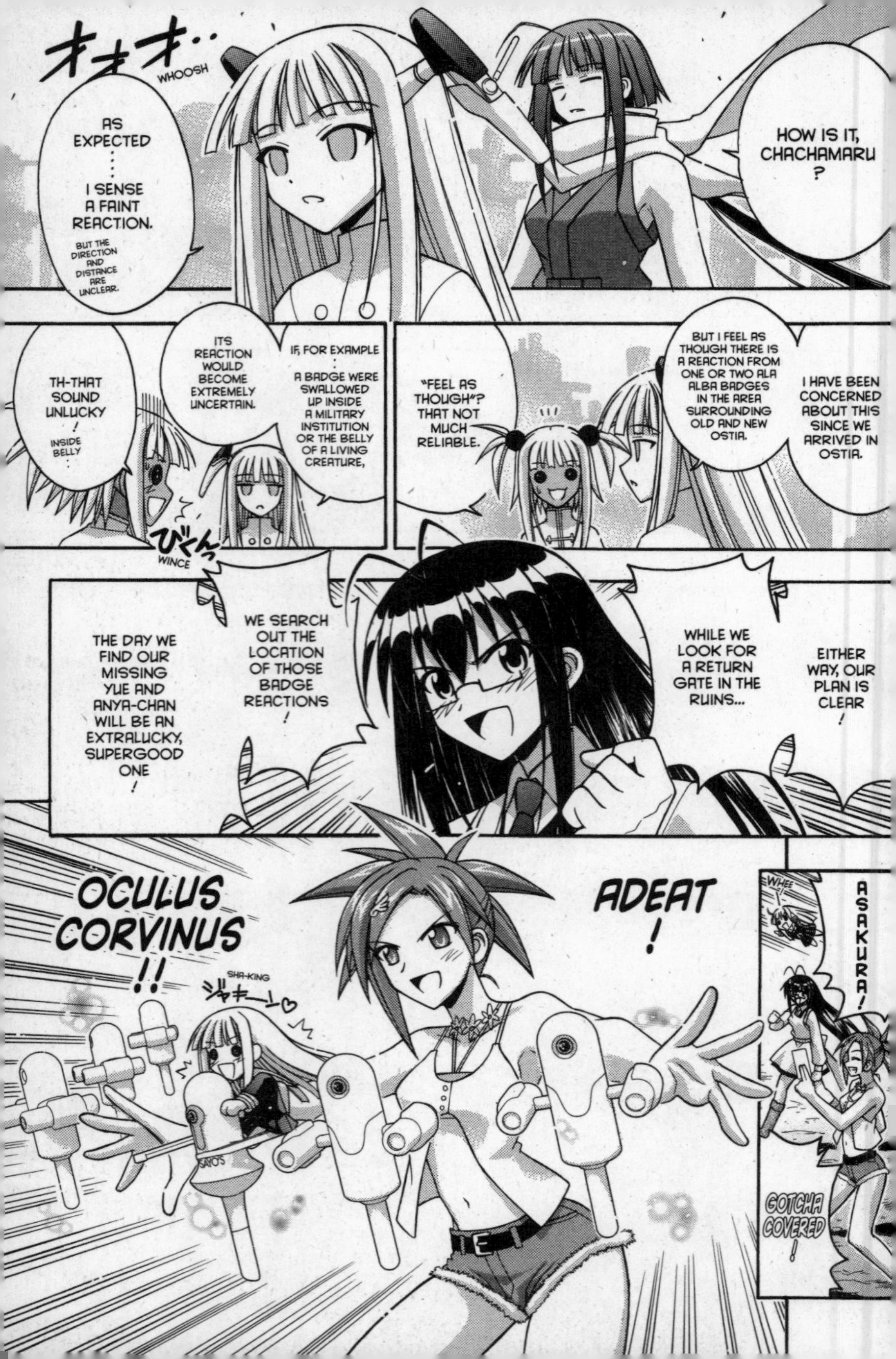

HOW IS IT, CHACHAMARU?
オオオ..
WHOOSH
AS EXPECTED... I SENSE A FAINT REACTION.
BUT THE DIRECTION AND DISTANCE ARE UNCLEAR.
I HAVE BEEN CONCERNED ABOUT THIS SINCE WE ARRIVED IN OSTIA.
BUT I FEEL AS THOUGH THERE IS A REACTION FROM ONE OR TWO ALA ALBA BADGES IN THE AREA SURROUNDING OLD AND NEW OSTIA.
"FEEL AS THOUGH"? THAT NOT MUCH RELIABLE.
IF, FOR EXAMPLE: A BADGE WERE SWALLOWED UP INSIDE A MILITARY INSTITUTION OR THE BELLY OF A LIVING CREATURE,
ITS REACTION WOULD BECOME EXTREMELY UNCERTAIN.
TH-THAT SOUND UNLUCKY!
INSIDE BELLY...
びくんっ
WINCE
EITHER WAY, OUR PLAN IS CLEAR!
WHILE WE LOOK FOR A RETURN GATE IN THE RUINS...
WE SEARCH OUT THE LOCATION OF THOSE BADGE REACTIONS!
THE DAY WE FIND OUR MISSING YUE AND ANYA-CHAN WILL BE AN EXTRALUCKY, SUPERGOOD ONE!
WHEE!
ASAKURA!
GOTCHA COVERED!
ADEAT!
OCULUS CORVINUS!!
SHA-KING
ジャキーン♡
SAYO'S

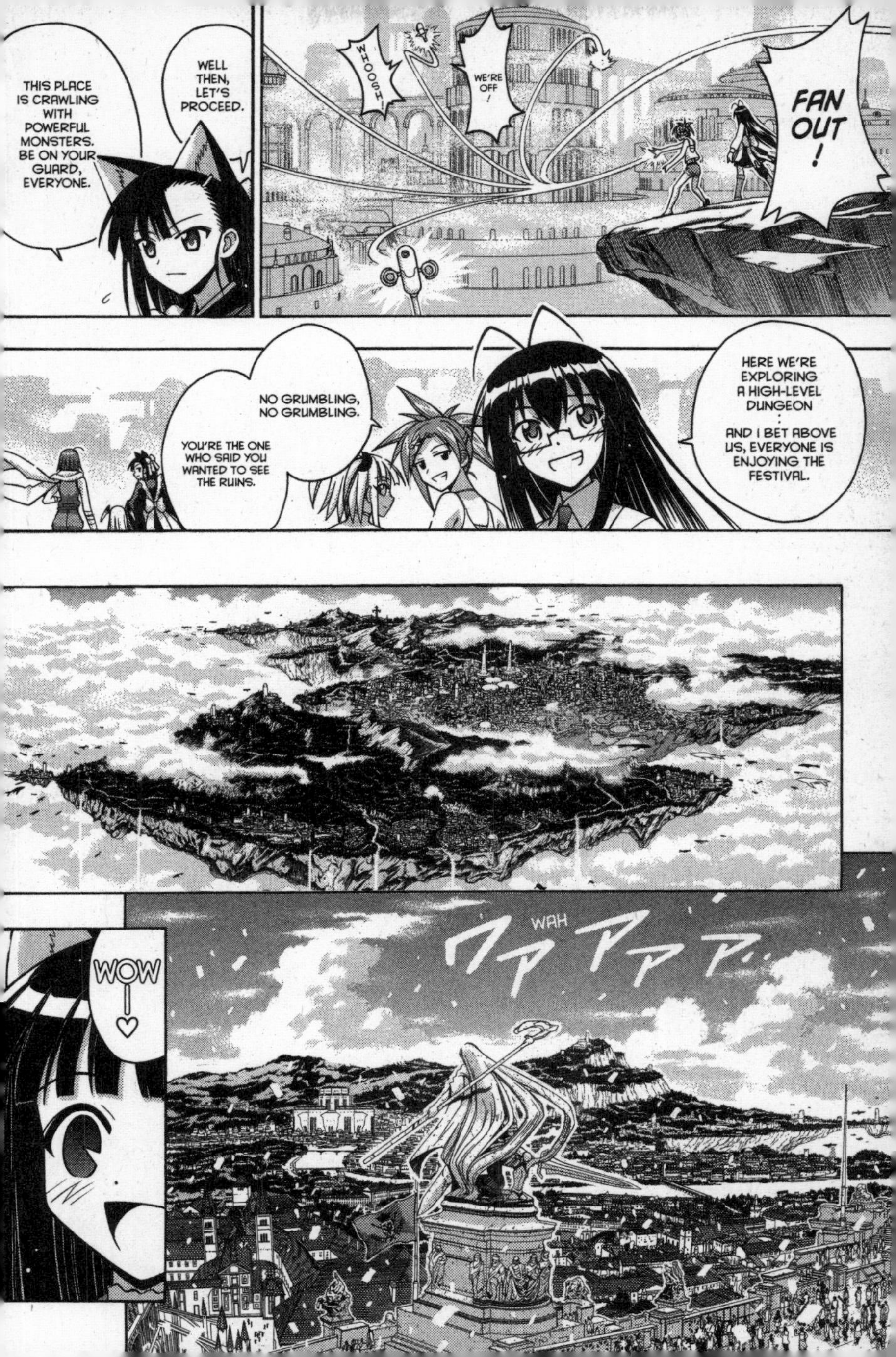
FAN OUT!
WE'RE OFF!
WHOOSH!
WELL THEN, LET'S PROCEED.
THIS PLACE IS CRAWLING WITH POWERFUL MONSTERS. BE ON YOUR GUARD, EVERYONE.
HERE WE'RE EXPLORING A HIGH-LEVEL DUNGEON: AND I BET ABOVE US, EVERYONE IS ENJOYING THE FESTIVAL.
NO GRUMBLING, NO GRUMBLING.
YOU'RE THE ONE WHO SAID YOU WANTED TO SEE THE RUINS.
WAH
WOW ♥

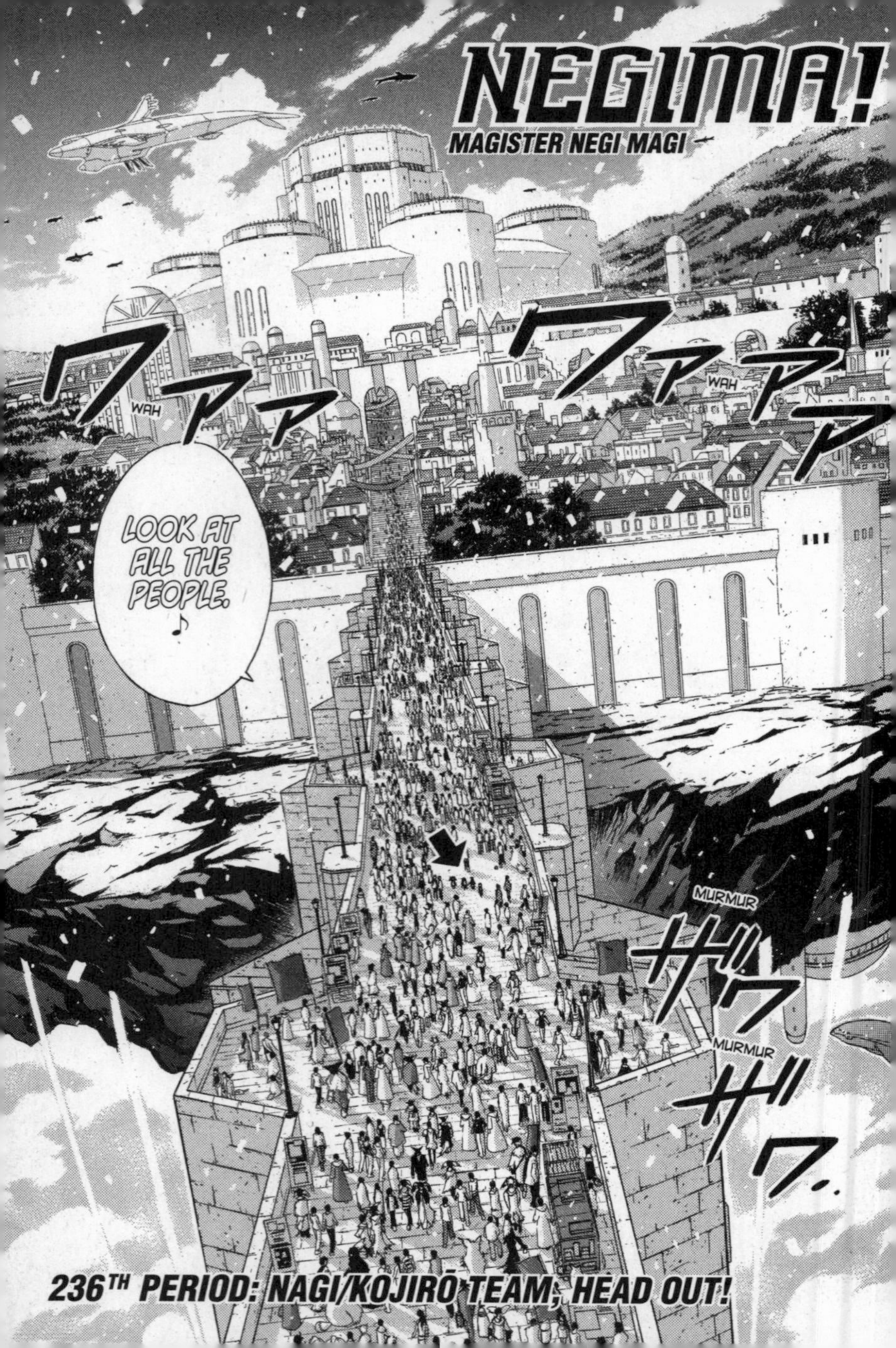
NEGIMA!
MAGISTER NEGI MAGI
WAH
WAH
LOOK AT ALL THE PEOPLE. ♪
MURMUR
MURMUR
236TH PERIOD: NAGI/KOJIRŌ TEAM, HEAD OUT!

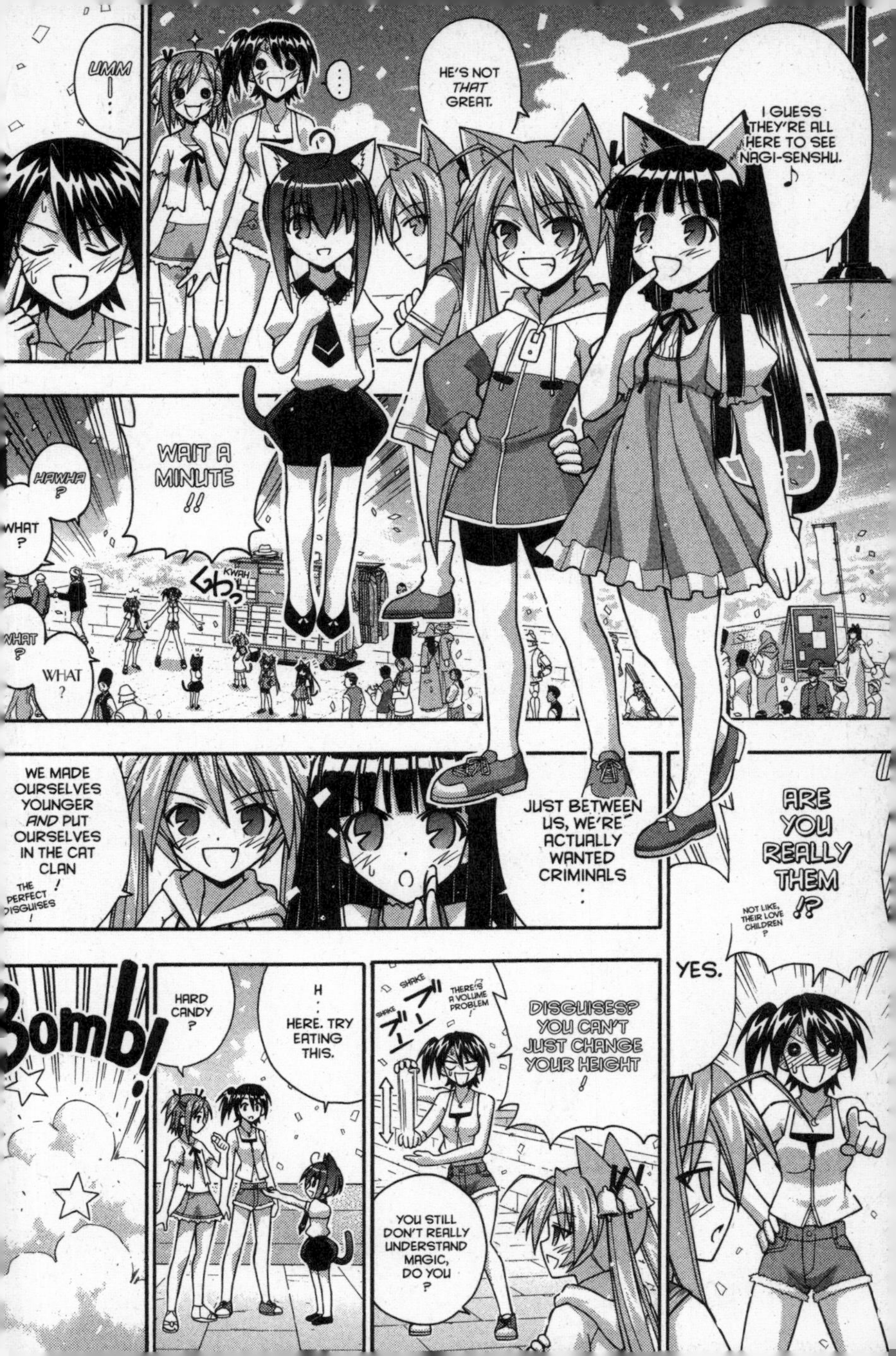
I GUESS THEY'RE ALL HERE TO SEE NAGI-SENSHU. ♪
HE'S NOT *THAT* GREAT.
…
UMM !…
WAIT A MINUTE !!
HAWHA ?
WHAT ?
KWAH
WHAT ?
WHAT ?
ARE YOU REALLY THEM !?
NOT LIKE, THEIR LOVE CHILDREN ?
JUST BETWEEN US, WE'RE ACTUALLY WANTED CRIMINALS ..
WE MADE OURSELVES YOUNGER *AND* PUT OURSELVES IN THE CAT CLAN !
THE PERFECT DISGUISES !
YES.
DISGUISES? YOU CAN'T JUST CHANGE YOUR HEIGHT !
THERE'S A VOLUME PROBLEM !
SHAKE
SHAKE
YOU STILL DON'T REALLY UNDERSTAND MAGIC, DO YOU ?
H.. HERE. TRY EATING THIS.
HARD CANDY ?
Bomb!

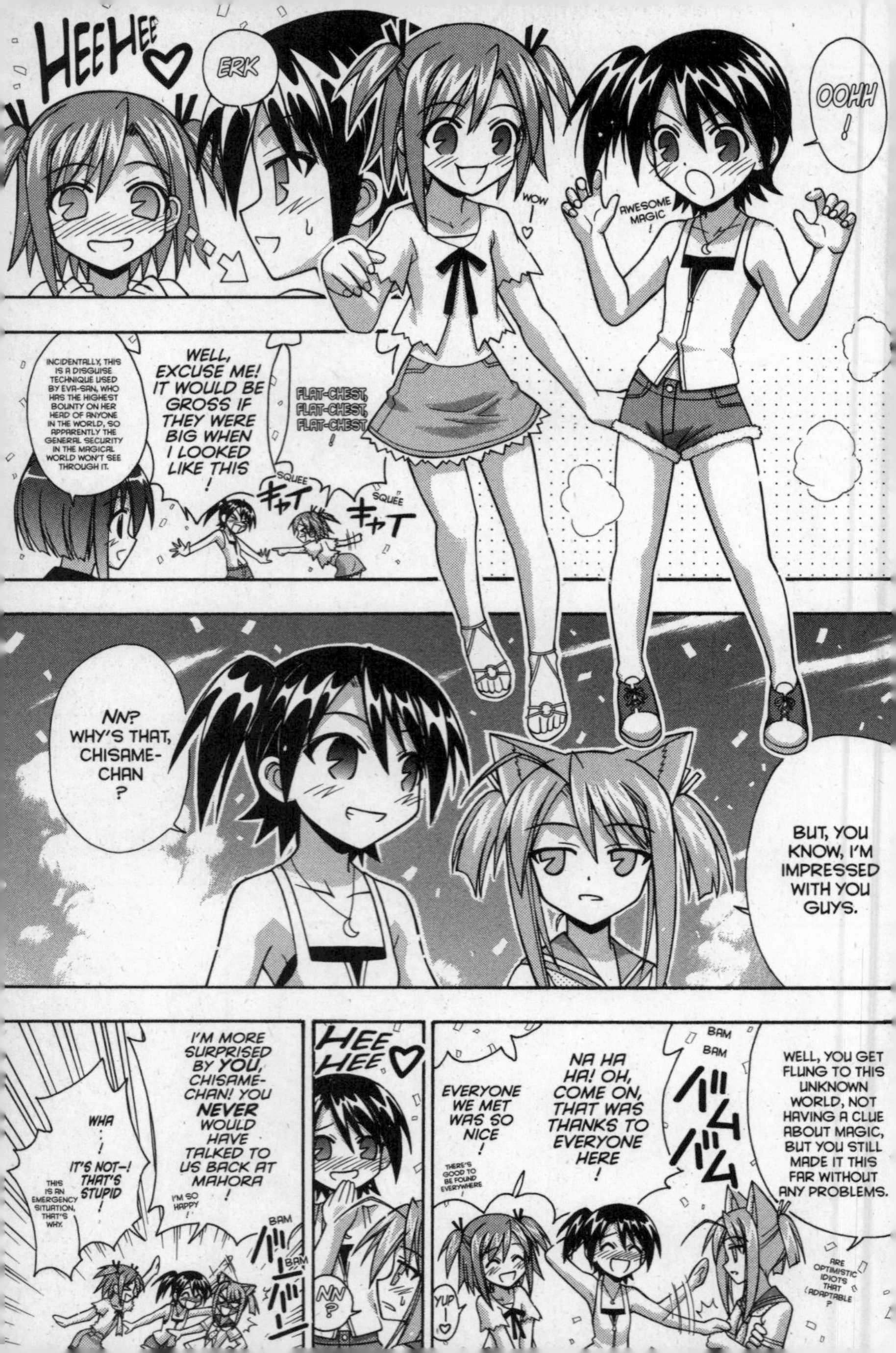
OOHH!
AWESOME MAGIC!
WOW!♥
ERK
HEEHEE♥
FLAT-CHEST, FLAT-CHEST, FLAT-CHEST!
WELL, EXCUSE ME! IT WOULD BE GROSS IF THEY WERE BIG WHEN I LOOKED LIKE THIS!
SQUEE
SQUEE
INCIDENTALLY, THIS IS A DISGUISE TECHNIQUE USED BY EVA-SAN, WHO HAS THE HIGHEST BOUNTY ON HER HEAD OF ANYONE IN THE WORLD, SO APPARENTLY THE GENERAL SECURITY IN THE MAGICAL WORLD WON'T SEE THROUGH IT.
BUT, YOU KNOW, I'M IMPRESSED WITH YOU GUYS.
NN? WHY'S THAT, CHISAME-CHAN?
WELL, YOU GET FLUNG TO THIS UNKNOWN WORLD, NOT HAVING A CLUE ABOUT MAGIC, BUT YOU STILL MADE IT THIS FAR WITHOUT ANY PROBLEMS.
ARE OPTIMISTIC IDIOTS THAT ADAPTABLE?
BAM
BAM
NA HA HA! OH, COME ON, THAT WAS THANKS TO EVERYONE HERE!
EVERYONE WE MET WAS SO NICE!
THERE'S GOOD TO BE FOUND EVERYWHERE!
YUP!♥
HEE HEE♥
I'M MORE SURPRISED BY YOU, CHISAME-CHAN! YOU NEVER WOULD HAVE TALKED TO US BACK AT MAHORA!
I'M SO HAPPY!
NN?
BAM
BAM
WHA...!
IT'S NOT-! THAT'S STUPID!
THIS IS AN EMERGENCY SITUATION, THAT'S WHY.

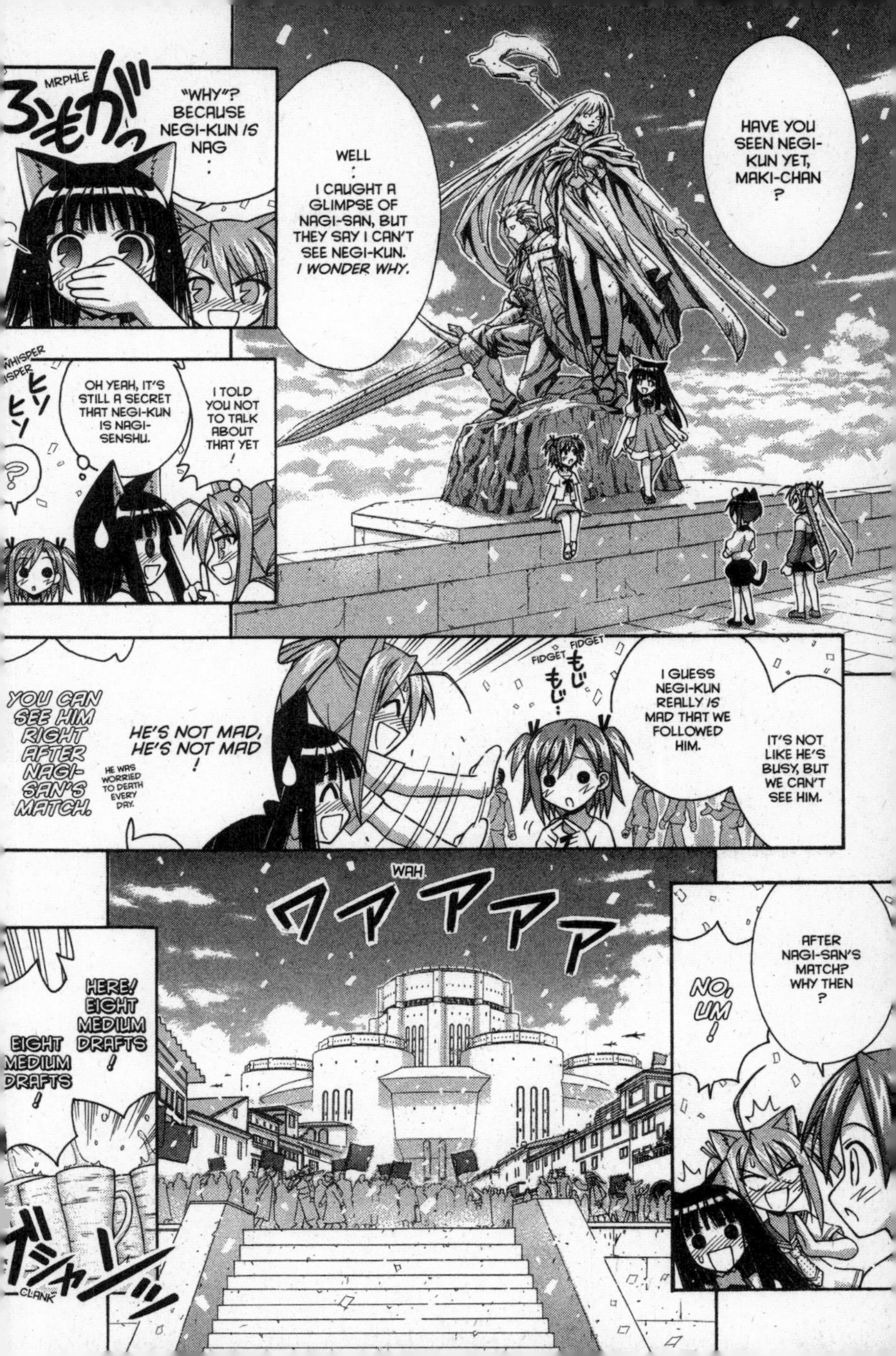
HAVE YOU SEEN NEGI-KUN YET, MAKI-CHAN?
WELL... I CAUGHT A GLIMPSE OF NAGI-SAN, BUT THEY SAY I CAN'T SEE NEGI-KUN. *I WONDER WHY.*
ふもがっ
MRPHLE
"WHY"? BECAUSE NEGI-KUN *IS* NAG...
ヒソ ヒソ
WHISPER WHISPER
OH YEAH, IT'S STILL A SECRET THAT NEGI-KUN IS NAGI-SENSHU.
I TOLD YOU NOT TO TALK ABOUT THAT YET!
?
もじ もじ
FIDGET FIDGET
I GUESS NEGI-KUN REALLY *IS* MAD THAT WE FOLLOWED HIM.
IT'S NOT LIKE HE'S BUSY, BUT WE CAN'T SEE HIM.
HE'S NOT MAD, HE'S NOT MAD!
HE WAS WORRIED TO DEATH EVERY DAY.
YOU CAN SEE HIM RIGHT AFTER NAGI-SAN'S MATCH.
AFTER NAGI-SAN'S MATCH? WHY THEN?
NO, UM!
ワァァァァ
WAH
HERE! EIGHT MEDIUM DRAFTS!
EIGHT MEDIUM DRAFTS!
ダシャーンッ
CLANK

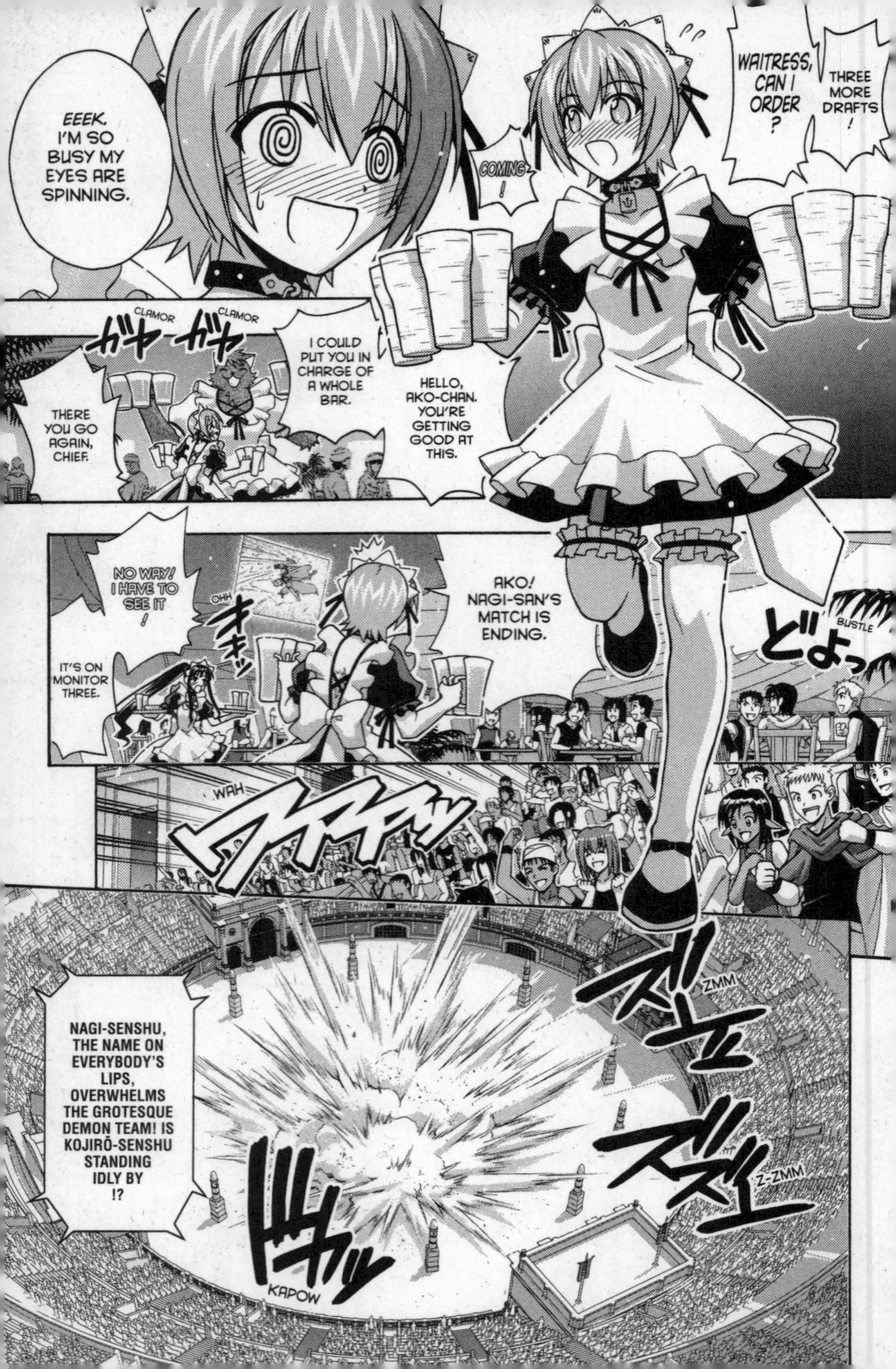
THREE MORE DRAFTS!
WAITRESS, CAN I ORDER?
COMING!
EEEK. I'M SO BUSY MY EYES ARE SPINNING.
CLAMOR
CLAMOR
HELLO, AKO-CHAN. YOU'RE GETTING GOOD AT THIS.
I COULD PUT YOU IN CHARGE OF A WHOLE BAR.
THERE YOU GO AGAIN, CHIEF.
BUSTLE
AKO! NAGI-SAN'S MATCH IS ENDING.
OHH
NO WAY! I HAVE TO SEE IT!
IT'S ON MONITOR THREE.
WAH
ZMM
Z-ZMM
KAPOW
NAGI-SENSHU, THE NAME ON EVERYBODY'S LIPS, OVERWHELMS THE GROTESQUE DEMON TEAM! IS KOJIRŌ-SENSHU STANDING IDLY BY!?

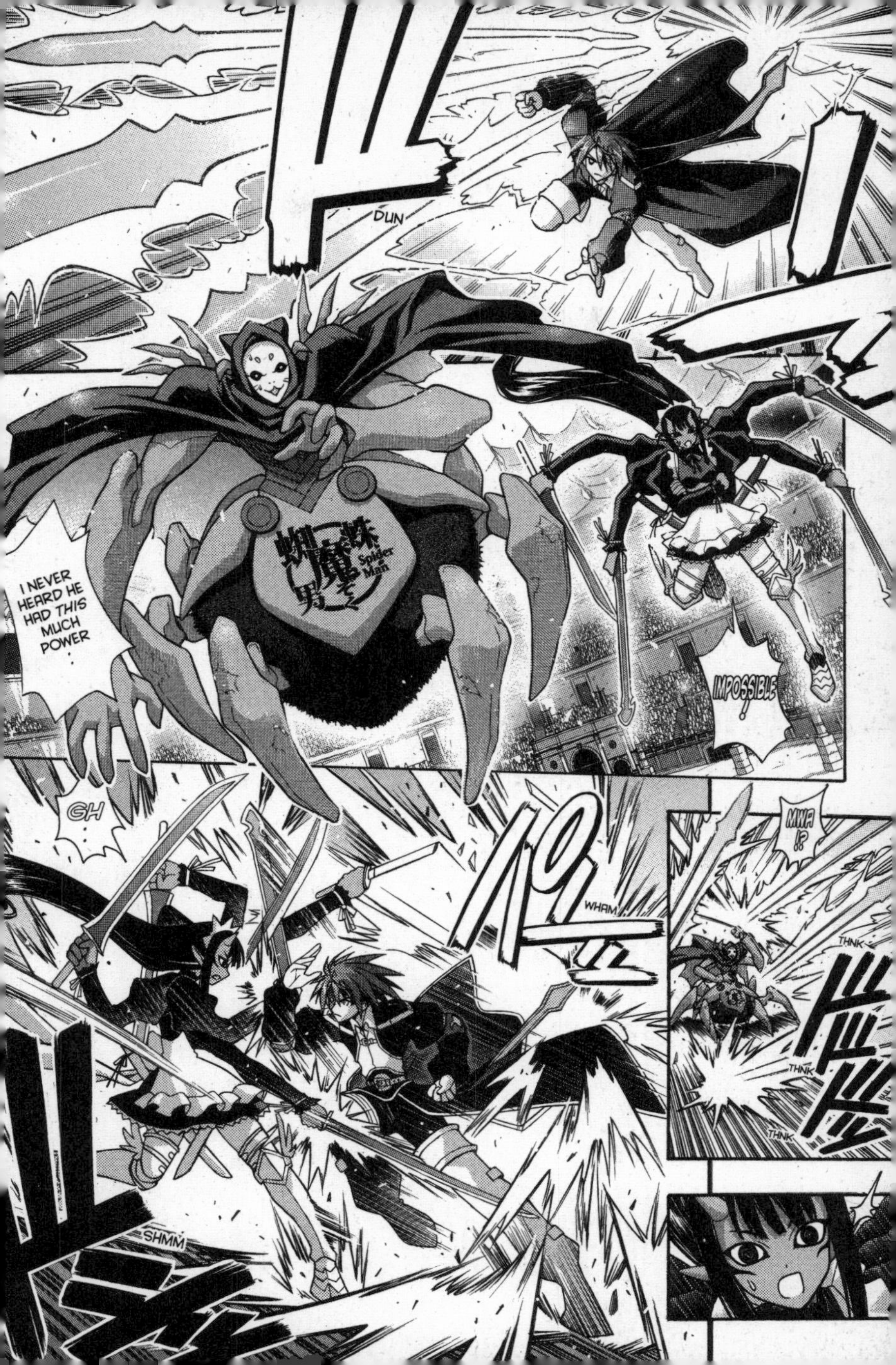
DUN
IMPOSSIBLE!
Spider Man
I NEVER HEARD HE HAD THIS MUCH POWER
MWA!?
THNK
THNK
THNK
WHAM
GH
SHMM

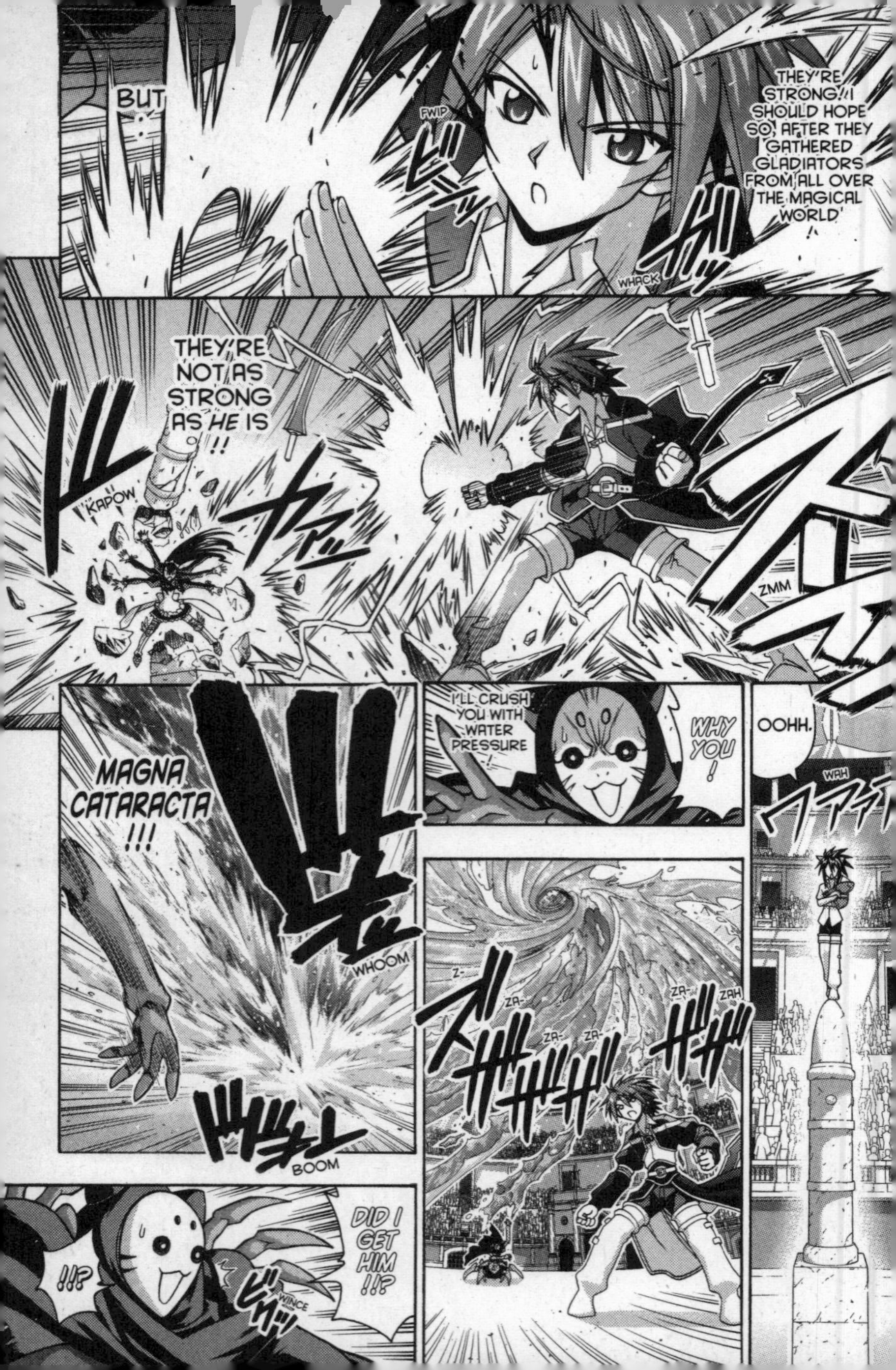
THEY'RE STRONG!! I SHOULD HOPE SO, AFTER THEY GATHERED GLADIATORS FROM ALL OVER THE MAGICAL WORLD!
WHACK
FWIP
BUT...
ZMM
THEY'RE NOT AS STRONG AS HE IS!!
KAPOW
OOHH.
WAH
WHY YOU!
I'LL CRUSH YOU WITH WATER PRESSURE!
MAGNA CATARACTA!!!
WHOOM
BOOM
Z-
ZA-
ZA-
ZA-
ZA-
ZAH
DID I GET HIM!!?
!!?
WINCE

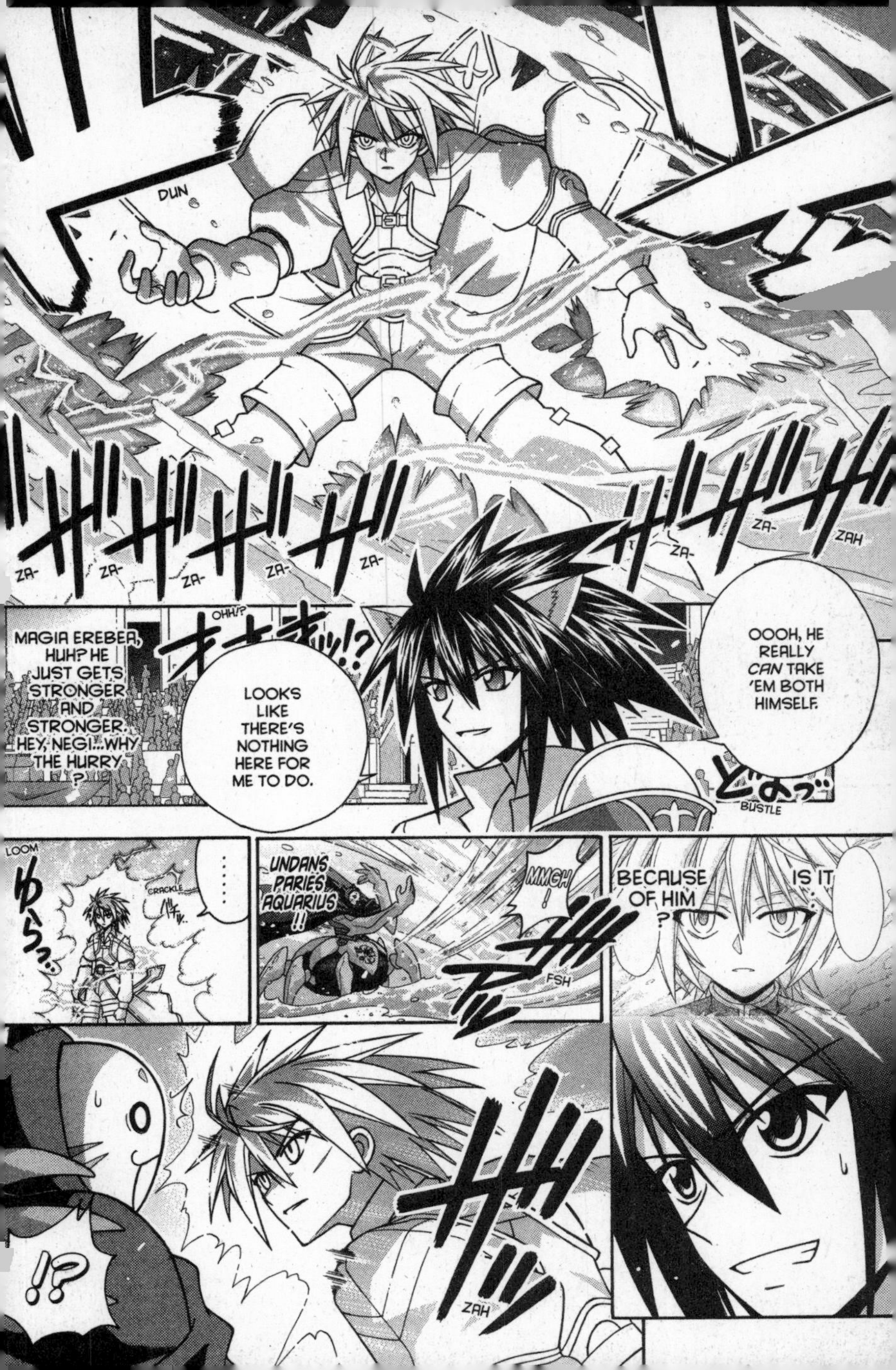
DUN
ZAH
ZA-
ZA-
ZA-
ZA-
ZA-
ZA-
ZA-
OOOH, HE REALLY CAN TAKE 'EM BOTH HIMSELF.
BUSTLE
LOOKS LIKE THERE'S NOTHING HERE FOR ME TO DO.
OHH!?
MAGIA EREBEA, HUH? HE JUST GETS STRONGER AND STRONGER. HEY, NEGI...WHY THE HURRY?
IS IT...
BECAUSE OF HIM?
MMGH!
FSH
UNDANS PARIES AQUARIUS!!
......
CRACKLE
LOOM
ZAH
!?

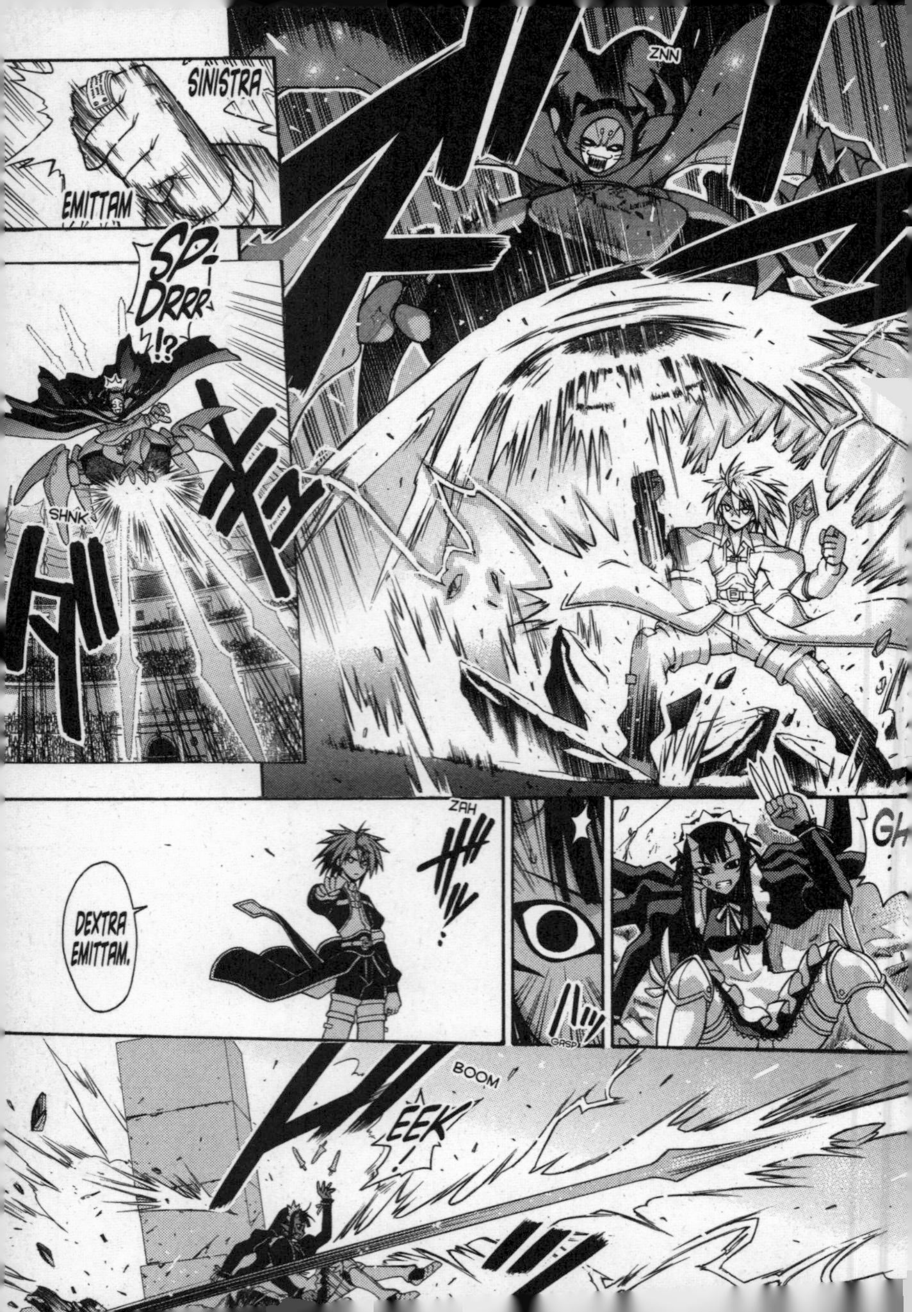
ZNN
SINISTRA
EMITTAM
SP-DRRR!?
SHNK
GH
GASP
ZAH
DEXTRA EMITTAM.
BOOM
EEK

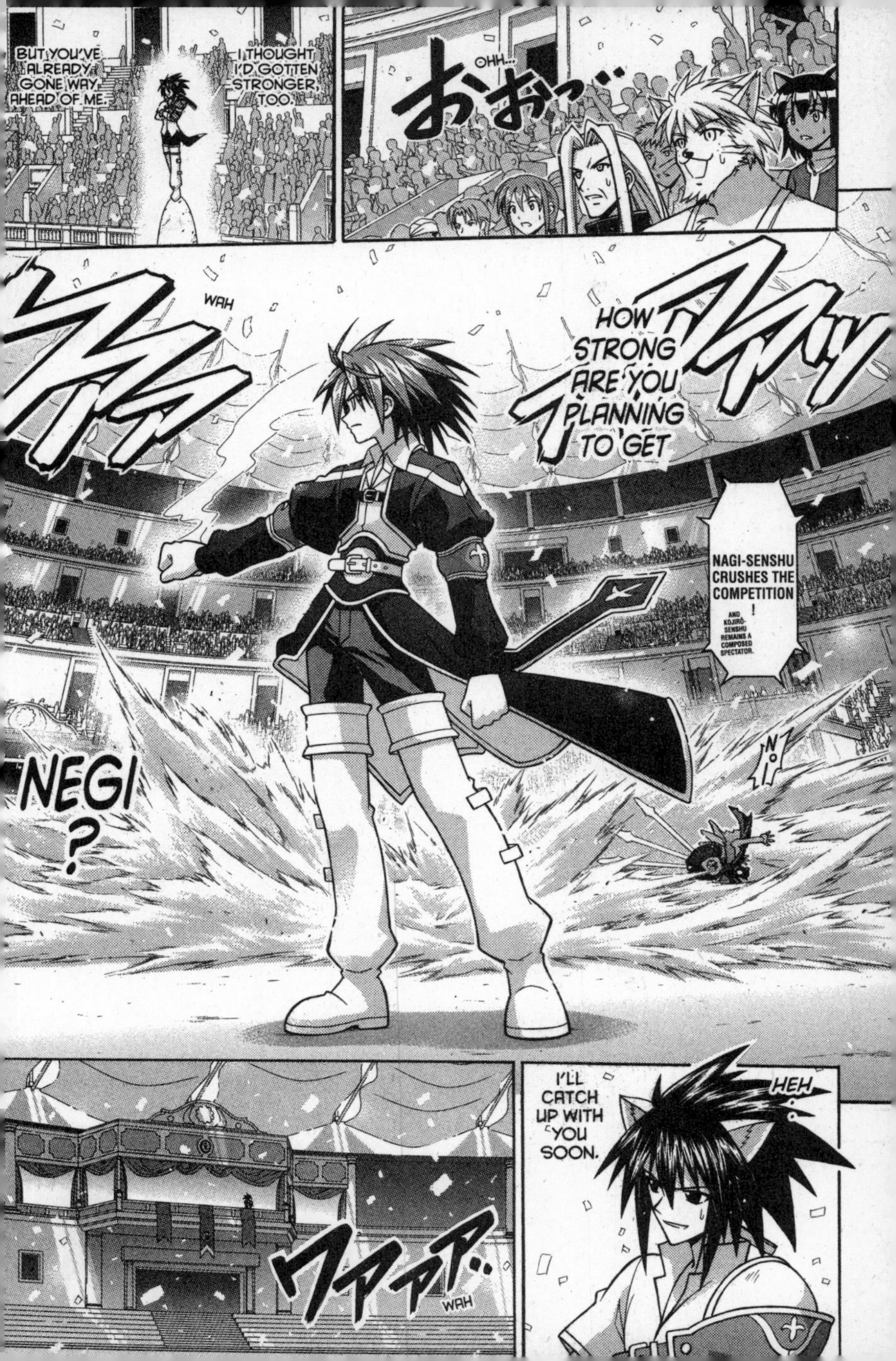

おおっ
OHH...
I THOUGHT I'D GOTTEN STRONGER, TOO.
BUT YOU'VE ALREADY GONE WAY AHEAD OF ME.
HOW STRONG ARE YOU PLANNING TO GET
NAGI-SENSHU CRUSHES THE COMPETITION!
AND KOJIRŌ-SENSHU REMAINS A COMPOSED SPECTATOR.
N...!
WAH
NEGI?
HEH
I'LL CATCH UP WITH YOU SOON.
ワァァ
WAH

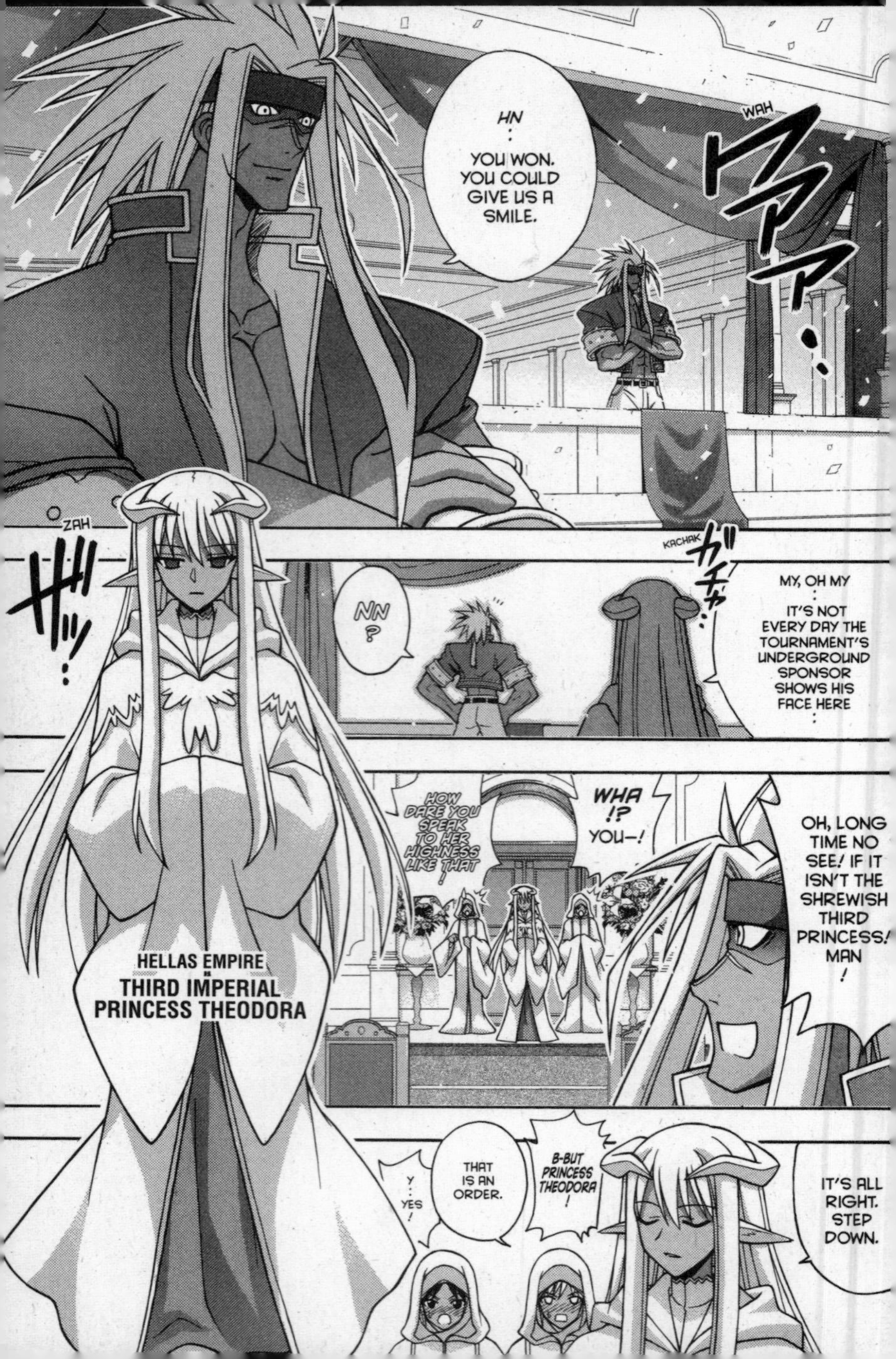
WAH
HN... YOU WON. YOU COULD GIVE US A SMILE.
KACHAK
MY, OH MY... IT'S NOT EVERY DAY THE TOURNAMENT'S UNDERGROUND SPONSOR SHOWS HIS FACE HERE...
NN?
OH, LONG TIME NO SEE! IF IT ISN'T THE SHREWISH THIRD PRINCESS! MAN!
WHA!? YOU—!
HOW DARE YOU SPEAK TO HER HIGHNESS LIKE THAT!
IT'S ALL RIGHT. STEP DOWN.
B-BUT PRINCESS THEODORA!
THAT IS AN ORDER.
Y... YES!
ZAH
HELLAS EMPIRE
THIRD IMPERIAL PRINCESS THEODORA

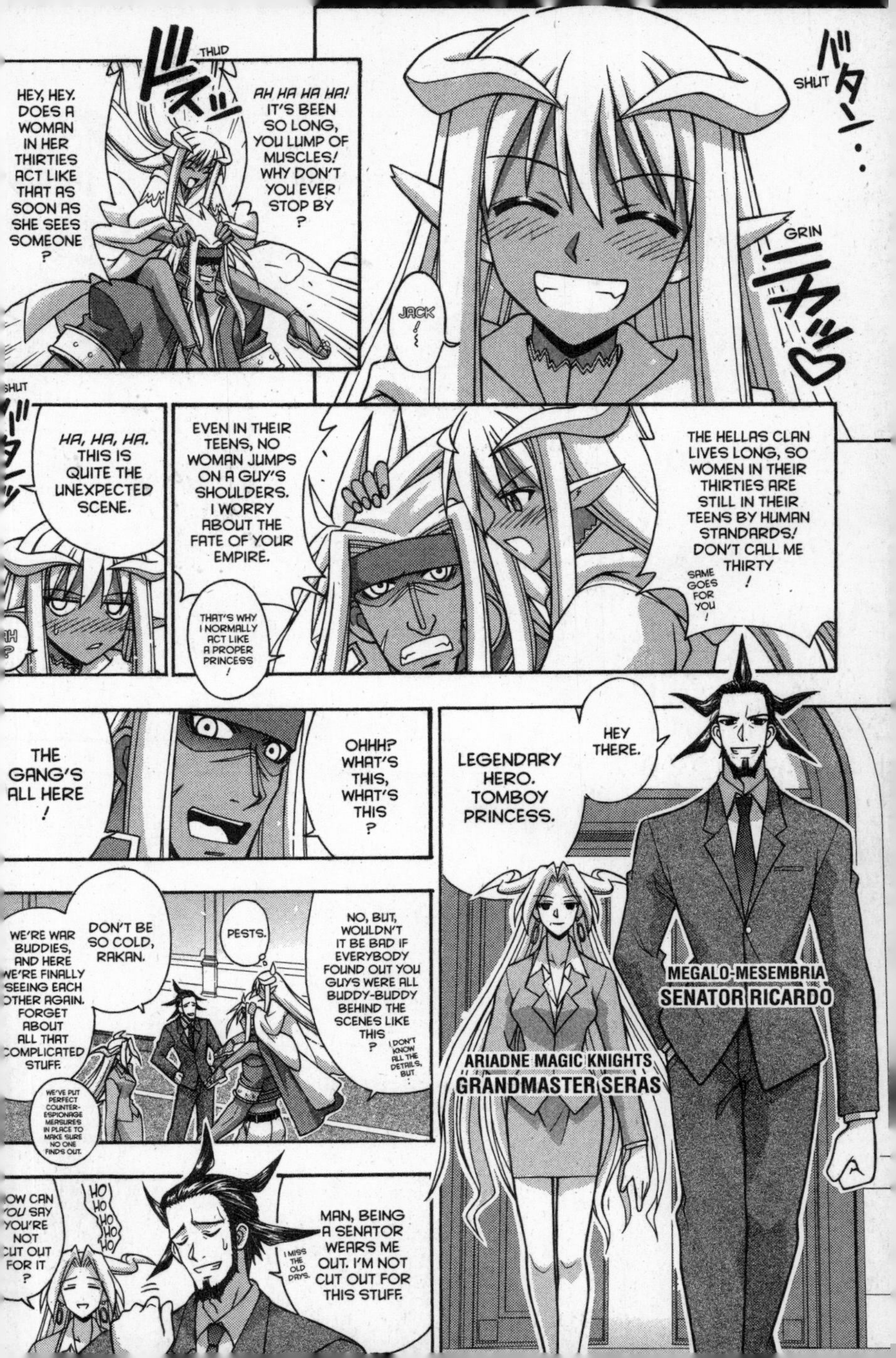
SHUT
GRIN
JACK!
THUD
AH HA HA HA! IT'S BEEN SO LONG, YOU LUMP OF MUSCLES! WHY DON'T YOU EVER STOP BY?
HEY, HEY. DOES A WOMAN IN HER THIRTIES ACT LIKE THAT AS SOON AS SHE SEES SOMEONE?
THE HELLAS CLAN LIVES LONG, SO WOMEN IN THEIR THIRTIES ARE STILL IN THEIR TEENS BY HUMAN STANDARDS! DON'T CALL ME THIRTY!
SAME GOES FOR YOU!
EVEN IN THEIR TEENS, NO WOMAN JUMPS ON A GUY'S SHOULDERS. I WORRY ABOUT THE FATE OF YOUR EMPIRE.
THAT'S WHY I NORMALLY ACT LIKE A PROPER PRINCESS!
SHUT
HA, HA, HA. THIS IS QUITE THE UNEXPECTED SCENE.
HEY THERE.
LEGENDARY HERO. TOMBOY PRINCESS.
MEGALO-MESEMBRIA
SENATOR RICARDO
ARIADNE MAGIC KNIGHTS
GRANDMASTER SERAS
OHHH? WHAT'S THIS, WHAT'S THIS?
THE GANG'S ALL HERE!
NO, BUT, WOULDN'T IT BE BAD IF EVERYBODY FOUND OUT YOU GUYS WERE ALL BUDDY-BUDDY BEHIND THE SCENES LIKE THIS?
I DON'T KNOW ALL THE DETAILS, BUT...
PESTS.
DON'T BE SO COLD, RAKAN.
WE'RE WAR BUDDIES, AND HERE WE'RE FINALLY SEEING EACH OTHER AGAIN. FORGET ABOUT ALL THAT COMPLICATED STUFF.
WE'VE PUT PERFECT COUNTER-ESPIONAGE MEASURES IN PLACE TO MAKE SURE NO ONE FINDS OUT.
MAN, BEING A SENATOR WEARS ME OUT. I'M NOT CUT OUT FOR THIS STUFF.
I MISS THE OLD DAYS.
HO HO HO HO HO
OW CAN YOU SAY YOU'RE NOT CUT OUT FOR IT?

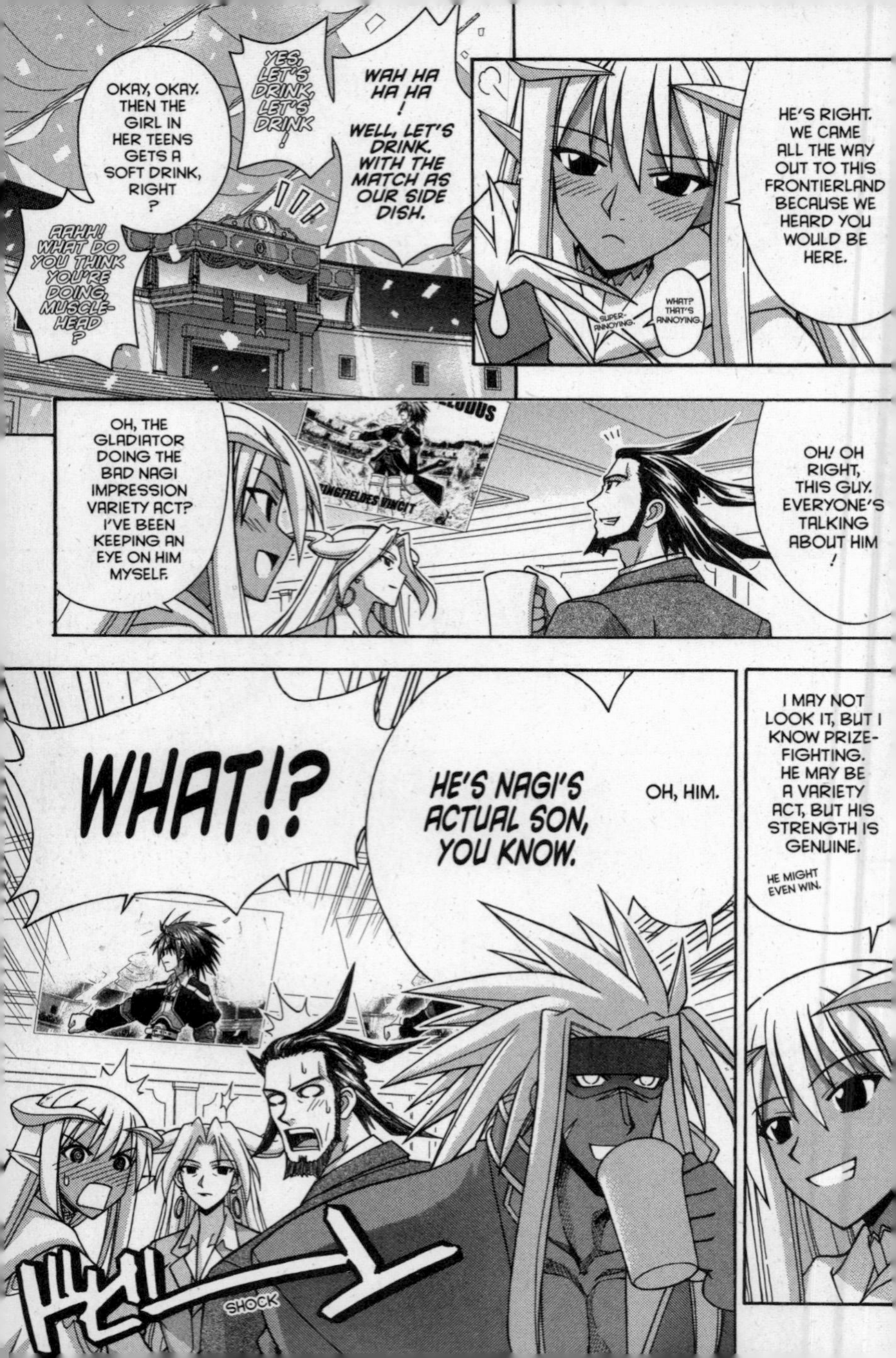
HE'S RIGHT. WE CAME ALL THE WAY OUT TO THIS FRONTIERLAND BECAUSE WE HEARD YOU WOULD BE HERE.
WHAT? THAT'S ANNOYING.
SUPER-ANNOYING.
WAH HA HA HA! WELL, LET'S DRINK. WITH THE MATCH AS OUR SIDE DISH.
YES, LET'S DRINK, LET'S DRINK!
OKAY, OKAY. THEN THE GIRL IN HER TEENS GETS A SOFT DRINK, RIGHT?
AAHH! WHAT DO YOU THINK YOU'RE DOING, MUSCLE-HEAD?
OH! OH RIGHT, THIS GUY. EVERYONE'S TALKING ABOUT HIM!
OH, THE GLADIATOR DOING THE BAD NAGI IMPRESSION VARIETY ACT? I'VE BEEN KEEPING AN EYE ON HIM MYSELF.
I MAY NOT LOOK IT, BUT I KNOW PRIZE-FIGHTING. HE MAY BE A VARIETY ACT, BUT HIS STRENGTH IS GENUINE.
HE MIGHT EVEN WIN.
OH, HIM.
HE'S NAGI'S ACTUAL SON, YOU KNOW.
WHAT!?
SHOCK

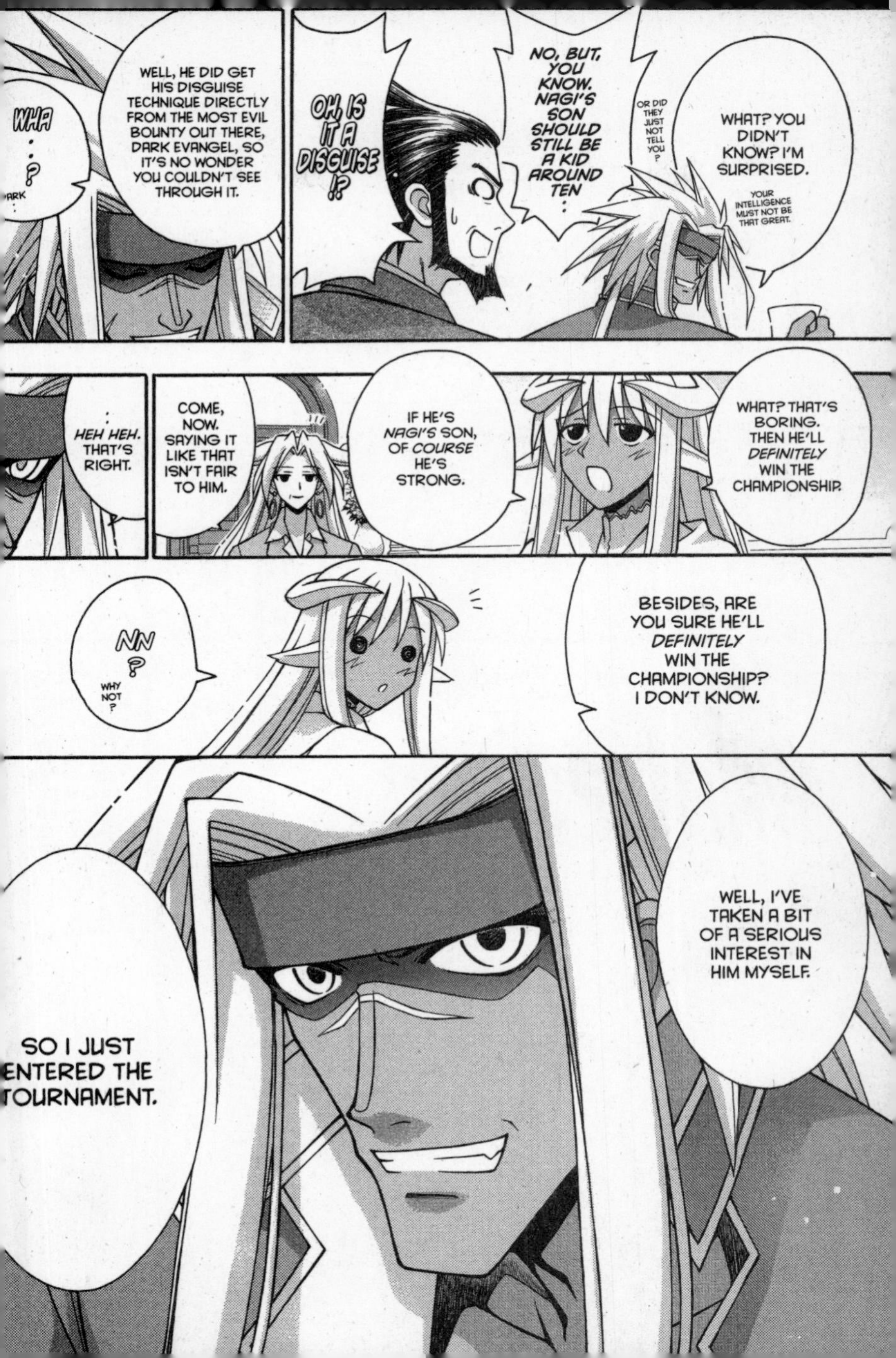
WHAT? YOU DIDN'T KNOW? I'M SURPRISED.
YOUR INTELLIGENCE MUST NOT BE THAT GREAT.
OR DID THEY JUST NOT TELL YOU?
NO, BUT, YOU KNOW. NAGI'S SON SHOULD STILL BE A KID AROUND TEN...
OH, IS IT A DISGUISE!?
WELL, HE DID GET HIS DISGUISE TECHNIQUE DIRECTLY FROM THE MOST EVIL BOUNTY OUT THERE, DARK EVANGEL, SO IT'S NO WONDER YOU COULDN'T SEE THROUGH IT.
WHA...?
WHAT? THAT'S BORING. THEN HE'LL DEFINITELY WIN THE CHAMPIONSHIP.
IF HE'S NAGI'S SON, OF COURSE HE'S STRONG.
COME, NOW. SAYING IT LIKE THAT ISN'T FAIR TO HIM.
HEH HEH. THAT'S RIGHT.
BESIDES, ARE YOU SURE HE'LL DEFINITELY WIN THE CHAMPIONSHIP? I DON'T KNOW.
NN?
WHY NOT?
WELL, I'VE TAKEN A BIT OF A SERIOUS INTEREST IN HIM MYSELF.
SO I JUST ENTERED THE TOURNAMENT.

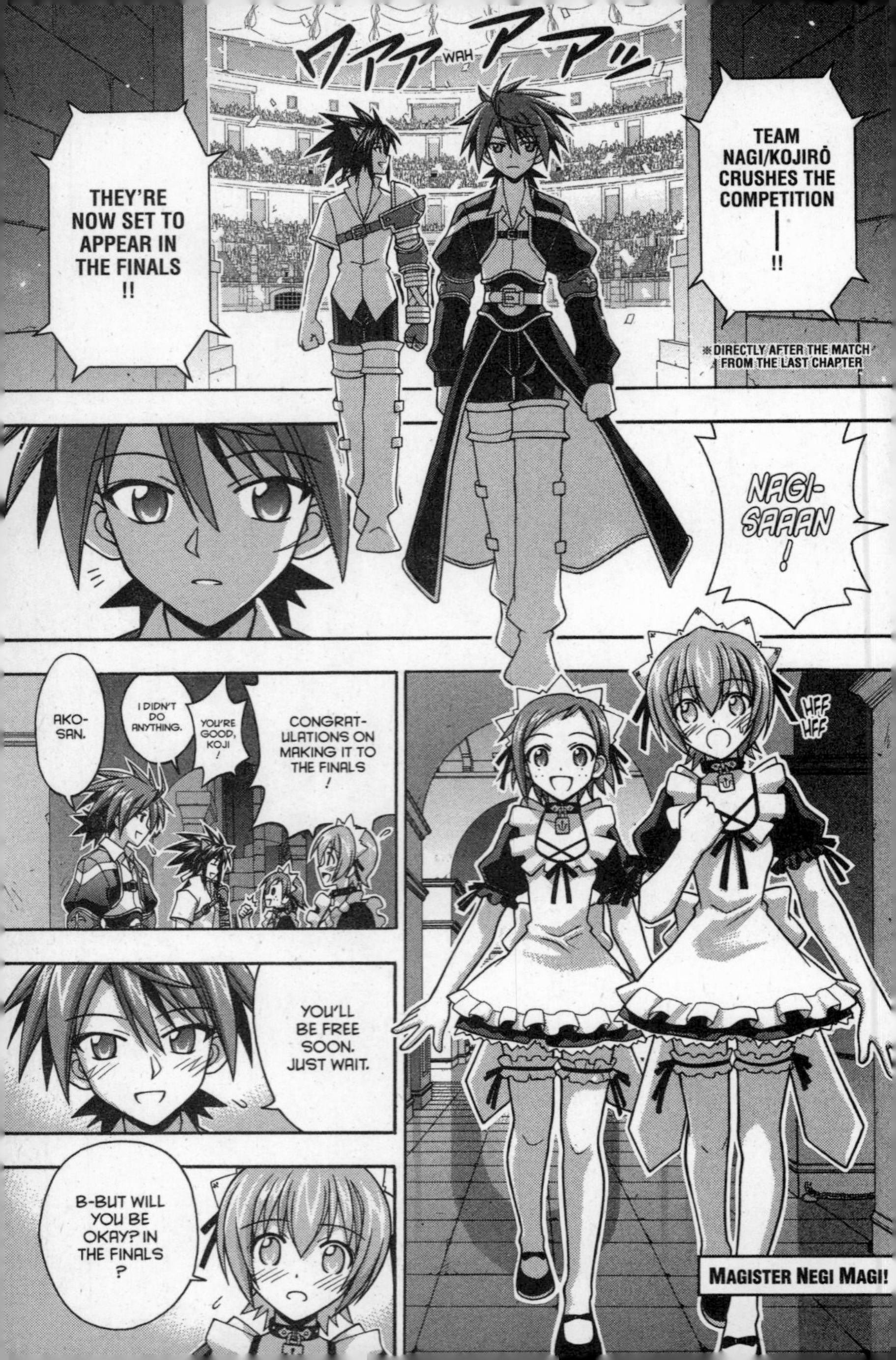
WAH
TEAM NAGI/KOJIRŌ CRUSHES THE COMPETITION —!!
THEY'RE NOW SET TO APPEAR IN THE FINALS !!
※DIRECTLY AFTER THE MATCH FROM THE LAST CHAPTER
NAGI-SAAAN!
HFF HFF
CONGRATULATIONS ON MAKING IT TO THE FINALS!
YOU'RE GOOD, KOJI!
I DIDN'T DO ANYTHING.
AKO-SAN.
YOU'LL BE FREE SOON. JUST WAIT.
B-BUT WILL YOU BE OKAY? IN THE FINALS?
MAGISTER NEGI MAGI!

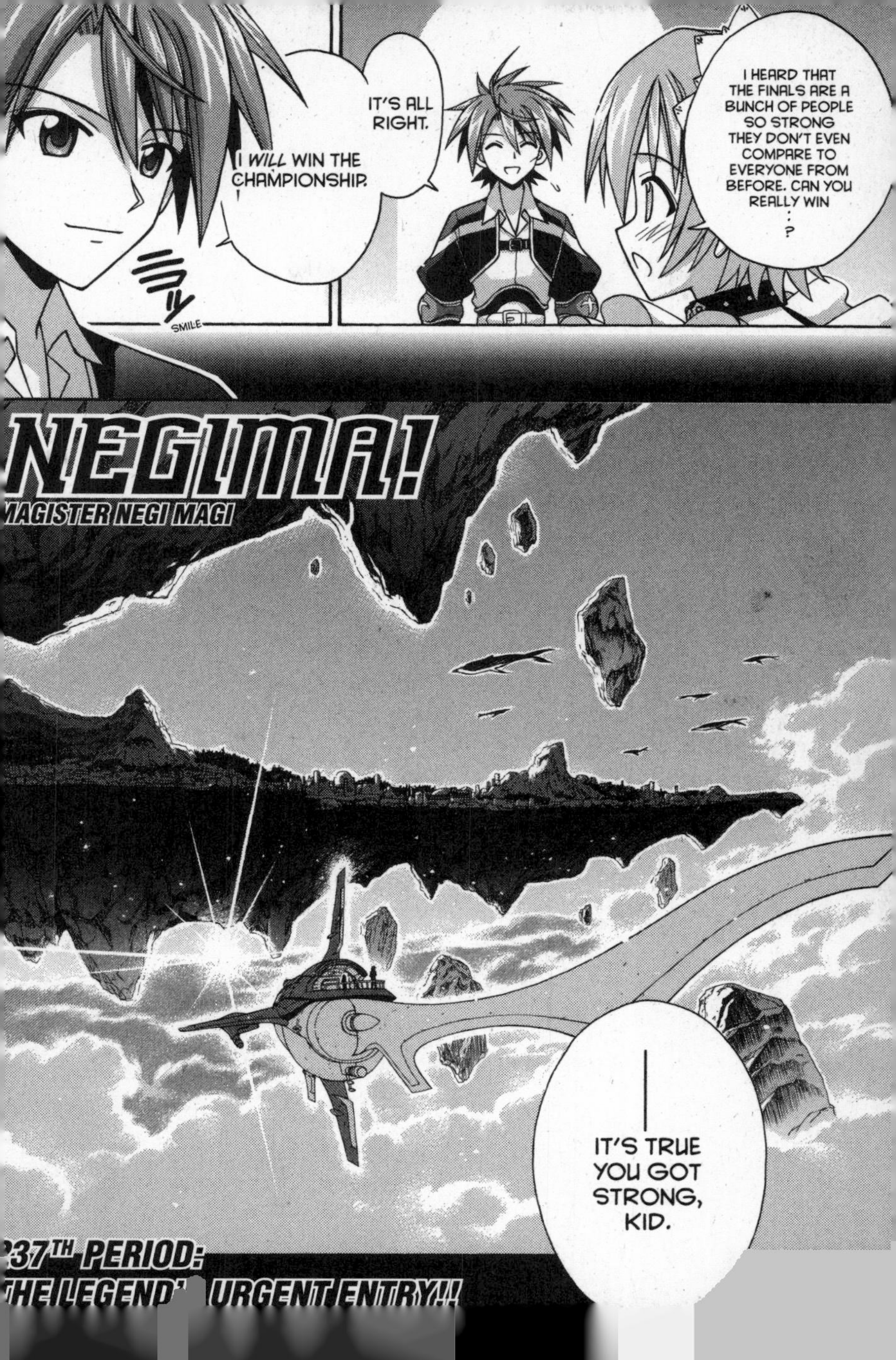
I HEARD THAT THE FINALS ARE A BUNCH OF PEOPLE SO STRONG THEY DON'T EVEN COMPARE TO EVERYONE FROM BEFORE. CAN YOU REALLY WIN . . . ?
IT'S ALL RIGHT.
I *WILL* WIN THE CHAMPIONSHIP.
SMILE
NEGIMA!
MAGISTER NEGI MAGI
IT'S TRUE YOU GOT STRONG, KID.
237TH PERIOD:
THE LEGEND' URGENT ENTRY!!

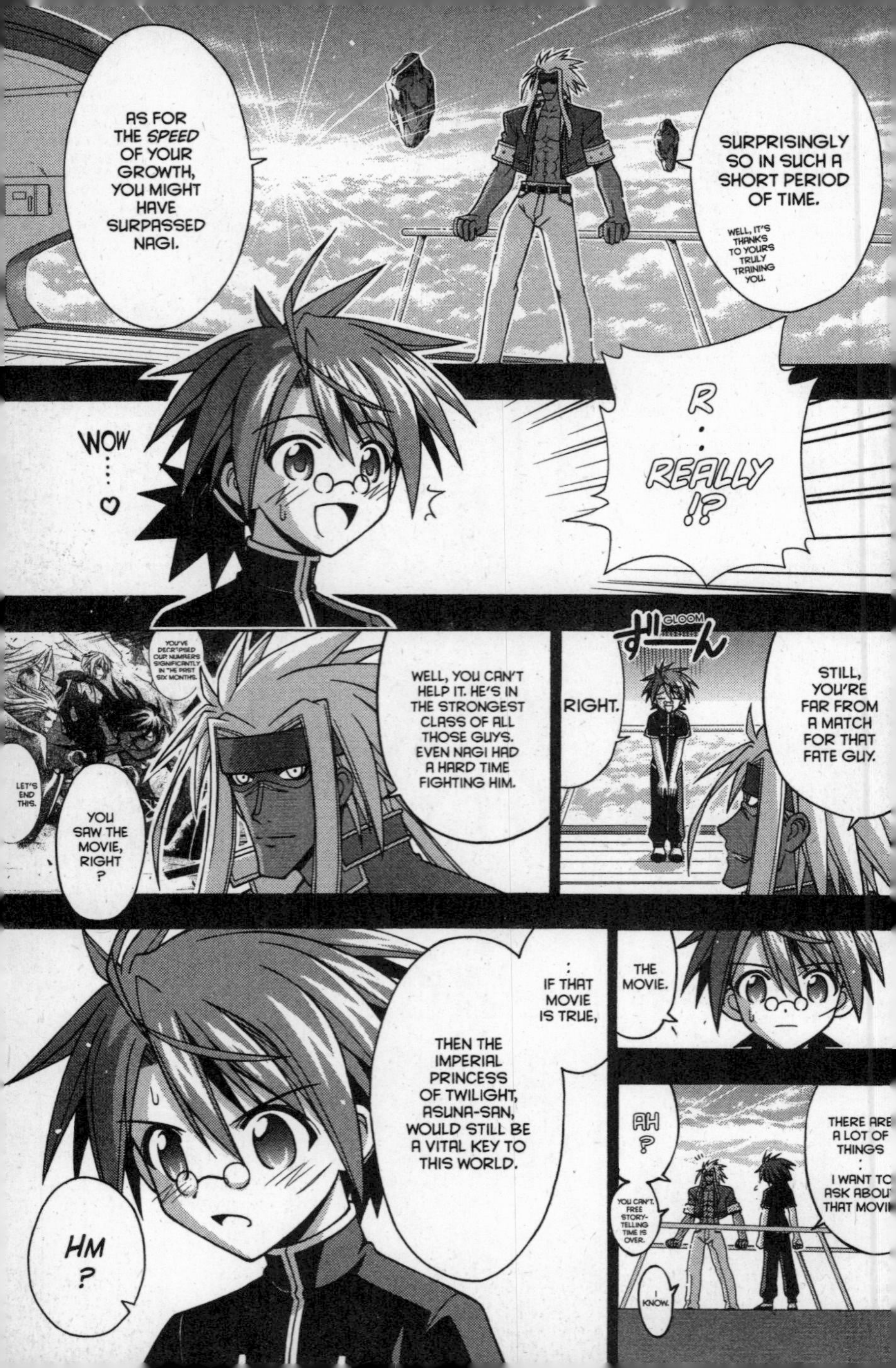

AS FOR THE SPEED OF YOUR GROWTH, YOU MIGHT HAVE SURPASSED NAGI.
SURPRISINGLY SO IN SUCH A SHORT PERIOD OF TIME.
WELL, IT'S THANKS TO YOURS TRULY TRAINING YOU.
R... REALLY!?
WOW... ♡
GLOOM
STILL, YOU'RE FAR FROM A MATCH FOR THAT FATE GUY.
RIGHT.
WELL, YOU CAN'T HELP IT. HE'S IN THE STRONGEST CLASS OF ALL THOSE GUYS. EVEN NAGI HAD A HARD TIME FIGHTING HIM.
YOU'VE DECREASED OUR NUMBERS SIGNIFICANTLY IN THE PAST SIX MONTHS.
LET'S END THIS.
YOU SAW THE MOVIE, RIGHT?
THE MOVIE.
THERE ARE A LOT OF THINGS... I WANT TO ASK ABOUT THAT MOVI
AH?
YOU CAN'T. FREE STORY-TELLING TIME IS OVER.
I KNOW.
: IF THAT MOVIE IS TRUE,
THEN THE IMPERIAL PRINCESS OF TWILIGHT, ASUNA-SAN, WOULD STILL BE A VITAL KEY TO THIS WORLD.
HM?

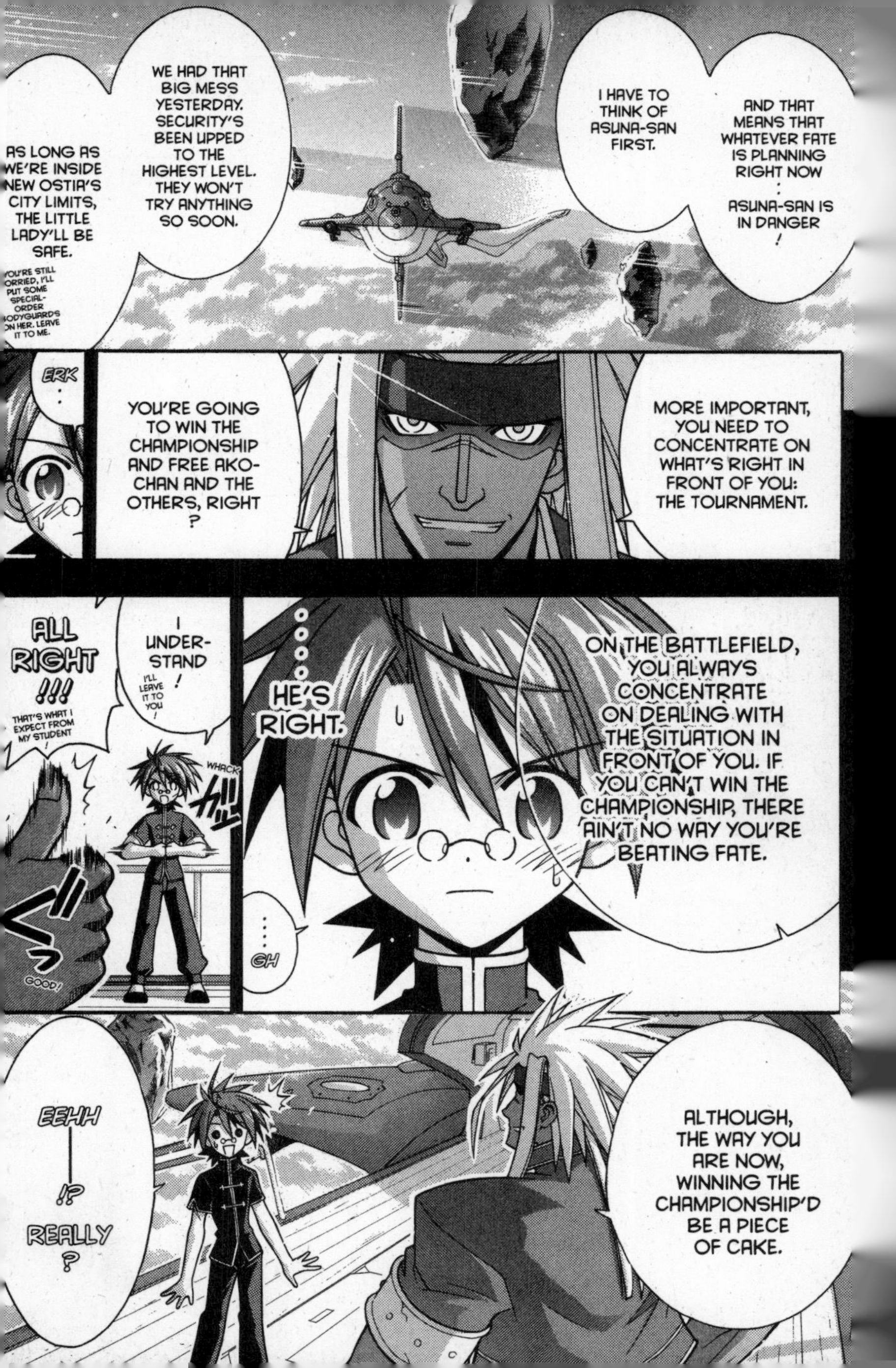
AND THAT MEANS THAT WHATEVER FATE IS PLANNING RIGHT NOW: ASUNA-SAN IS IN DANGER!
I HAVE TO THINK OF ASUNA-SAN FIRST.
WE HAD THAT BIG MESS YESTERDAY. SECURITY'S BEEN UPPED TO THE HIGHEST LEVEL. THEY WON'T TRY ANYTHING SO SOON.
AS LONG AS WE'RE INSIDE NEW OSTIA'S CITY LIMITS, THE LITTLE LADY'LL BE SAFE.
YOU'RE STILL ORRIED, I'LL PUT SOME SPECIAL-ORDER ODYGUARDS ON HER. LEAVE IT TO ME.
MORE IMPORTANT, YOU NEED TO CONCENTRATE ON WHAT'S RIGHT IN FRONT OF YOU: THE TOURNAMENT.
YOU'RE GOING TO WIN THE CHAMPIONSHIP AND FREE AKO-CHAN AND THE OTHERS, RIGHT?
ERK...
ON THE BATTLEFIELD, YOU ALWAYS CONCENTRATE ON DEALING WITH THE SITUATION IN FRONT OF YOU. IF YOU CAN'T WIN THE CHAMPIONSHIP, THERE AIN'T NO WAY YOU'RE BEATING FATE.
.....HE'S RIGHT.
....GH
I UNDERSTAND!
I'LL LEAVE IT TO YOU!
ALL RIGHT!!!
THAT'S WHAT I EXPECT FROM MY STUDENT!
WHACK
GOOD!
ALTHOUGH, THE WAY YOU ARE NOW, WINNING THE CHAMPIONSHIP'D BE A PIECE OF CAKE.
EEHH—!?
REALLY?

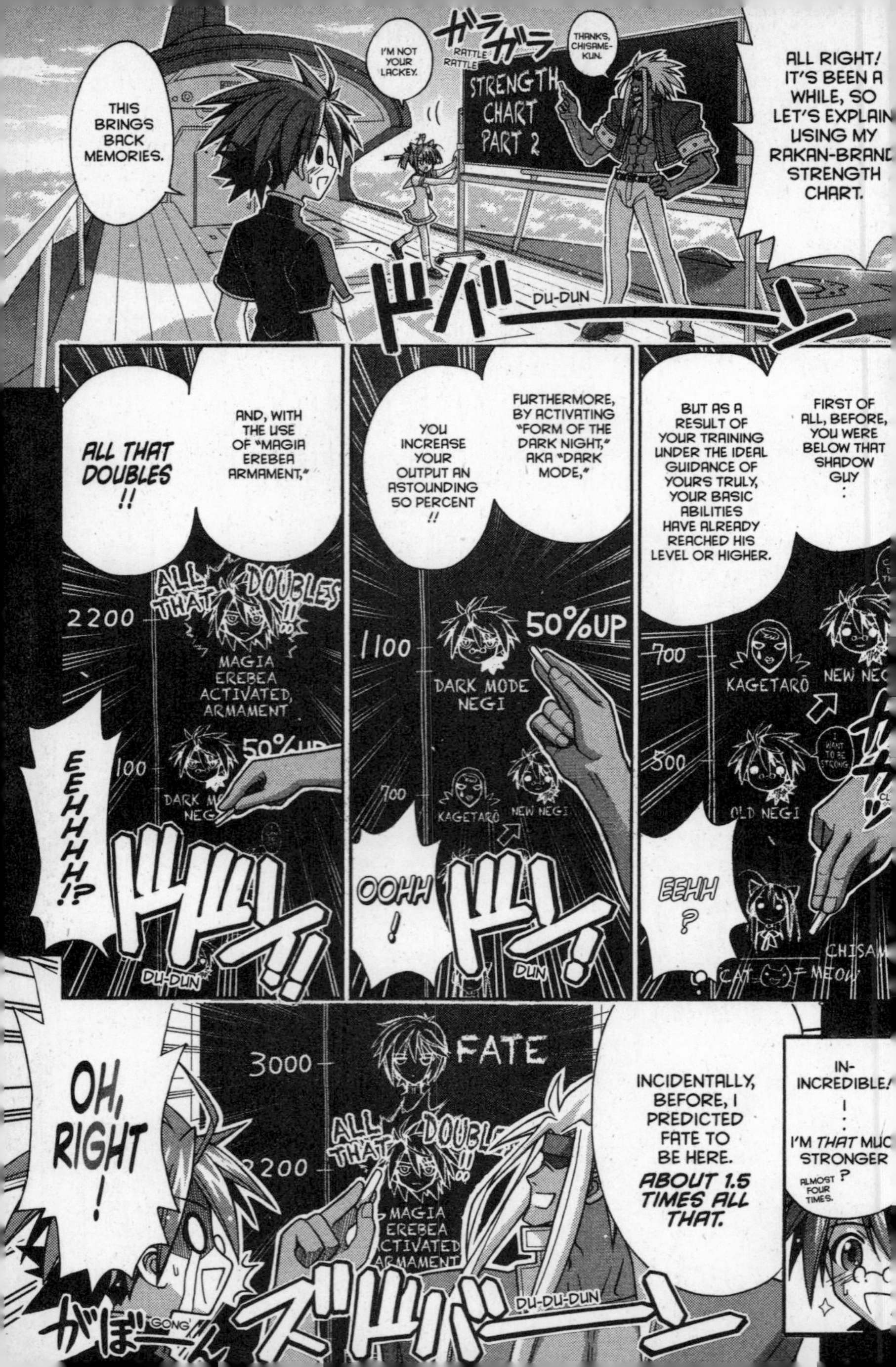
ALL RIGHT! IT'S BEEN A WHILE, SO LET'S EXPLAIN USING MY RAKAN-BRAND STRENGTH CHART.
THANKS, CHISAME-KUN.
ガラガラ
RATTLE RATTLE
I'M NOT YOUR LACKEY.
STRENGTH CHART PART 2
THIS BRINGS BACK MEMORIES.
DU-DUN
FIRST OF ALL, BEFORE, YOU WERE BELOW THAT SHADOW GUY...
BUT AS A RESULT OF YOUR TRAINING UNDER THE IDEAL GUIDANCE OF YOURS TRULY, YOUR BASIC ABILITIES HAVE ALREADY REACHED HIS LEVEL OR HIGHER.
700
KAGETARŌ
NEW NEGI
500
I WANT TO BE STRONG.
OLD NEGI
EEHH?
CAT = MEOW
FURTHERMORE, BY ACTIVATING "FORM OF THE DARK NIGHT," AKA "DARK MODE,"
YOU INCREASE YOUR OUTPUT AN ASTOUNDING 50 PERCENT!!
1100
50%UP
DARK MODE NEGI
700
KAGETARŌ
NEW NEGI
OOHH!
DUN
AND, WITH THE USE OF "MAGIA EREBEA ARMAMENT,"
ALL THAT DOUBLES!!
2200
ALL THAT DOUBLES!!
MAGIA EREBEA ACTIVATED, ARMAMENT
100
50%UP
DARK MODE NEGI
EEHHHHH!?
DU-DUN
IN-INCREDIBLE!... I'M THAT MUCH STRONGER?
ALMOST FOUR TIMES.
INCIDENTALLY, BEFORE, I PREDICTED FATE TO BE HERE.
ABOUT 1.5 TIMES ALL THAT.
3000
FATE
2200
ALL THAT DOUBLES!!
MAGIA EREBEA ACTIVATED ARMAMENT
DU-DU-DUN
OH, RIGHT!
GONG

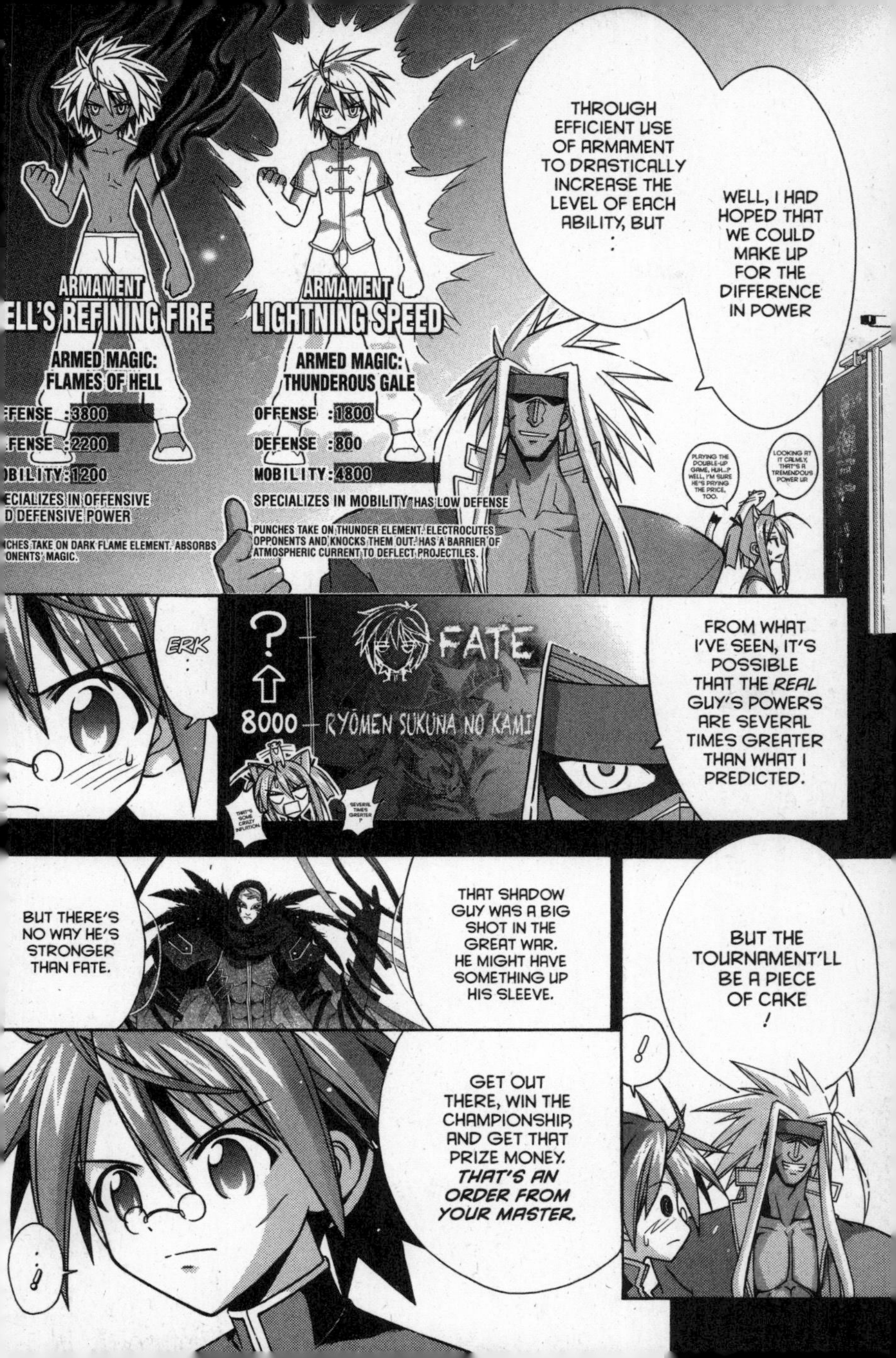

WELL, I HAD HOPED THAT WE COULD MAKE UP FOR THE DIFFERENCE IN POWER
THROUGH EFFICIENT USE OF ARMAMENT TO DRASTICALLY INCREASE THE LEVEL OF EACH ABILITY, BUT
LOOKING AT IT CALMLY, THAT'S A TREMENDOUS POWER UP.
PLAYING THE DOUBLE-UP GAME, HUH...? WELL, I'M SURE HE'S PAYING THE PRICE, TOO.
ARMAMENT
LIGHTNING SPEED
ARMED MAGIC: THUNDEROUS GALE
OFFENSE :1800
DEFENSE :800
MOBILITY:4800
SPECIALIZES IN MOBILITY. HAS LOW DEFENSE
PUNCHES TAKE ON THUNDER ELEMENT. ELECTROCUTES OPPONENTS AND KNOCKS THEM OUT. HAS A BARRIER OF ATMOSPHERIC CURRENT TO DEFLECT PROJECTILES.
ARMAMENT
ELL'S REFINING FIRE
ARMED MAGIC: FLAMES OF HELL
FENSE :3800
FENSE :2200
OBILITY:1200
ECIALIZES IN OFFENSIVE
D DEFENSIVE POWER
NCHES TAKE ON DARK FLAME ELEMENT. ABSORBS
ONENTS' MAGIC.
FROM WHAT I'VE SEEN, IT'S POSSIBLE THAT THE REAL GUY'S POWERS ARE SEVERAL TIMES GREATER THAN WHAT I PREDICTED.
?
FATE
8000 RYŌMEN SUKUNA NO KAMI
SEVERAL TIMES GREATER?
THAT'S SOME CRAZY INFLATION.
ERK
BUT THE TOURNAMENT'LL BE A PIECE OF CAKE!
THAT SHADOW GUY WAS A BIG SHOT IN THE GREAT WAR. HE MIGHT HAVE SOMETHING UP HIS SLEEVE.
BUT THERE'S NO WAY HE'S STRONGER THAN FATE.
!
GET OUT THERE, WIN THE CHAMPIONSHIP, AND GET THAT PRIZE MONEY. THAT'S AN ORDER FROM YOUR MASTER.
...!

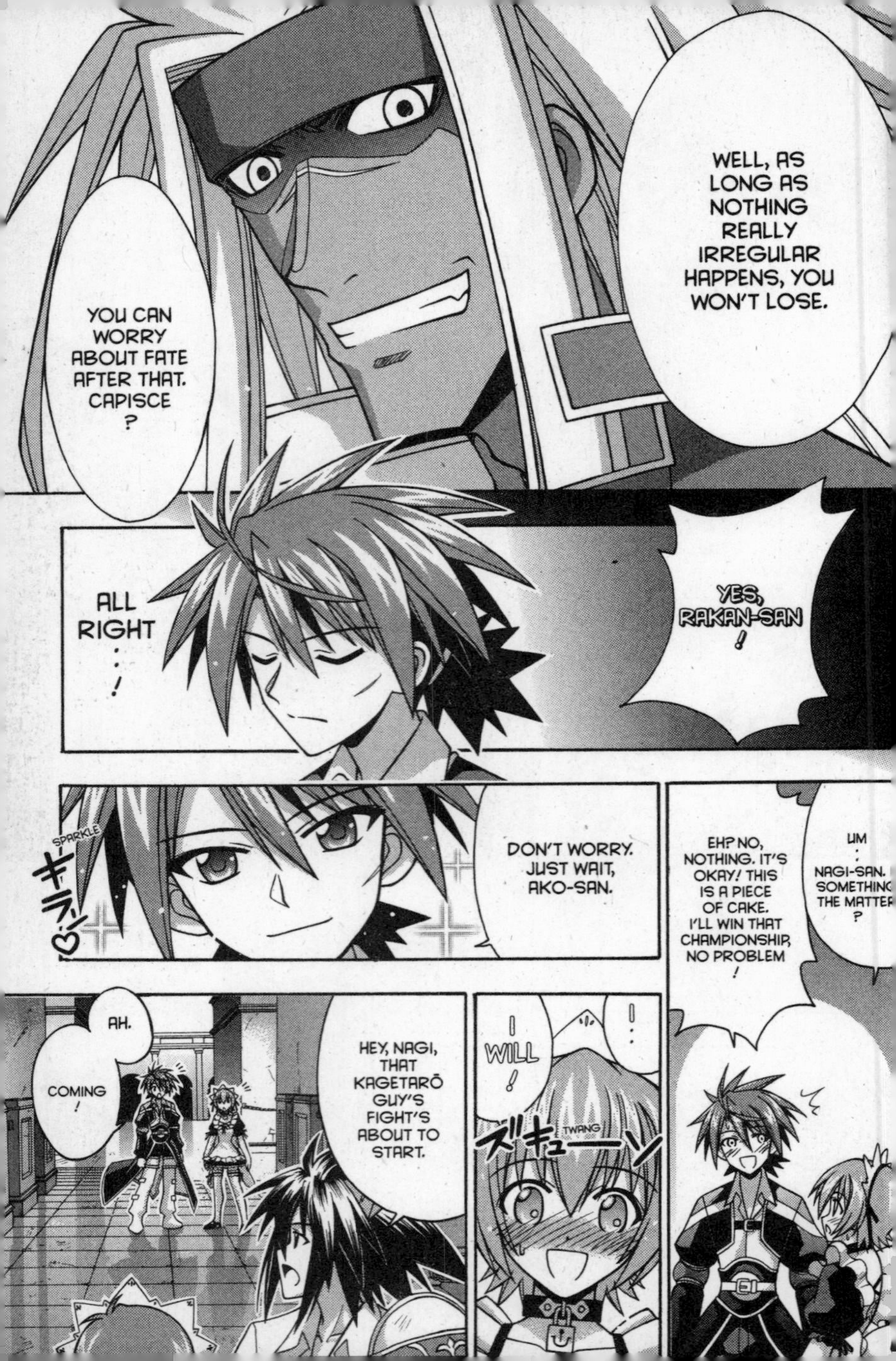

WELL, AS LONG AS NOTHING REALLY IRREGULAR HAPPENS, YOU WON'T LOSE.
YOU CAN WORRY ABOUT FATE AFTER THAT. CAPISCE?
YES, RAKAN-SAN!
ALL RIGHT...!
UM... NAGI-SAN. SOMETHING THE MATTER?
EH? NO, NOTHING. IT'S OKAY! THIS IS A PIECE OF CAKE. I'LL WIN THAT CHAMPIONSHIP, NO PROBLEM!
DON'T WORRY. JUST WAIT, AKO-SAN.
SPARKLE
キラ
!..
I WILL!
TWANG
ズキューン
HEY, NAGI, THAT KAGETARŌ GUY'S FIGHT'S ABOUT TO START.
AH.
COMING!

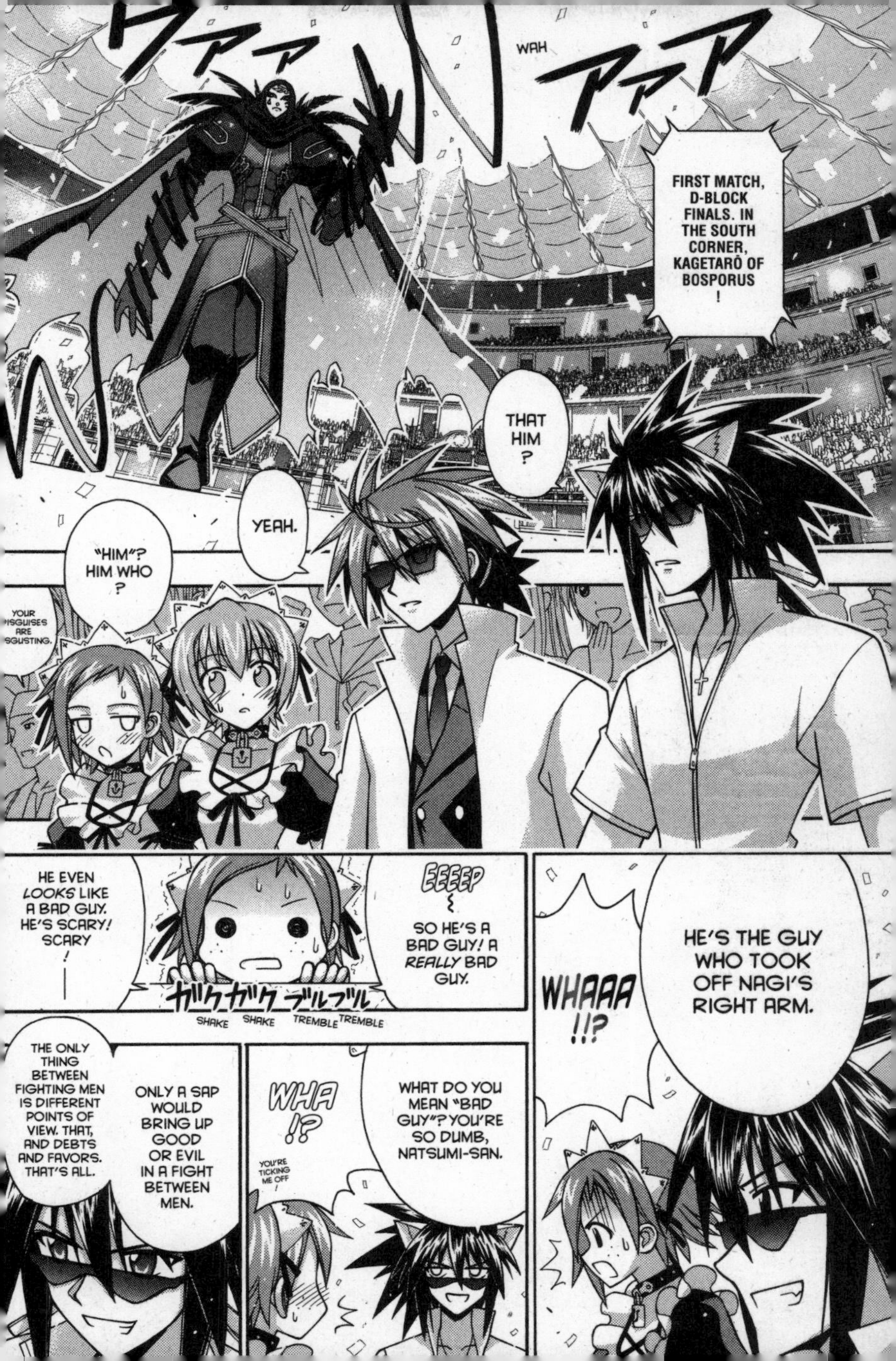
ワァァァ
WAH
アァァ
FIRST MATCH, D-BLOCK FINALS. IN THE SOUTH CORNER, KAGETARÔ OF BOSPORUS!
THAT HIM?
YEAH.
"HIM"? HIM WHO?
YOUR ISGUISES ARE SGUSTING.
HE'S THE GUY WHO TOOK OFF NAGI'S RIGHT ARM.
WHAAA!!?
EEEEP
SO HE'S A BAD GUY! A *REALLY* BAD GUY.
HE EVEN *LOOKS* LIKE A BAD GUY. HE'S SCARY! SCARY!
ガクガク ブルブル
SHAKE SHAKE TREMBLE TREMBLE
WHAT DO YOU MEAN "BAD GUY"? YOU'RE SO DUMB, NATSUMI-SAN.
WHA!?
YOU'RE TICKING ME OFF!
ONLY A SAP WOULD BRING UP GOOD OR EVIL IN A FIGHT BETWEEN MEN.
THE ONLY THING BETWEEN FIGHTING MEN IS DIFFERENT POINTS OF VIEW. THAT, AND DEBTS AND FAVORS. THAT'S ALL.

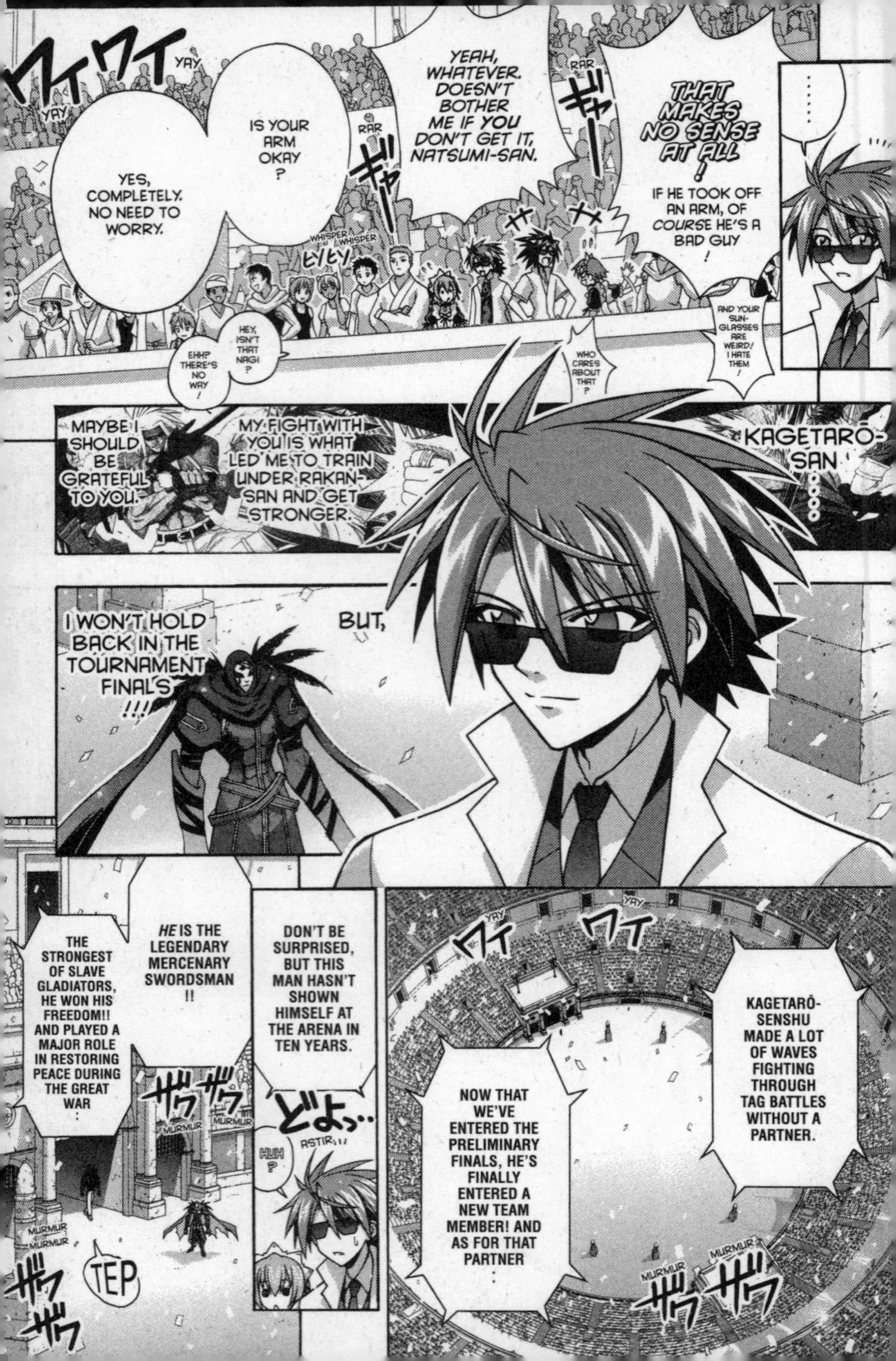
......
AND YOUR SUNGLASSES ARE WEIRD! I HATE THEM!
THAT MAKES NO SENSE AT ALL!
IF HE TOOK OFF AN ARM, OF COURSE HE'S A BAD GUY!
RAR
YEAH, WHATEVER. DOESN'T BOTHER ME IF YOU DON'T GET IT, NATSUMI-SAN.
WHO CARES ABOUT THAT?
RAR
IS YOUR ARM OKAY?
WHISPER WHISPER
YES, COMPLETELY. NO NEED TO WORRY.
HEY, ISN'T THAT NAGI?
EHH? THERE'S NO WAY!
YAY
YAY
KAGETARŌ-SAN......
MY FIGHT WITH YOU IS WHAT LED ME TO TRAIN UNDER RAKAN-SAN AND GET STRONGER.
MAYBE I SHOULD BE GRATEFUL TO YOU.
BUT,
I WON'T HOLD BACK IN THE TOURNAMENT FINALS!!!
YAY
YAY
KAGETARŌ-SENSHU MADE A LOT OF WAVES FIGHTING THROUGH TAG BATTLES WITHOUT A PARTNER.
NOW THAT WE'VE ENTERED THE PRELIMINARY FINALS, HE'S FINALLY ENTERED A NEW TEAM MEMBER! AND AS FOR THAT PARTNER:
MURMUR MURMUR
DON'T BE SURPRISED, BUT THIS MAN HASN'T SHOWN HIMSELF AT THE ARENA IN TEN YEARS.
ASTIR
HUH?
HE IS THE LEGENDARY MERCENARY SWORDSMAN!!
THE STRONGEST OF SLAVE GLADIATORS, HE WON HIS FREEDOM!! AND PLAYED A MAJOR ROLE IN RESTORING PEACE DURING THE GREAT WAR:
MURMUR MURMUR
MURMUR MURMUR
TEP

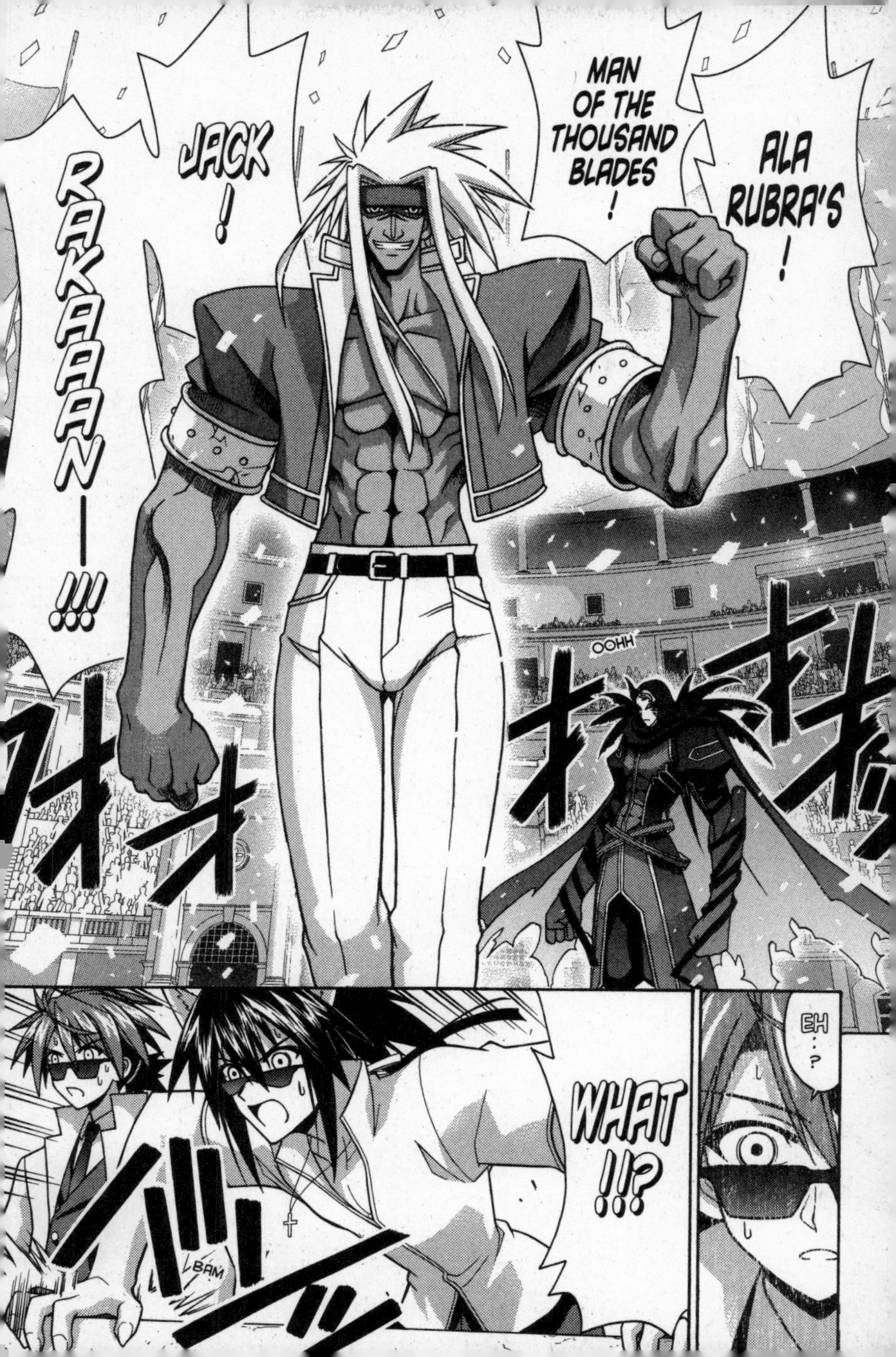
ALA RUBRA'S!
MAN OF THE THOUSAND BLADES!
JACK!
RAKAAAAAN—!!!
OOHH
EH...?
WHAT!!?
BAM

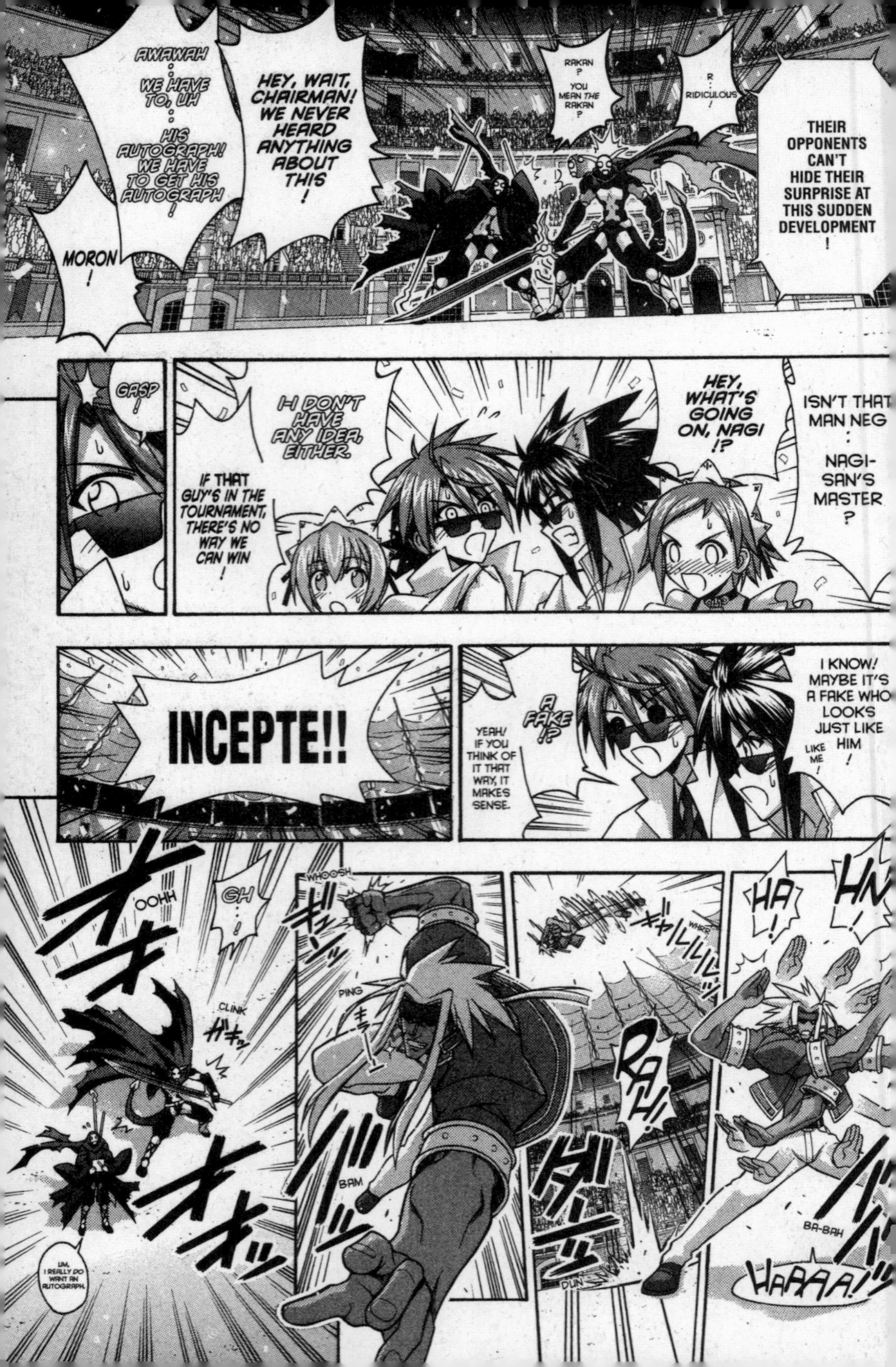
THEIR OPPONENTS CAN'T HIDE THEIR SURPRISE AT THIS SUDDEN DEVELOPMENT!
R... RIDICULOUS!
RAKAN? YOU MEAN *THE* RAKAN?
HEY, WAIT, CHAIRMAN! WE NEVER HEARD ANYTHING ABOUT THIS!
AWAWAH... WE HAVE TO, UH... HIS AUTOGRAPH! WE HAVE TO GET HIS AUTOGRAPH!
MORON!
ISN'T THAT MAN NEG... NAGI-SAN'S MASTER?
HEY, WHAT'S GOING ON, NAGI!?
I-I DON'T HAVE ANY IDEA, EITHER.
IF THAT GUY'S IN THE TOURNAMENT, THERE'S NO WAY WE CAN WIN!
GASP!
I KNOW! MAYBE IT'S A FAKE WHO LOOKS JUST LIKE HIM!
LIKE ME
A FAKE!?
YEAH! IF YOU THINK OF IT THAT WAY, IT MAKES SENSE.
INCEPTE!!
HN!
HA!
BA-BAH
HAAAA!!
WHRR
RAH!
DUN
WHOOSH
PING
BAM
OOHH
GH...!
CLINK
UM, I REALLY *DO* WANT AN AUTOGRAPH.

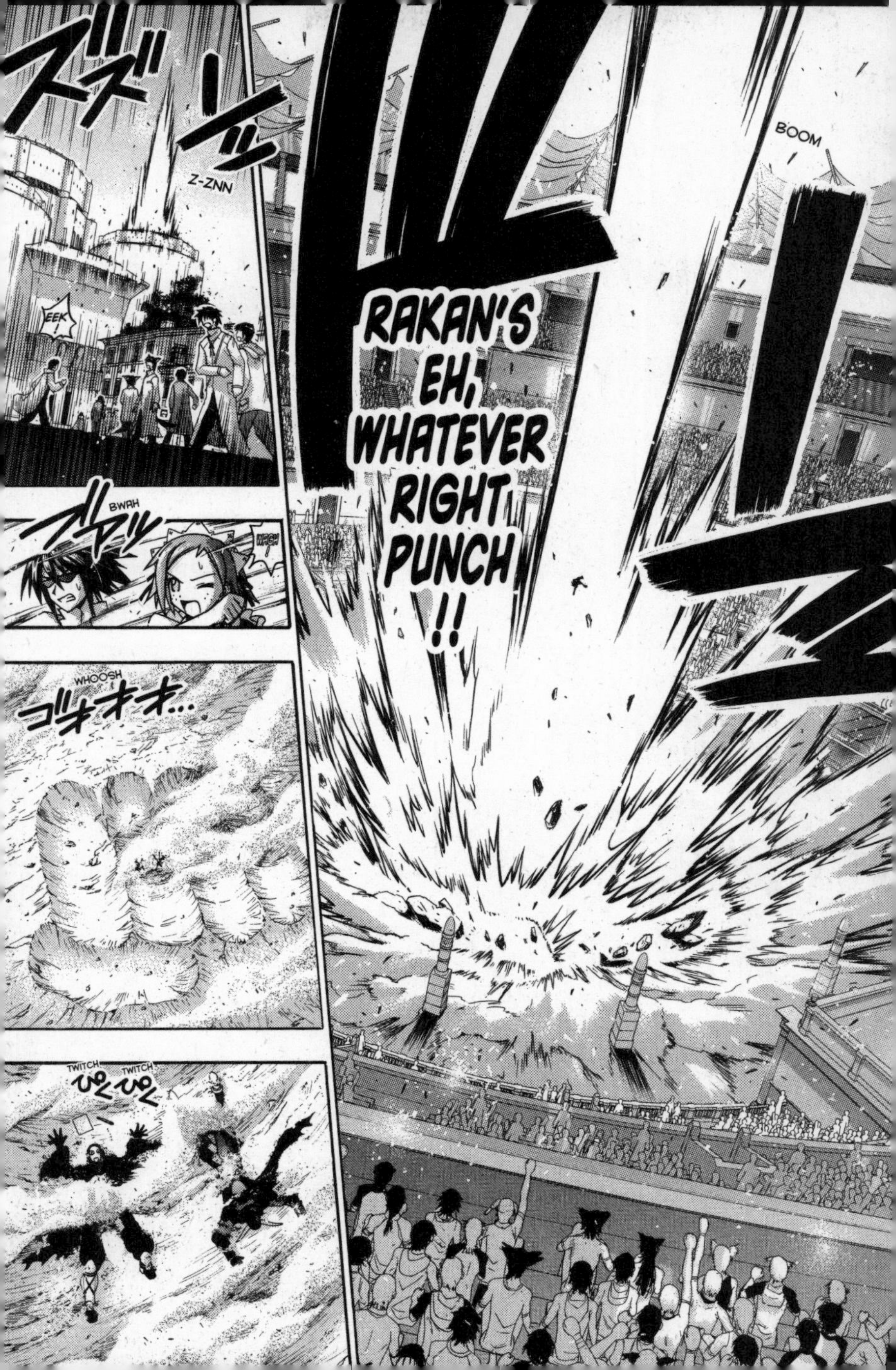
BOOM
RAKAN'S EH, WHATEVER RIGHT PUNCH!!
Z-ZNN
EEK!
BWAH
WAGH!
WHOOSH
TWITCH TWITCH

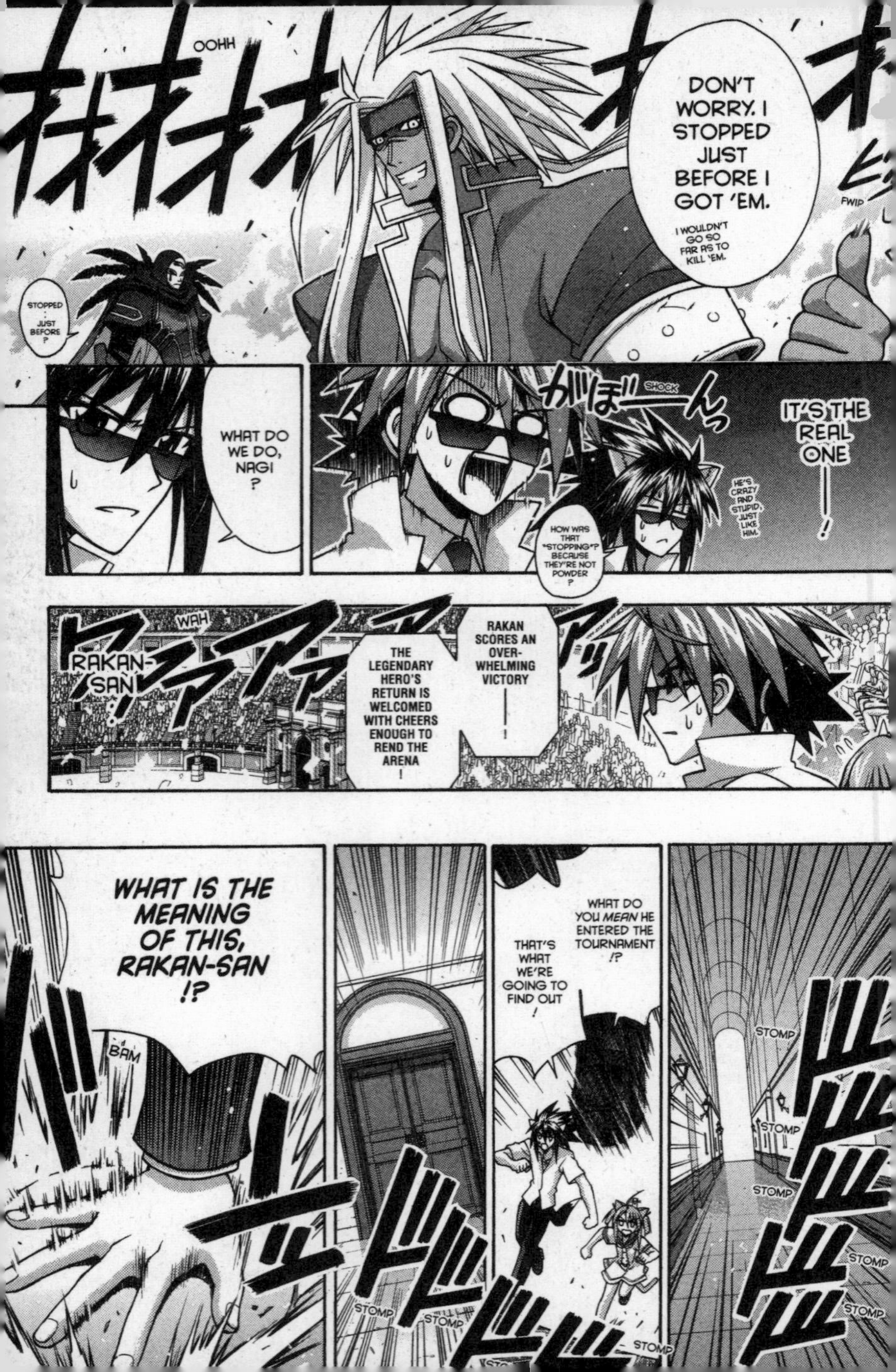
FWIP
DON'T WORRY. I STOPPED JUST BEFORE I GOT 'EM.
I WOULDN'T GO SO FAR AS TO KILL 'EM.
OOHH
STOPPED... JUST BEFORE?
SHOCK
IT'S THE REAL ONE—!
HE'S CRAZY AND STUPID, JUST LIKE HIM.
HOW WAS THAT "STOPPING"? BECAUSE THEY'RE NOT POWDER?
WHAT DO WE DO, NAGI?
RAKAN SCORES AN OVER-WHELMING VICTORY—!
THE LEGENDARY HERO'S RETURN IS WELCOMED WITH CHEERS ENOUGH TO REND THE ARENA!
WAH
RAKAN-SAN!
STOMP
STOMP
STOMP
STOMP
STOMP
WHAT DO YOU MEAN HE ENTERED THE TOURNAMENT!?
THAT'S WHAT WE'RE GOING TO FIND OUT!
STOMP
STOMP
STOMP
WHAT IS THE MEANING OF THIS, RAKAN-SAN!?
BAM

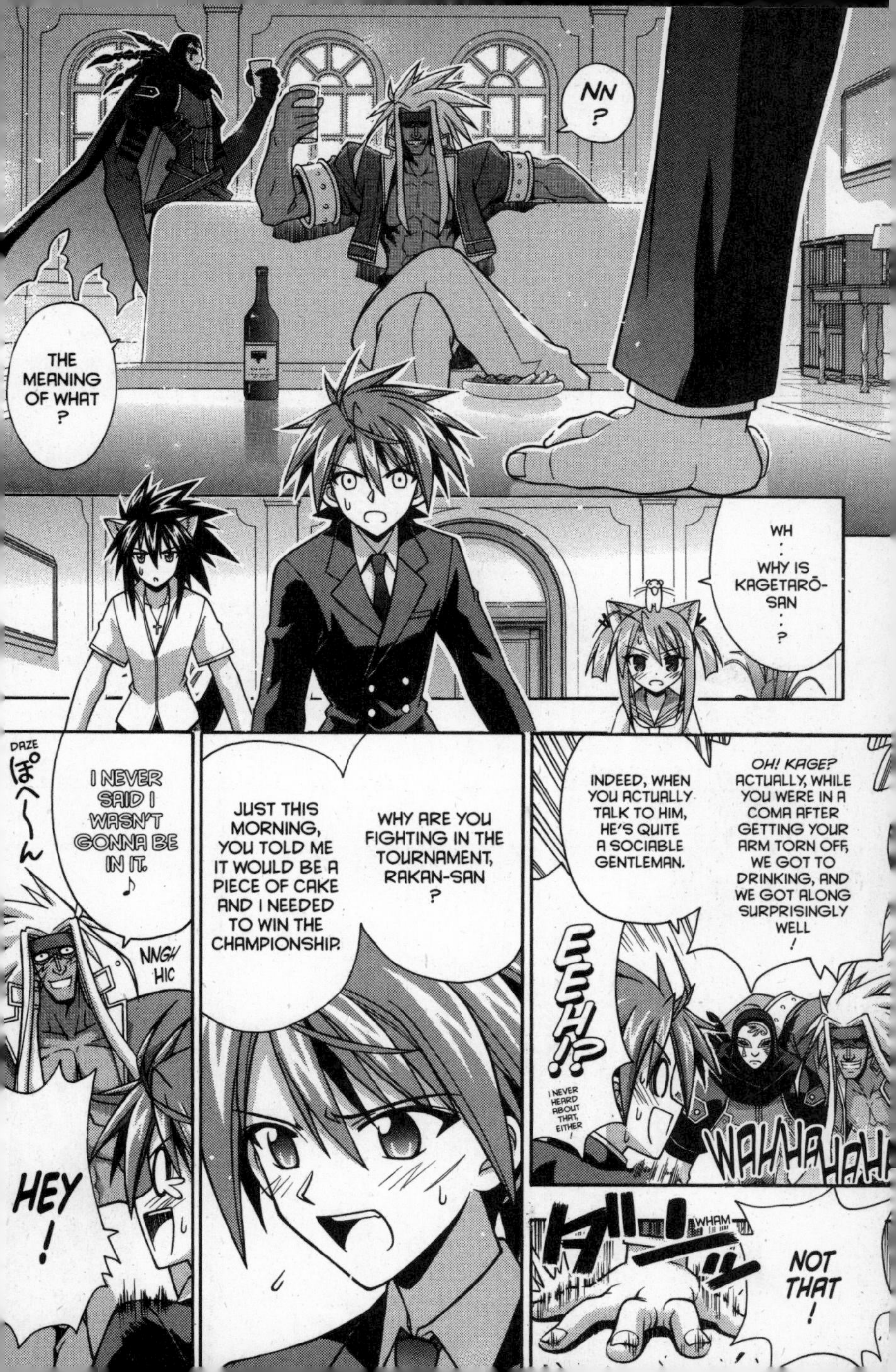
NN?
THE MEANING OF WHAT?
WH... WHY IS KAGETARŌ-SAN...?
OH! KAGE? ACTUALLY, WHILE YOU WERE IN A COMA AFTER GETTING YOUR ARM TORN OFF, WE GOT TO DRINKING, AND WE GOT ALONG SURPRISINGLY WELL!
INDEED, WHEN YOU ACTUALLY TALK TO HIM, HE'S QUITE A SOCIABLE GENTLEMAN.
EEH!?
I NEVER HEARD ABOUT THAT, EITHER!
WAH HA HA HA
WHAM
NOT THAT!
WHY ARE YOU FIGHTING IN THE TOURNAMENT, RAKAN-SAN?
JUST THIS MORNING, YOU TOLD ME IT WOULD BE A PIECE OF CAKE AND I NEEDED TO WIN THE CHAMPIONSHIP.
I NEVER SAID I WASN'T GONNA BE IN IT. ♪
DAZE
ぽへ～ん
NNGH HIC
HEY!

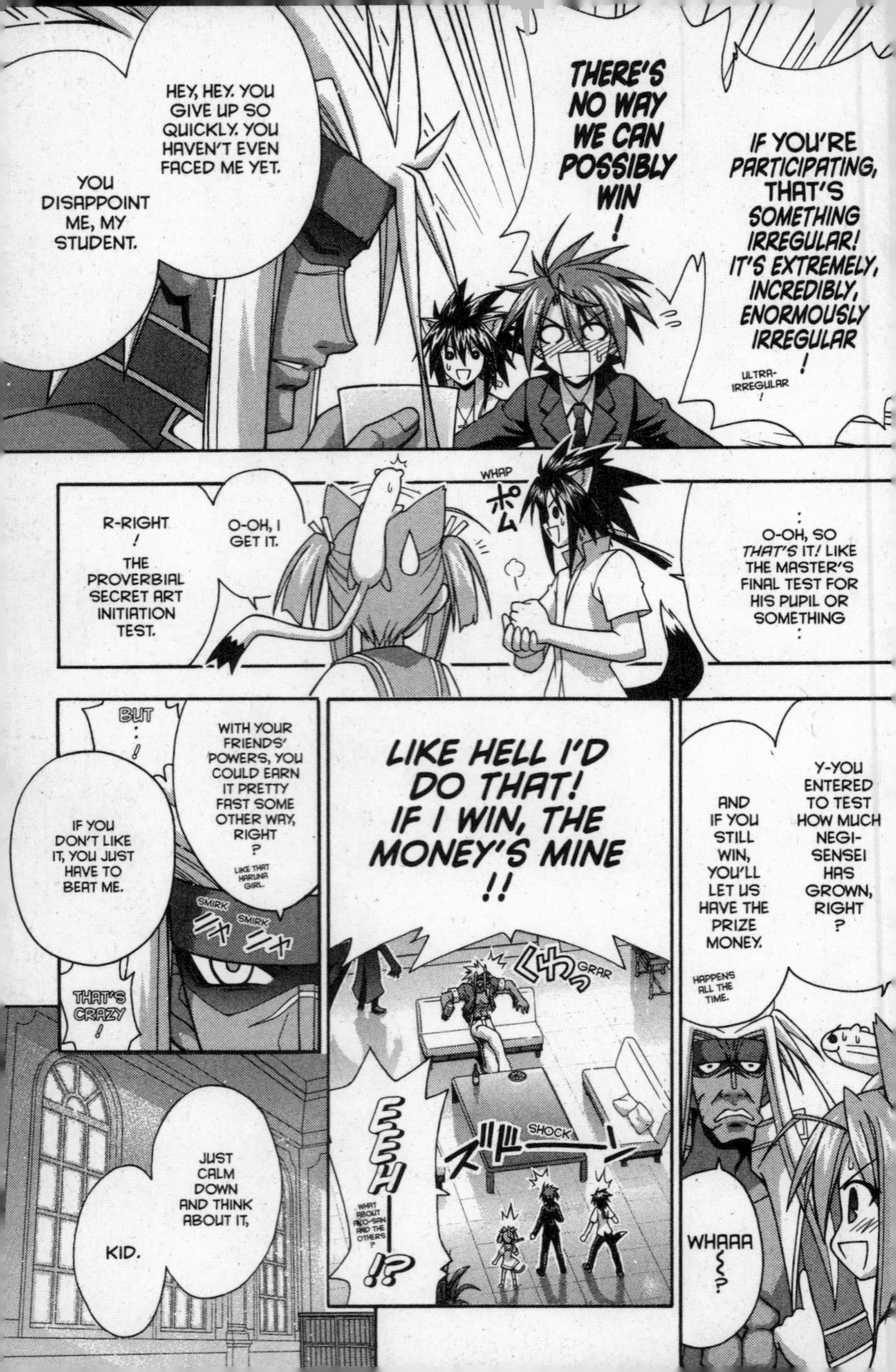
IF YOU'RE PARTICIPATING, THAT'S SOMETHING IRREGULAR! IT'S EXTREMELY, INCREDIBLY, ENORMOUSLY IRREGULAR!
ULTRA-IRREGULAR!
THERE'S NO WAY WE CAN POSSIBLY WIN!
HEY, HEY. YOU GIVE UP SO QUICKLY. YOU HAVEN'T EVEN FACED ME YET.
YOU DISAPPOINT ME, MY STUDENT.
O-OH, SO THAT'S IT! LIKE THE MASTER'S FINAL TEST FOR HIS PUPIL OR SOMETHING
WHAP ポム
O-OH, I GET IT.
R-RIGHT! THE PROVERBIAL SECRET ART INITIATION TEST.
Y-YOU ENTERED TO TEST HOW MUCH NEGI-SENSEI HAS GROWN, RIGHT?
AND IF YOU STILL WIN, YOU'LL LET US HAVE THE PRIZE MONEY.
HAPPENS ALL THE TIME.
WHAAA~?
LIKE HELL I'D DO THAT! IF I WIN, THE MONEY'S MINE!!
くわっ GRAR
SHOCK ズドーン
EEEH—!?
WHAT ABOUT AKO-SAN AND THE OTHERS?
WITH YOUR FRIENDS' POWERS, YOU COULD EARN IT PRETTY FAST SOME OTHER WAY, RIGHT?
LIKE THAT HARUNA GIRL.
BUT...!
IF YOU DON'T LIKE IT, YOU JUST HAVE TO BEAT ME.
SMIRK SMIRK ニヤ ニヤ
THAT'S CRAZY!
JUST CALM DOWN AND THINK ABOUT IT,
KID.

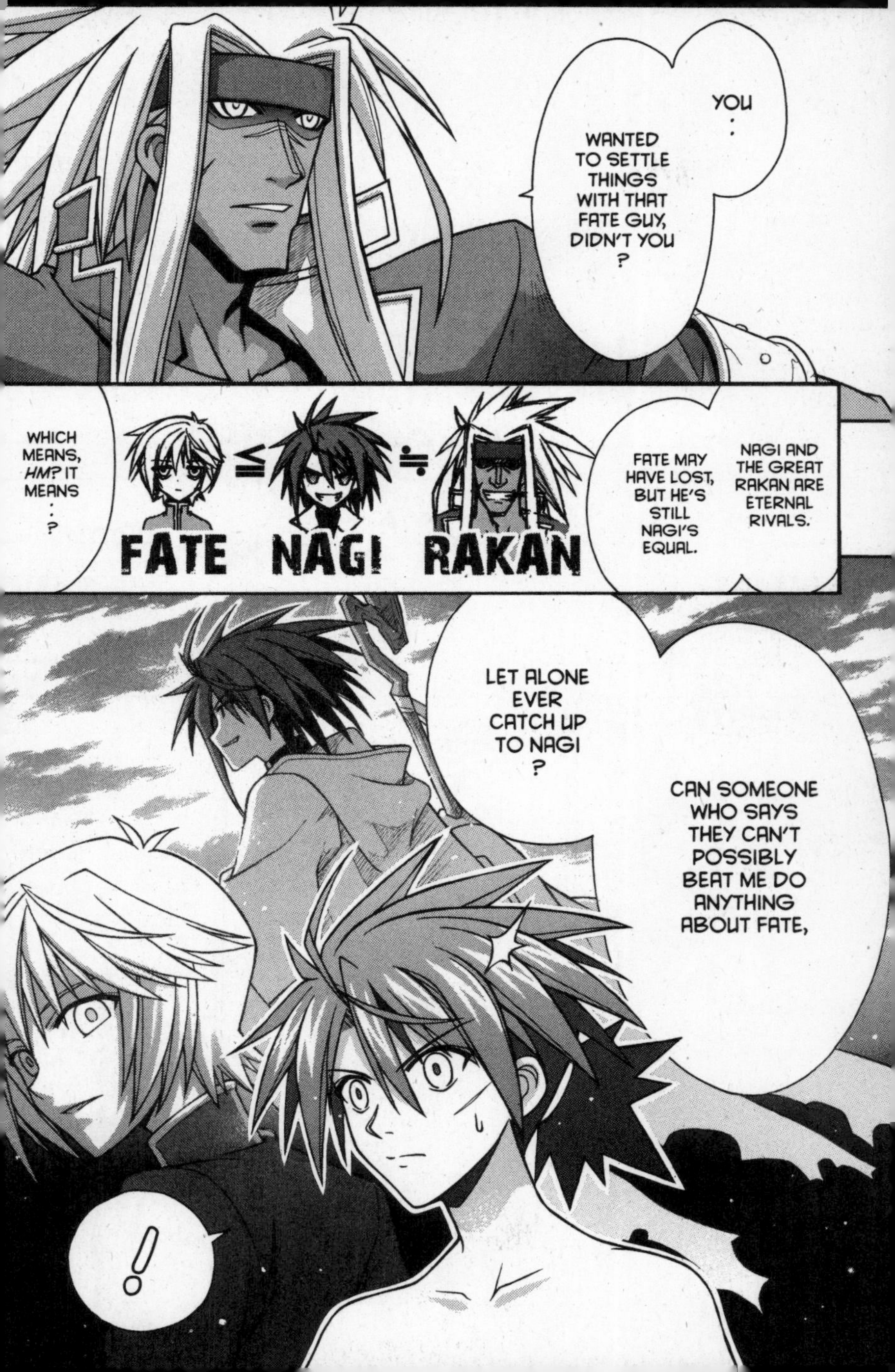
YOU . . . WANTED TO SETTLE THINGS WITH THAT FATE GUY, DIDN'T YOU ?
NAGI AND THE GREAT RAKAN ARE ETERNAL RIVALS.
FATE MAY HAVE LOST, BUT HE'S STILL NAGI'S EQUAL.
FATE ≤ NAGI ≒ RAKAN
WHICH MEANS, *HM?* IT MEANS . . . ?
CAN SOMEONE WHO SAYS THEY CAN'T POSSIBLY BEAT ME DO ANYTHING ABOUT FATE,
LET ALONE EVER CATCH UP TO NAGI ?
!

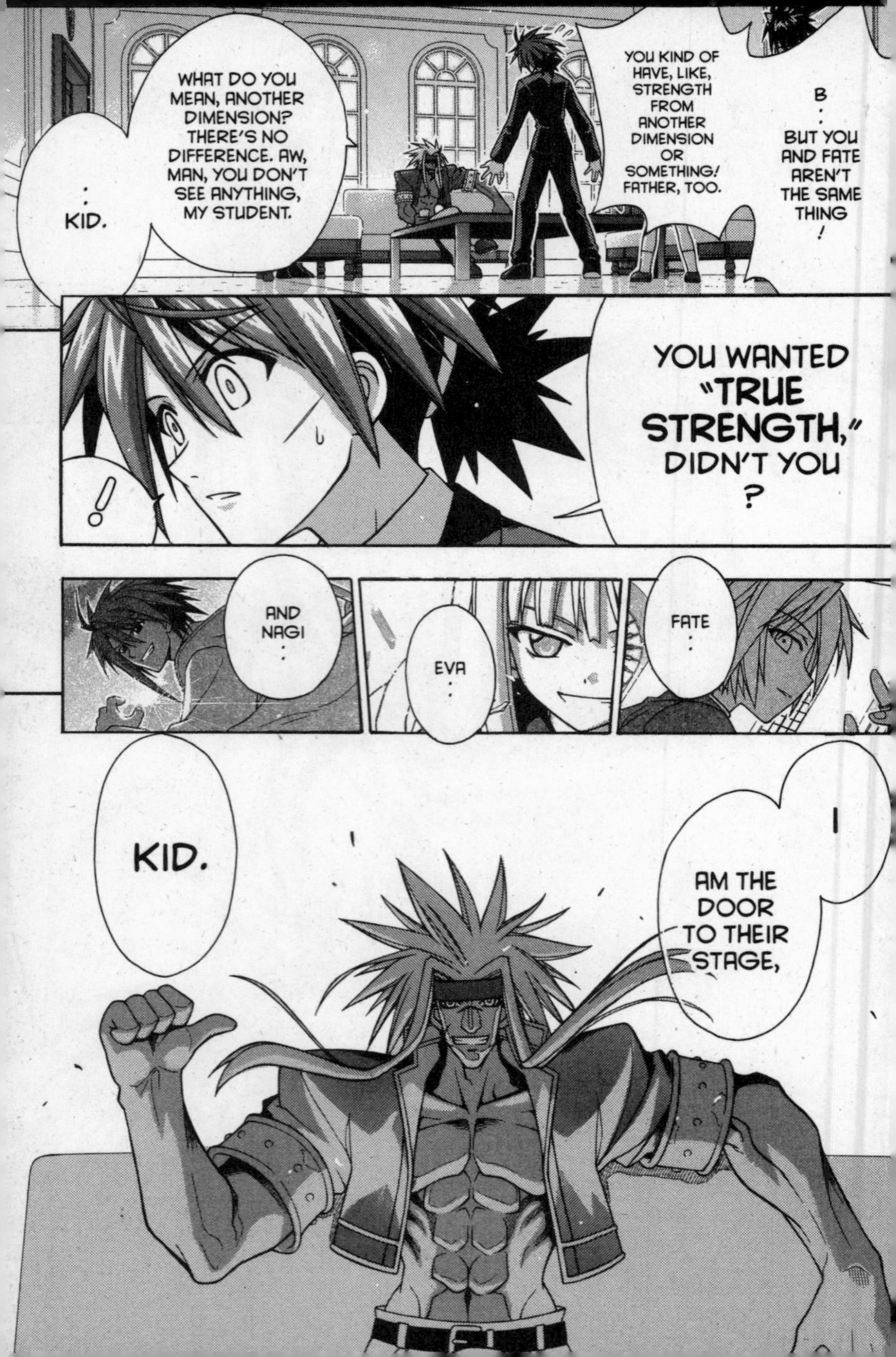
B... BUT YOU AND FATE AREN'T THE SAME THING!
YOU KIND OF HAVE, LIKE, STRENGTH FROM ANOTHER DIMENSION OR SOMETHING! FATHER, TOO.
WHAT DO YOU MEAN, ANOTHER DIMENSION? THERE'S NO DIFFERENCE. AW, MAN, YOU DON'T SEE ANYTHING, MY STUDENT.
...KID.
YOU WANTED "TRUE STRENGTH," DIDN'T YOU?
!
FATE...
EVA...
AND NAGI...
I AM THE DOOR TO THEIR STAGE,
KID.

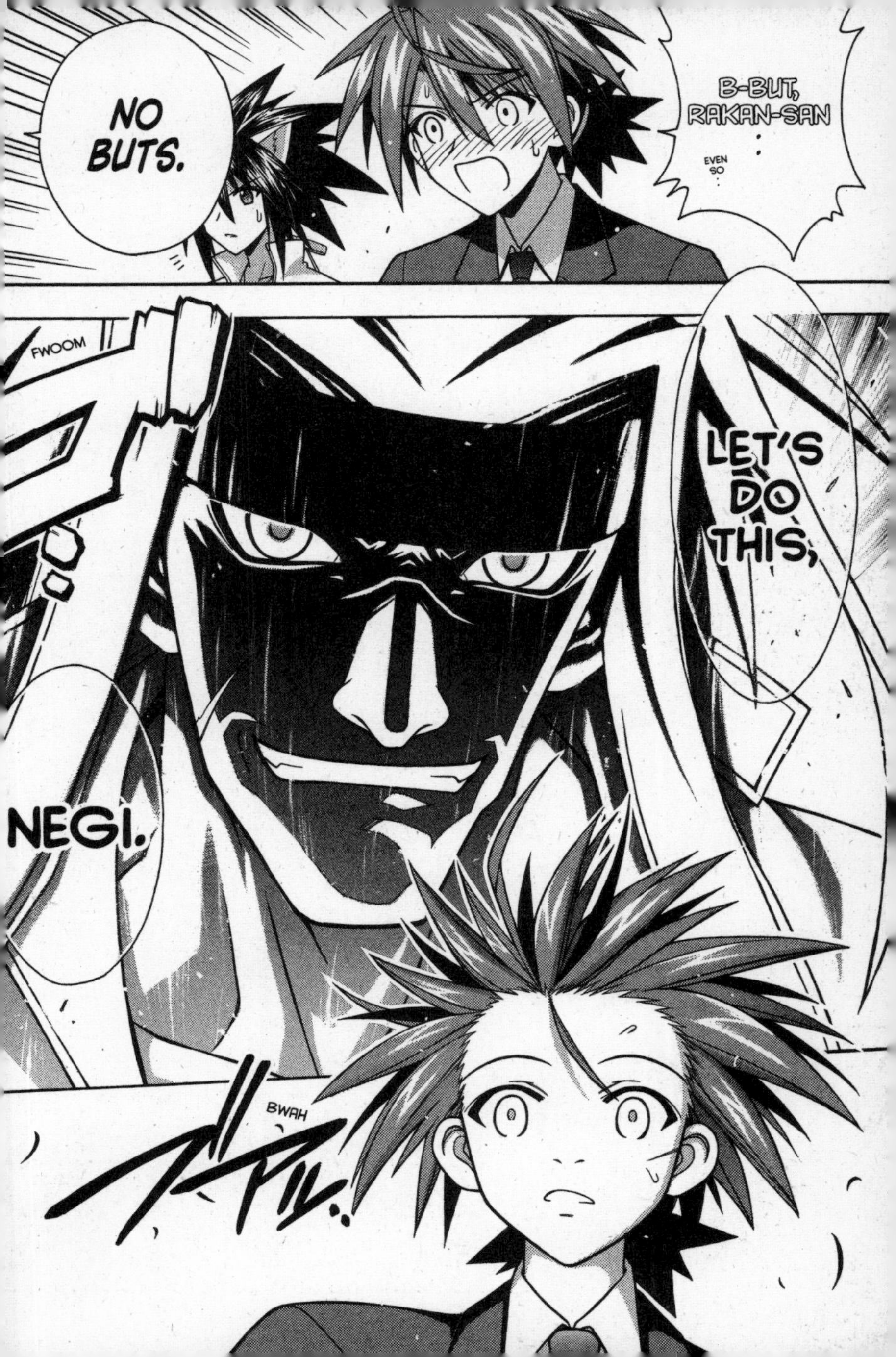
B-BUT, RAKAN-SAN . . .
EVEN SO . . .
NO BUTS.
FWOOM
LET'S DO THIS,
NEGI.
BWAH

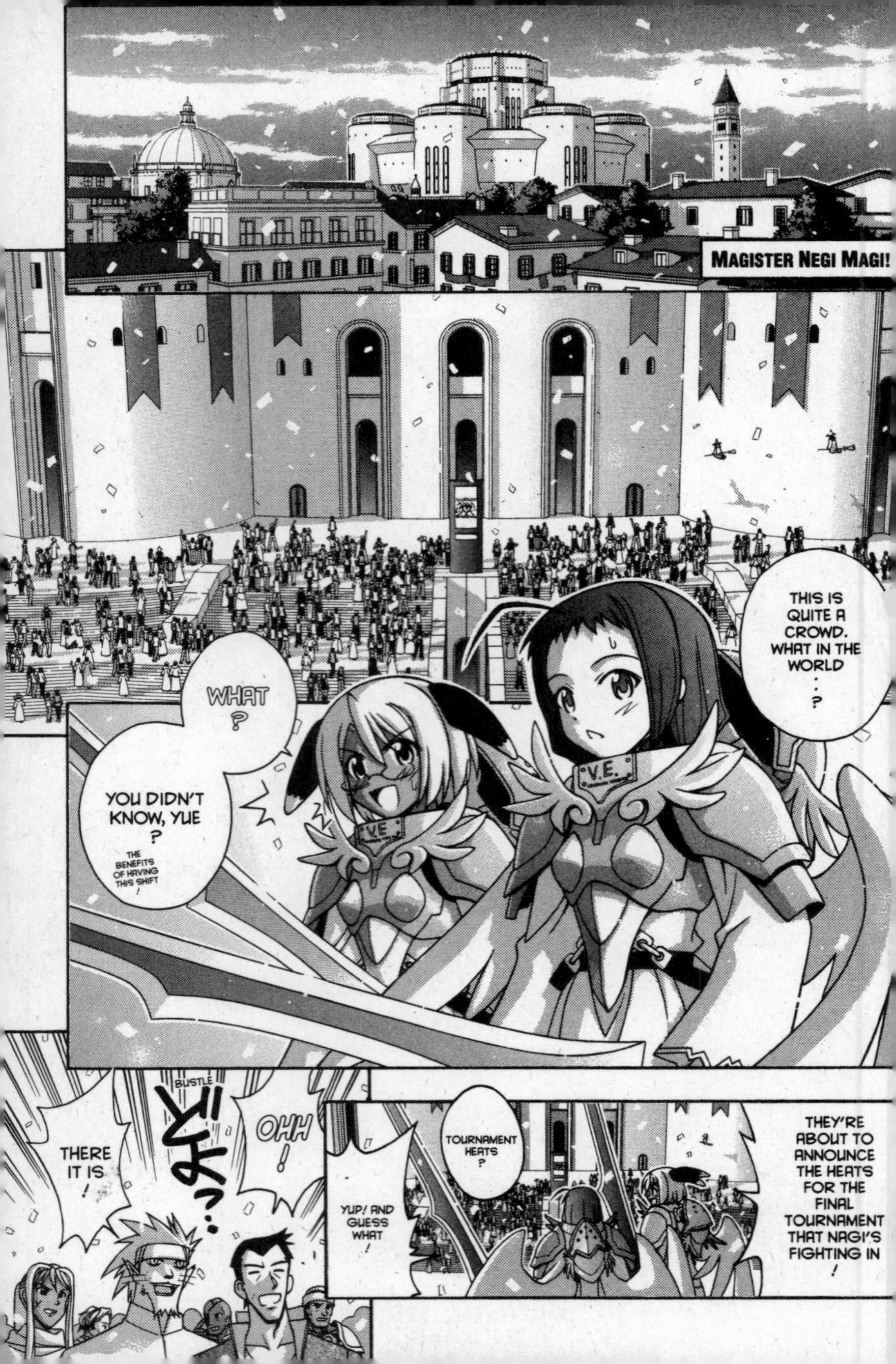
MAGISTER NEGI MAGI!
THIS IS QUITE A CROWD. WHAT IN THE WORLD . . . ?
WHAT ?
YOU DIDN'T KNOW, YUE ?
THE BENEFITS OF HAVING THIS SHIFT !
THEY'RE ABOUT TO ANNOUNCE THE HEATS FOR THE FINAL TOURNAMENT THAT NAGI'S FIGHTING IN !
TOURNAMENT HEATS ?
YUP! AND GUESS WHAT !
OHH !
BUSTLE
どよっ
THERE IT IS !

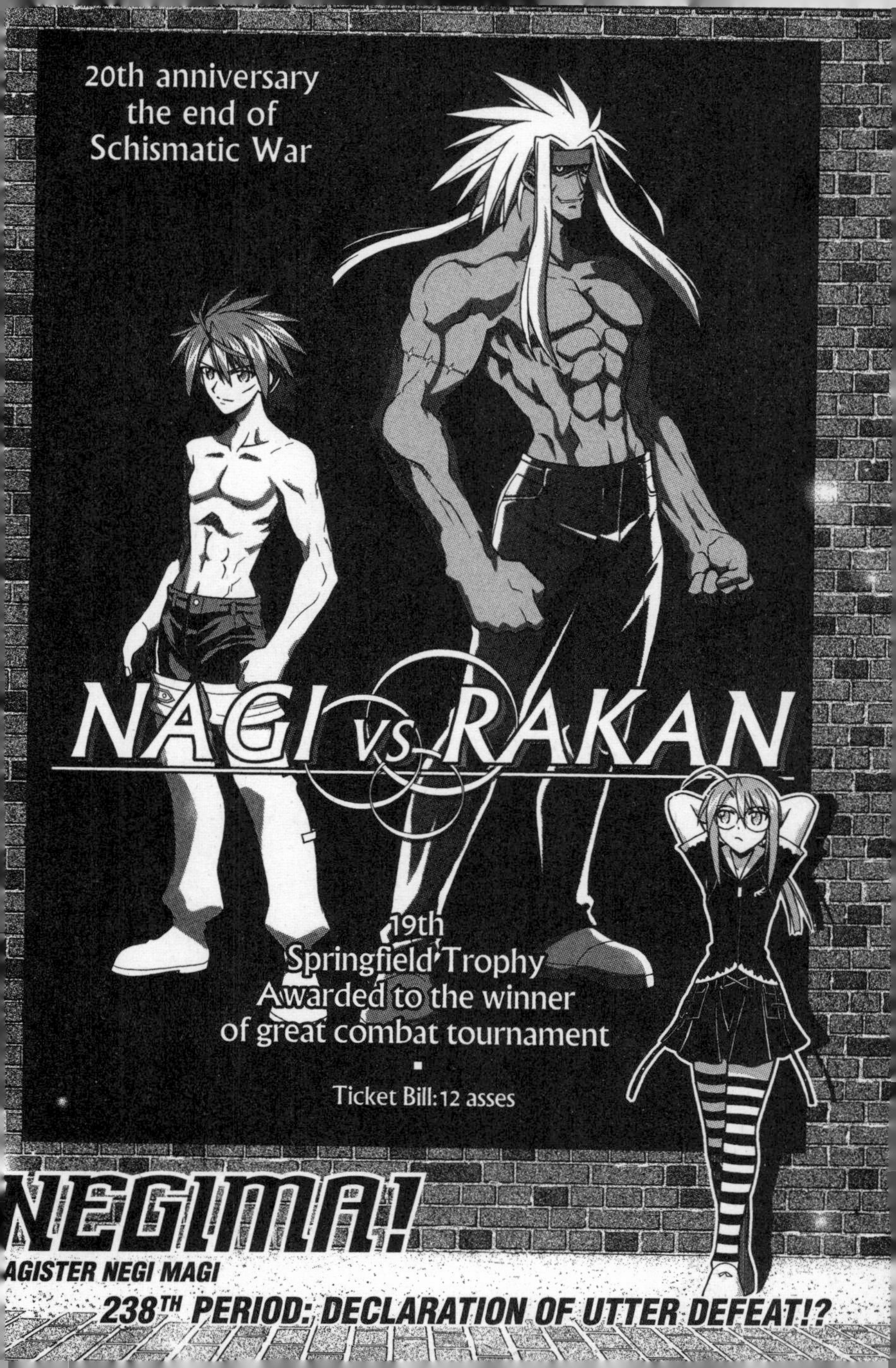
20th anniversary
the end of
Schismatic War
NAGI vs RAKAN
19th
Springfield Trophy
Awarded to the winner
of great combat tournament
Ticket Bill: 12 asses
NEGIMA!
AGISTER NEGI MAGI
238TH PERIOD: DECLARATION OF UTTER DEFEAT!?

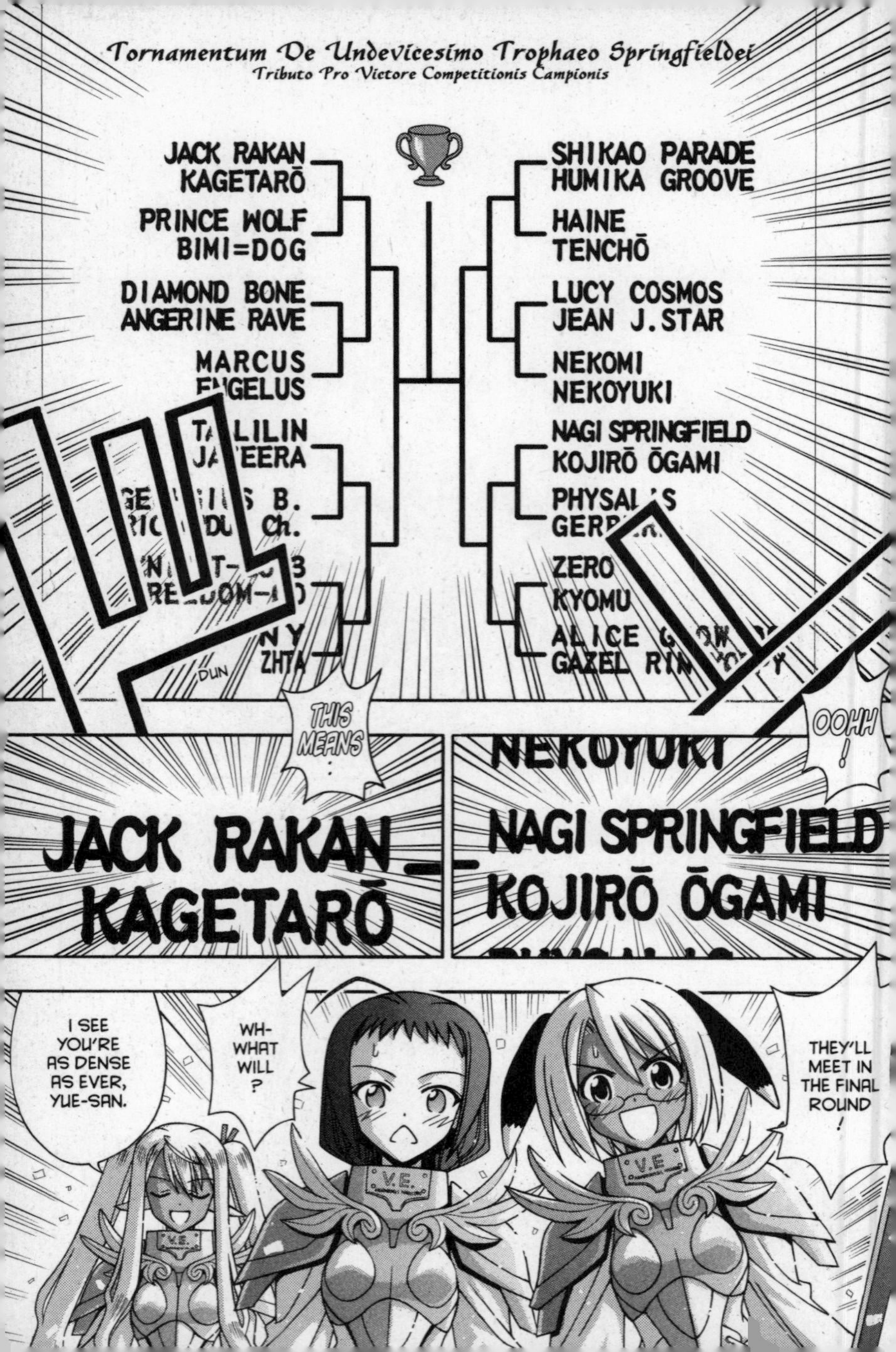
Tornamentum De Undevicesimo Trophaeo Springfieldei
Tributo Pro Victore Competitionis Campionis
JACK RAKAN
KAGETARŌ
PRINCE WOLF
BIMI=DOG
DIAMOND BONE
ANGERINE RAVE
MARCUS
SHIKAO PARADE
HUMIKA GROOVE
HAINE
TENCHŌ
LUCY COSMOS
JEAN J. STAR
NEKOMI
NEKOYUKI
NAGI SPRINGFIELD
KOJIRŌ ŌGAMI
ZERO
KYOMU
GAZEL
DUN
OOHH!
NEKOYUKI
NAGI SPRINGFIELD
KOJIRŌ ŌGAMI
THIS MEANS:
JACK RAKAN
KAGETARŌ
THEY'LL MEET IN THE FINAL ROUND!
WH- WHAT WILL?
I SEE YOU'RE AS DENSE AS EVER, YUE-SAN.

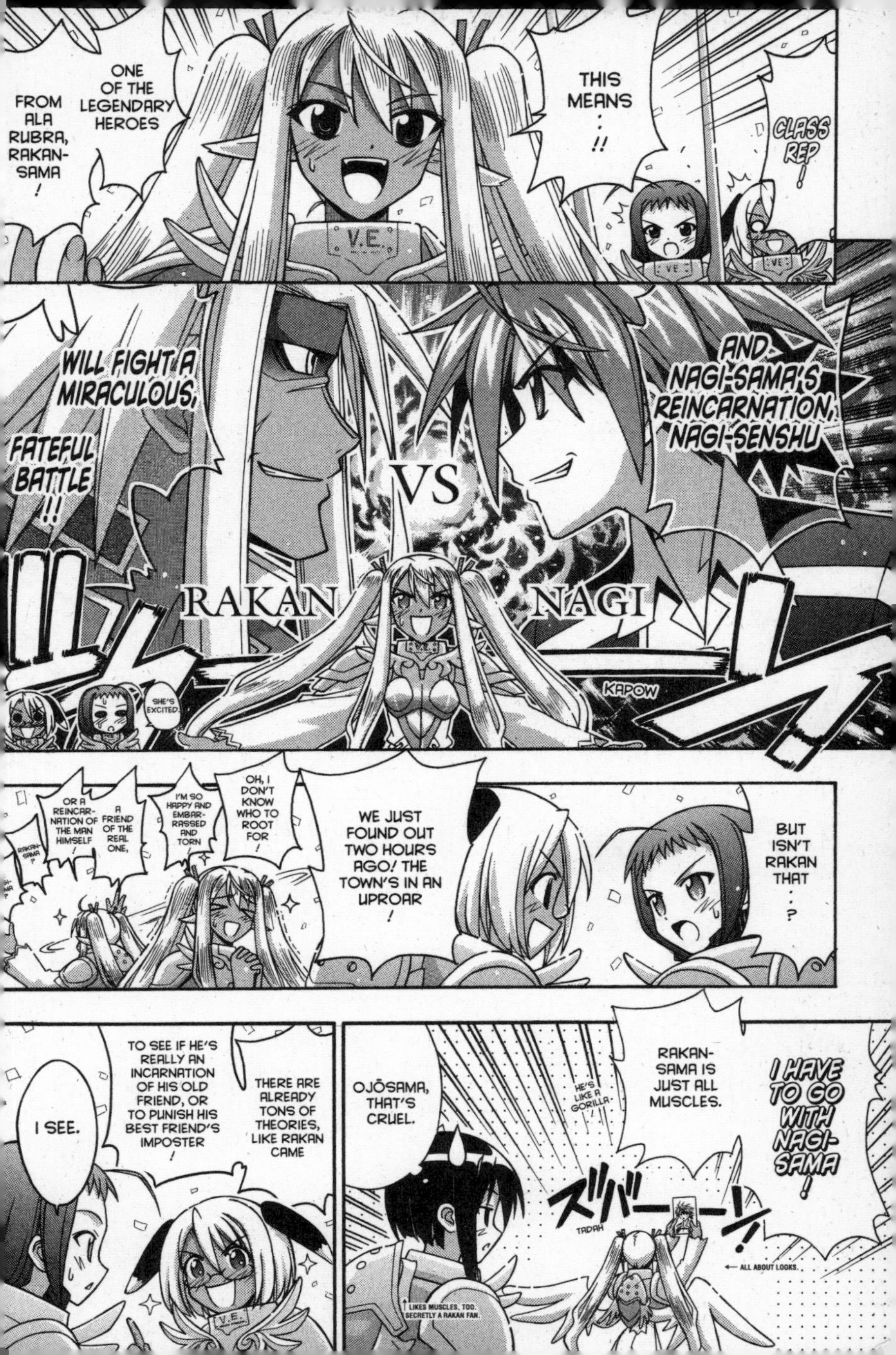
CLASS REP!
THIS MEANS...!!
ONE OF THE LEGENDARY HEROES
FROM ALA RUBRA, RAKAN-SAMA!
AND NAGI-SAMA'S REINCARNATION, NAGI-SENSHU
WILL FIGHT A MIRACULOUS, FATEFUL BATTLE!!
RAKAN
VS
NAGI
KAPOW
SHE'S EXCITED.
BUT ISN'T RAKAN THAT...?
WE JUST FOUND OUT TWO HOURS AGO! THE TOWN'S IN AN UPROAR!
OH, I DON'T KNOW WHO TO ROOT FOR!
I'M SO HAPPY AND EMBARRASSED AND TORN
A FRIEND OF THE REAL ONE,
OR A REINCARNATION OF THE MAN HIMSELF!
RAKAN-SAMA?
I HAVE TO GO WITH NAGI-SAMA!
RAKAN-SAMA IS JUST ALL MUSCLES.
HE'S LIKE A GORILLA!
OJŌSAMA, THAT'S CRUEL.
TADAH
ALL ABOUT LOOKS.
LIKES MUSCLES, TOO. SECRETLY A RAKAN FAN.
THERE ARE ALREADY TONS OF THEORIES, LIKE RAKAN CAME
TO SEE IF HE'S REALLY AN INCARNATION OF HIS OLD FRIEND, OR TO PUNISH HIS BEST FRIEND'S IMPOSTER!
I SEE.

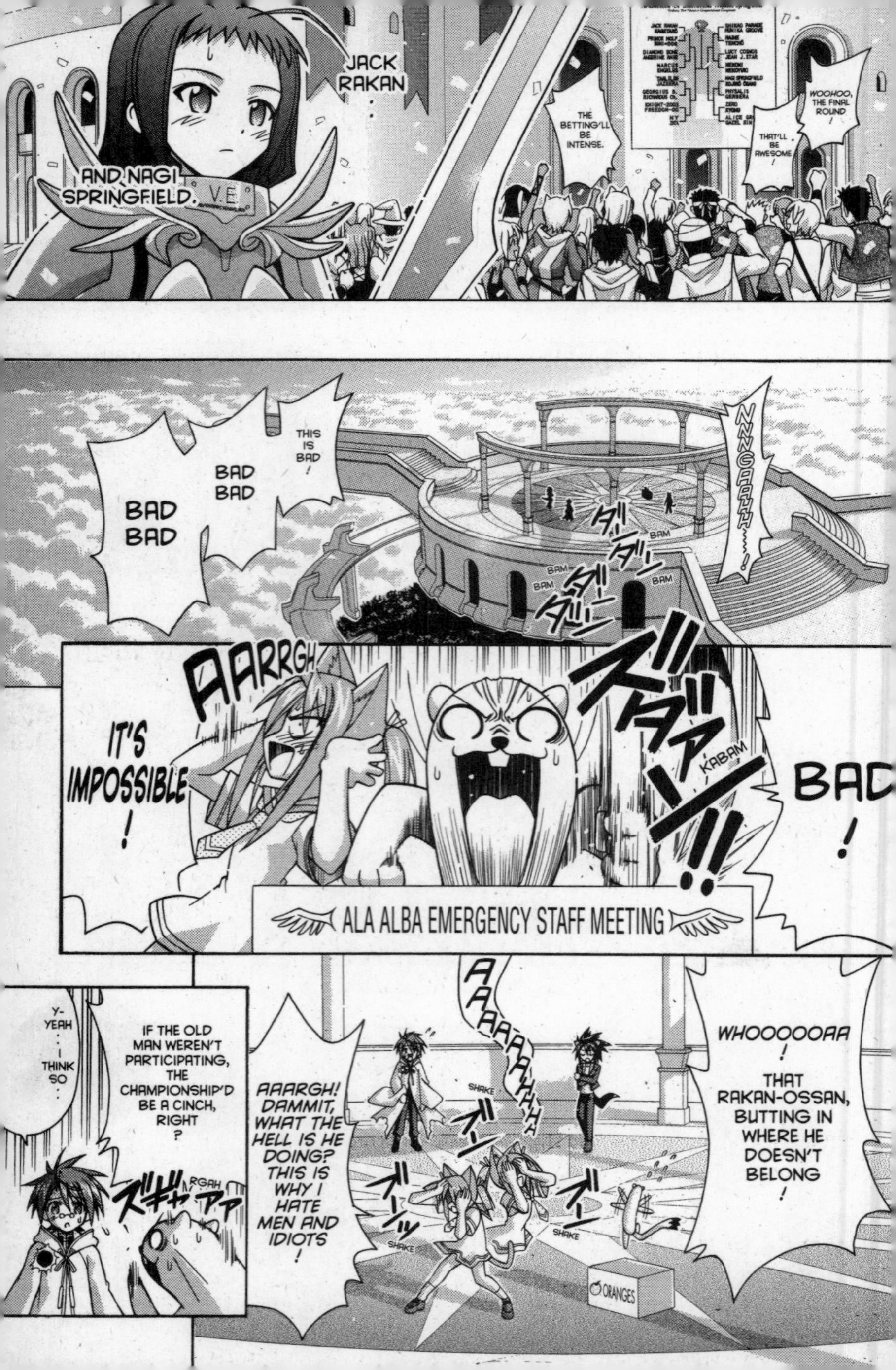

WOOHOO, THE FINAL ROUND!
THAT'LL BE AWESOME!
THE BETTING'LL BE INTENSE.
JACK RAKAN.
AND NAGI SPRINGFIELD.
V.E.
NNNGAAAHH...!
BAM
BAM
BAM
BAM
THIS IS BAD!
BAD BAD
BAD BAD
BAD!
KABAM
AARRGH
IT'S IMPOSSIBLE!
ALA ALBA EMERGENCY STAFF MEETING
WHOOOOOAA! THAT RAKAN-OSSAN, BUTTING IN WHERE HE DOESN'T BELONG!
AAAAAAAHHH
SHAKE
SHAKE
SHAKE
AAARGH! DAMMIT, WHAT THE HELL IS HE DOING? THIS IS WHY I HATE MEN AND IDIOTS!
ORANGES
IF THE OLD MAN WEREN'T PARTICIPATING, THE CHAMPIONSHIP'D BE A CINCH, RIGHT?
Y-YEAH... I THINK SO...
RGAH

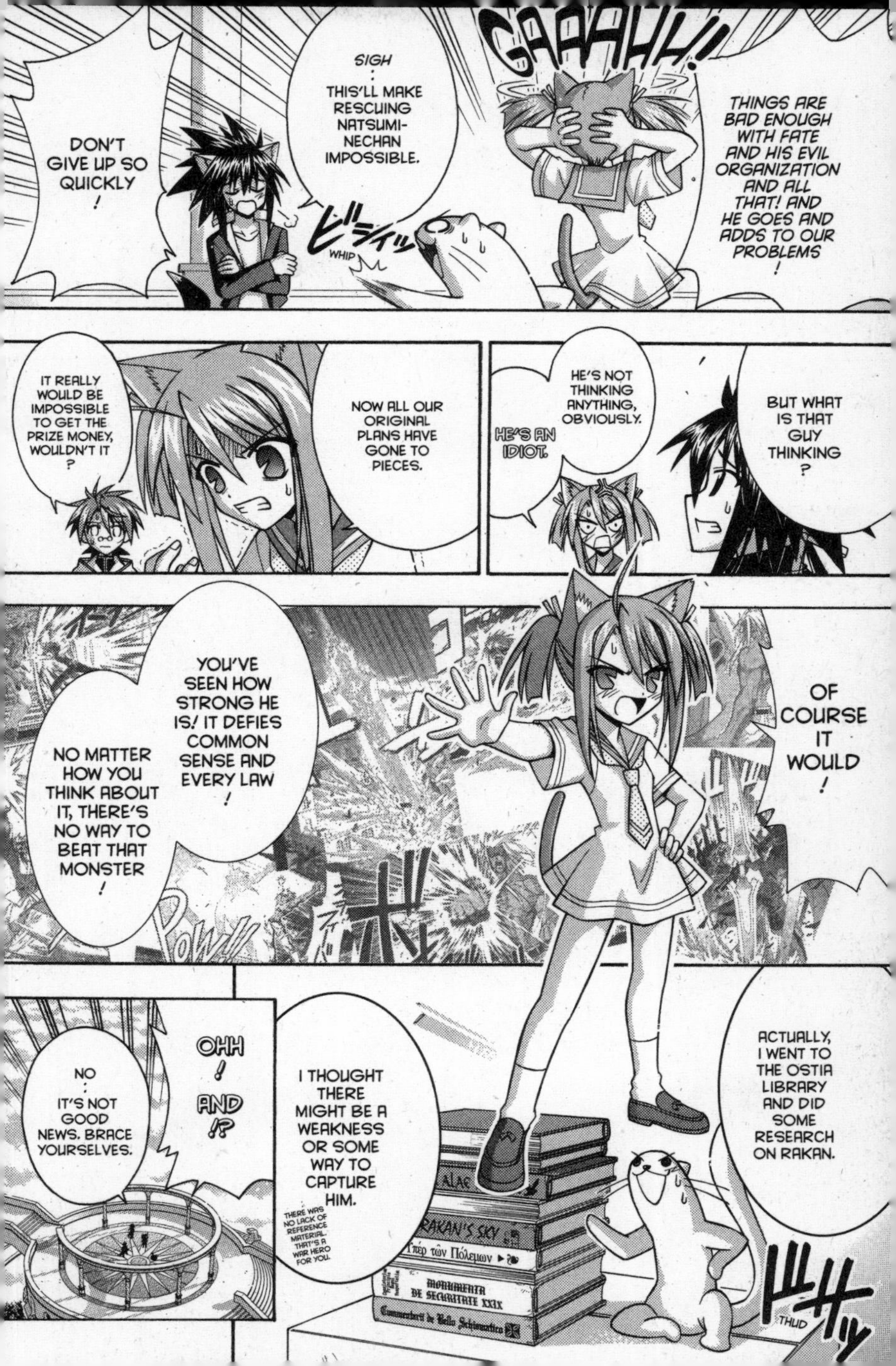
GAAAHH!!
THINGS ARE BAD ENOUGH WITH FATE AND HIS EVIL ORGANIZATION AND ALL THAT! AND HE GOES AND ADDS TO OUR PROBLEMS!
SIGH : THIS'LL MAKE RESCUING NATSUMI-NECHAN IMPOSSIBLE.
WHIP
DON'T GIVE UP SO QUICKLY!
BUT WHAT IS THAT GUY THINKING?
HE'S NOT THINKING ANYTHING, OBVIOUSLY.
HE'S AN IDIOT.
NOW ALL OUR ORIGINAL PLANS HAVE GONE TO PIECES.
IT REALLY WOULD BE IMPOSSIBLE TO GET THE PRIZE MONEY, WOULDN'T IT?
OF COURSE IT WOULD!
YOU'VE SEEN HOW STRONG HE IS! IT DEFIES COMMON SENSE AND EVERY LAW!
NO MATTER HOW YOU THINK ABOUT IT, THERE'S NO WAY TO BEAT THAT MONSTER!
POW
ACTUALLY, I WENT TO THE OSTIA LIBRARY AND DID SOME RESEARCH ON RAKAN.
THUD
I THOUGHT THERE MIGHT BE A WEAKNESS OR SOME WAY TO CAPTURE HIM.
THERE WAS NO LACK OF REFERENCE MATERIAL. THAT'S A WAR HERO FOR YOU.
ALAE
RAKAN'S SKY
Υπέρ τῶν Πολέμων
MONUMENTA DE SECURITATE XXIX
Commentarii de Bello Schismatico
OHH! AND!?
NO : IT'S NOT GOOD NEWS. BRACE YOURSELVES.

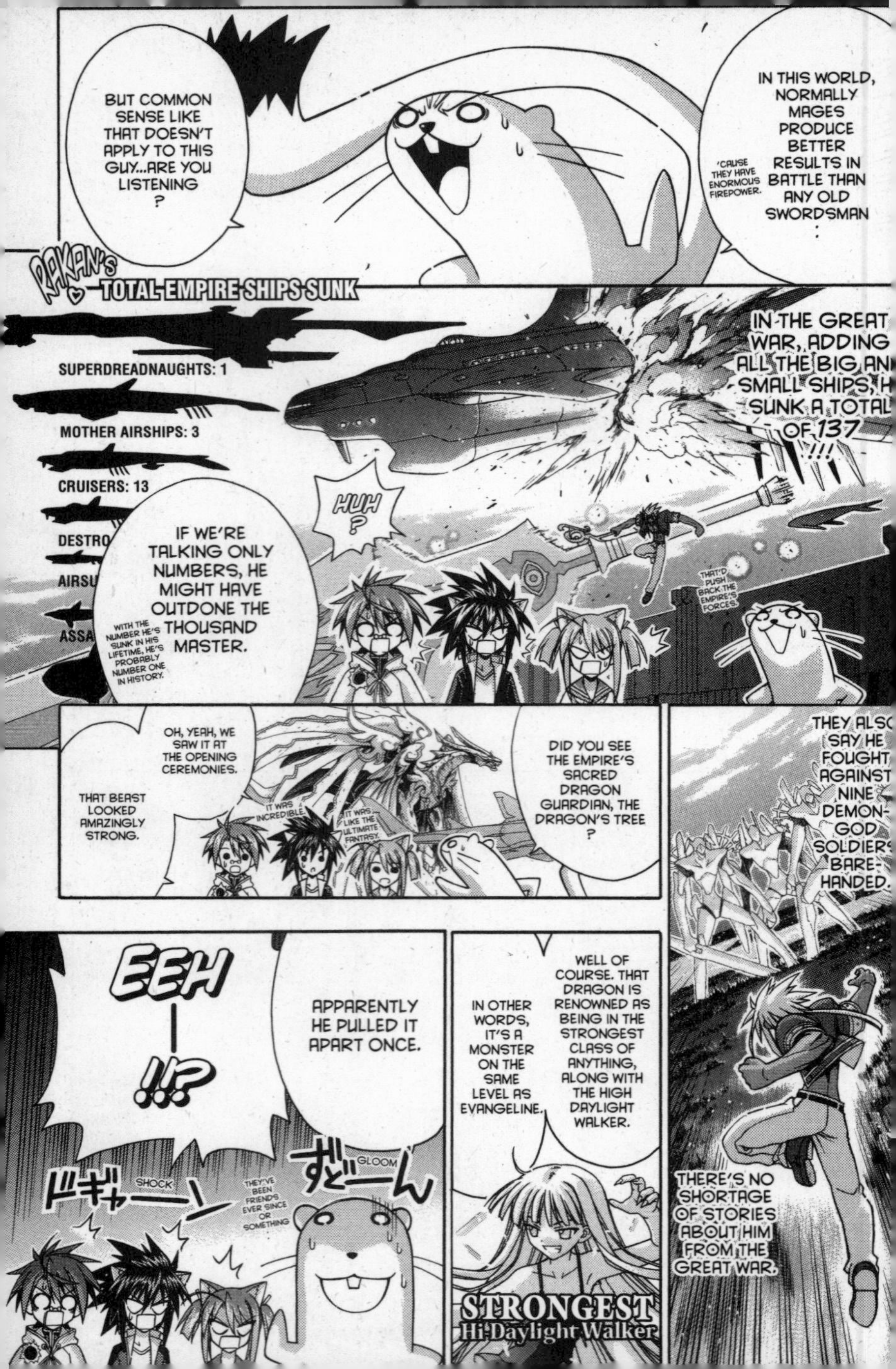
IN THIS WORLD, NORMALLY MAGES PRODUCE BETTER RESULTS IN BATTLE THAN ANY OLD SWORDSMAN :
'CAUSE THEY HAVE ENORMOUS FIREPOWER.
BUT COMMON SENSE LIKE THAT DOESN'T APPLY TO THIS GUY...ARE YOU LISTENING ?
RAKAN'S TOTAL EMPIRE SHIPS SUNK
SUPERDREADNAUGHTS: 1
MOTHER AIRSHIPS: 3
CRUISERS: 13
DESTRO
AIRSU
ASSA
IN THE GREAT WAR, ADDING ALL THE BIG AN SMALL SHIPS, H SUNK A TOTAL OF 137 !!!
THAT'D PUSH BACK THE EMPIRE'S FORCES.
HUH ?
IF WE'RE TALKING ONLY NUMBERS, HE MIGHT HAVE OUTDONE THE THOUSAND MASTER.
WITH THE NUMBER HE'S SUNK IN HIS LIFETIME, HE'S PROBABLY NUMBER ONE IN HISTORY.
THEY ALSO SAY HE FOUGHT AGAINST NINE DEMON-GOD SOLDIERS BARE-HANDED.
THERE'S NO SHORTAGE OF STORIES ABOUT HIM FROM THE GREAT WAR.
DID YOU SEE THE EMPIRE'S SACRED DRAGON GUARDIAN, THE DRAGON'S TREE ?
OH, YEAH, WE SAW IT AT THE OPENING CEREMONIES.
IT WAS INCREDIBLE.
IT WAS LIKE THE ULTIMATE FANTASY.
THAT BEAST LOOKED AMAZINGLY STRONG.
WELL OF COURSE. THAT DRAGON IS RENOWNED AS BEING IN THE STRONGEST CLASS OF ANYTHING, ALONG WITH THE HIGH DAYLIGHT WALKER.
IN OTHER WORDS, IT'S A MONSTER ON THE SAME LEVEL AS EVANGELINE.
STRONGEST Hi-Daylight Walker
APPARENTLY HE PULLED IT APART ONCE.
EEH — !!?
ずどーん GLOOM
ドギャーン SHOCK
THEY'VE BEEN FRIENDS EVER SINCE OR SOMETHING

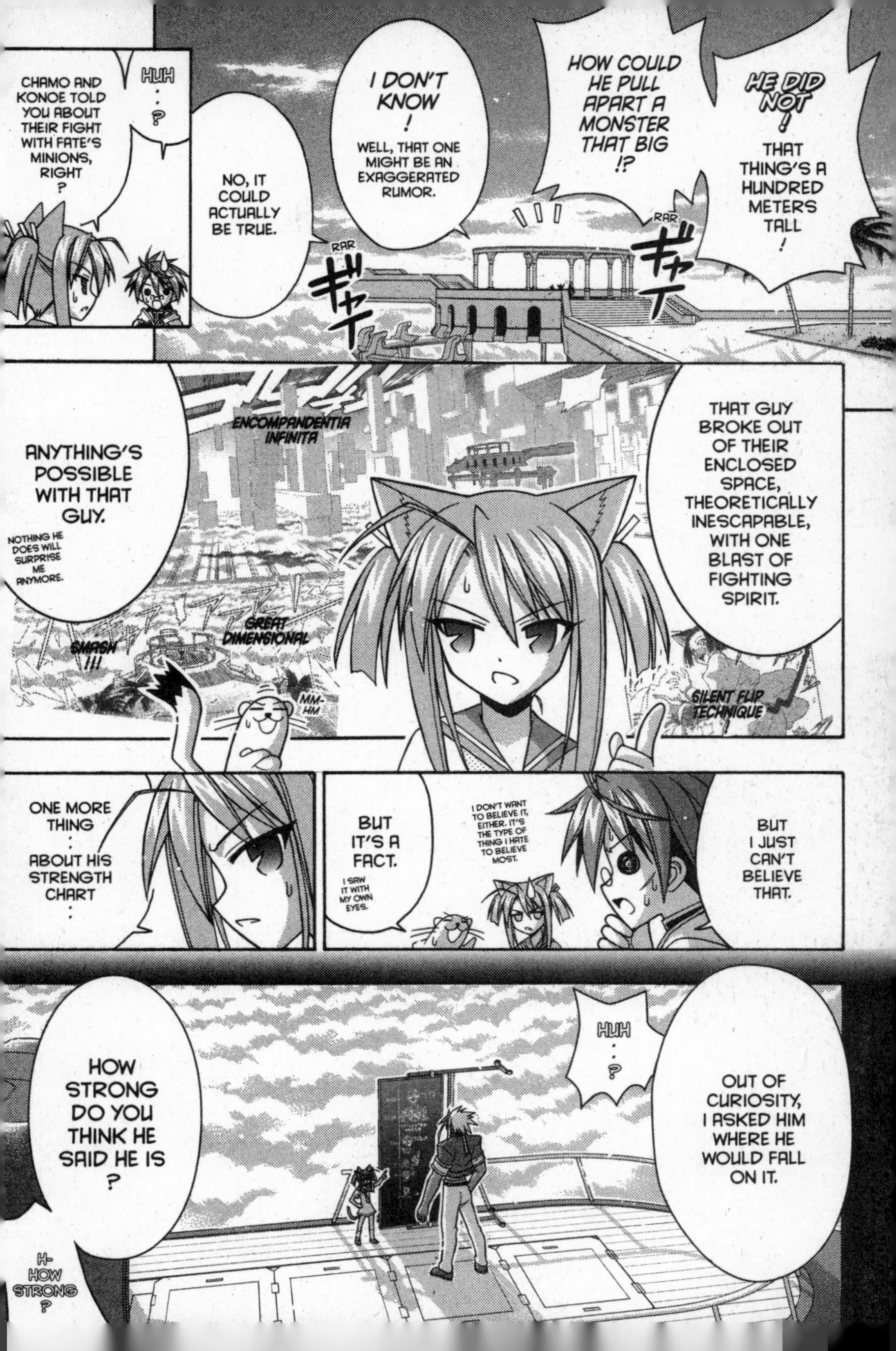
HE DID NOT! THAT THING'S A HUNDRED METERS TALL!
HOW COULD HE PULL APART A MONSTER THAT BIG!?
RAR
!!!
I DON'T KNOW! WELL, THAT ONE MIGHT BE AN EXAGGERATED RUMOR.
RAR
NO, IT COULD ACTUALLY BE TRUE.
HUH..?
CHAMO AND KONOE TOLD YOU ABOUT THEIR FIGHT WITH FATE'S MINIONS, RIGHT?
THAT GUY BROKE OUT OF THEIR ENCLOSED SPACE, THEORETICALLY INESCAPABLE, WITH ONE BLAST OF FIGHTING SPIRIT.
SILENT FLIP TECHNIQUE
MM-HM
GREAT DIMENSIONAL
ENCOMPANDENTIA INFINITA
SMASH!!!
ANYTHING'S POSSIBLE WITH THAT GUY.
NOTHING HE DOES WILL SURPRISE ME ANYMORE.
BUT I JUST CAN'T BELIEVE THAT.
I DON'T WANT TO BELIEVE IT, EITHER. IT'S THE TYPE OF THING I HATE TO BELIEVE MOST.
BUT IT'S A FACT.
I SAW IT WITH MY OWN EYES.
ONE MORE THING: ABOUT HIS STRENGTH CHART..
HUH..?
OUT OF CURIOSITY, I ASKED HIM WHERE HE WOULD FALL ON IT.
HOW STRONG DO YOU THINK HE SAID HE IS?
H-HOW STRONG?

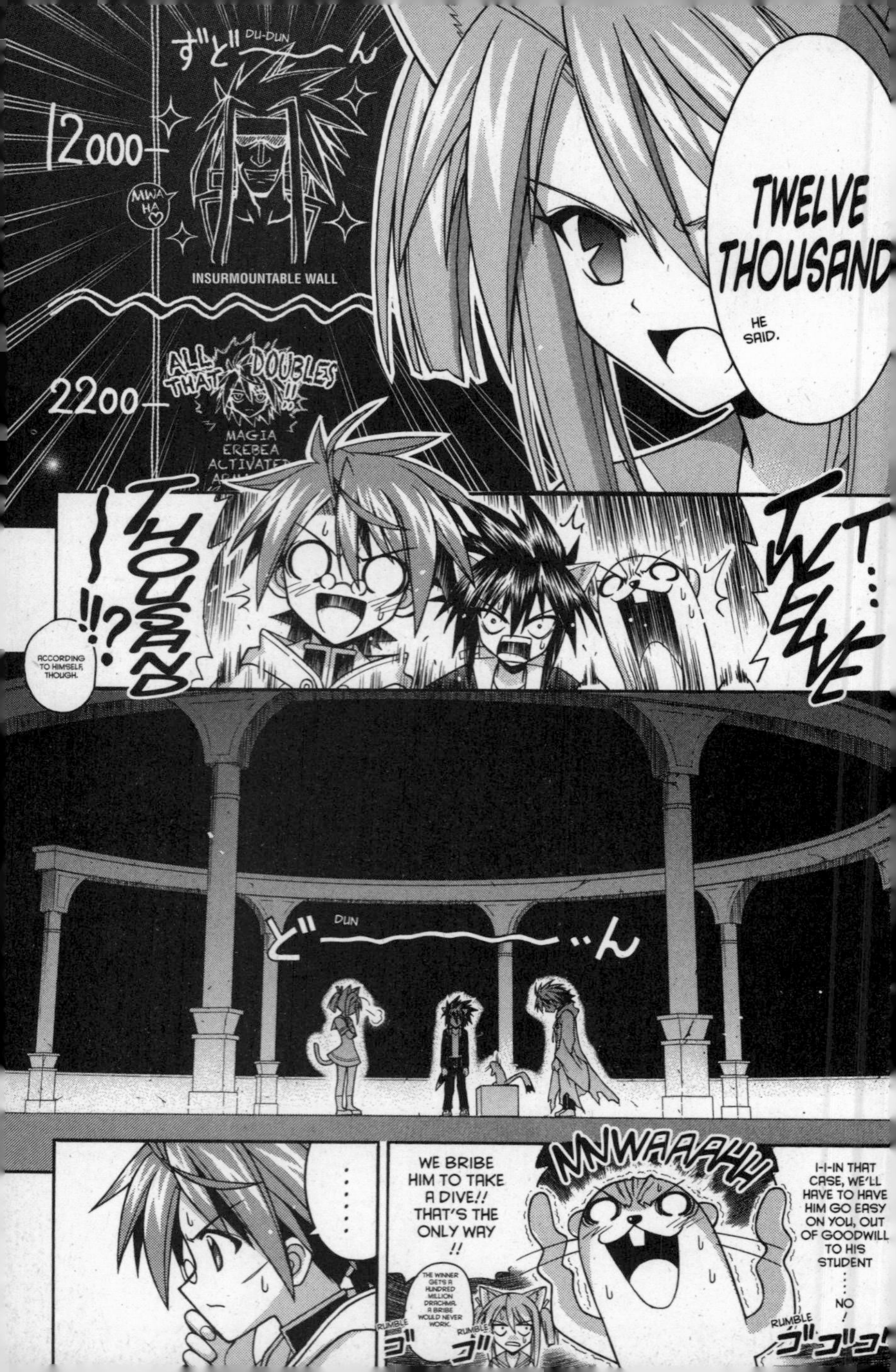
TWELVE THOUSAND
HE SAID.
ずど〜〜ん
DU-DUN
12000
MWA HA♡
INSURMOUNTABLE WALL
2200
ALL THAT DOUBLES!!
MAGIA EREBEA ACTIVATED
TWELVE...
THOUSAND~!!?
ACCORDING TO HIMSELF, THOUGH.
ど――ん
DUN
MNWAAAHH
I-I-IN THAT CASE, WE'LL HAVE TO HAVE HIM GO EASY ON YOU, OUT OF GOODWILL TO HIS STUDENT
......NO!
RUMBLE
ゴゴゴ
WE BRIBE HIM TO TAKE A DIVE!! THAT'S THE ONLY WAY!!
THE WINNER GETS A HUNDRED MILLION DRACHMA. A BRIBE WOULD NEVER WORK.
RUMBLE
ゴ
RUMBLE
ゴ
......

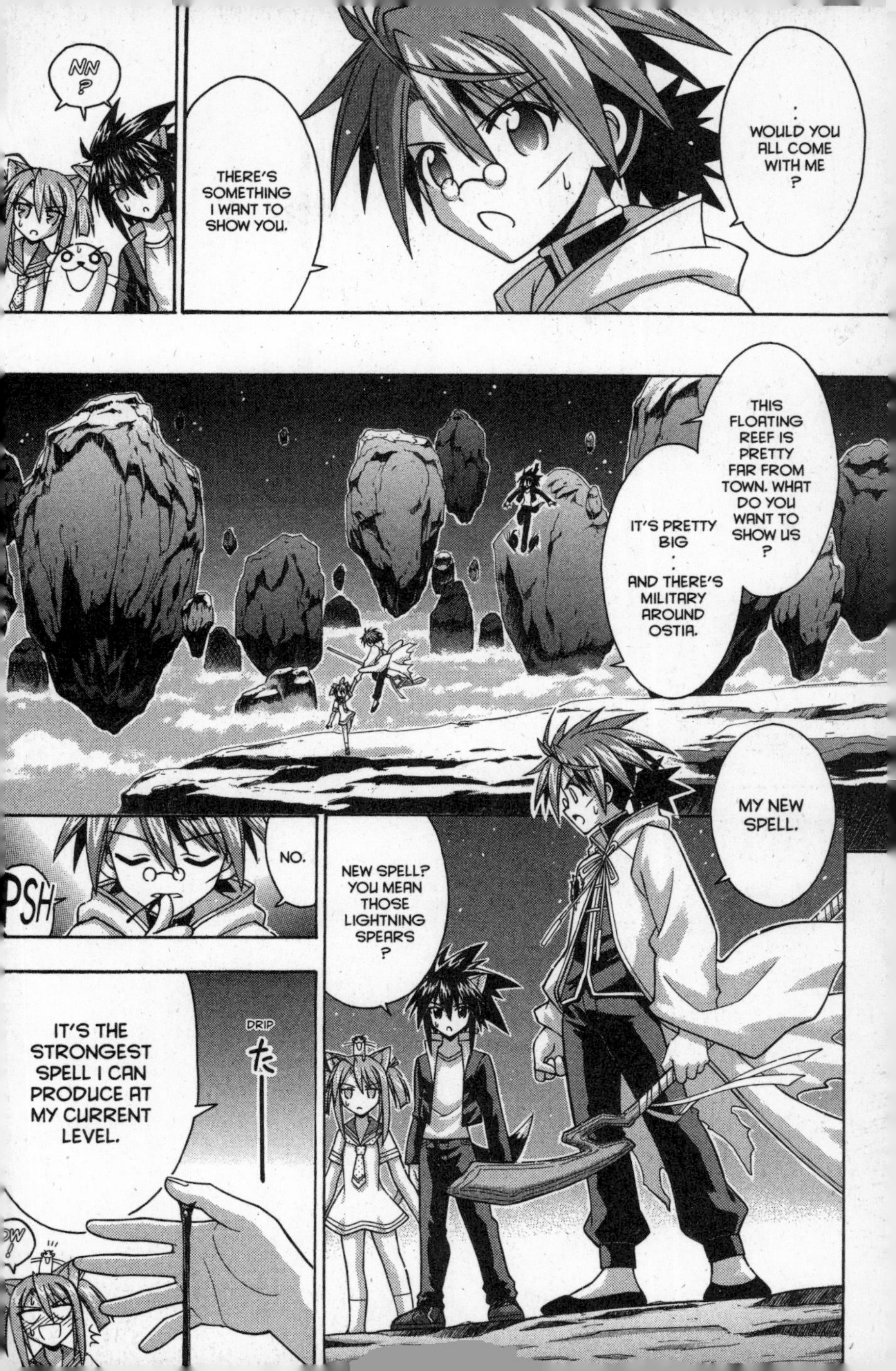
WOULD YOU ALL COME WITH ME?
THERE'S SOMETHING I WANT TO SHOW YOU.
NN?
THIS FLOATING REEF IS PRETTY FAR FROM TOWN. WHAT DO YOU WANT TO SHOW US?
IT'S PRETTY BIG... AND THERE'S MILITARY AROUND OSTIA.
MY NEW SPELL.
NEW SPELL? YOU MEAN THOSE LIGHTNING SPEARS?
NO.
PSH
IT'S THE STRONGEST SPELL I CAN PRODUCE AT MY CURRENT LEVEL.
DRIP
た

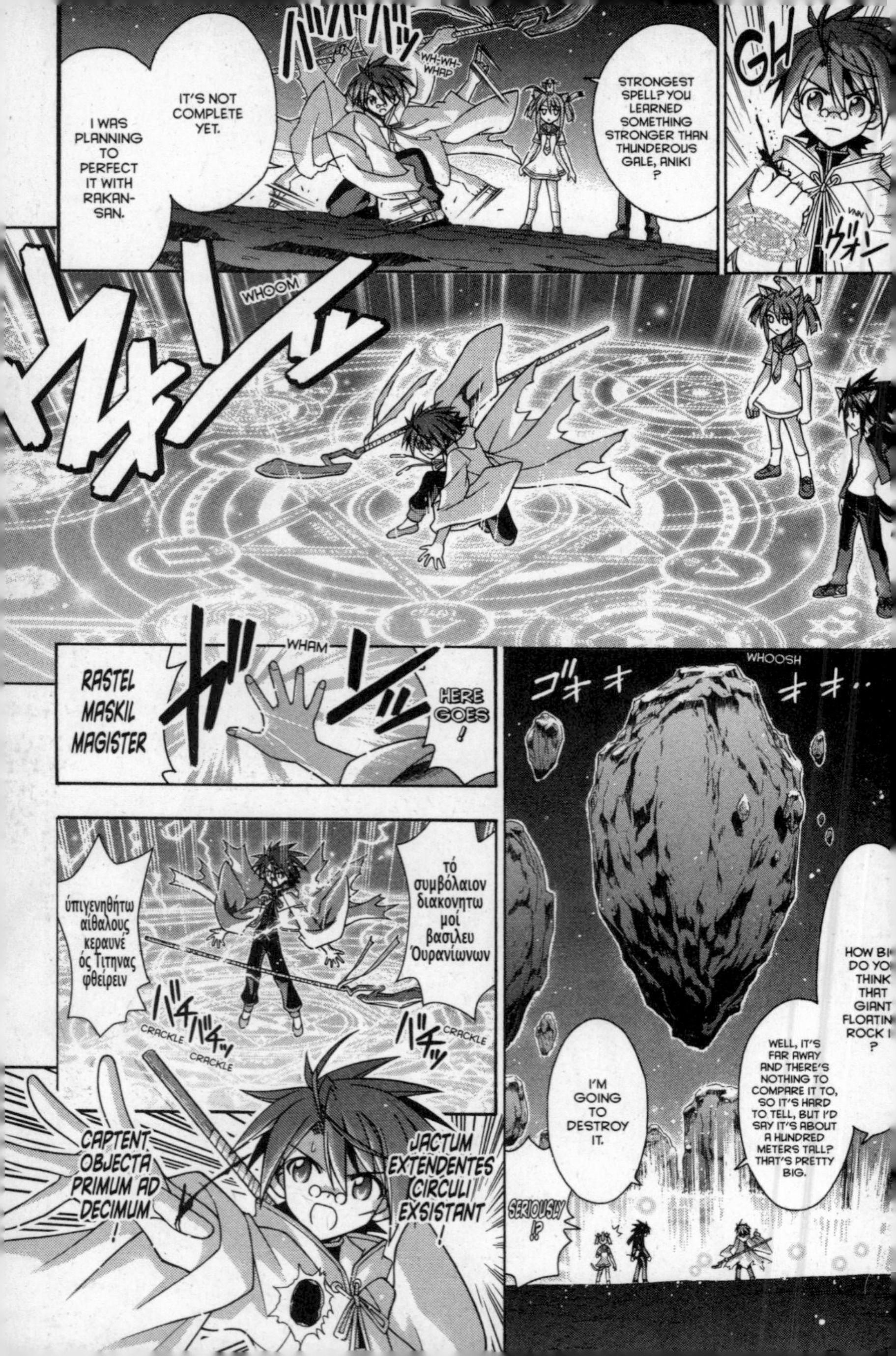

GH
VNN
WH-WH-WHAP
STRONGEST SPELL? YOU LEARNED SOMETHING STRONGER THAN THUNDEROUS GALE, ANIKI ?
IT'S NOT COMPLETE YET.
I WAS PLANNING TO PERFECT IT WITH RAKAN-SAN.
WHOOM
WHOOSH
HOW BIG DO YOU THINK THAT GIANT FLOATING ROCK IS ?
WELL, IT'S FAR AWAY AND THERE'S NOTHING TO COMPARE IT TO, SO IT'S HARD TO TELL, BUT I'D SAY IT'S ABOUT A HUNDRED METERS TALL? THAT'S PRETTY BIG.
I'M GOING TO DESTROY IT.
SERIOUSLY !?
HERE GOES !
WHAM
RASTEL MASKIL MAGISTER
τό συμβόλαιον διακονητω μοί βασιλευ Ουρανίωνων
ύπιγενηθήτω αίθαλους κεραυνέ ός Τιτηνας φθείρειν
CRACKLE
CRACKLE
CRACKLE
JACTUM EXTENDENTES CIRCULI EXSISTANT !
CAPTENT OBJECTA PRIMUM AD DECIMUM !

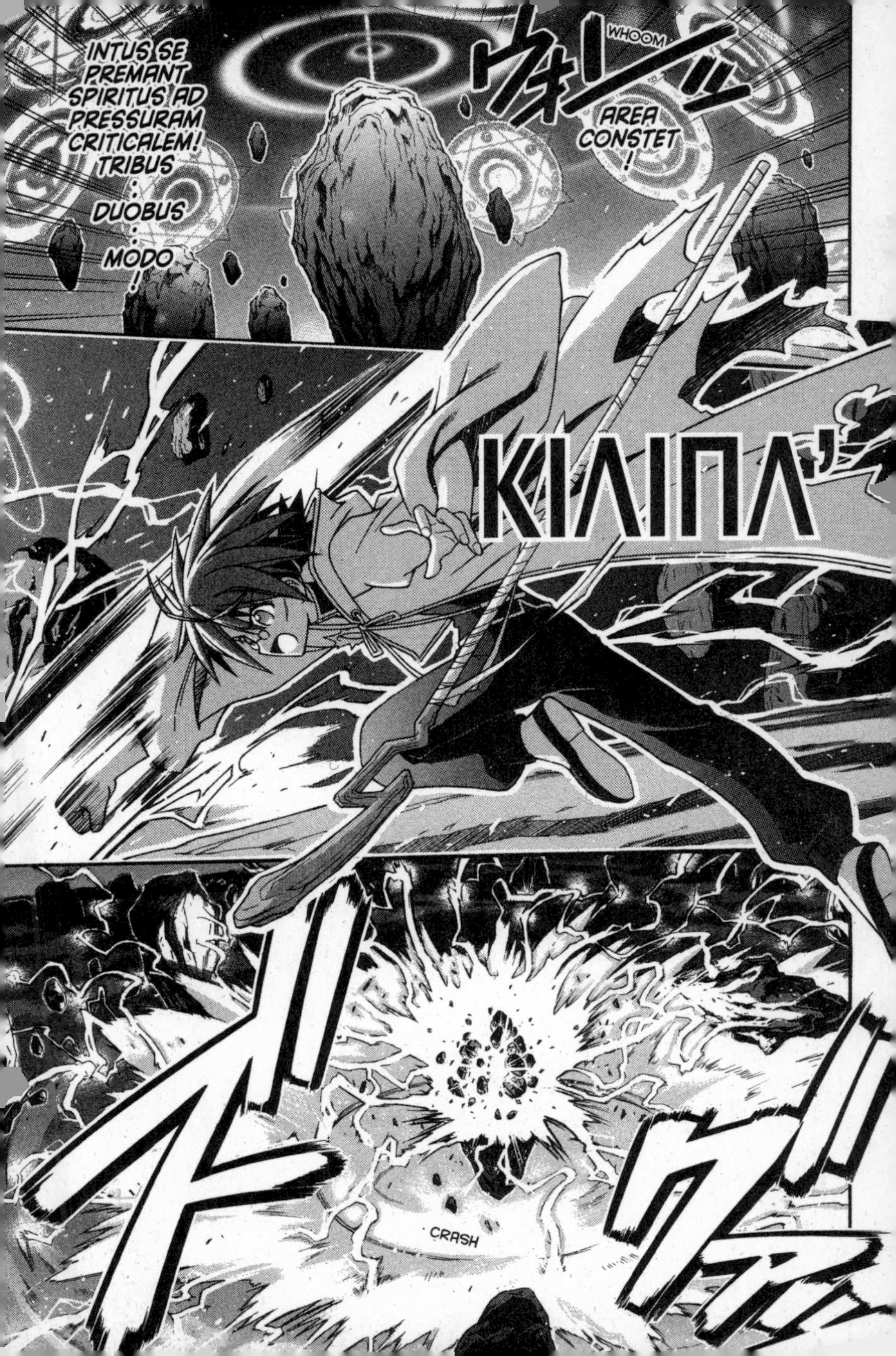
WHOOM
AREA CONSTET !
INTUS SE PREMANT SPIRITUS AD PRESSURAM CRITICALEM! TRIBUS . . . DUOBUS . . . MODO !
KIAINA'
CRASH

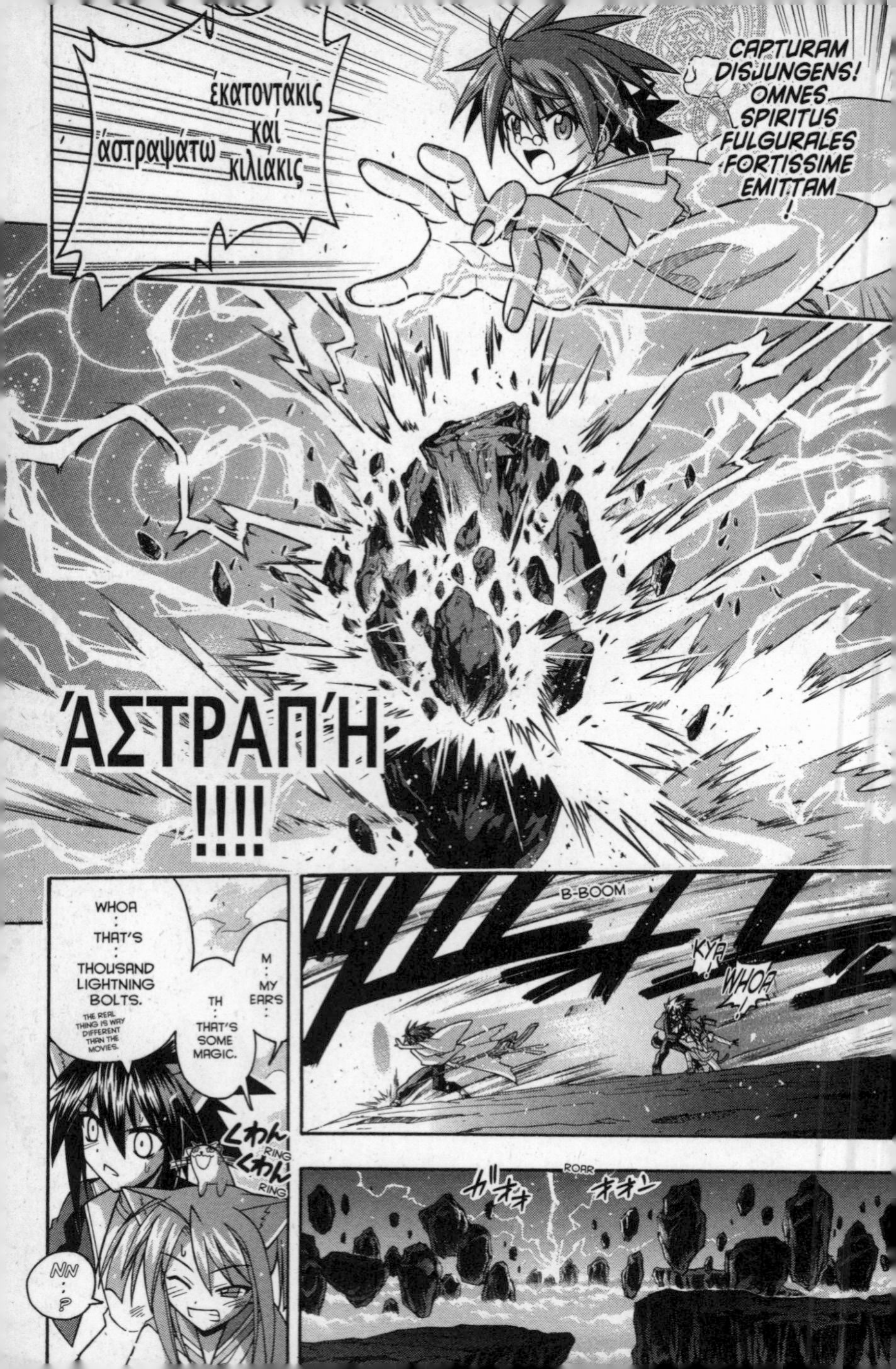
CAPTURAM DISJUNGENS! OMNES SPIRITUS FULGURALES FORTISSIME EMITTAM!
έκατοντάκις καί κιλιάκις ἀστραψάτω
ΆΣΤΡΑΠ'Η !!!!
B-BOOM
KYA! WHOA!
ガオオ オオー
ROAR
WHOA... THAT'S... THOUSAND LIGHTNING BOLTS.
THE REAL THING IS WAY DIFFERENT THAN THE MOVIES.
M... MY EARS...
TH... THAT'S SOME MAGIC.
くわん くわん
RING RING
NN...?

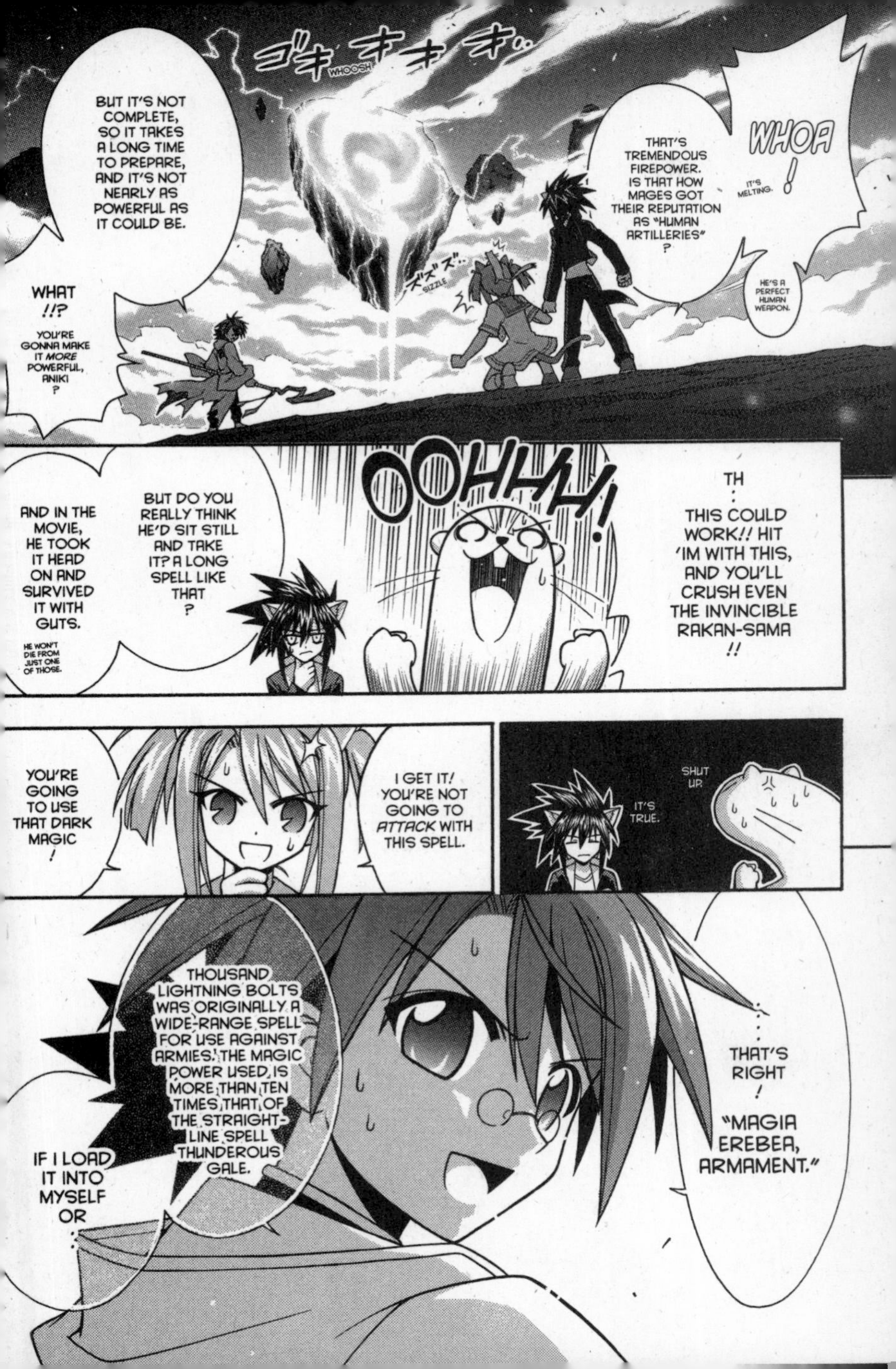

WHOA!
IT'S MELTING.
THAT'S TREMENDOUS FIREPOWER. IS THAT HOW MAGES GOT THEIR REPUTATION AS "HUMAN ARTILLERIES"?
HE'S A PERFECT HUMAN WEAPON.
ゴオオオ.. WHOOSH
BUT IT'S NOT COMPLETE, SO IT TAKES A LONG TIME TO PREPARE, AND IT'S NOT NEARLY AS POWERFUL AS IT COULD BE.
ズズズ.. SIZZLE
WHAT!!?
YOU'RE GONNA MAKE IT *MORE* POWERFUL, ANIKI?
TH... THIS COULD WORK!! HIT 'IM WITH THIS, AND YOU'LL CRUSH EVEN THE INVINCIBLE RAKAN-SAMA!!
OOHHH!
BUT DO YOU REALLY THINK HE'D SIT STILL AND TAKE IT? A LONG SPELL LIKE THAT?
AND IN THE MOVIE, HE TOOK IT HEAD ON AND SURVIVED IT WITH GUTS.
HE WON'T DIE FROM JUST ONE OF THOSE.
SHUT UP.
IT'S TRUE.
I GET IT! YOU'RE NOT GOING TO *ATTACK* WITH THIS SPELL.
YOU'RE GOING TO USE THAT DARK MAGIC!
...THAT'S RIGHT! "MAGIA EREBEA, ARMAMENT."
THOUSAND LIGHTNING BOLTS WAS ORIGINALLY A WIDE-RANGE SPELL FOR USE AGAINST ARMIES. THE MAGIC POWER USED IS MORE THAN TEN TIMES THAT OF THE STRAIGHT-LINE SPELL THUNDEROUS GALE.
IF I LOAD IT INTO MYSELF OR...

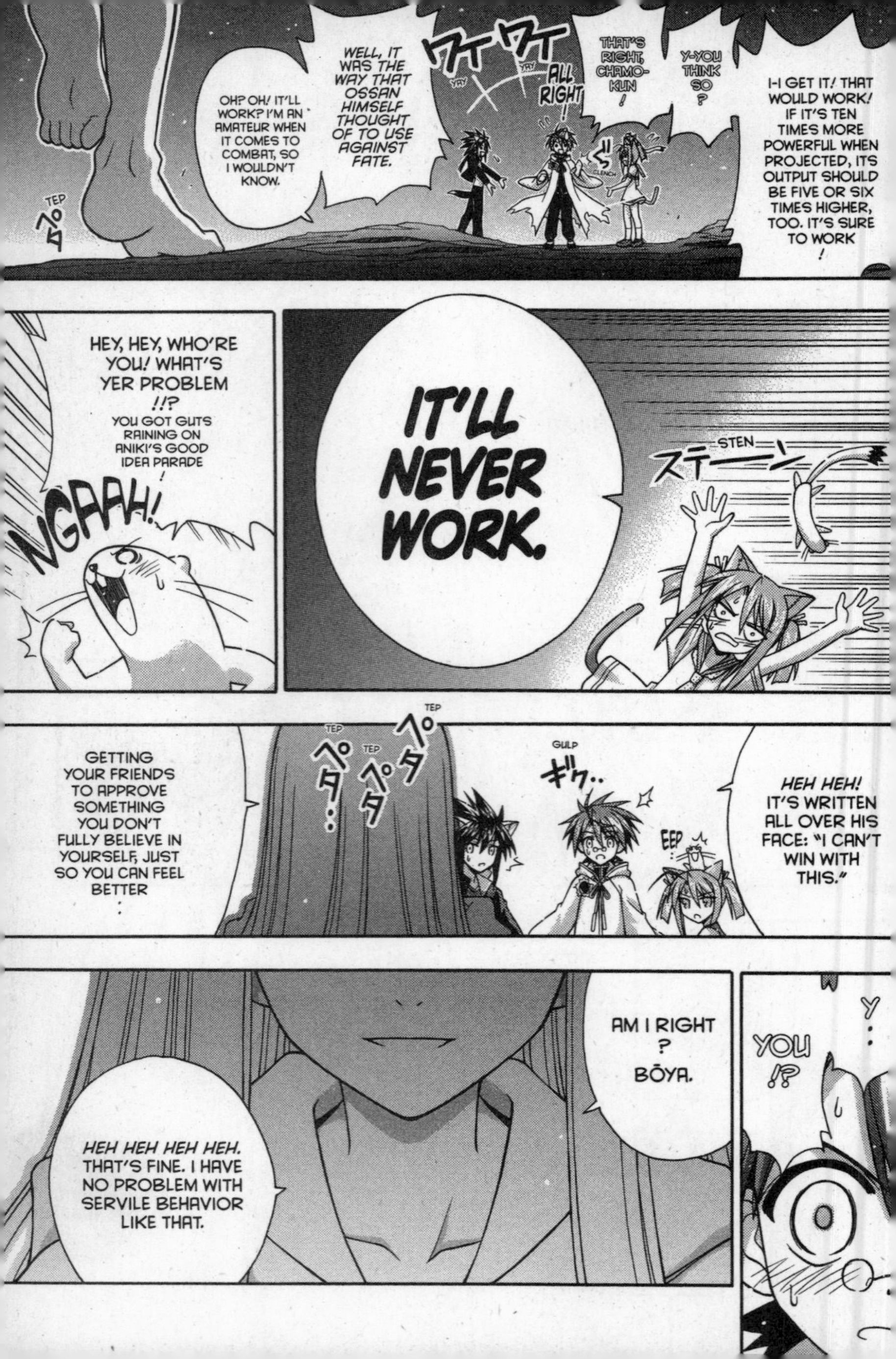
I-I GET IT! THAT WOULD WORK! IF IT'S TEN TIMES MORE POWERFUL WHEN PROJECTED, ITS OUTPUT SHOULD BE FIVE OR SIX TIMES HIGHER, TOO. IT'S SURE TO WORK!
Y-YOU THINK SO?
THAT'S RIGHT, CHAMO-KUN!
CLENCH
ALL RIGHT!
YAY
YAY
WELL, IT WAS THE WAY THAT OSSAN HIMSELF THOUGHT OF TO USE AGAINST FATE.
OH? OH! IT'LL WORK? I'M AN AMATEUR WHEN IT COMES TO COMBAT, SO I WOULDN'T KNOW.
TEP
STEN
IT'LL NEVER WORK.
HEY, HEY, WHO'RE YOU! WHAT'S YER PROBLEM!!?
YOU GOT GUTS RAINING ON ANIKI'S GOOD IDEA PARADE!
NGAAAH!
HEH HEH! IT'S WRITTEN ALL OVER HIS FACE: "I CAN'T WIN WITH THIS."
EEP
GULP
TEP
TEP
TEP
GETTING YOUR FRIENDS TO APPROVE SOMETHING YOU DON'T FULLY BELIEVE IN YOURSELF, JUST SO YOU CAN FEEL BETTER...
Y... YOU!?
AM I RIGHT? BŌYA.
HEH HEH HEH HEH. THAT'S FINE. I HAVE NO PROBLEM WITH SERVILE BEHAVIOR LIKE THAT.

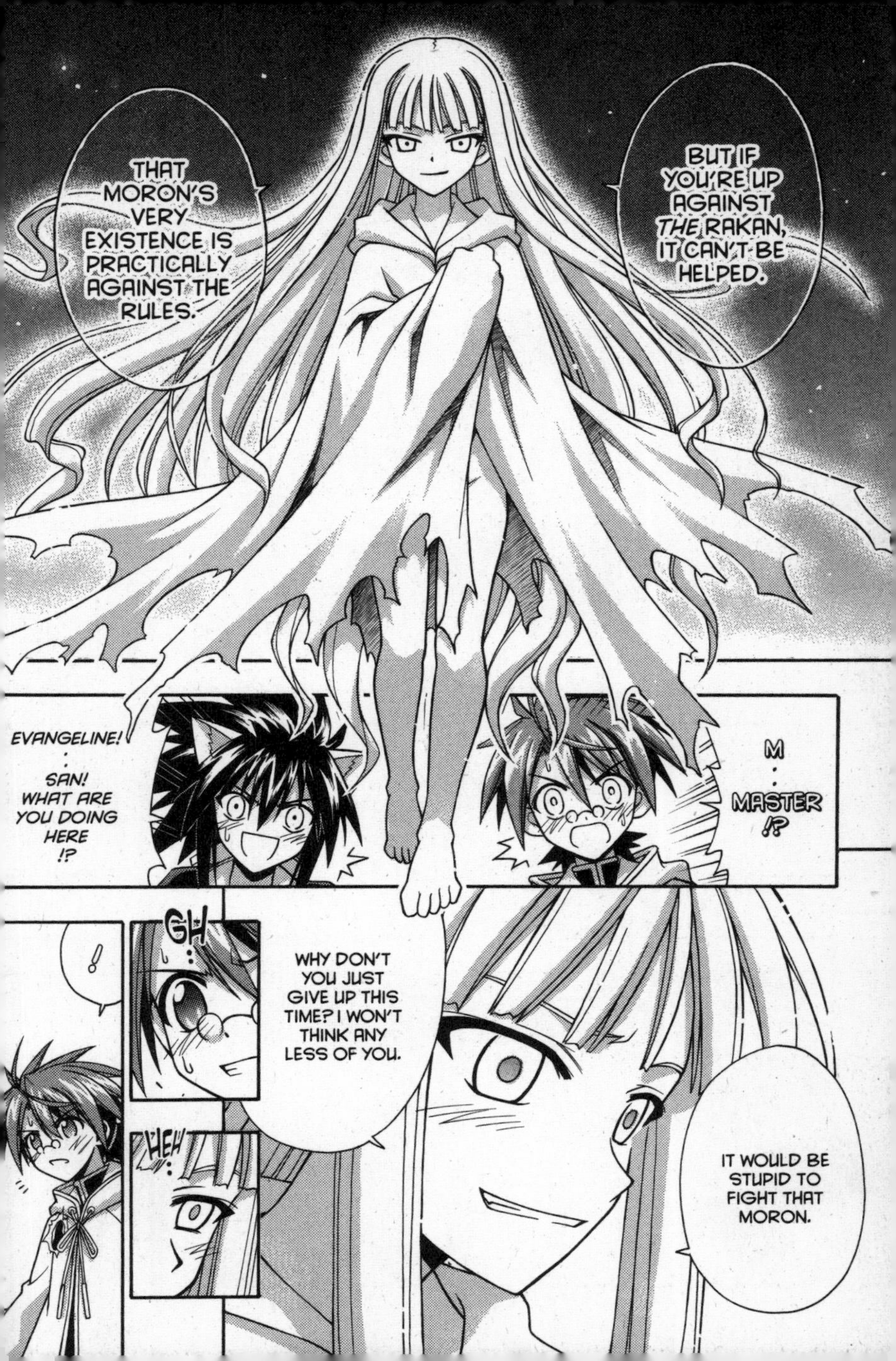
BUT IF YOU'RE UP AGAINST THE RAKAN, IT CAN'T BE HELPED.
THAT MORON'S VERY EXISTENCE IS PRACTICALLY AGAINST THE RULES.
M . . MASTER !?
EVANGELINE! . . SAN! WHAT ARE YOU DOING HERE !?
IT WOULD BE STUPID TO FIGHT THAT MORON.
WHY DON'T YOU JUST GIVE UP THIS TIME? I WON'T THINK ANY LESS OF YOU.
GH . .
HEH . .
!

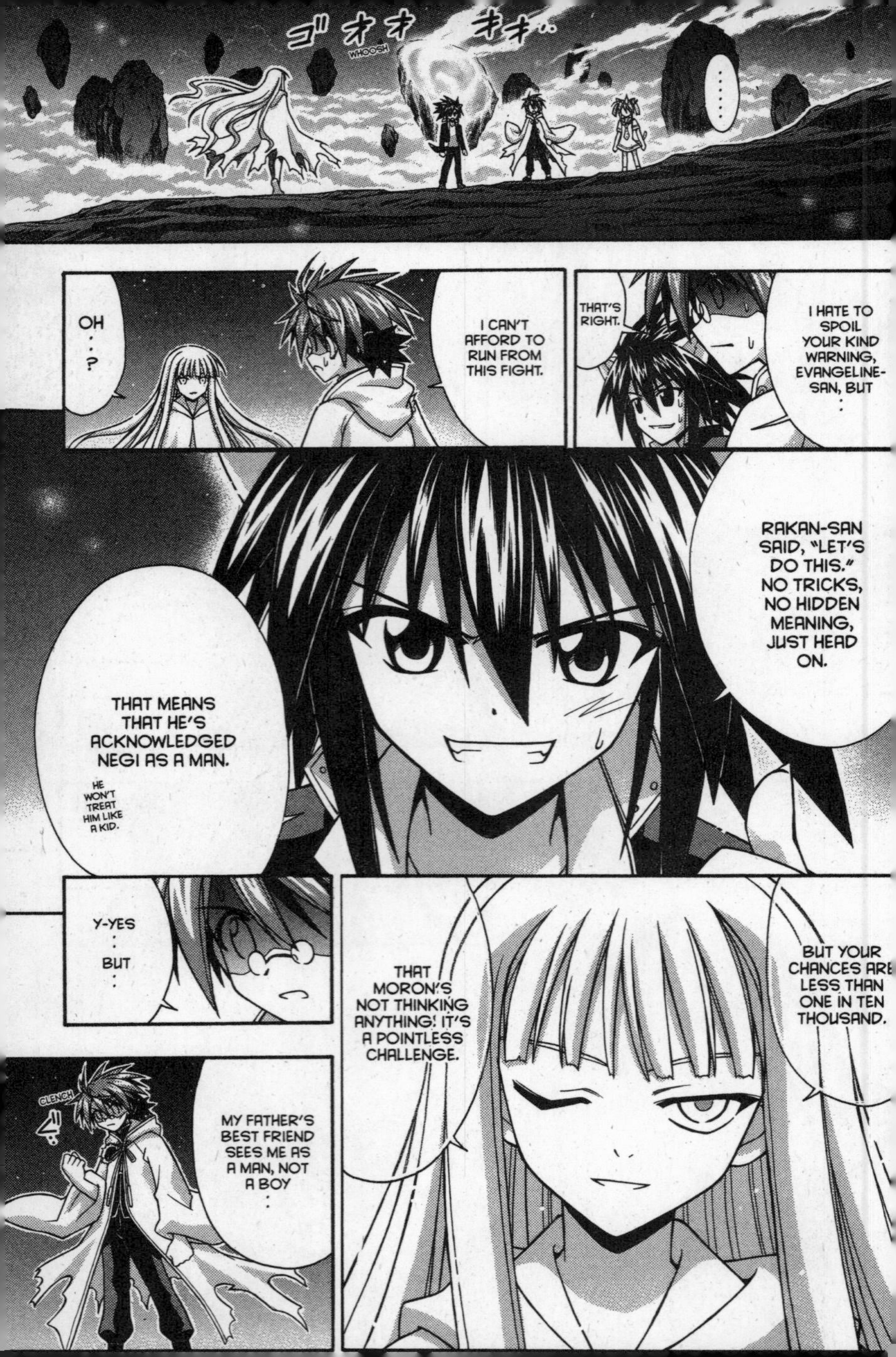
ゴオオ オオ
WHOOSH
. . . . . .
I HATE TO SPOIL YOUR KIND WARNING, EVANGELINE-SAN, BUT . . .
THAT'S RIGHT.
I CAN'T AFFORD TO RUN FROM THIS FIGHT.
OH . . . ?
RAKAN-SAN SAID, "LET'S DO THIS." NO TRICKS, NO HIDDEN MEANING, JUST HEAD ON.
THAT MEANS THAT HE'S ACKNOWLEDGED NEGI AS A MAN.
HE WON'T TREAT HIM LIKE A KID.
BUT YOUR CHANCES ARE LESS THAN ONE IN TEN THOUSAND.
THAT MORON'S NOT THINKING ANYTHING! IT'S A POINTLESS CHALLENGE.
Y-YES . . BUT . . .
CLENCH
MY FATHER'S BEST FRIEND SEES ME AS A MAN, NOT A BOY . . .

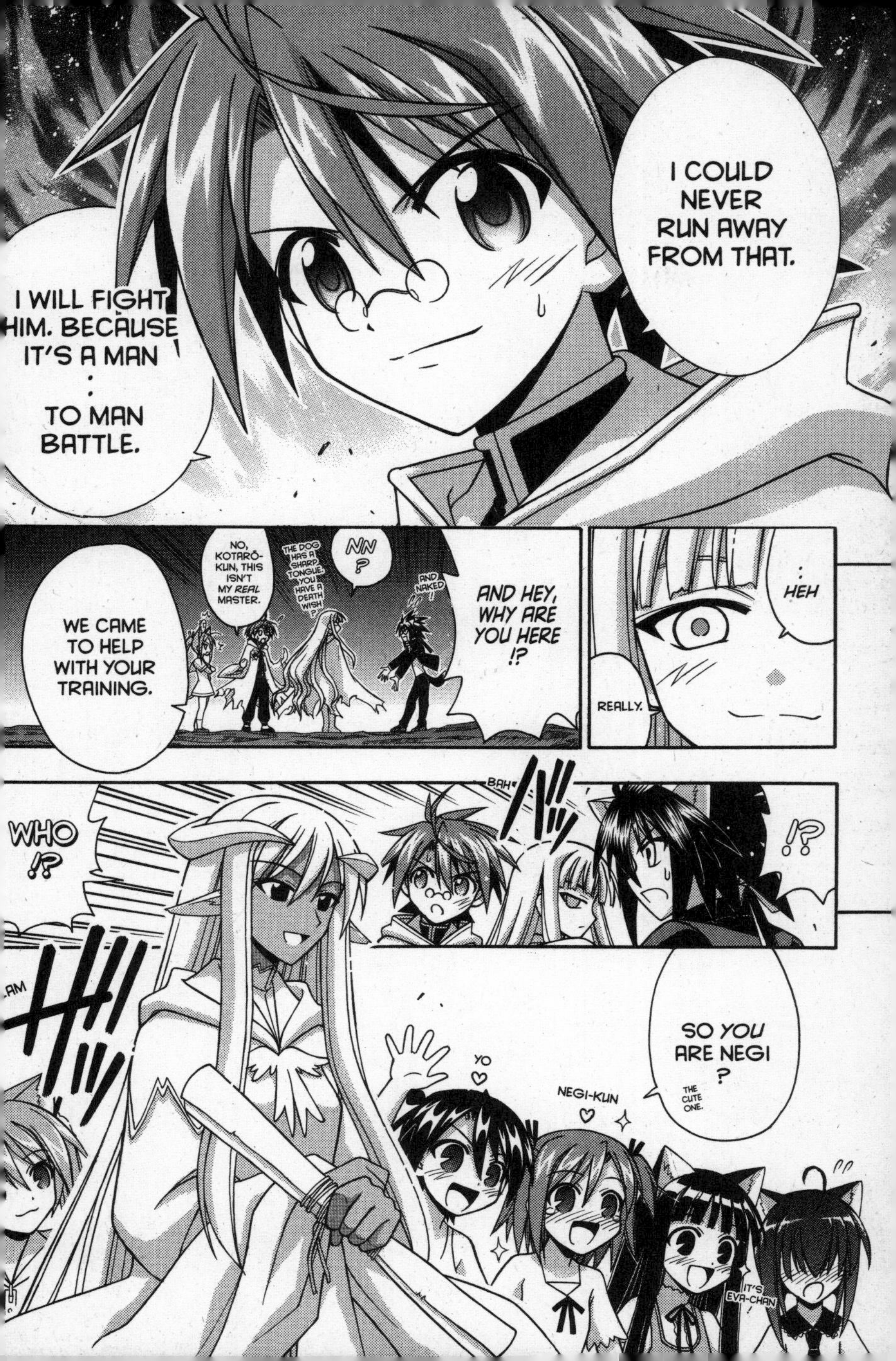
I COULD NEVER RUN AWAY FROM THAT.
I WILL FIGHT HIM. BECAUSE IT'S A MAN : TO MAN BATTLE.
: HEH
REALLY.
AND HEY, WHY ARE YOU HERE !?
AND NAKED !
NN ?
THE DOG HAS A SHARP TONGUE. YOU HAVE A DEATH WISH ?
NO, KOTARŌ-KUN, THIS ISN'T MY REAL MASTER.
WE CAME TO HELP WITH YOUR TRAINING.
!?
BAH
WHO !?
SO YOU ARE NEGI ?
THE CUTE ONE.
NEGI-KUN
YO
IT'S EVA-CHAN !

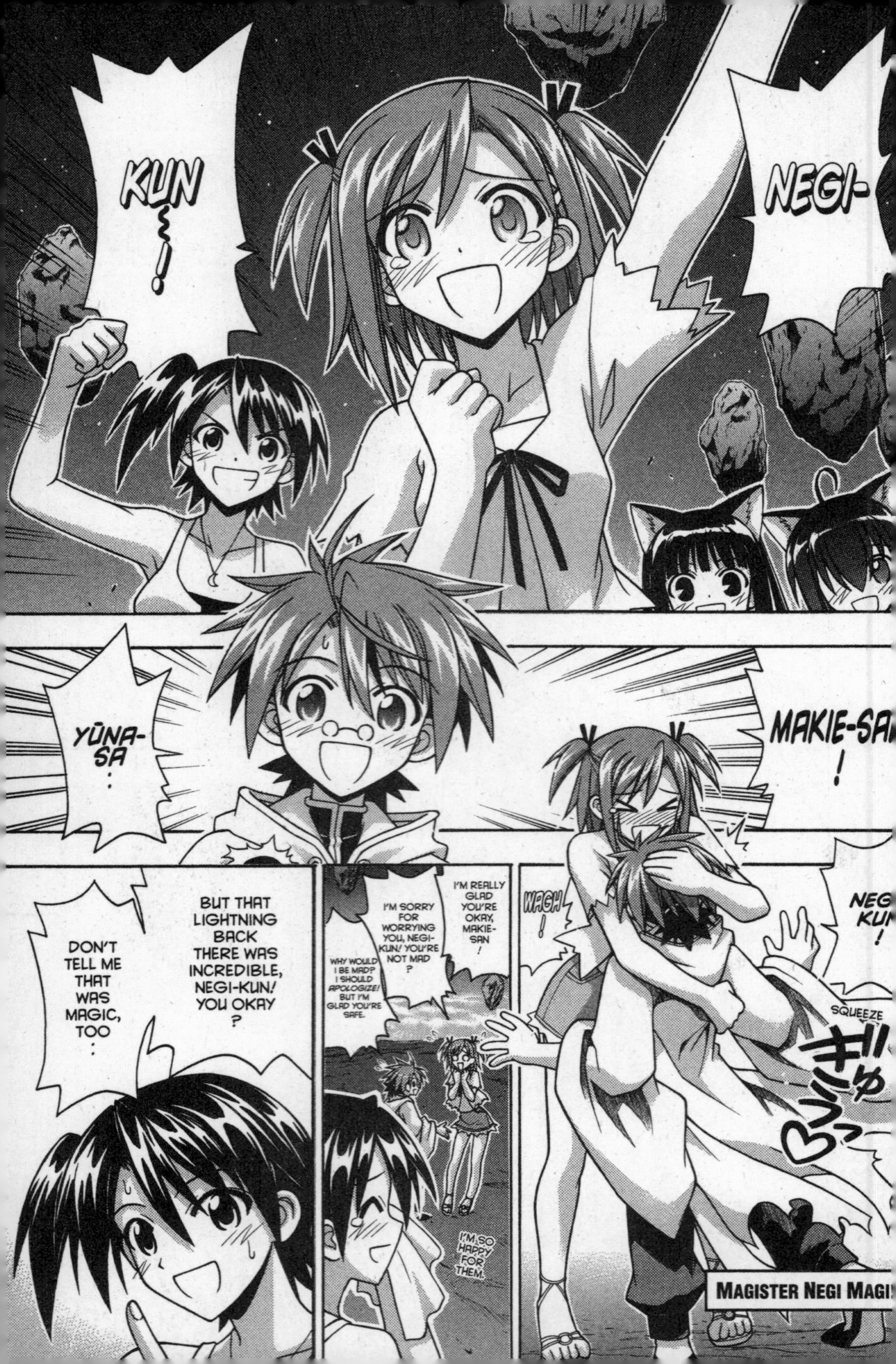
NEGI-
KUN~!
MAKIE-SA
!
YŪNA-SA...
NEGI-KUN!
WAGH!
SQUEEZE
ぎゅうっ♡
I'M REALLY GLAD YOU'RE OKAY, MAKIE-SAN!
I'M SORRY FOR WORRYING YOU, NEGI-KUN! YOU'RE NOT MAD?
WHY WOULD I BE MAD? I SHOULD APOLOGIZE! BUT I'M GLAD YOU'RE SAFE.
I'M SO HAPPY FOR THEM.
BUT THAT LIGHTNING BACK THERE WAS INCREDIBLE, NEGI-KUN! YOU OKAY?
DON'T TELL ME THAT WAS MAGIC, TOO...
MAGISTER NEGI MAGI

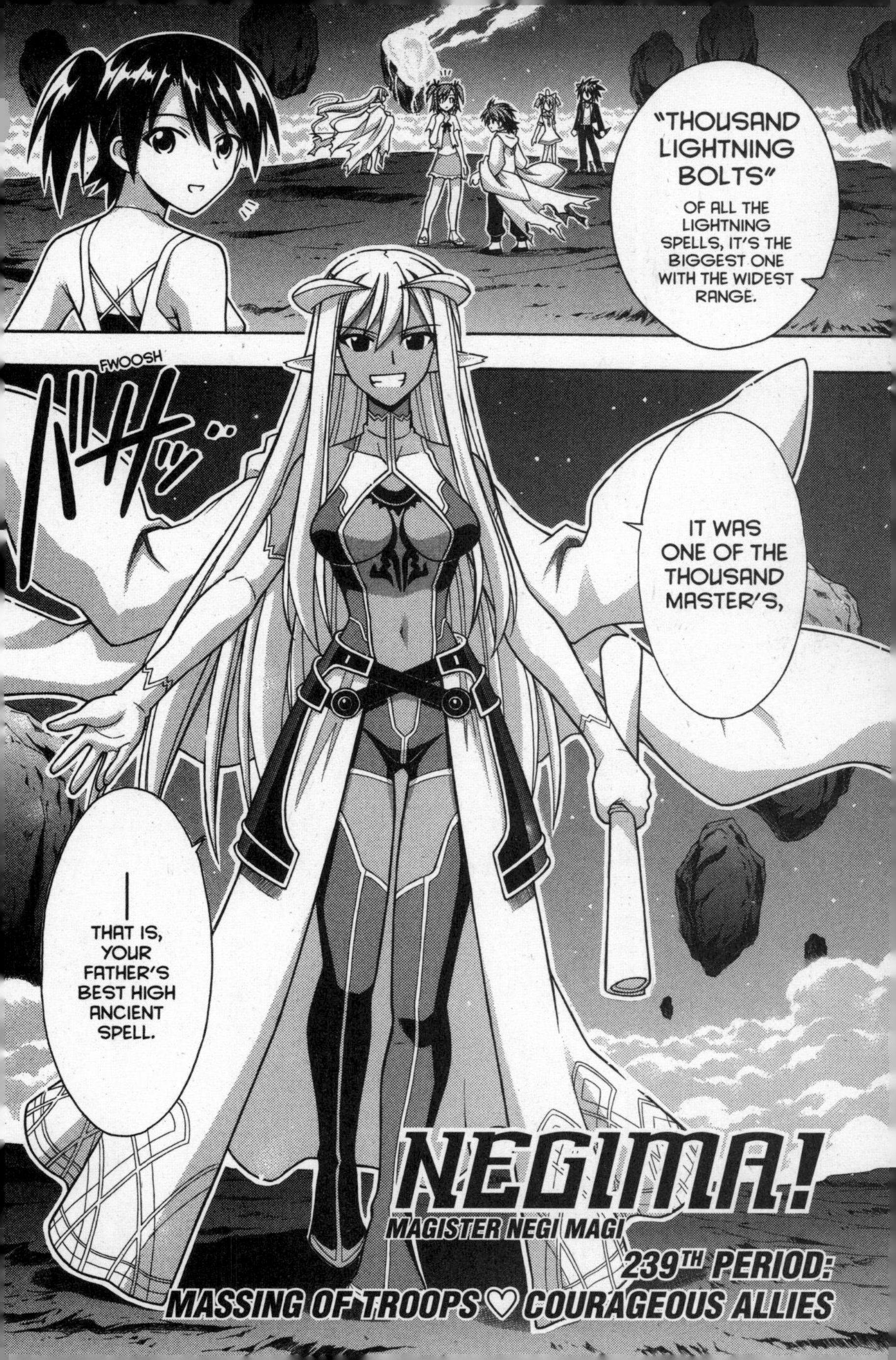
"THOUSAND LIGHTNING BOLTS" OF ALL THE LIGHTNING SPELLS, IT'S THE BIGGEST ONE WITH THE WIDEST RANGE.
IT WAS ONE OF THE THOUSAND MASTER'S,
FWOOSH
—THAT IS, YOUR FATHER'S BEST HIGH ANCIENT SPELL.
NEGIMA!
MAGISTER NEGI MAGI
239TH PERIOD:
MASSING OF TROOPS ♥ COURAGEOUS ALLIES

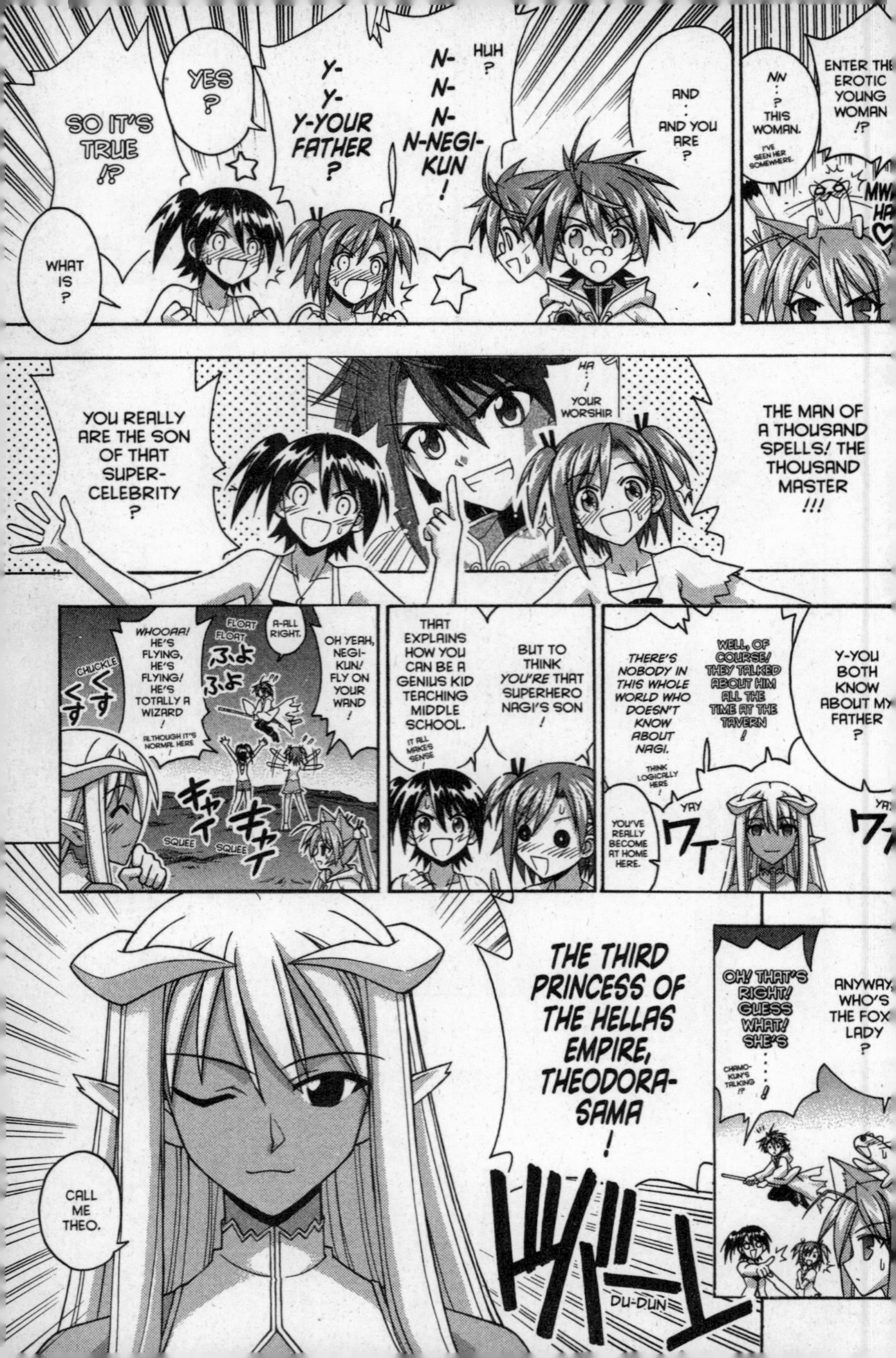

ENTER THE EROTIC YOUNG WOMAN !?
NN . . . ? THIS WOMAN.
I'VE SEEN HER SOMEWHERE.
MWA HA ♥
AND . . . AND YOU ARE ?
HUH ?
N-N-N-N-NEGI-KUN !
Y-Y-Y-YOUR FATHER ?
YES ?
SO IT'S TRUE !?
WHAT IS ?
THE MAN OF A THOUSAND SPELLS! THE THOUSAND MASTER !!!
HA ! YOUR WORSHIP.
YOU REALLY ARE THE SON OF THAT SUPER-CELEBRITY ?
Y-YOU BOTH KNOW ABOUT MY FATHER ?
YAY ワー
WELL, OF COURSE! THEY TALKED ABOUT HIM ALL THE TIME AT THE TAVERN !
THERE'S NOBODY IN THIS WHOLE WORLD WHO DOESN'T KNOW ABOUT NAGI.
YAY ワー
THINK LOGICALLY HERE !
YOU'VE REALLY BECOME AT HOME HERE.
BUT TO THINK YOU'RE THAT SUPERHERO NAGI'S SON !
THAT EXPLAINS HOW YOU CAN BE A GENIUS KID TEACHING MIDDLE SCHOOL.
IT ALL MAKES SENSE
OH YEAH, NEGI-KUN! FLY ON YOUR WAND !
A-ALL RIGHT.
FLOAT FLOAT ふよふよ
WHOOAA! HE'S FLYING, HE'S FLYING! HE'S TOTALLY A WIZARD !
ALTHOUGH IT'S NORMAL HERE !
CHUCKLE くすくす
キャイ キャイ SQUEE SQUEE
ANYWAY, WHO'S THE FOX LADY ?
OH! THAT'S RIGHT! GUESS WHAT! SHE'S
CHAMO-KUN'S TALKING !?
THE THIRD PRINCESS OF THE HELLAS EMPIRE, THEODORA-SAMA !
DU-DUN
CALL ME THEO.

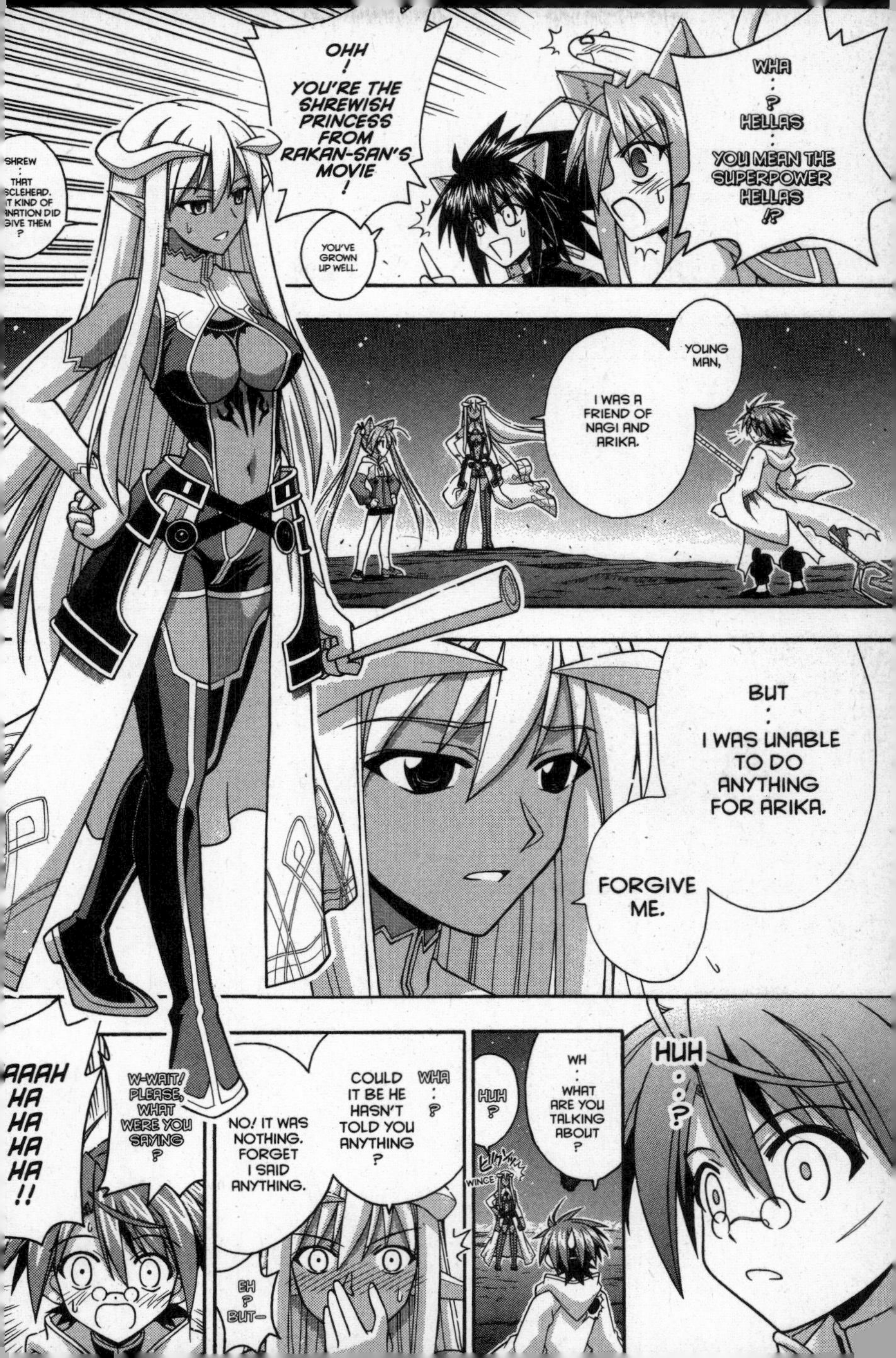
WHA... ? HELLAS... YOU MEAN THE SUPERPOWER HELLAS !?
YOU'VE GROWN UP WELL.
OHH! YOU'RE THE SHREWISH PRINCESS FROM RAKAN-SAN'S MOVIE!
SHREW: THAT SCLEHEAD. T KIND OF NATION DID GIVE THEM ?
YOUNG MAN,
I WAS A FRIEND OF NAGI AND ARIKA.
BUT... I WAS UNABLE TO DO ANYTHING FOR ARIKA.
FORGIVE ME.
HUH...?
WH... WHAT ARE YOU TALKING ABOUT?
HUH?
WINCE
WHA...?
COULD IT BE HE HASN'T TOLD YOU ANYTHING?
NO! IT WAS NOTHING. FORGET I SAID ANYTHING.
EH? BUT—
W-WAIT! PLEASE, WHAT WERE YOU SAYING?
AAAH HA HA HA HA!!

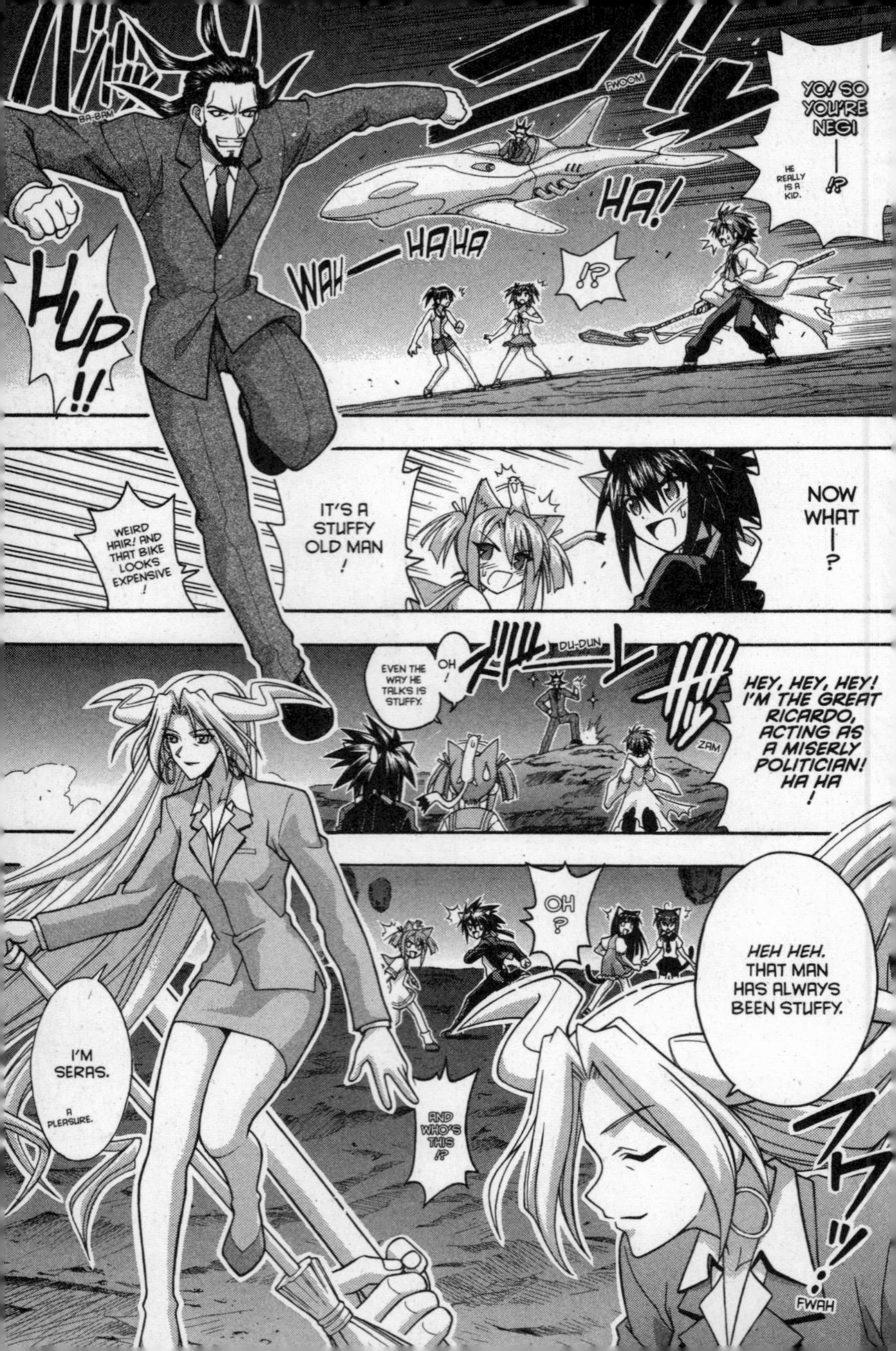
YO! SO YOU'RE NEGI—!?
HE REALLY IS A KID.
HA!
FWOOM
!?
WAH—HA HA
BA-BAM
HUP!!
NOW WHAT—?
IT'S A STUFFY OLD MAN!
WEIRD HAIR! AND THAT BIKE LOOKS EXPENSIVE!
HEY, HEY, HEY! I'M THE GREAT RICARDO, ACTING AS A MISERLY POLITICIAN! HA HA!
ZAM
DU-DUN
OH!
EVEN THE WAY HE TALKS IS STUFFY.
FWAH
HEH HEH. THAT MAN HAS ALWAYS BEEN STUFFY.
OH?
AND WHO'S THIS!?
I'M SERAS.
A PLEASURE.

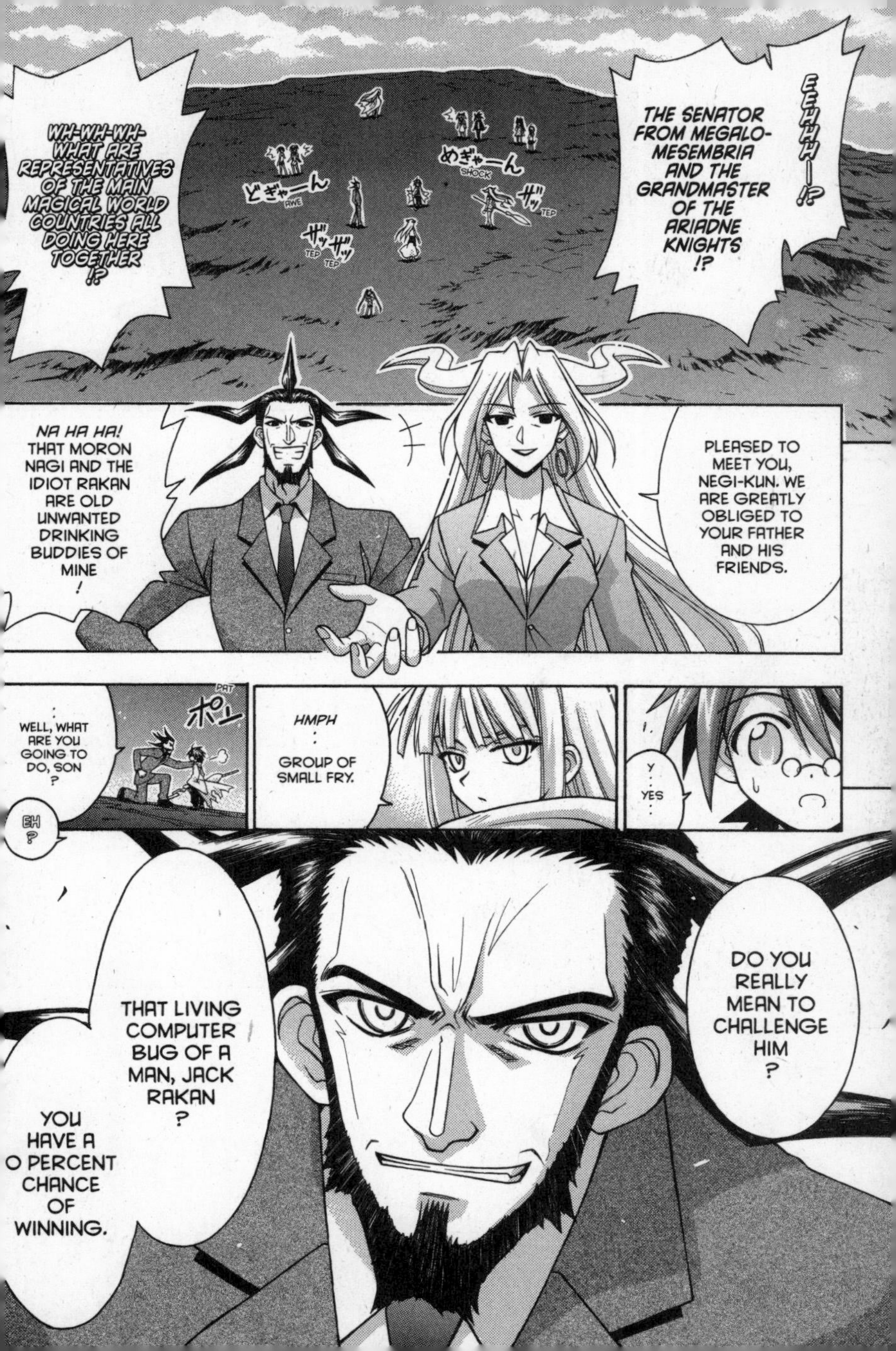
EEHHHH—!?
THE SENATOR FROM MEGALO-MESEMBRIA AND THE GRANDMASTER OF THE ARIADNE KNIGHTS!?
めぎゃーん
SHOCK
ザッ
TEP
どぎゃーん
AWE
ザッザッ
TEP TEP
WH-WH-WH-WHAT ARE REPRESENTATIVES OF THE MAIN MAGICAL WORLD COUNTRIES ALL DOING HERE TOGETHER!?
PLEASED TO MEET YOU, NEGI-KUN. WE ARE GREATLY OBLIGED TO YOUR FATHER AND HIS FRIENDS.
NA HA HA! THAT MORON NAGI AND THE IDIOT RAKAN ARE OLD UNWANTED DRINKING BUDDIES OF MINE!
Y... YES...
HMPH: GROUP OF SMALL FRY.
PAT
ポッ
: WELL, WHAT ARE YOU GOING TO DO, SON?
EH?
DO YOU REALLY MEAN TO CHALLENGE HIM?
THAT LIVING COMPUTER BUG OF A MAN, JACK RAKAN?
YOU HAVE A 0 PERCENT CHANCE OF WINNING.

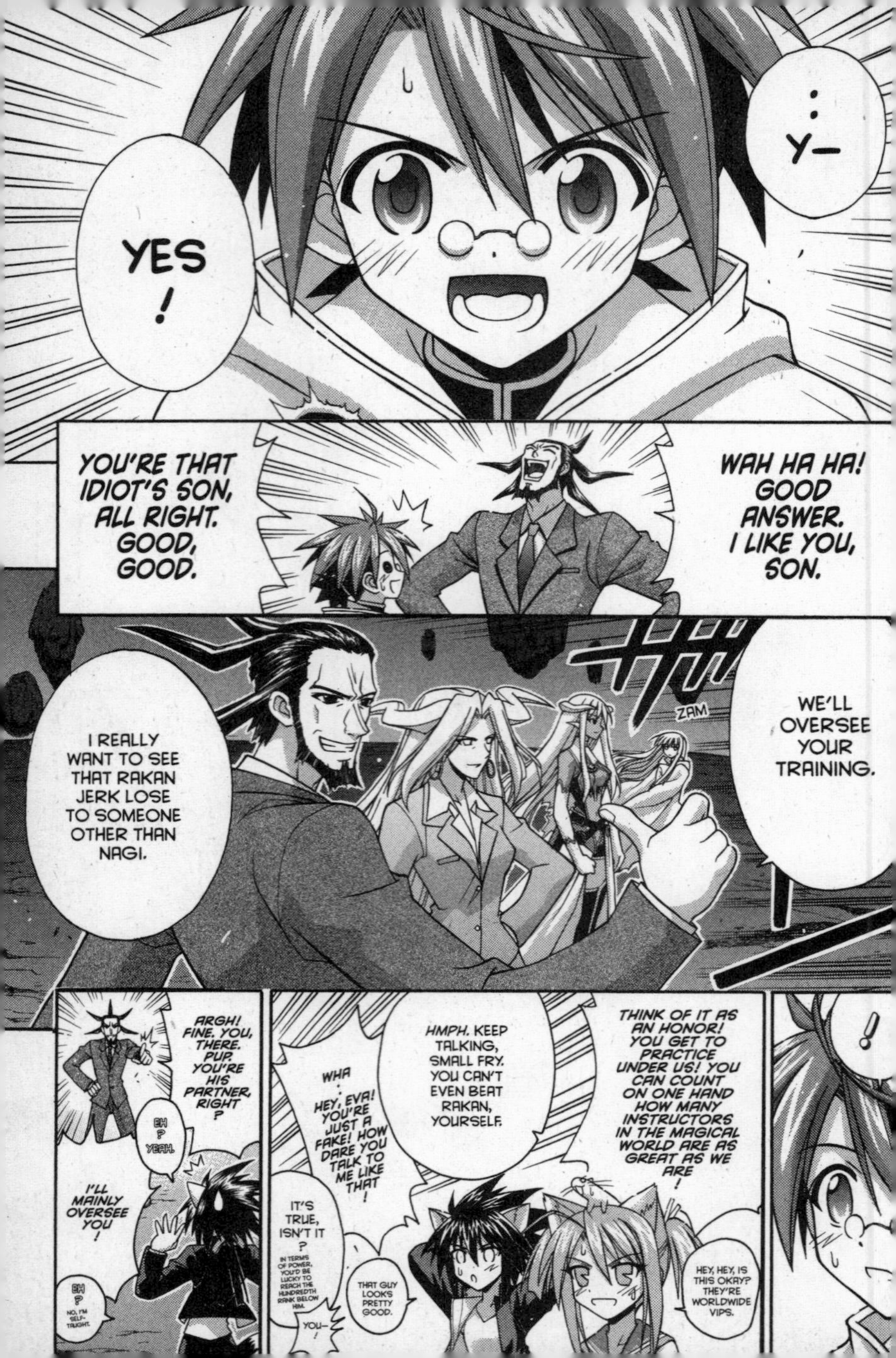

: Y—
YES !
WAH HA HA! GOOD ANSWER. I LIKE YOU, SON.
YOU'RE THAT IDIOT'S SON, ALL RIGHT. GOOD, GOOD.
WE'LL OVERSEE YOUR TRAINING.
ZAM
I REALLY WANT TO SEE THAT RAKAN JERK LOSE TO SOMEONE OTHER THAN NAGI.
!
THINK OF IT AS AN HONOR! YOU GET TO PRACTICE UNDER US! YOU CAN COUNT ON ONE HAND HOW MANY INSTRUCTORS IN THE MAGICAL WORLD ARE AS GREAT AS WE ARE !
HMPH. KEEP TALKING, SMALL FRY. YOU CAN'T EVEN BEAT RAKAN, YOURSELF.
WHA :
HEY, EVA! YOU'RE JUST A FAKE! HOW DARE YOU TALK TO ME LIKE THAT !
HEY, HEY, IS THIS OKAY? THEY'RE WORLDWIDE VIPS.
THAT GUY LOOKS PRETTY GOOD.
IT'S TRUE, ISN'T IT ?
IN TERMS OF POWER, YOU'D BE LUCKY TO REACH THE HUNDREDTH RANK BELOW HIM.
YOU—
ARGH! FINE. YOU, THERE. PUP. YOU'RE HIS PARTNER, RIGHT ?
EH ? YEAH.
I'LL MAINLY OVERSEE YOU !
EH ?
NO, I'M SELF-TAUGHT.

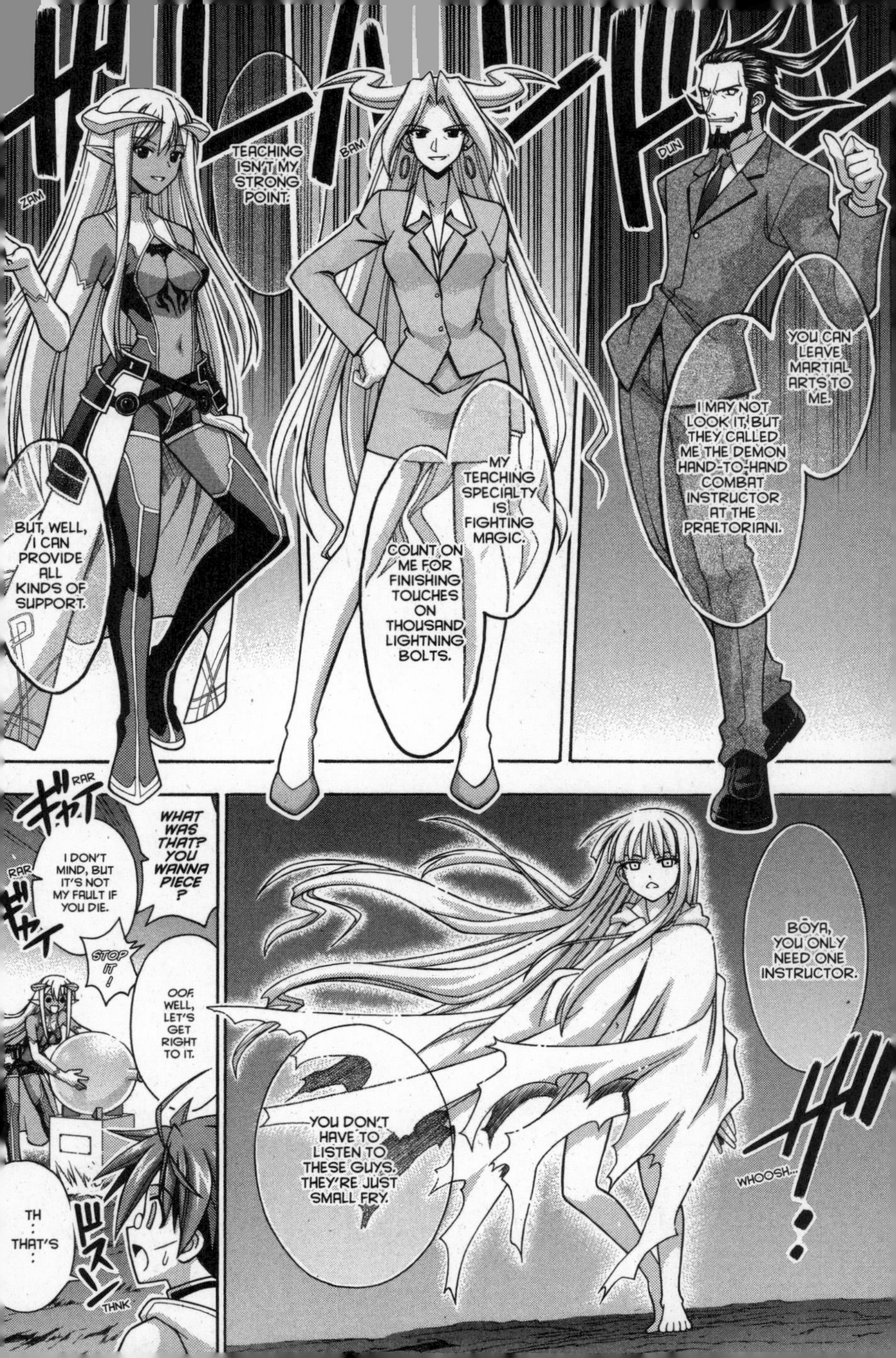
DUN
YOU CAN LEAVE MARTIAL ARTS TO ME.
I MAY NOT LOOK IT, BUT THEY CALLED ME THE DEMON HAND-TO-HAND COMBAT INSTRUCTOR AT THE PRAETORIANI.
BAM
MY TEACHING SPECIALTY IS FIGHTING MAGIC.
COUNT ON ME FOR FINISHING TOUCHES ON THOUSAND LIGHTNING BOLTS.
ZAM
TEACHING ISN'T MY STRONG POINT.
BUT, WELL, I CAN PROVIDE ALL KINDS OF SUPPORT.
BŌYA, YOU ONLY NEED ONE INSTRUCTOR.
WHOOSH...
YOU DON'T HAVE TO LISTEN TO THESE GUYS. THEY'RE JUST SMALL FRY.
RAR
RAR
WHAT WAS THAT? YOU WANNA PIECE?
I DON'T MIND, BUT IT'S NOT MY FAULT IF YOU DIE.
STOP IT!
OOF. WELL, LET'S GET RIGHT TO IT.
THNK
TH... THAT'S...

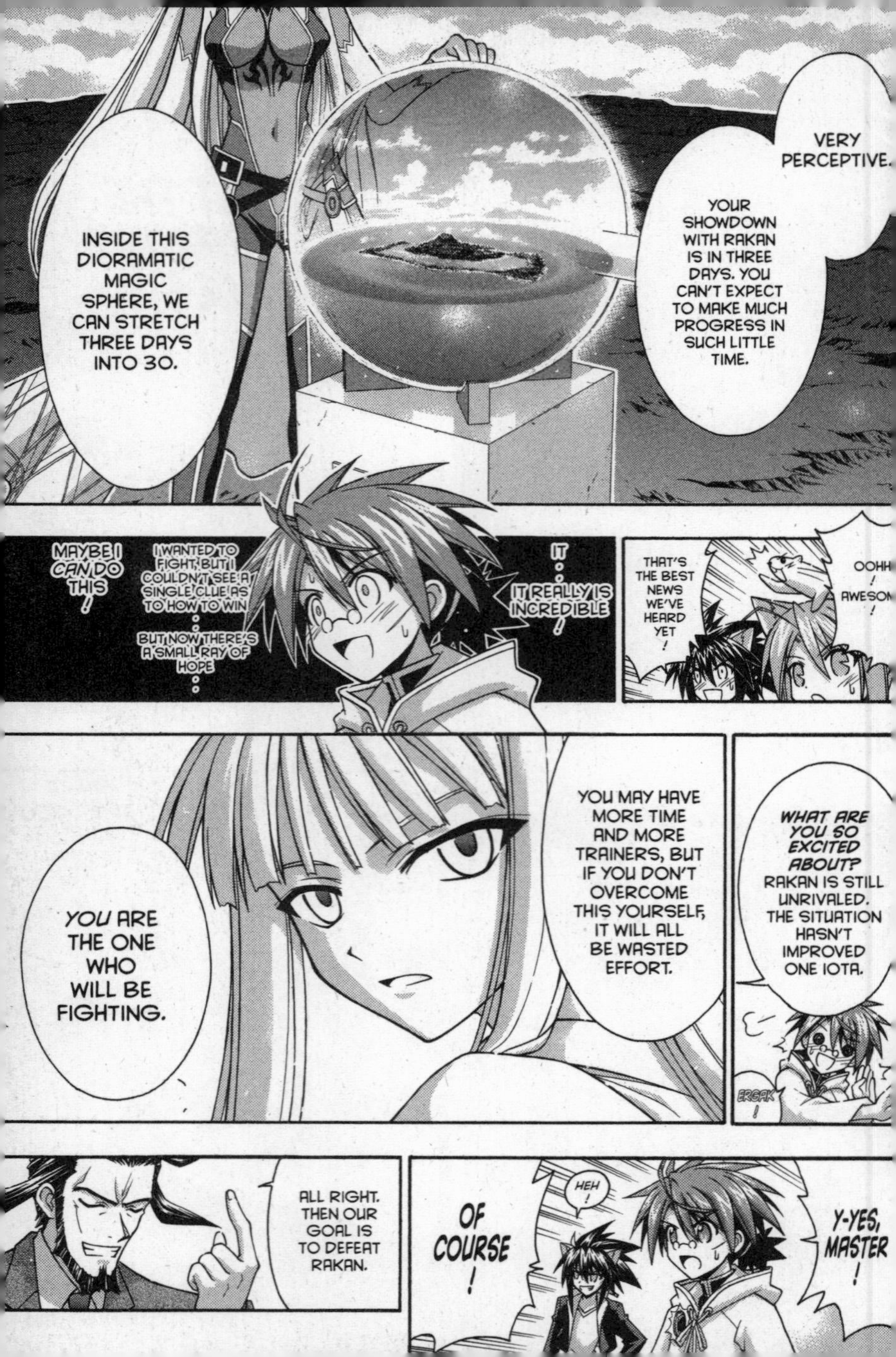
VERY PERCEPTIVE.
YOUR SHOWDOWN WITH RAKAN IS IN THREE DAYS. YOU CAN'T EXPECT TO MAKE MUCH PROGRESS IN SUCH LITTLE TIME.
INSIDE THIS DIORAMATIC MAGIC SPHERE, WE CAN STRETCH THREE DAYS INTO 30.
OOHH! AWESOM!
THAT'S THE BEST NEWS WE'VE HEARD YET!
IT... IT REALLY IS INCREDIBLE!
I WANTED TO FIGHT, BUT I COULDN'T SEE A SINGLE CLUE AS TO HOW TO WIN...
BUT NOW THERE'S A SMALL RAY OF HOPE...
MAYBE I CAN DO THIS!
WHAT ARE YOU SO EXCITED ABOUT? RAKAN IS STILL UNRIVALED. THE SITUATION HASN'T IMPROVED ONE IOTA.
ERGAK!
YOU MAY HAVE MORE TIME AND MORE TRAINERS, BUT IF YOU DON'T OVERCOME THIS YOURSELF, IT WILL ALL BE WASTED EFFORT.
YOU ARE THE ONE WHO WILL BE FIGHTING.
Y-YES, MASTER!
HEH!
OF COURSE!
ALL RIGHT. THEN OUR GOAL IS TO DEFEAT RAKAN.

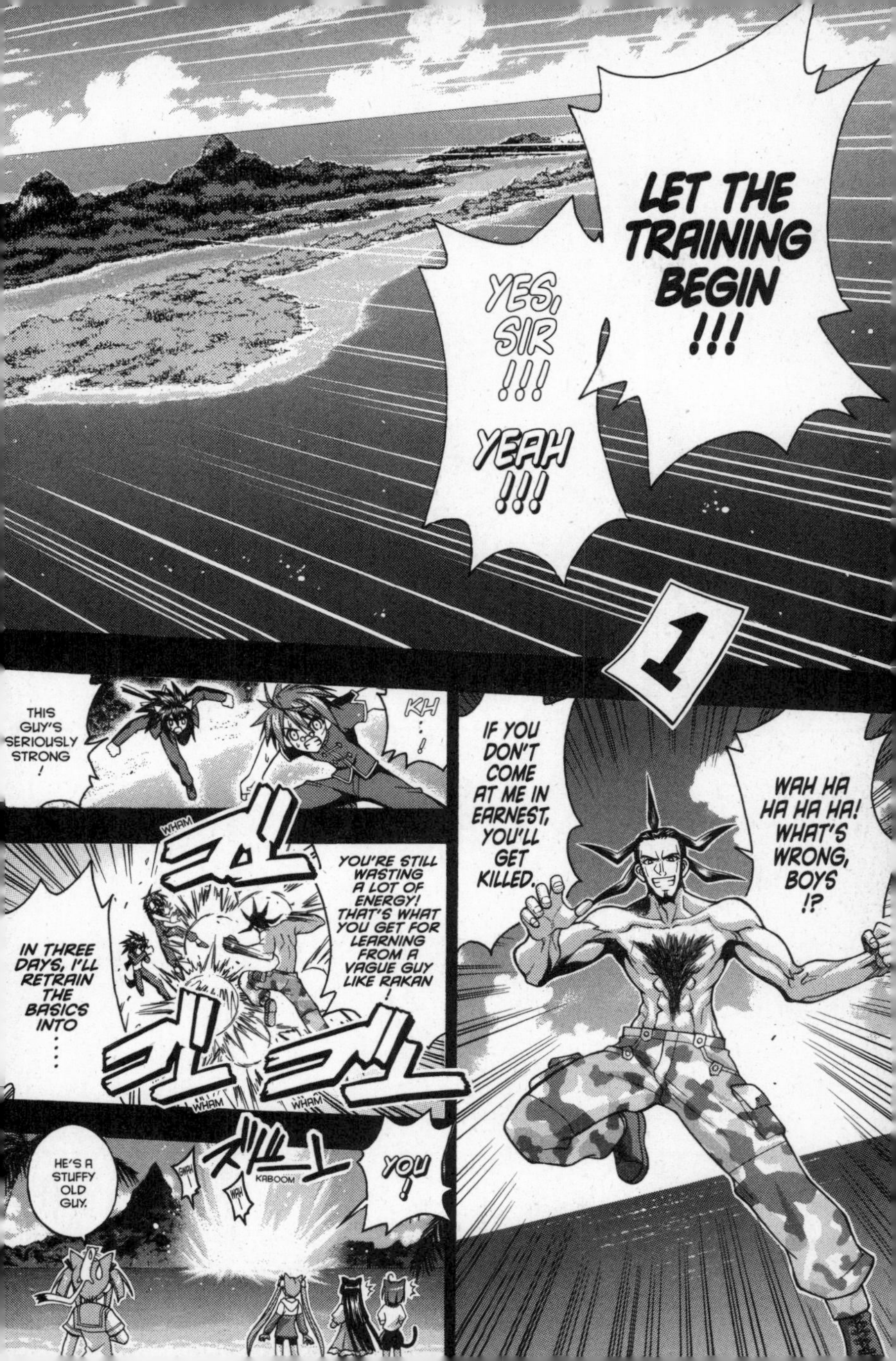
LET THE TRAINING BEGIN!!!
YES, SIR!!!
YEAH!!!
1
WAH HA HA HA HA! WHAT'S WRONG, BOYS!?
IF YOU DON'T COME AT ME IN EARNEST, YOU'LL GET KILLED.
KH...!
THIS GUY'S SERIOUSLY STRONG!
WHAM
YOU'RE STILL WASTING A LOT OF ENERGY! THAT'S WHAT YOU GET FOR LEARNING FROM A VAGUE GUY LIKE RAKAN!
IN THREE DAYS, I'LL RETRAIN THE BASICS INTO.....
WHAM
WHAM
YOU!
KABOOM
WAH!
GWAH!
HE'S A STUFFY OLD GUY.

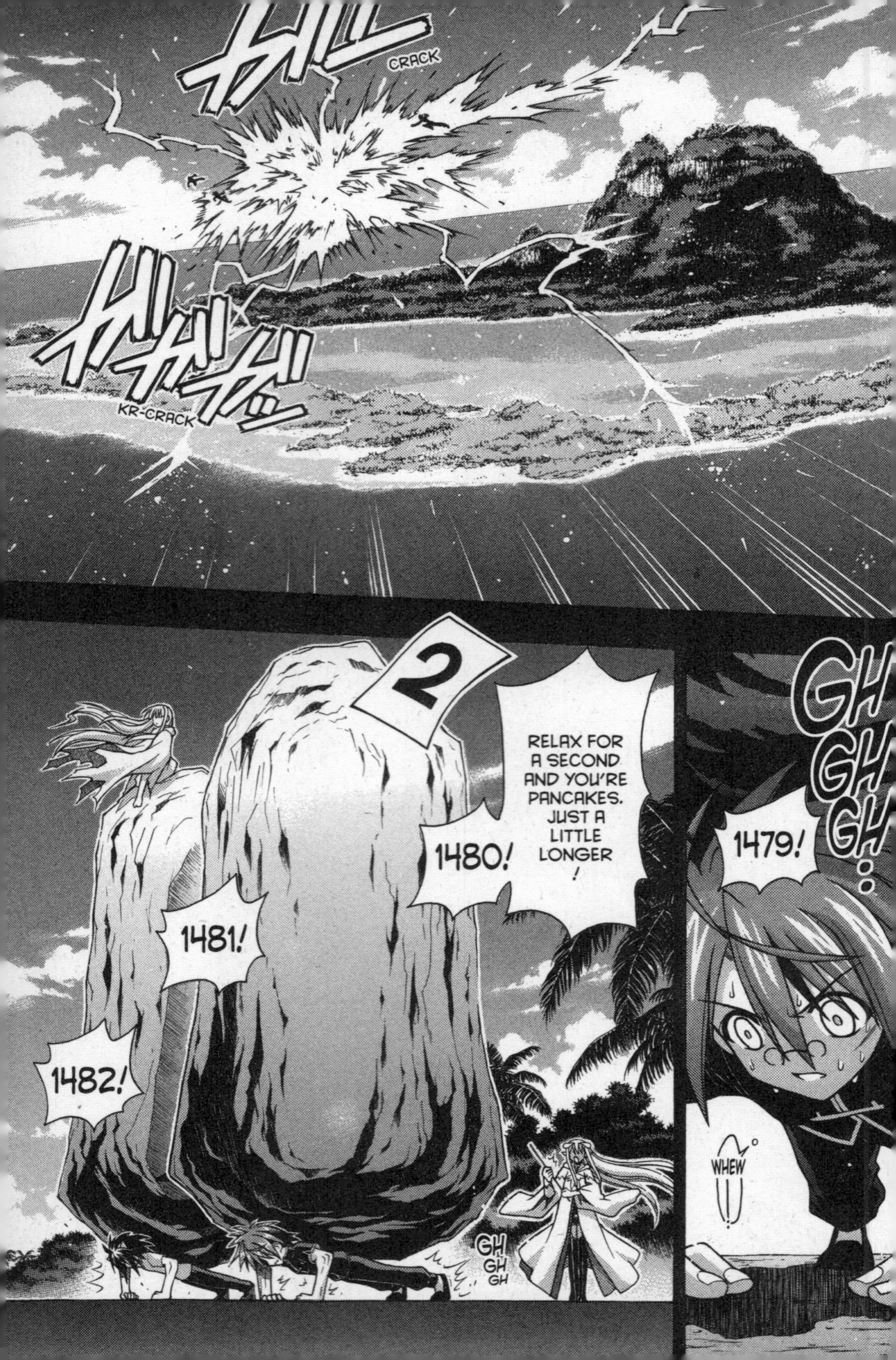
CRACK
KR-CRACK
GH GH GH...
1479!
WHEW
2
RELAX FOR A SECOND AND YOU'RE PANCAKES. JUST A LITTLE LONGER!
1480!
1481!
1482!
GH GH GH

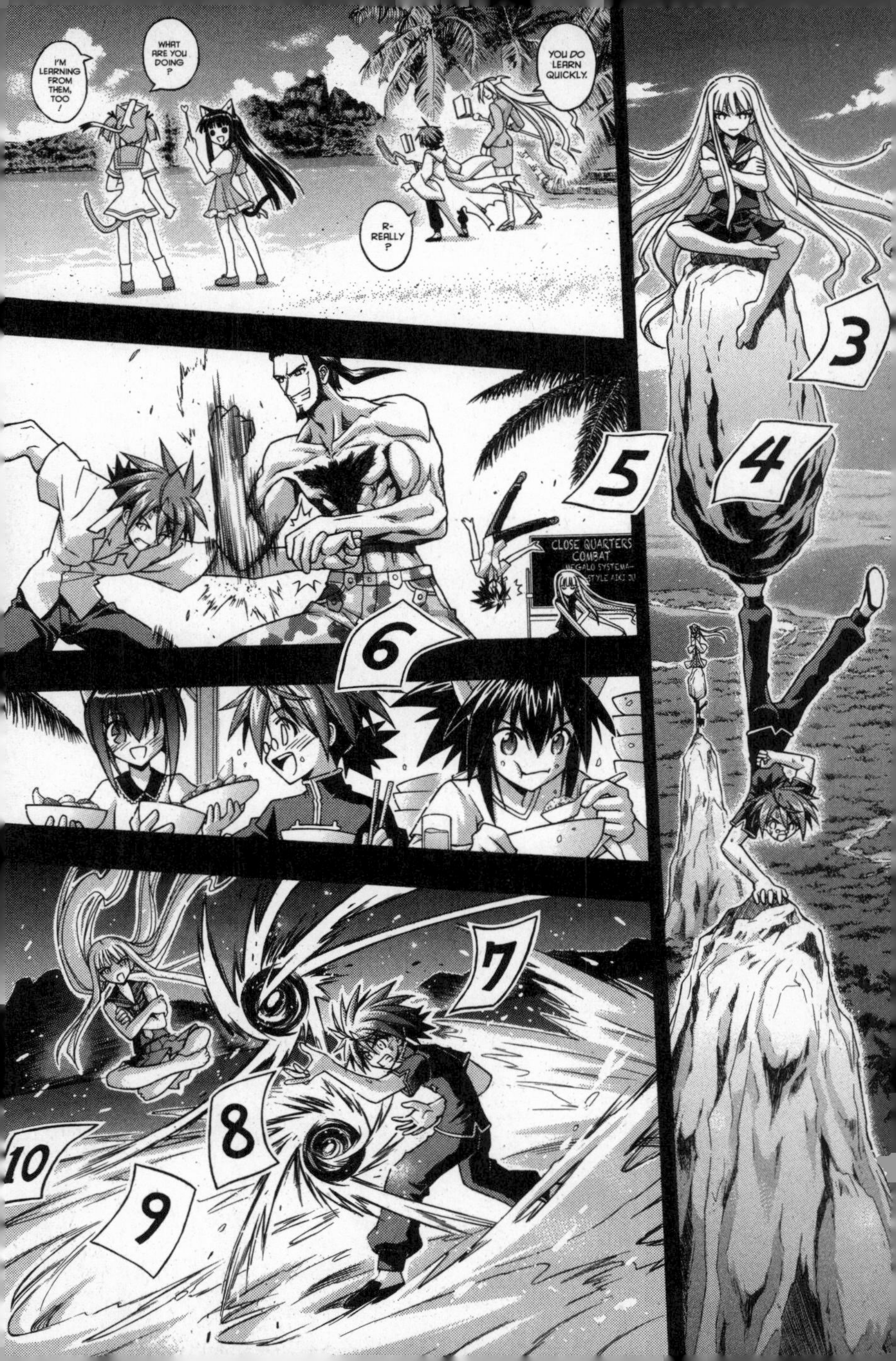
3
4
YOU DO LEARN QUICKLY.
R-REALLY?
WHAT ARE YOU DOING?
I'M LEARNING FROM THEM, TOO!
5
CLOSE QUARTERS COMBAT
MEGALO SYSTEMA-STYLE AIKI JU
6
7
8
9
10

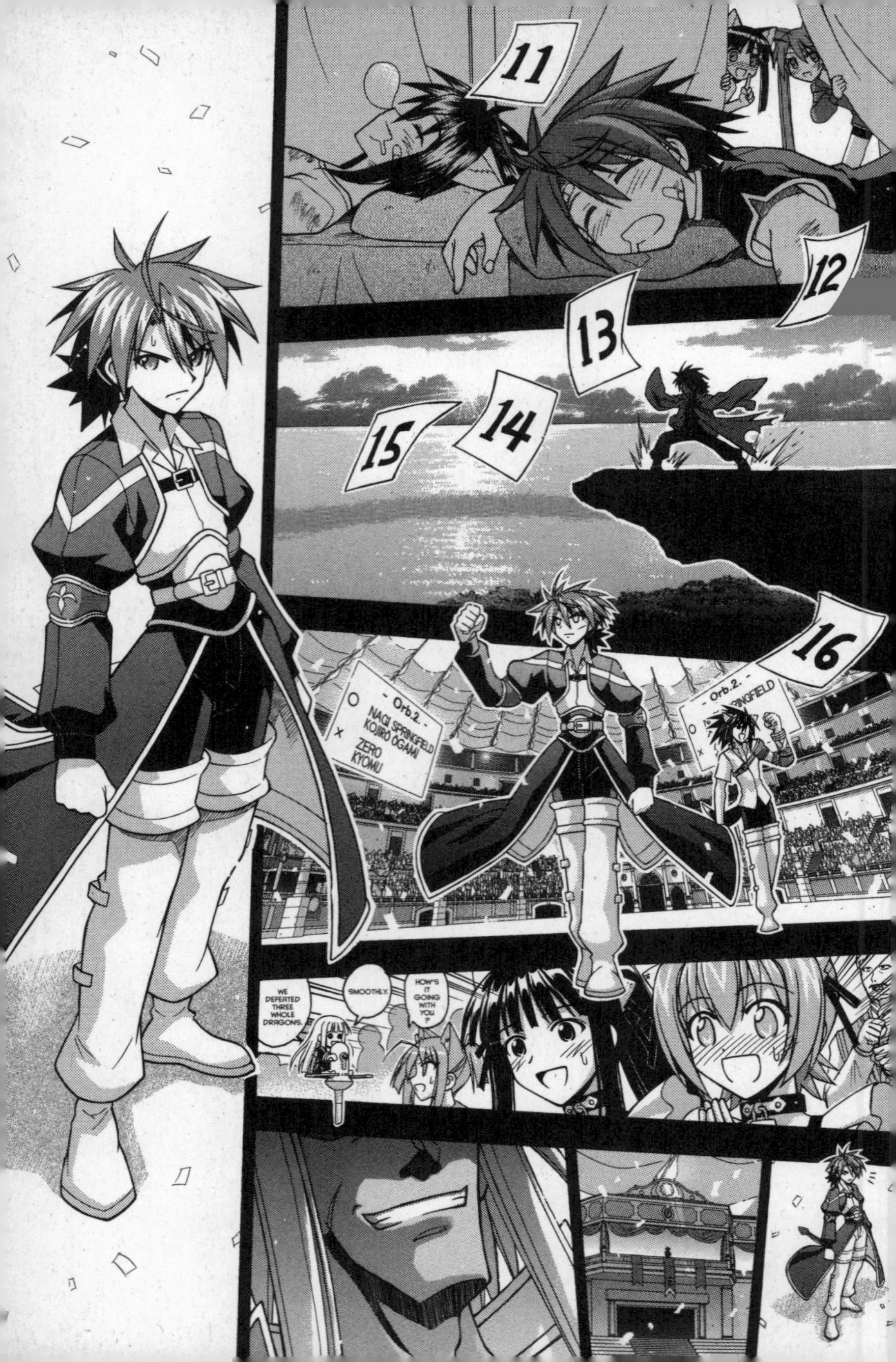
11
12
13
14
15
16
- Orb.2. -
- Orb.2. -
NAGI SPRINGFIELD
KOJIRŌ ŌGAMI
ZERO
KYOMU
HOW'S IT GOING WITH YOU?
SMOOTHLY.
WE DEFEATED THREE WHOLE DRAGONS.

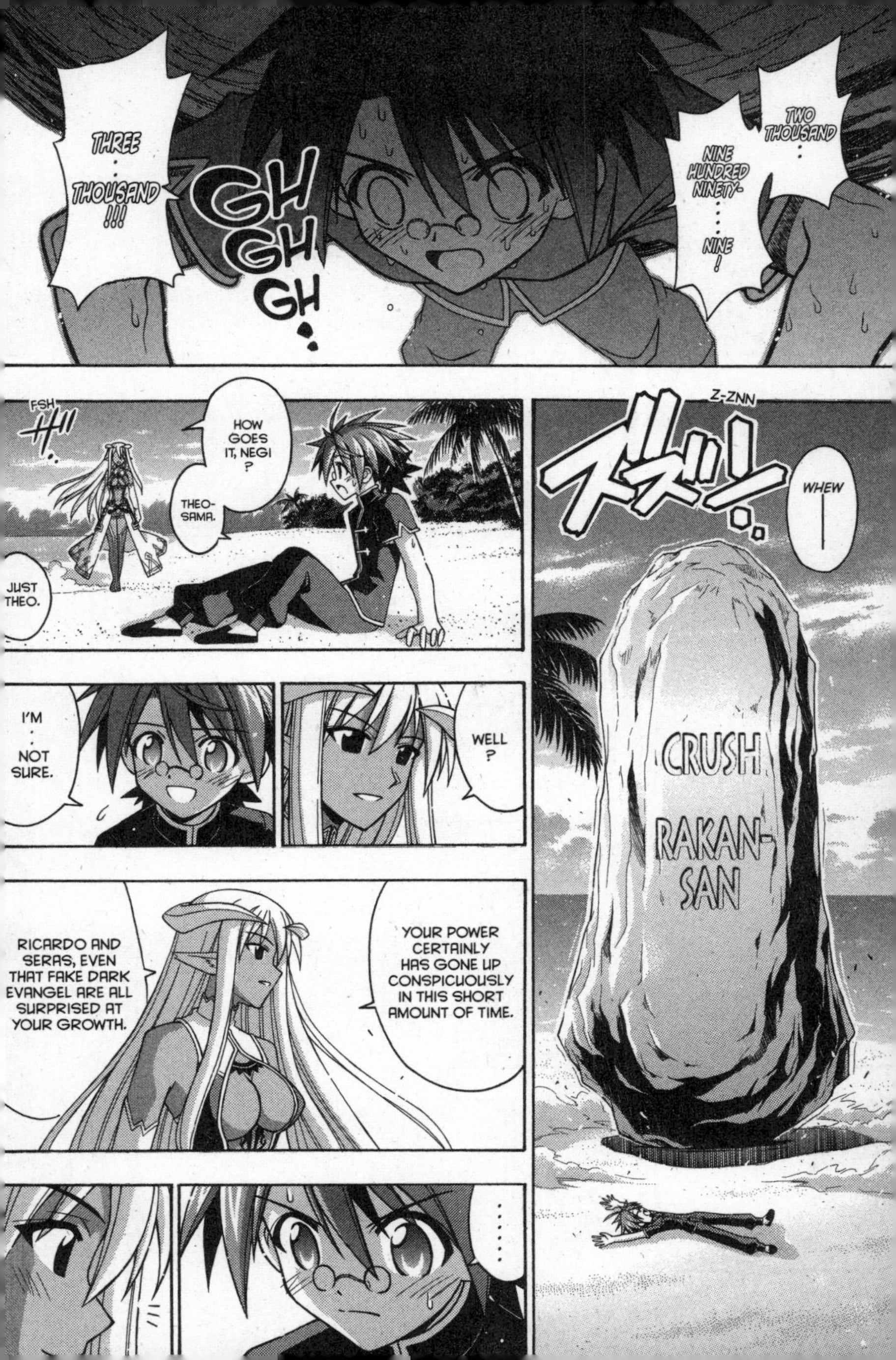
TWO THOUSAND . . .
NINE HUNDRED NINETY- . . . . NINE !
GH GH GH
THREE . . . THOUSAND !!!
Z-ZNN
WHEW
CRUSH RAKAN-SAN
HOW GOES IT, NEGI ?
THEO-SAMA.
FSH
JUST THEO.
WELL ?
I'M . . NOT SURE.
YOUR POWER CERTAINLY HAS GONE UP CONSPICUOUSLY IN THIS SHORT AMOUNT OF TIME.
RICARDO AND SERAS, EVEN THAT FAKE DARK EVANGEL ARE ALL SURPRISED AT YOUR GROWTH.
. . . . . .

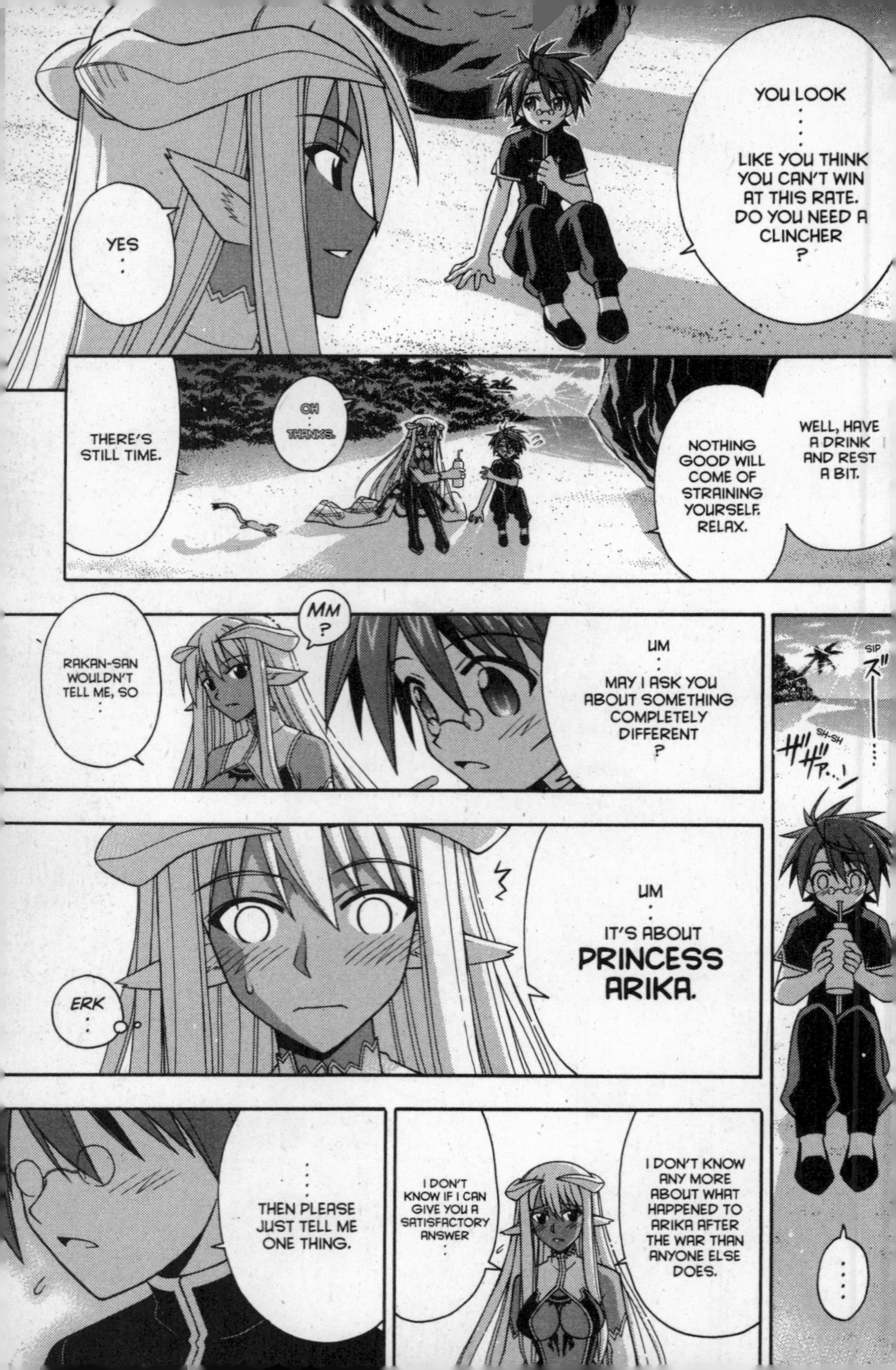
YOU LOOK... LIKE YOU THINK YOU CAN'T WIN AT THIS RATE. DO YOU NEED A CLINCHER?
YES...
WELL, HAVE A DRINK AND REST A BIT.
NOTHING GOOD WILL COME OF STRAINING YOURSELF. RELAX.
OH... THANKS.
THERE'S STILL TIME.
SIP
ズー…
SH-SH
ザザァ…!
UM... MAY I ASK YOU ABOUT SOMETHING COMPLETELY DIFFERENT?
MM?
RAKAN-SAN WOULDN'T TELL ME, SO...
UM... IT'S ABOUT PRINCESS ARIKA.
ERK...
....
I DON'T KNOW ANY MORE ABOUT WHAT HAPPENED TO ARIKA AFTER THE WAR THAN ANYONE ELSE DOES.
I DON'T KNOW IF I CAN GIVE YOU A SATISFACTORY ANSWER...
...THEN PLEASE JUST TELL ME ONE THING.

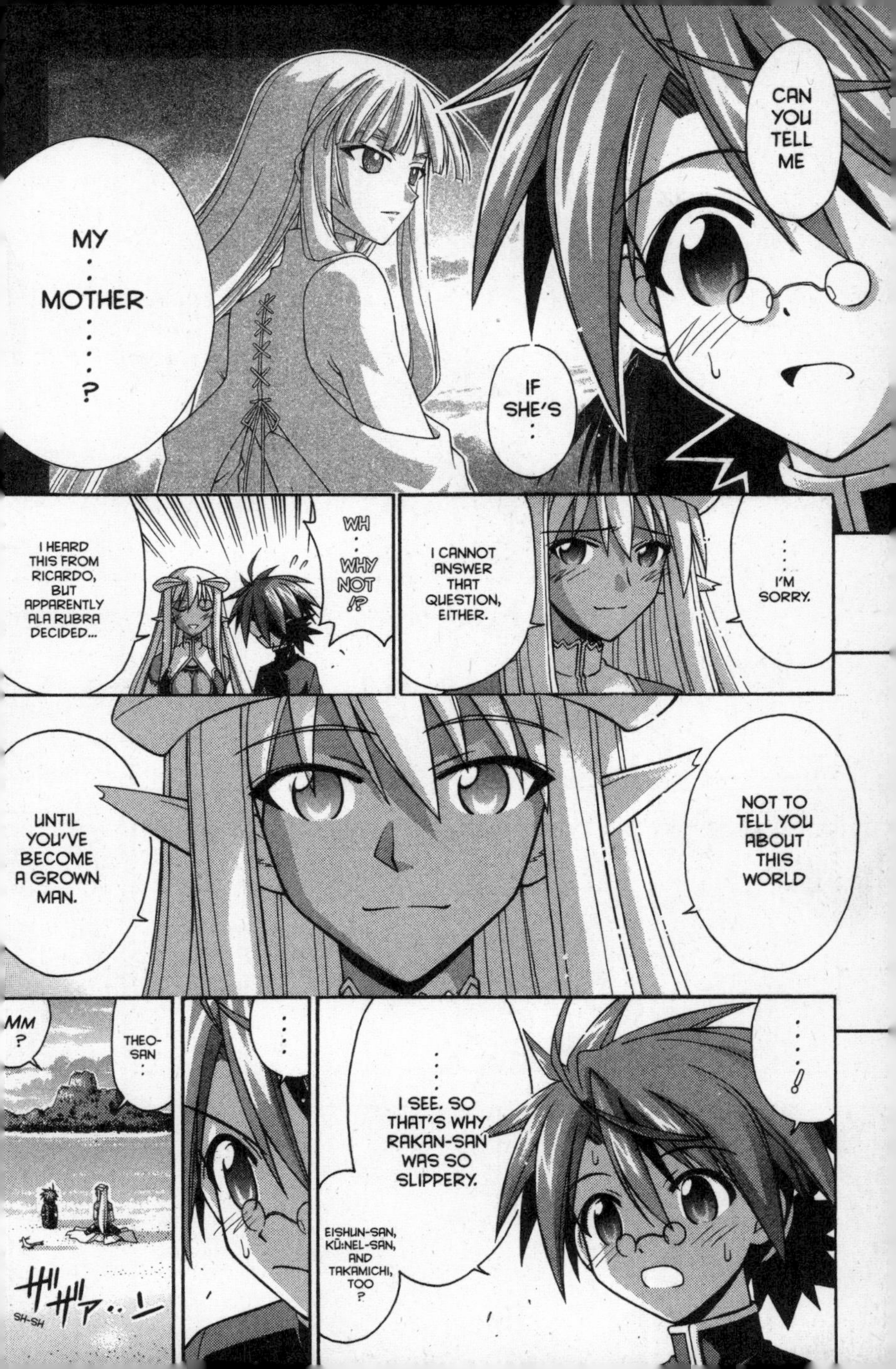
CAN YOU TELL ME
IF SHE'S . . .
MY . . . MOTHER . . . . . ?
. . . I'M SORRY.
I CANNOT ANSWER THAT QUESTION, EITHER.
WH . . . WHY NOT !?
I HEARD THIS FROM RICARDO, BUT APPARENTLY ALA RUBRA DECIDED...
NOT TO TELL YOU ABOUT THIS WORLD
UNTIL YOU'VE BECOME A GROWN MAN.
. . . . !
. . . I SEE. SO THAT'S WHY RAKAN-SAN WAS SO SLIPPERY.
EISHUN-SAN, KŪ:NEL-SAN, AND TAKAMICHI, TOO?
. . . .
THEO-SAN . .
MM ?
SH-SH

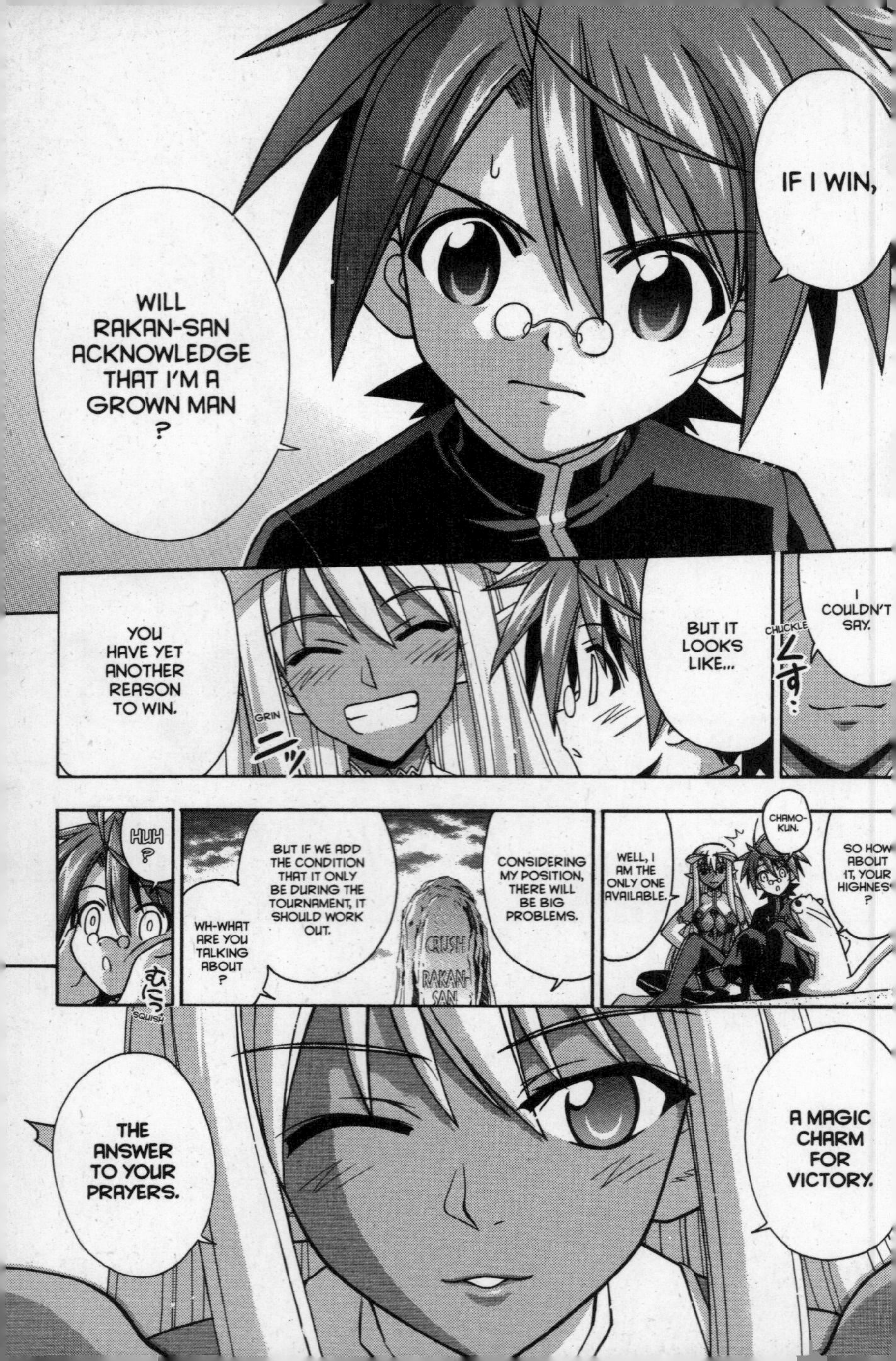
IF I WIN,
WILL RAKAN-SAN ACKNOWLEDGE THAT I'M A GROWN MAN ?
I COULDN'T SAY.
CHUCKLE
くす…
BUT IT LOOKS LIKE...
YOU HAVE YET ANOTHER REASON TO WIN.
GRIN
ニッ
SO HOW ABOUT IT, YOUR HIGHNES ?
CHAMO-KUN.
WELL, I AM THE ONLY ONE AVAILABLE.
CONSIDERING MY POSITION, THERE WILL BE BIG PROBLEMS.
BUT IF WE ADD THE CONDITION THAT IT ONLY BE DURING THE TOURNAMENT, IT SHOULD WORK OUT.
CRUSH RAKAN-SAN
WH-WHAT ARE YOU TALKING ABOUT ?
HUH ?
SQUISH
A MAGIC CHARM FOR VICTORY.
THE ANSWER TO YOUR PRAYERS.

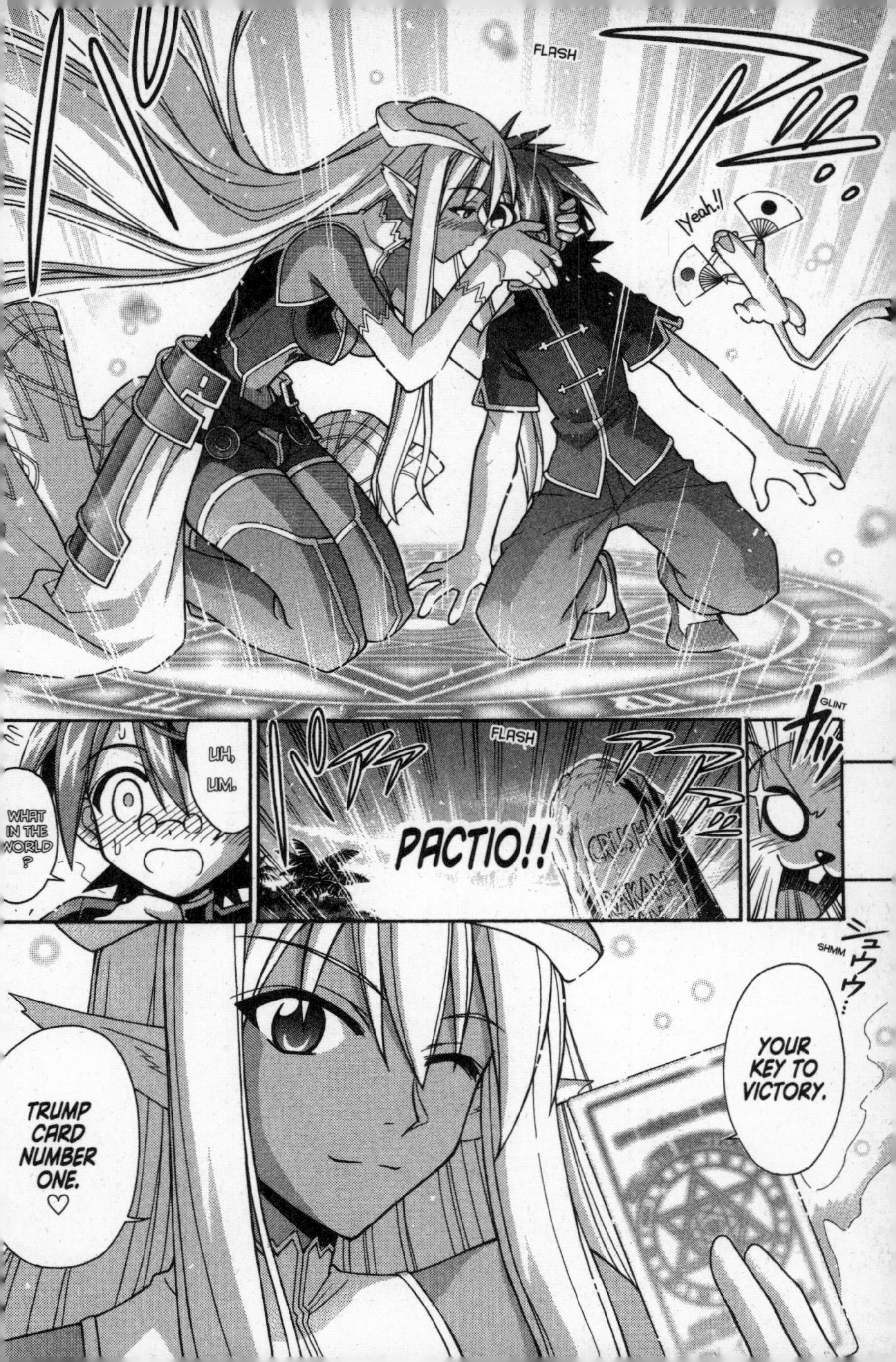
FLASH
Yeah!!
GLINT
FLASH
PACTIO!!
UH, UM.
WHAT IN THE WORLD?
SHMM
YOUR KEY TO VICTORY.
TRUMP CARD NUMBER ONE. ♡

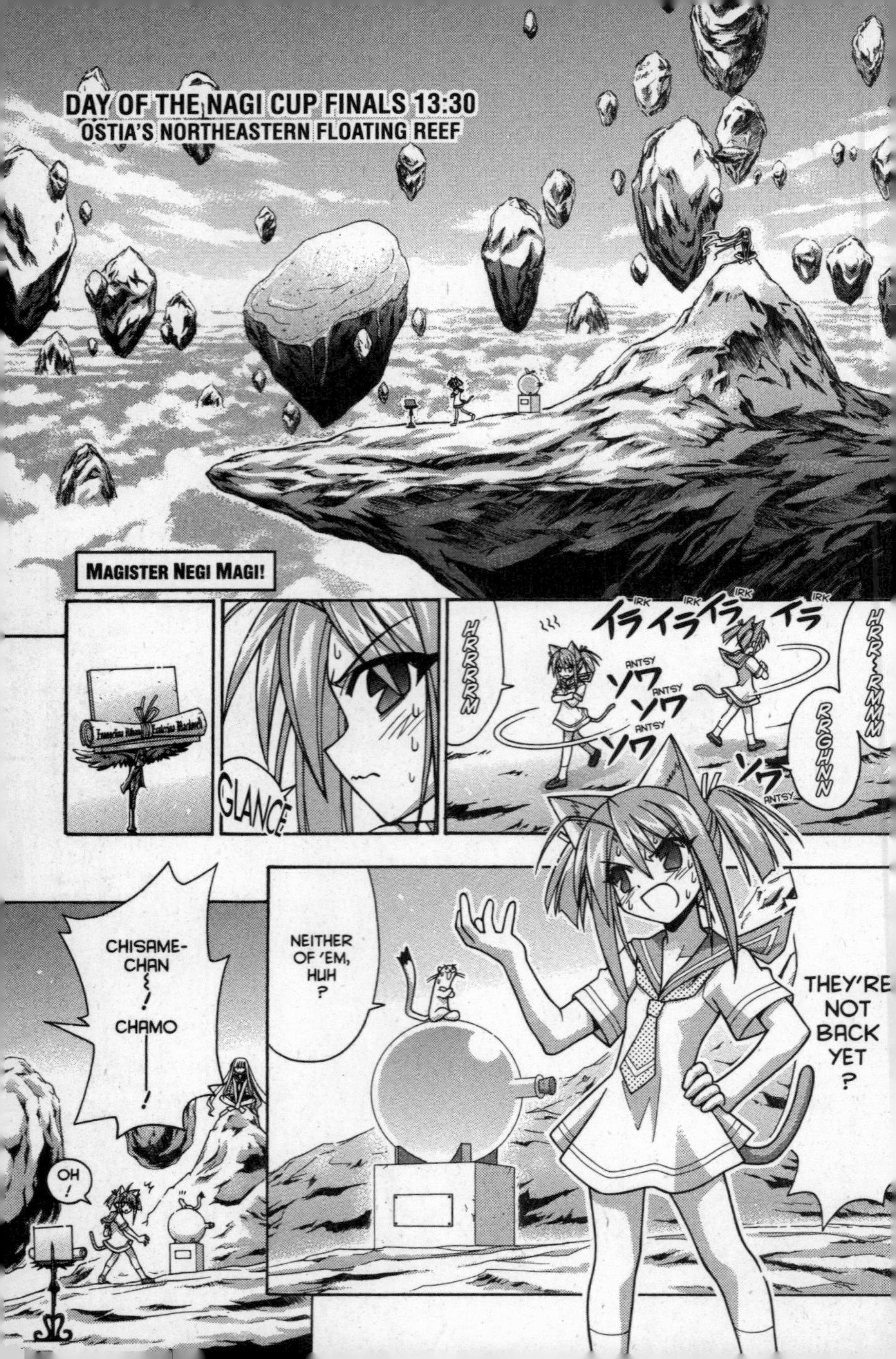
DAY OF THE NAGI CUP FINALS 13:30
OSTIA'S NORTHEASTERN FLOATING REEF
MAGISTER NEGI MAGI!
HRR-RMMM
RRGHNN
IRK イラ IRK イラ IRK イラ IRK イラ
ANTSY ソワ ANTSY ソワ ANTSY ソワ ANTSY ソワ
HRRRRM
GLANCE
THEY'RE NOT BACK YET?
NEITHER OF 'EM, HUH?
CHISAME-CHAN~! CHAMO—!
OH!

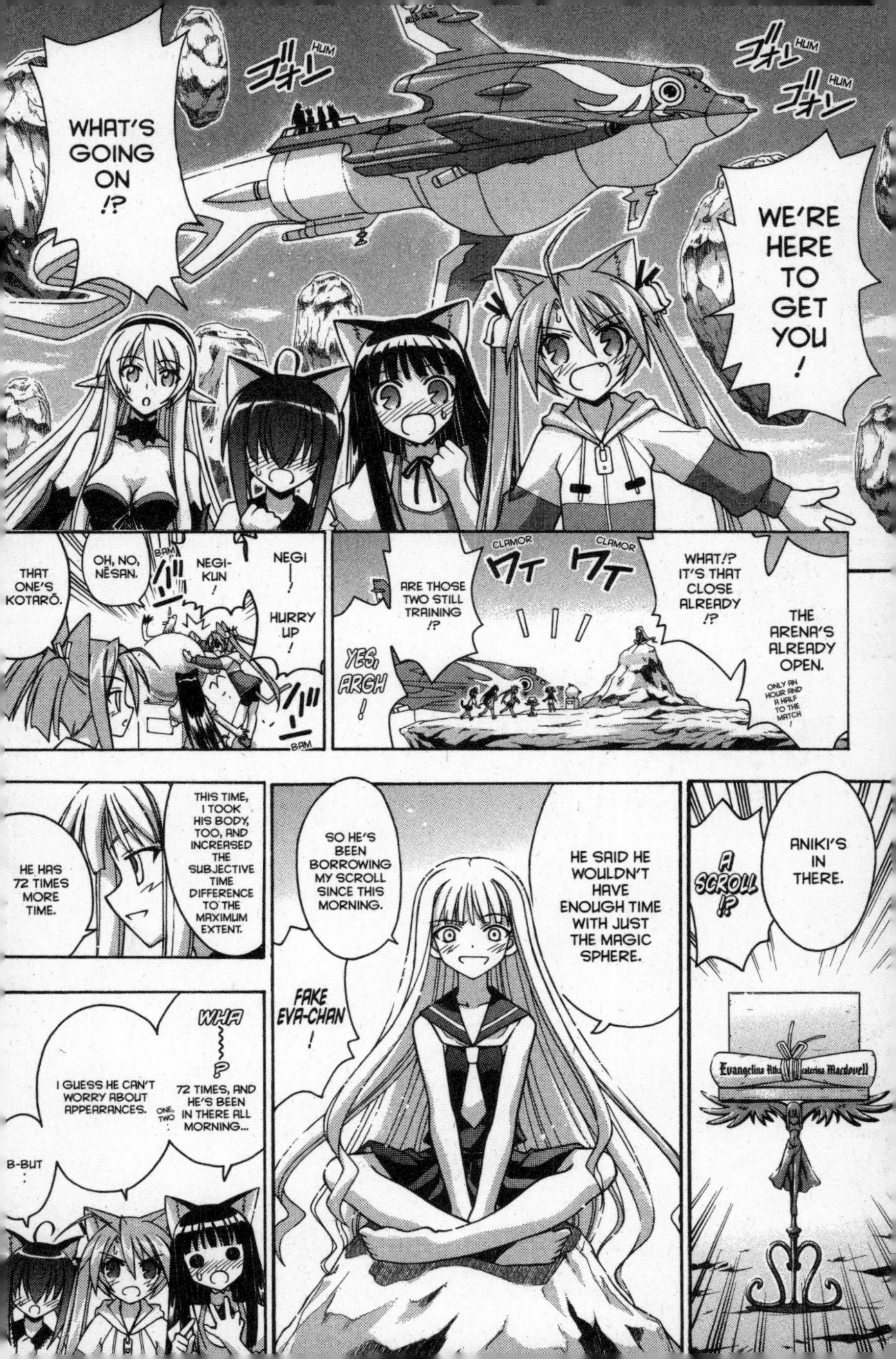
ゴォン HUM
ゴォン HUM
WE'RE HERE TO GET YOU!
ゴォン HUM
WHAT'S GOING ON!?
ワァ CLAMOR
ワァ CLAMOR
WHAT!? IT'S THAT CLOSE ALREADY!?
THE ARENA'S ALREADY OPEN.
ONLY AN HOUR AND A HALF TO THE MATCH!
ARE THOSE TWO STILL TRAINING!?
YES, ARGH!
NEGI! HURRY UP!
NEGI-KUN!
BAM
OH, NO, NĒSAN.
THAT ONE'S KOTARŌ.
BAM
ANIKI'S IN THERE.
A SCROLL!?
HE SAID HE WOULDN'T HAVE ENOUGH TIME WITH JUST THE MAGIC SPHERE.
SO HE'S BEEN BORROWING MY SCROLL SINCE THIS MORNING.
FAKE EVA-CHAN!
THIS TIME, I TOOK HIS BODY, TOO, AND INCREASED THE SUBJECTIVE TIME DIFFERENCE TO THE MAXIMUM EXTENT.
HE HAS 72 TIMES MORE TIME.
WHA~~~?
72 TIMES, AND HE'S BEEN IN THERE ALL MORNING...
ONE, TWO...
I GUESS HE CAN'T WORRY ABOUT APPEARANCES.
B-BUT...

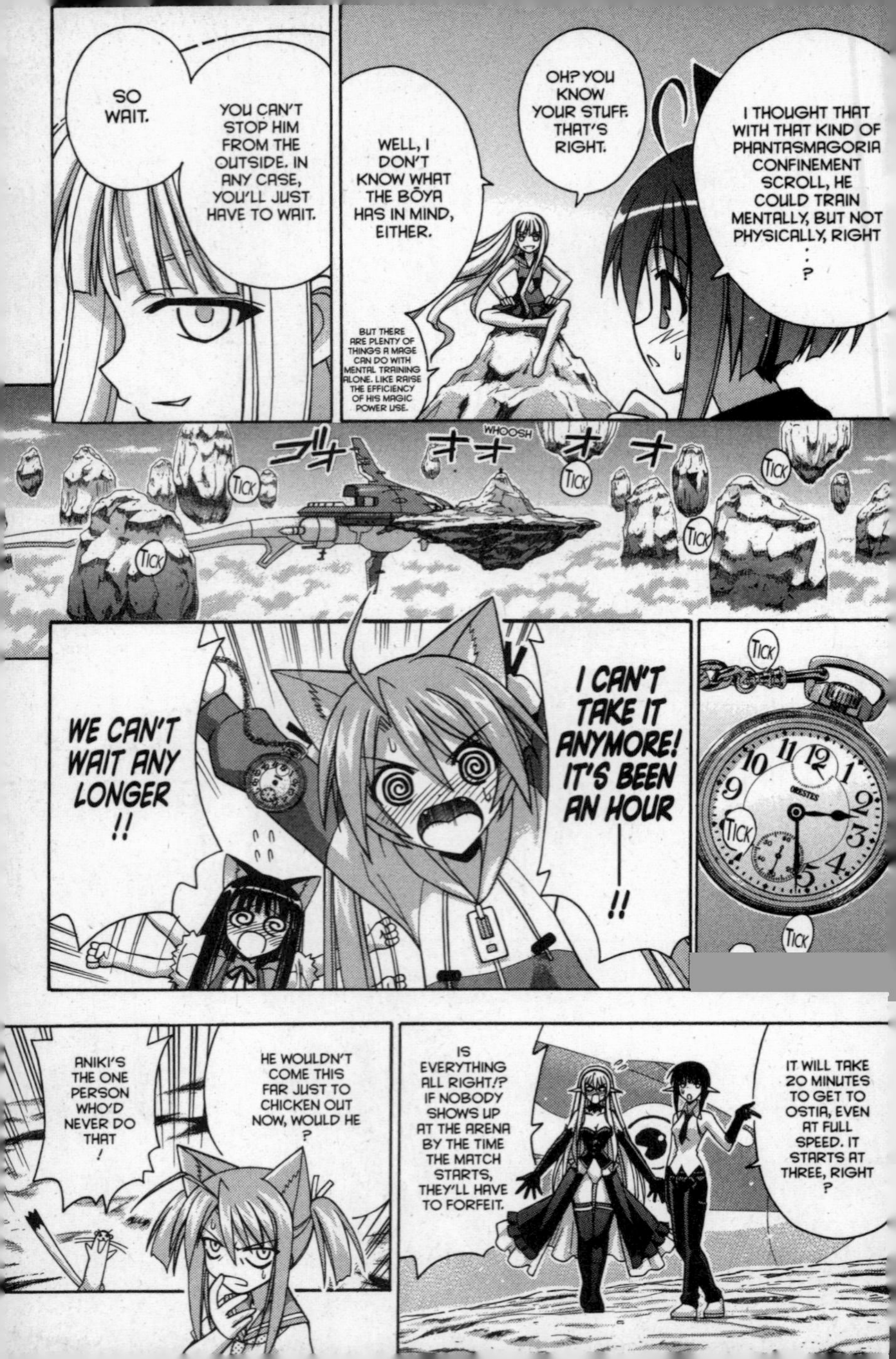
I THOUGHT THAT WITH THAT KIND OF PHANTASMAGORIA CONFINEMENT SCROLL, HE COULD TRAIN MENTALLY, BUT NOT PHYSICALLY, RIGHT...?
OH? YOU KNOW YOUR STUFF. THAT'S RIGHT.
WELL, I DON'T KNOW WHAT THE BŌYA HAS IN MIND, EITHER.
BUT THERE ARE PLENTY OF THINGS A MAGE CAN DO WITH MENTAL TRAINING ALONE. LIKE RAISE THE EFFICIENCY OF HIS MAGIC POWER USE.
YOU CAN'T STOP HIM FROM THE OUTSIDE. IN ANY CASE, YOU'LL JUST HAVE TO WAIT.
SO WAIT.
ゴォォォ
WHOOSH
TICK
TICK
TICK
TICK
TICK
TICK
ORESTES
TICK
TICK
I CAN'T TAKE IT ANYMORE! IT'S BEEN AN HOUR—!!
WE CAN'T WAIT ANY LONGER!!
IT WILL TAKE 20 MINUTES TO GET TO OSTIA, EVEN AT FULL SPEED. IT STARTS AT THREE, RIGHT?
IS EVERYTHING ALL RIGHT!? IF NOBODY SHOWS UP AT THE ARENA BY THE TIME THE MATCH STARTS, THEY'LL HAVE TO FORFEIT.
HE WOULDN'T COME THIS FAR JUST TO CHICKEN OUT NOW, WOULD HE?
ANIKI'S THE ONE PERSON WHO'D NEVER DO THAT!

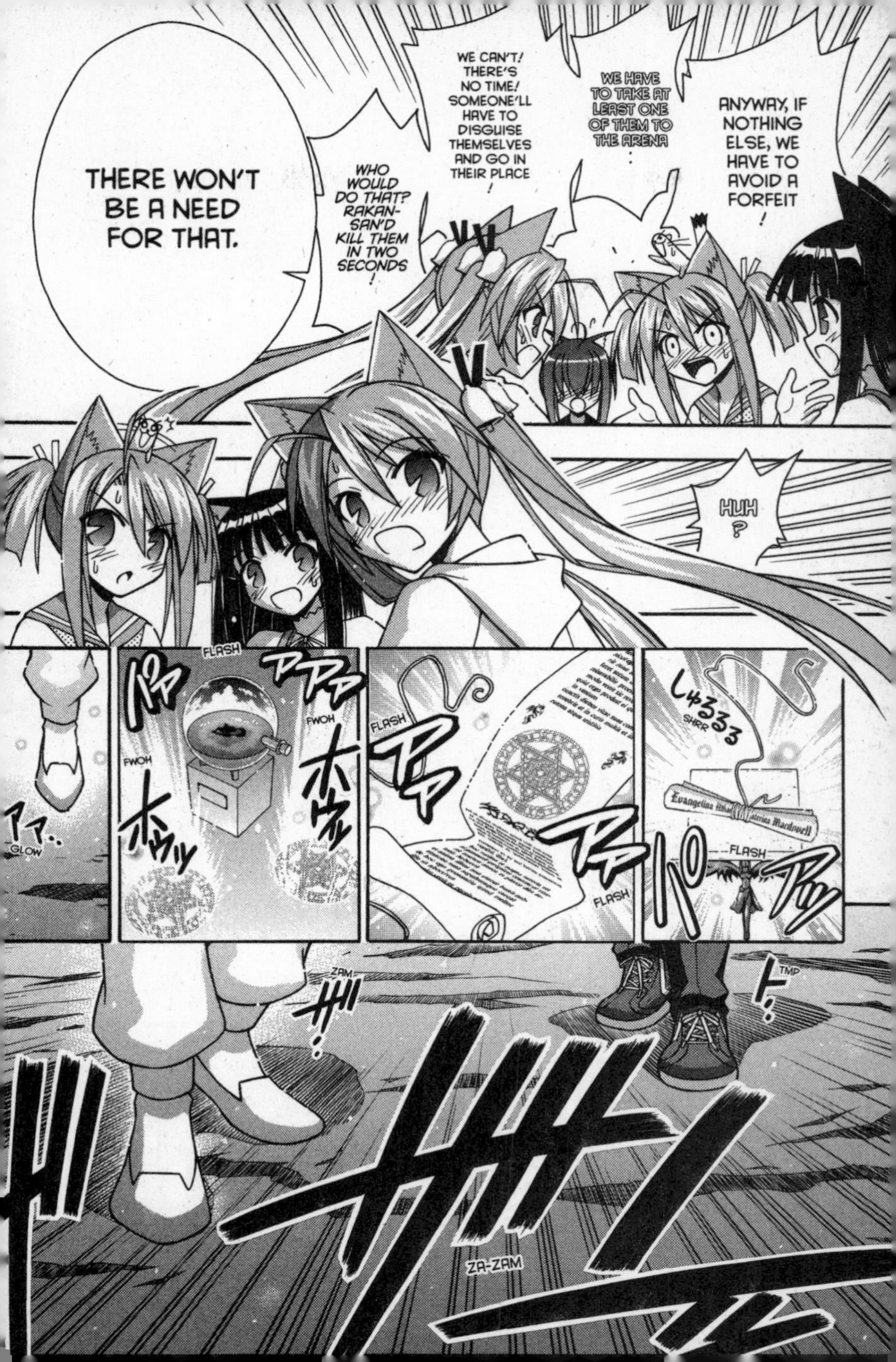
ANYWAY, IF NOTHING ELSE, WE HAVE TO AVOID A FORFEIT!
WE HAVE TO TAKE AT LEAST ONE OF THEM TO THE ARENA
WE CAN'T! THERE'S NO TIME! SOMEONE'LL HAVE TO DISGUISE THEMSELVES AND GO IN THEIR PLACE!
WHO WOULD DO THAT? RAKAN-SAN'D KILL THEM IN TWO SECONDS!
THERE WON'T BE A NEED FOR THAT.
HUH?
しゅるるる
SHRR
FLASH
FLASH
FLASH
FLASH
FWOH
FWOH
GLOW
TMP
ZAM
ZA-ZAM

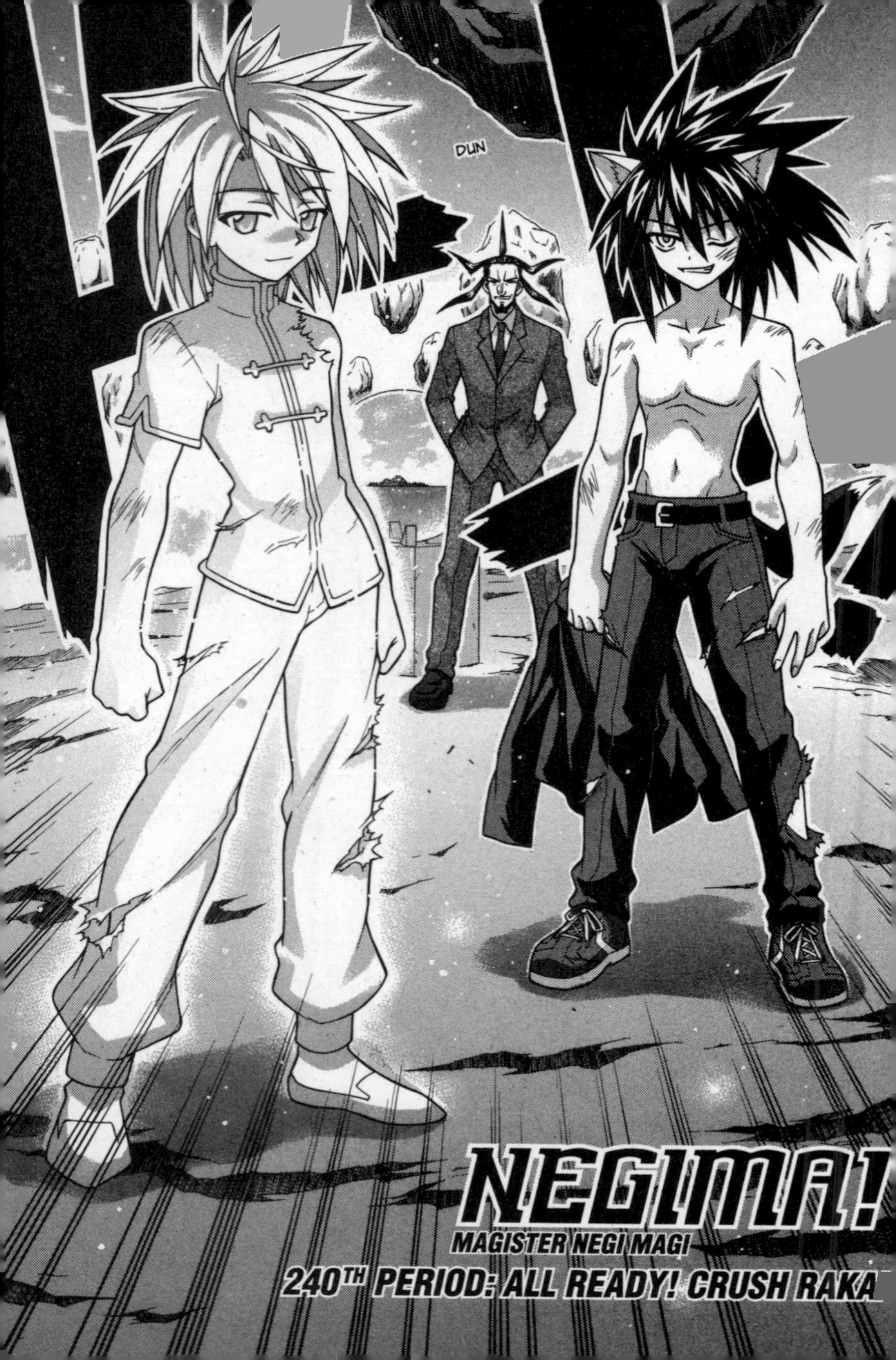
DUN
NEGIMA!
MAGISTER NEGI MAGI
240TH PERIOD: ALL READY! CRUSH RAKA

NE

I'M SORRY TO KEEP YOU WAITING.

WELL? HOW ARE YOU FEELING, NEGI?

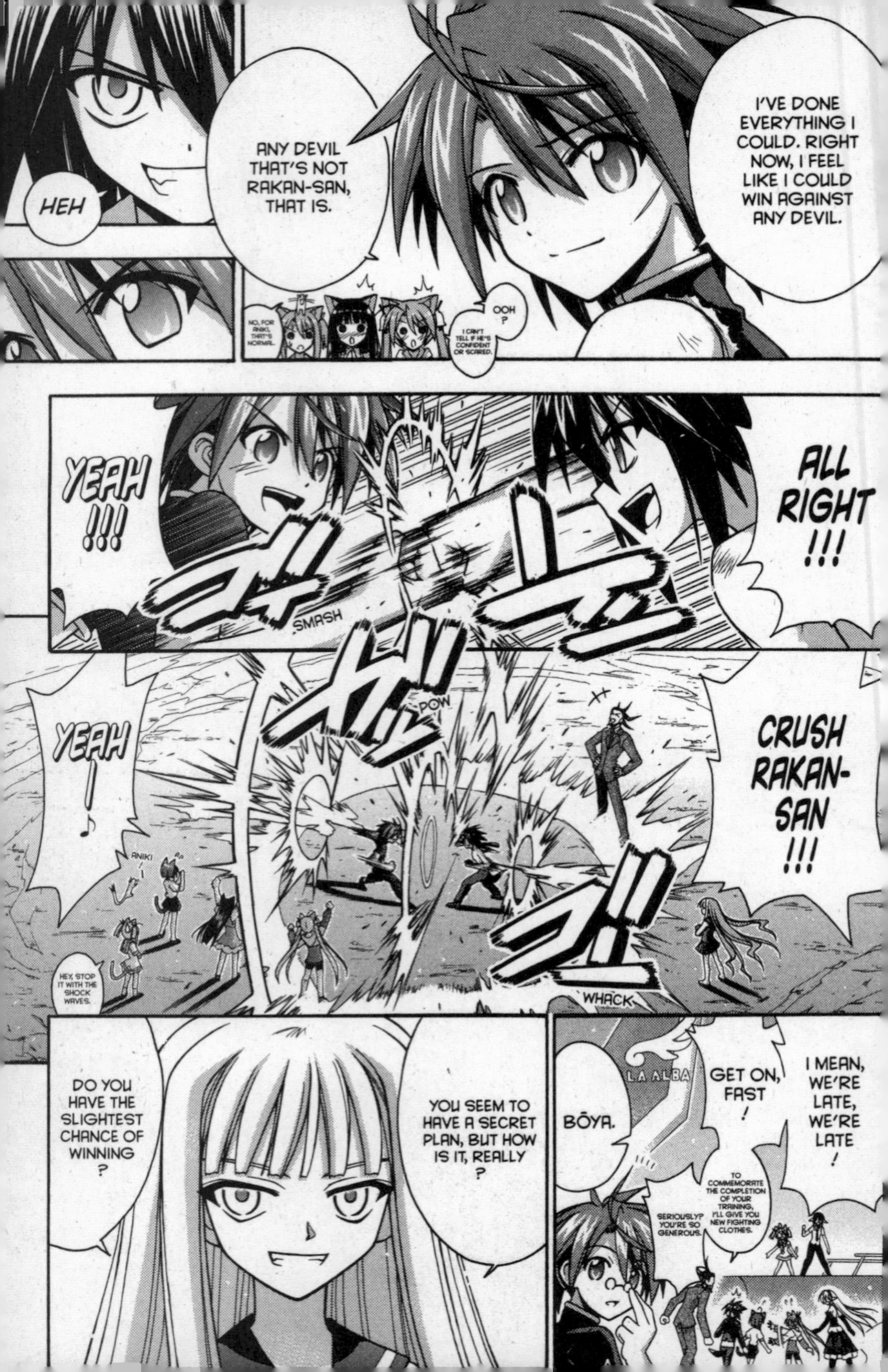
I'VE DONE EVERYTHING I COULD. RIGHT NOW, I FEEL LIKE I COULD WIN AGAINST ANY DEVIL.
ANY DEVIL THAT'S NOT RAKAN-SAN, THAT IS.
OOH?
I CAN'T TELL IF HE'S CONFIDENT OR SCARED.
NO, FOR ANIKI, THAT'S NORMAL.
HEH
ALL RIGHT!!!
YEAH!!!
SMASH
CRUSH RAKAN-SAN!!!
POW
WHACK
YEAH! ♪
ANIKI!
HEY, STOP IT WITH THE SHOCK WAVES.
I MEAN, WE'RE LATE, WE'RE LATE!
GET ON, FAST!
LA ALBA
BŌYA.
TO COMMEMORATE THE COMPLETION OF YOUR TRAINING, I'LL GIVE YOU NEW FIGHTING CLOTHES.
SERIOUSLY? YOU'RE SO GENEROUS.
YOU SEEM TO HAVE A SECRET PLAN, BUT HOW IS IT, REALLY?
DO YOU HAVE THE SLIGHTEST CHANCE OF WINNING?

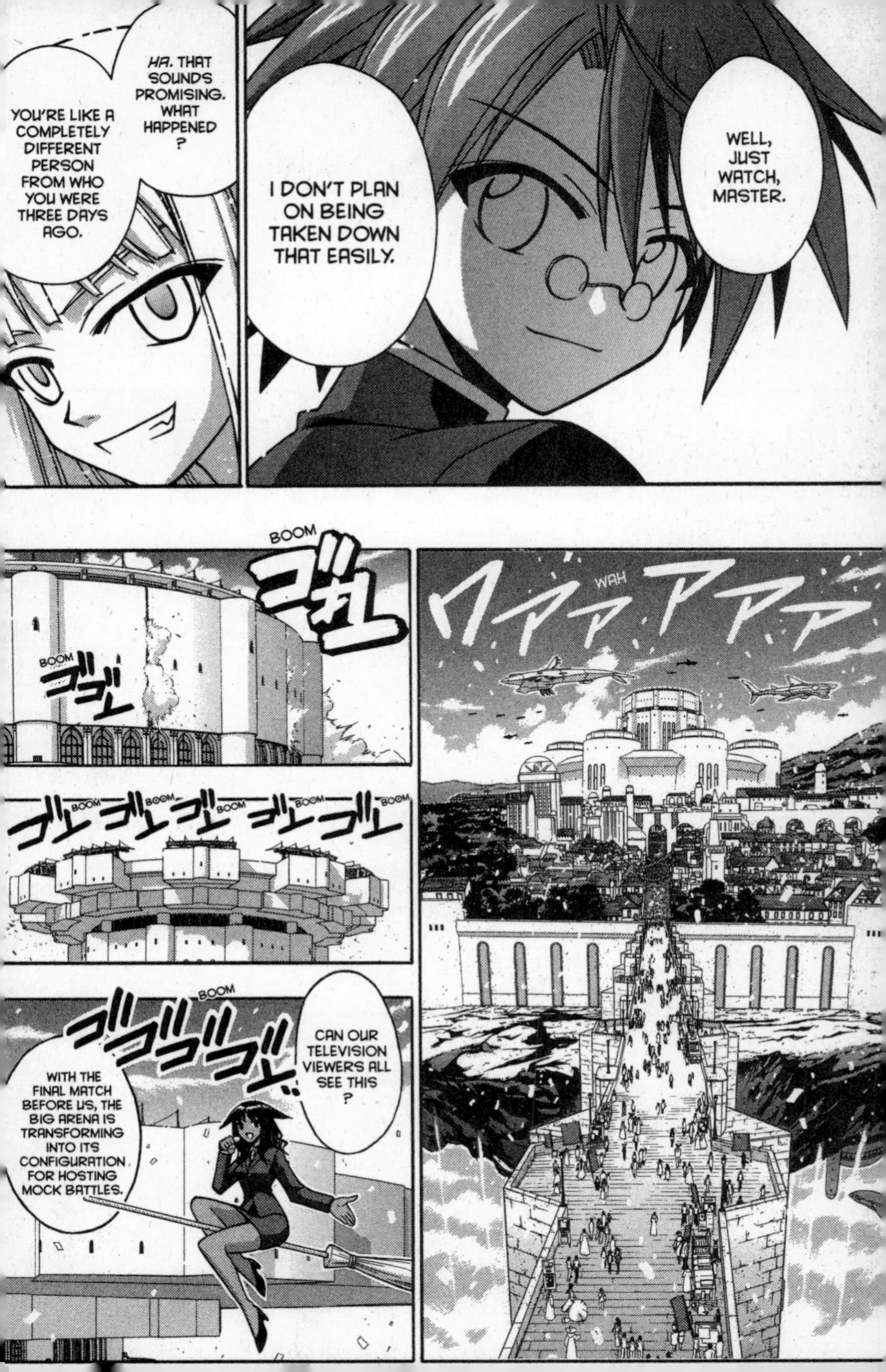
WELL, JUST WATCH, MASTER.
I DON'T PLAN ON BEING TAKEN DOWN THAT EASILY.
HA. THAT SOUNDS PROMISING. WHAT HAPPENED?
YOU'RE LIKE A COMPLETELY DIFFERENT PERSON FROM WHO YOU WERE THREE DAYS AGO.
WAH
BOOM
BOOM
BOOM
BOOM
BOOM
BOOM
BOOM
BOOM
CAN OUR TELEVISION VIEWERS ALL SEE THIS?
WITH THE FINAL MATCH BEFORE US, THE BIG ARENA IS TRANSFORMING INTO ITS CONFIGURATION FOR HOSTING MOCK BATTLES.

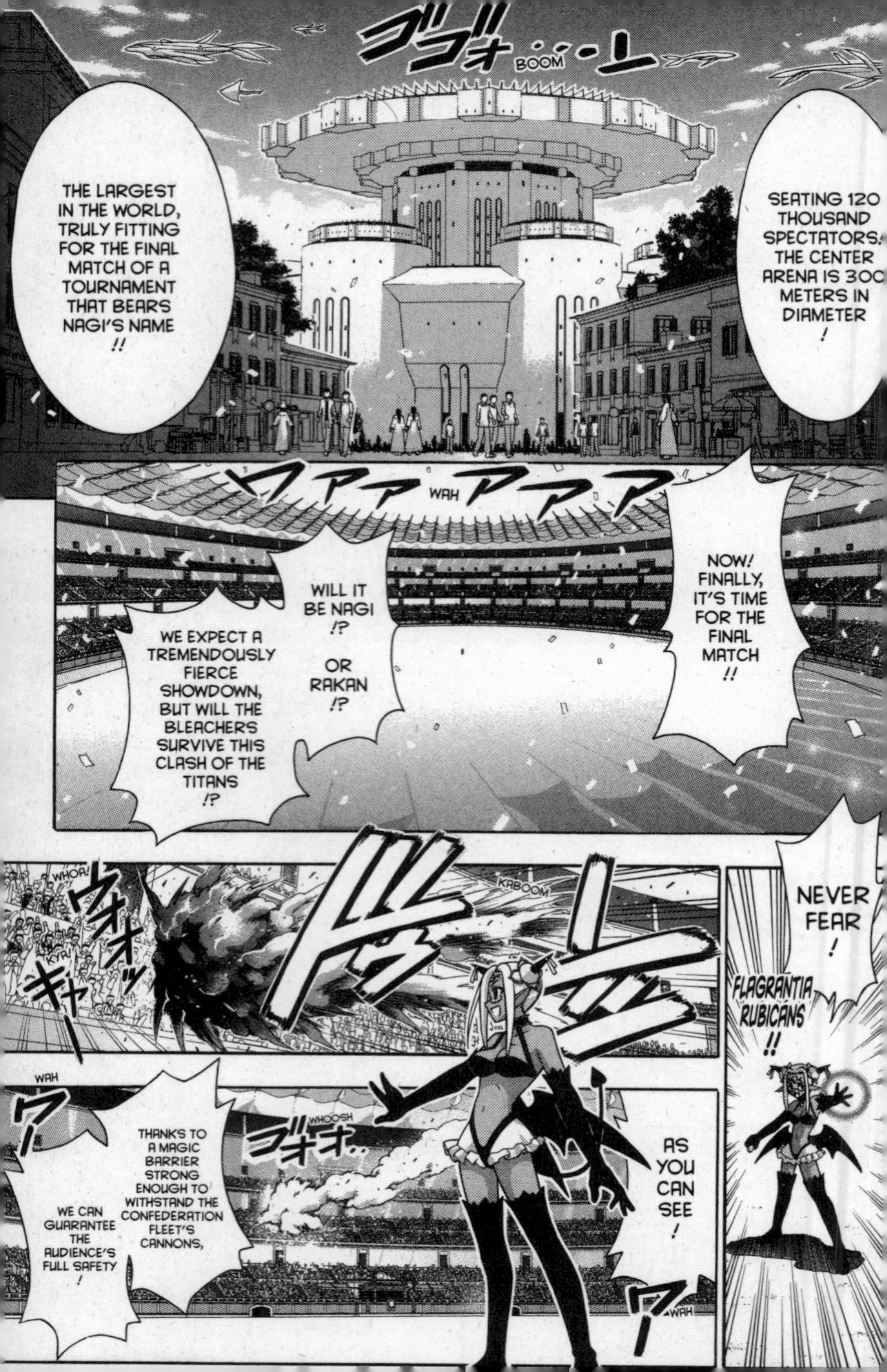
BOOM
SEATING 120 THOUSAND SPECTATORS. THE CENTER ARENA IS 300 METERS IN DIAMETER!
THE LARGEST IN THE WORLD, TRULY FITTING FOR THE FINAL MATCH OF A TOURNAMENT THAT BEARS NAGI'S NAME!!
WAH
NOW! FINALLY, IT'S TIME FOR THE FINAL MATCH!!
WILL IT BE NAGI!? OR RAKAN!?
WE EXPECT A TREMENDOUSLY FIERCE SHOWDOWN, BUT WILL THE BLEACHERS SURVIVE THIS CLASH OF THE TITANS!?
NEVER FEAR!
FLAGRANTIA RUBICANS!!
KABOOM
WHOA!
KYA!
AS YOU CAN SEE!
WHOOSH
THANKS TO A MAGIC BARRIER STRONG ENOUGH TO WITHSTAND THE CONFEDERATION FLEET'S CANNONS,
WE CAN GUARANTEE THE AUDIENCE'S FULL SAFETY!
WAH
WAH

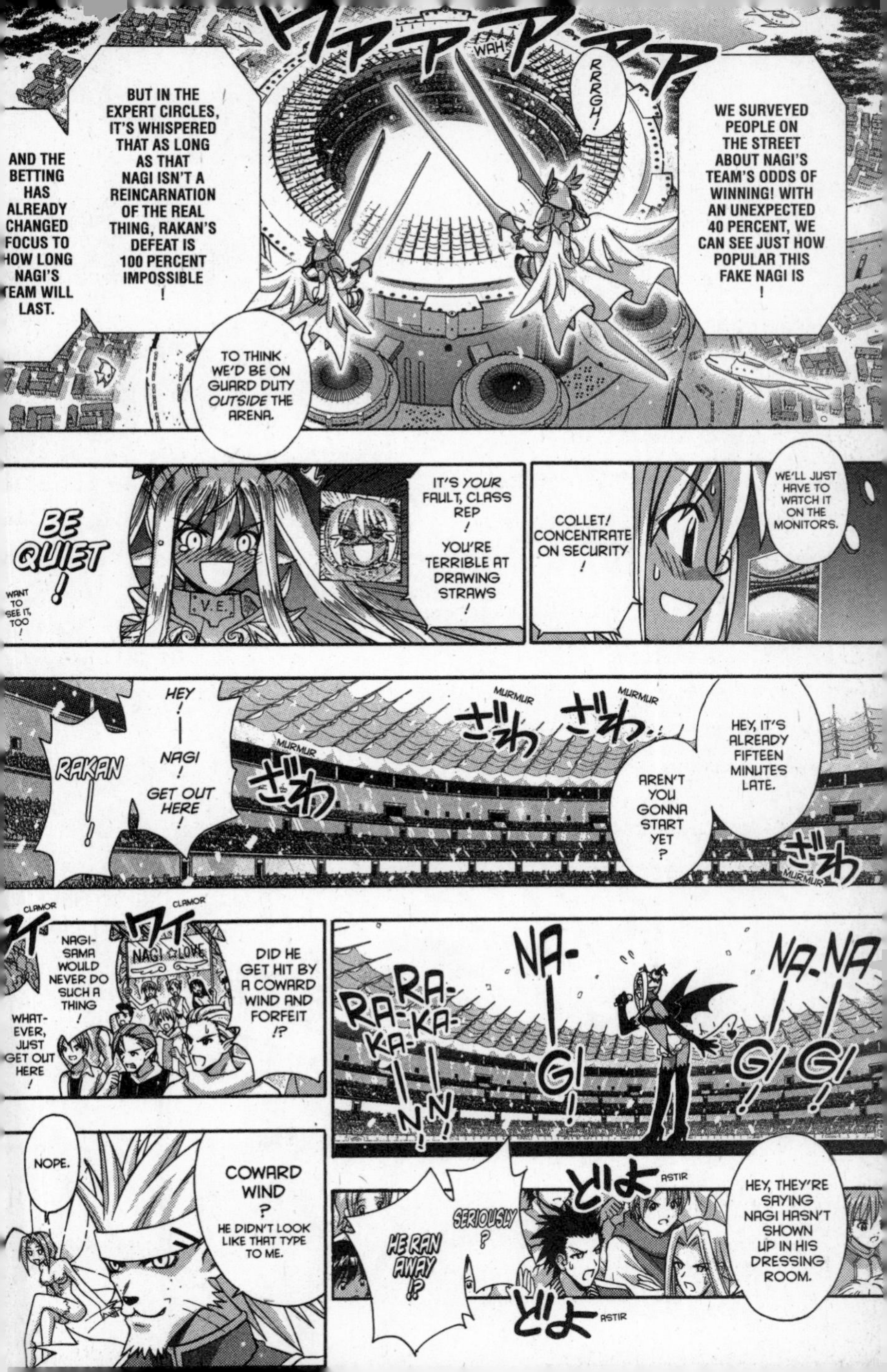
WE SURVEYED PEOPLE ON THE STREET ABOUT NAGI'S TEAM'S ODDS OF WINNING! WITH AN UNEXPECTED 40 PERCENT, WE CAN SEE JUST HOW POPULAR THIS FAKE NAGI IS!
RRRGH!
WAH!
BUT IN THE EXPERT CIRCLES, IT'S WHISPERED THAT AS LONG AS THAT NAGI ISN'T A REINCARNATION OF THE REAL THING, RAKAN'S DEFEAT IS 100 PERCENT IMPOSSIBLE!
AND THE BETTING HAS ALREADY CHANGED FOCUS TO HOW LONG NAGI'S TEAM WILL LAST.
TO THINK WE'D BE ON GUARD DUTY *OUTSIDE* THE ARENA.
WE'LL JUST HAVE TO WATCH IT ON THE MONITORS.
COLLET! CONCENTRATE ON SECURITY!
IT'S *YOUR* FAULT, CLASS REP! YOU'RE TERRIBLE AT DRAWING STRAWS!
V.E.
BE QUIET!
WANT TO SEE IT, TOO!
HEY, IT'S ALREADY FIFTEEN MINUTES LATE.
AREN'T YOU GONNA START YET?
ざわ MURMUR
ざわ MURMUR
ざわ MURMUR
ざわ MURMUR
HEY! NAGI! GET OUT HERE!
RAKAN!!
NA-NA-GI! NA-GI!
NA-GI!
RA-KA-N! RA-KA-N!
ワイ CLAMOR
ワイ CLAMOR
DID HE GET HIT BY A COWARD WIND AND FORFEIT!?
NAGI☆LOVE
NAGI-SAMA WOULD NEVER DO SUCH A THING!
WHATEVER, JUST GET OUT HERE!
HEY, THEY'RE SAYING NAGI HASN'T SHOWN UP IN HIS DRESSING ROOM.
どよ ASTIR
SERIOUSLY?
HE RAN AWAY!?
どよ ASTIR
COWARD WIND? HE DIDN'T LOOK LIKE THAT TYPE TO ME.
NOPE.

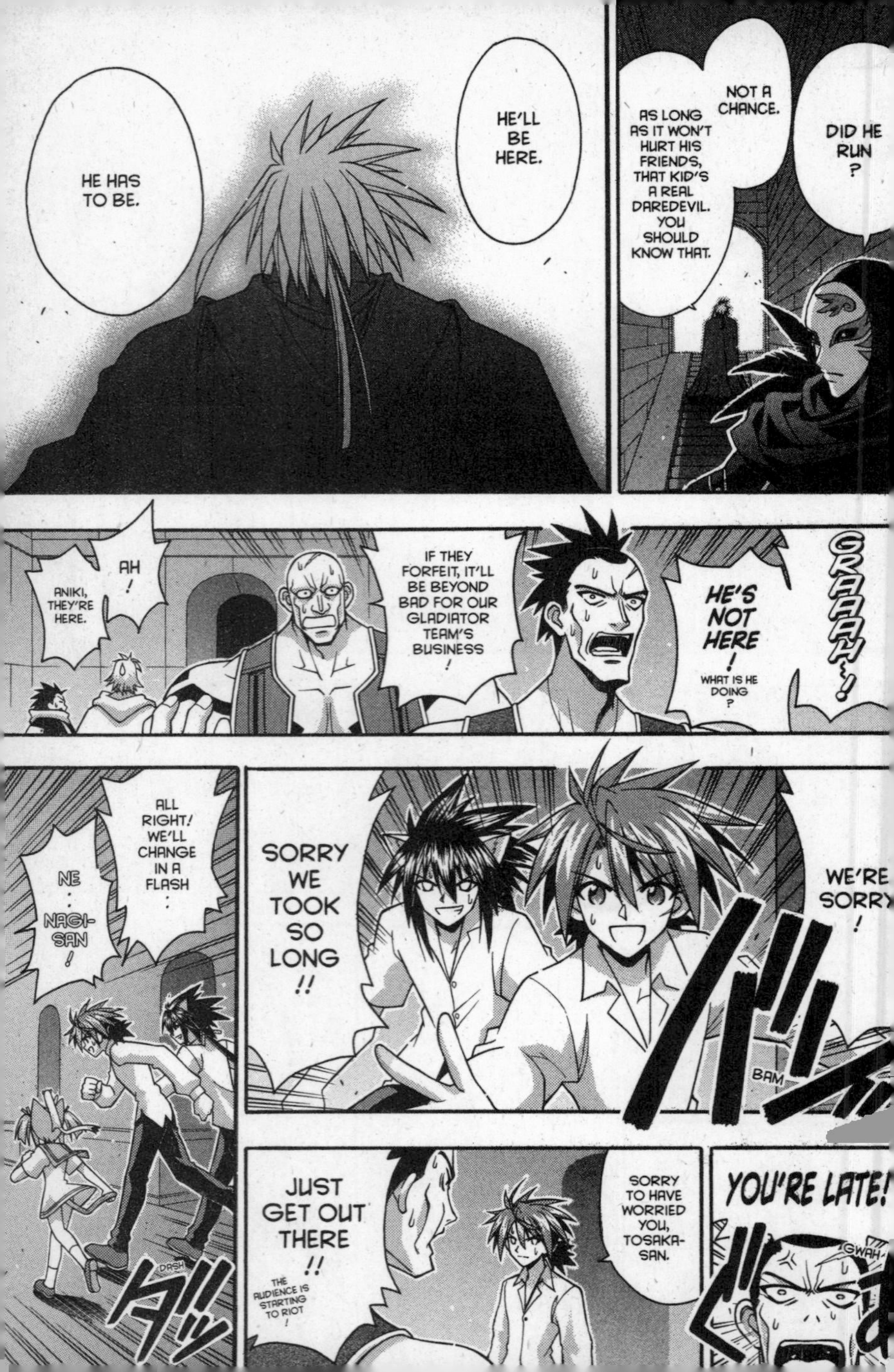
DID HE RUN?
NOT A CHANCE.
AS LONG AS IT WON'T HURT HIS FRIENDS, THAT KID'S A REAL DAREDEVIL. YOU SHOULD KNOW THAT.
HE'LL BE HERE.
HE HAS TO BE.
GRAAAAH!
HE'S NOT HERE! WHAT IS HE DOING?
IF THEY FORFEIT, IT'LL BE BEYOND BAD FOR OUR GLADIATOR TEAM'S BUSINESS!
AH!
ANIKI, THEY'RE HERE.
WE'RE SORRY!
BAM
SORRY WE TOOK SO LONG!!
YOU'RE LATE!
GWAH
SORRY TO HAVE WORRIED YOU, TOSAKA-SAN.
JUST GET OUT THERE!!
THE AUDIENCE IS STARTING TO RIOT!
ALL RIGHT! WE'LL CHANGE IN A FLASH..
NE.. NAGI-SAN!
DASH

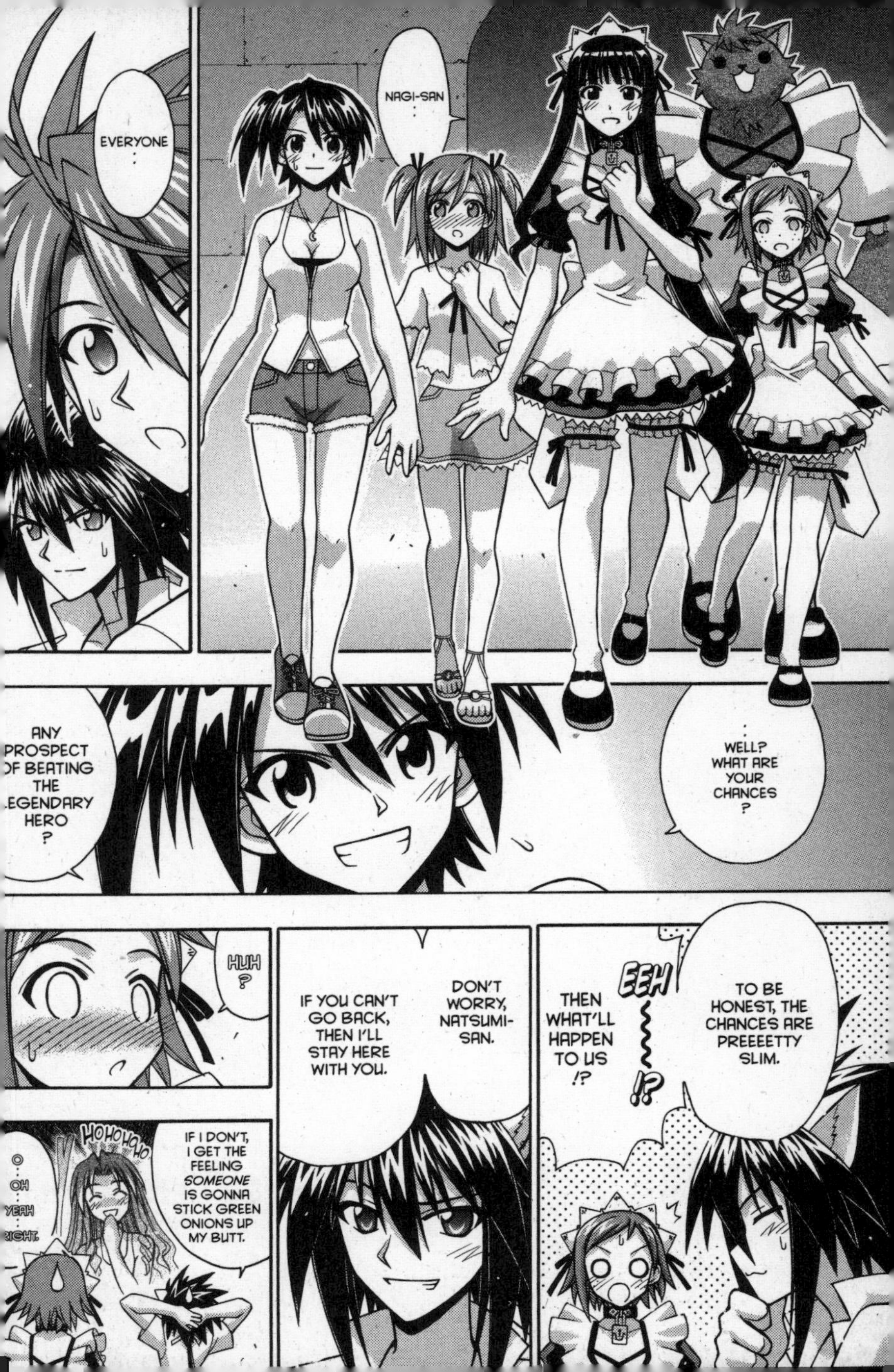
NAGI-SAN ...
EVERYONE ...
... WELL? WHAT ARE YOUR CHANCES?
ANY PROSPECT OF BEATING THE LEGENDARY HERO?
TO BE HONEST, THE CHANCES ARE PREEEETTY SLIM.
EEH !?
THEN WHAT'LL HAPPEN TO US !?
DON'T WORRY, NATSUMI-SAN.
IF YOU CAN'T GO BACK, THEN I'LL STAY HERE WITH YOU.
HUH ?
IF I DON'T, I GET THE FEELING *SOMEONE* IS GONNA STICK GREEN ONIONS UP MY BUTT.
HOHOHOHO
O... OH YEAH... RIGHT.

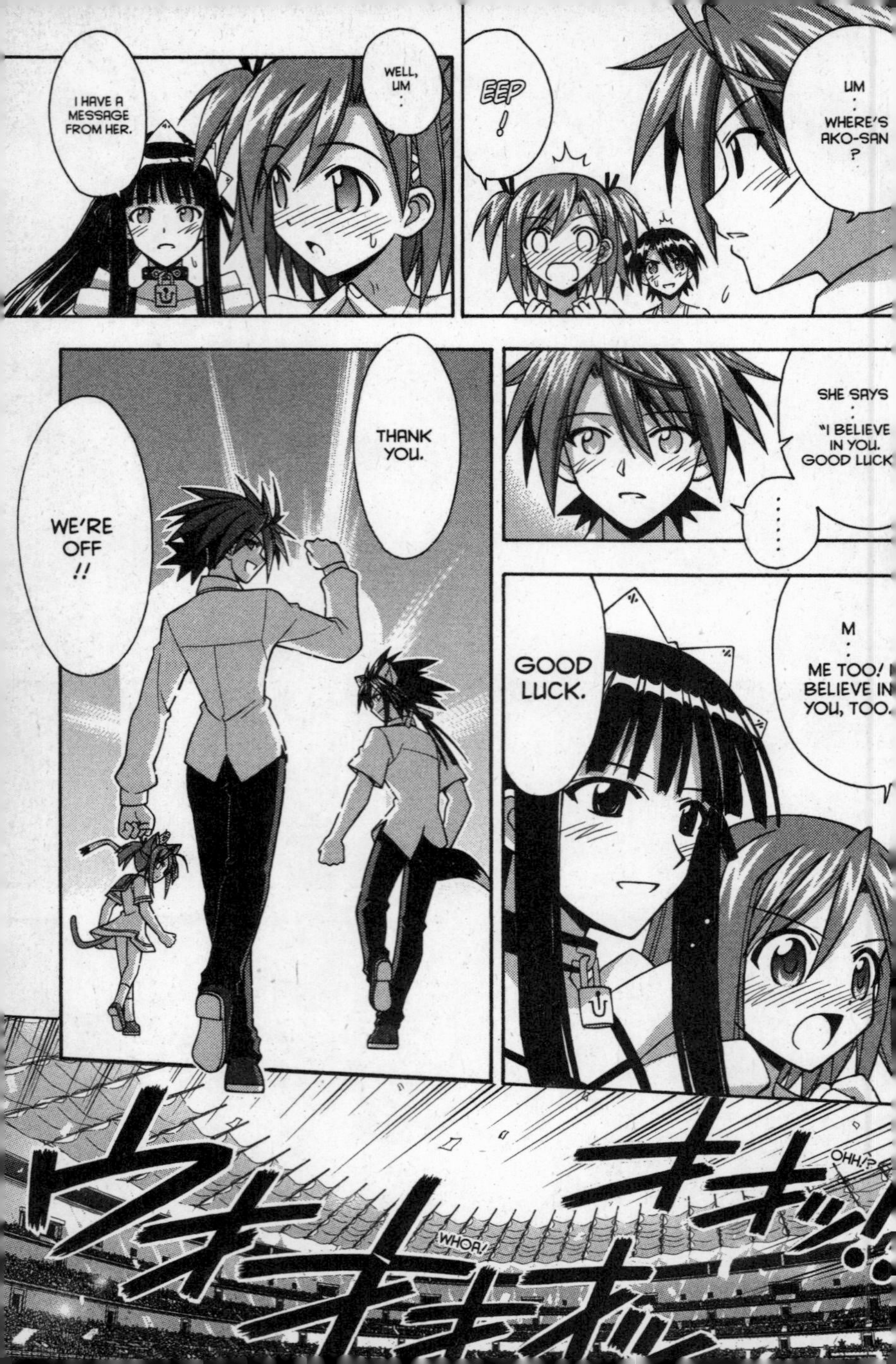
UM : WHERE'S AKO-SAN ?
EEP !
WELL, UM :
I HAVE A MESSAGE FROM HER.
SHE SAYS : "I BELIEVE IN YOU. GOOD LUCK
......
M : ME TOO! I BELIEVE IN YOU, TOO.
GOOD LUCK.
THANK YOU.
WE'RE OFF !!
OHH!?
WHOA!

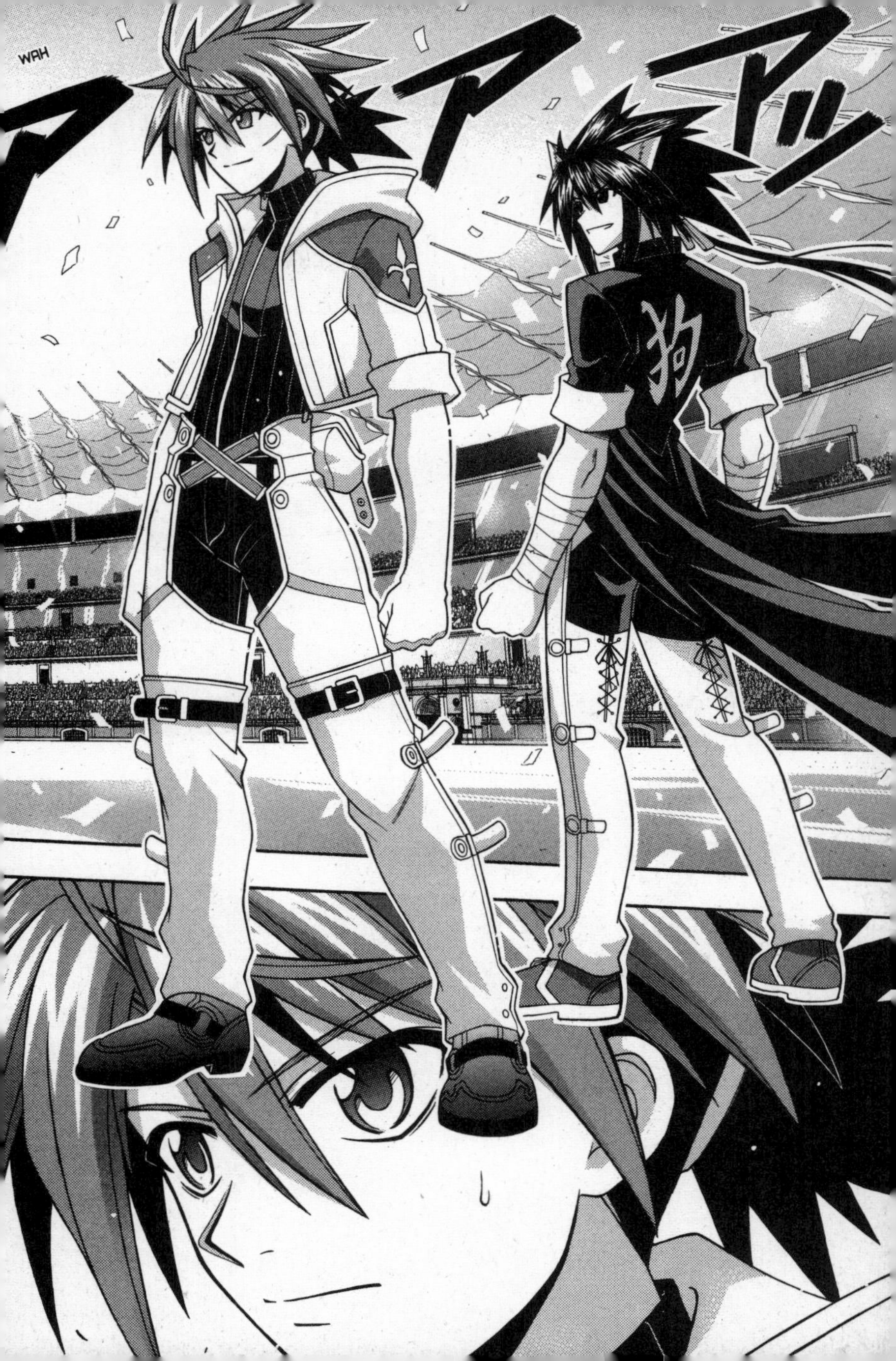
WAH
アアアアッ

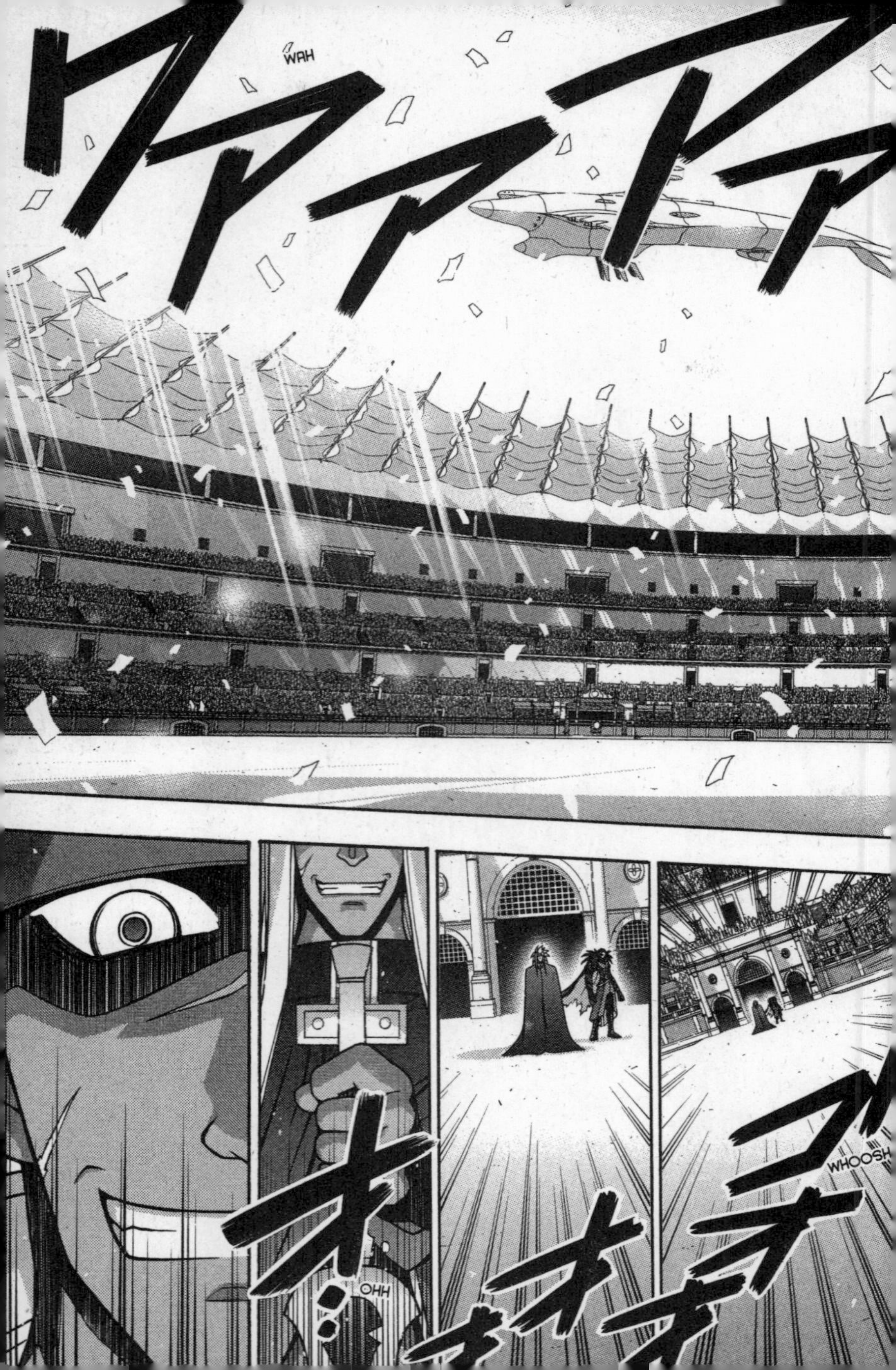
WAH
WHOOSH
OHH

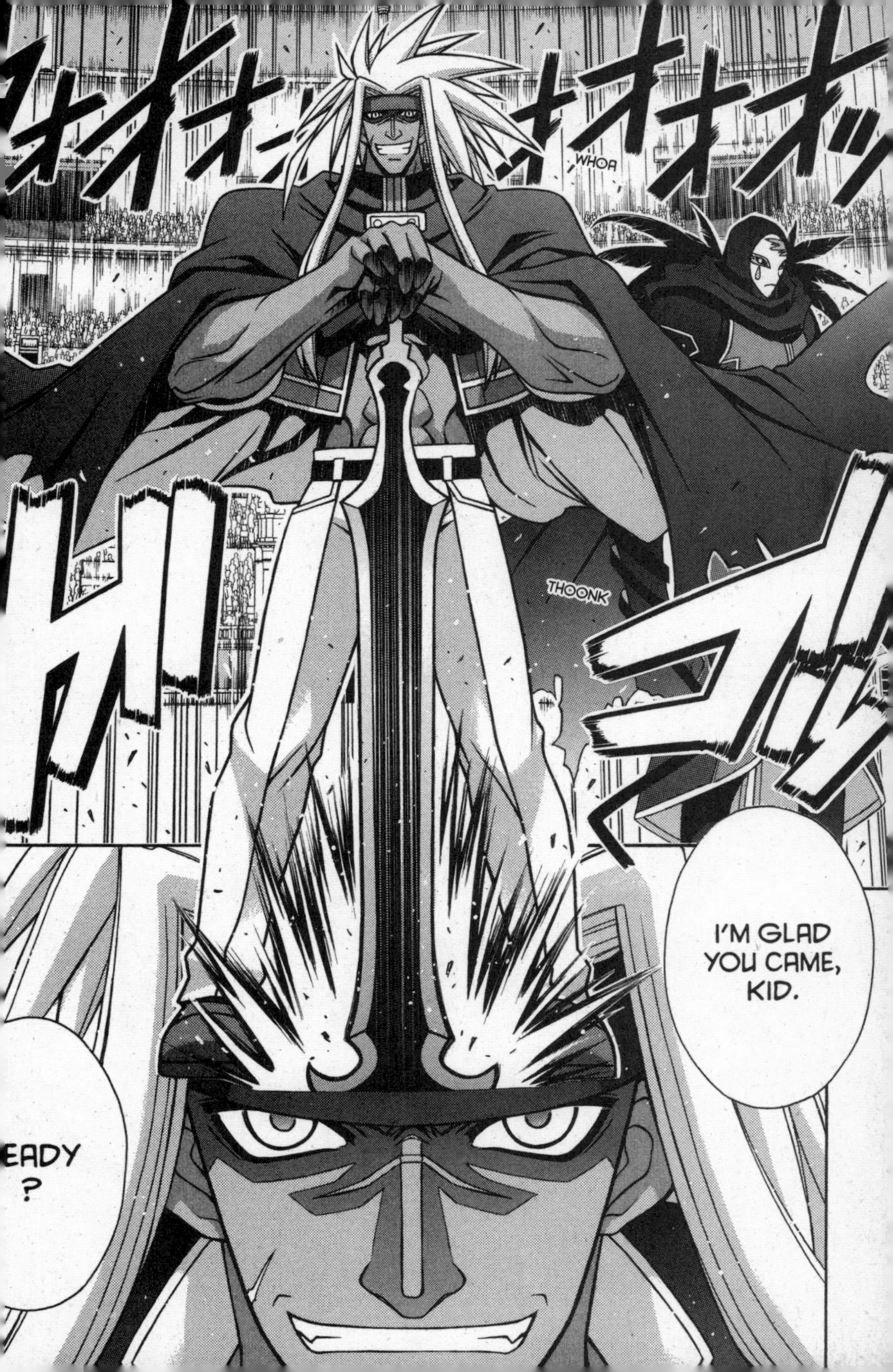
WHOA
THOONK
I'M GLAD YOU CAME, KID.
EADY ?

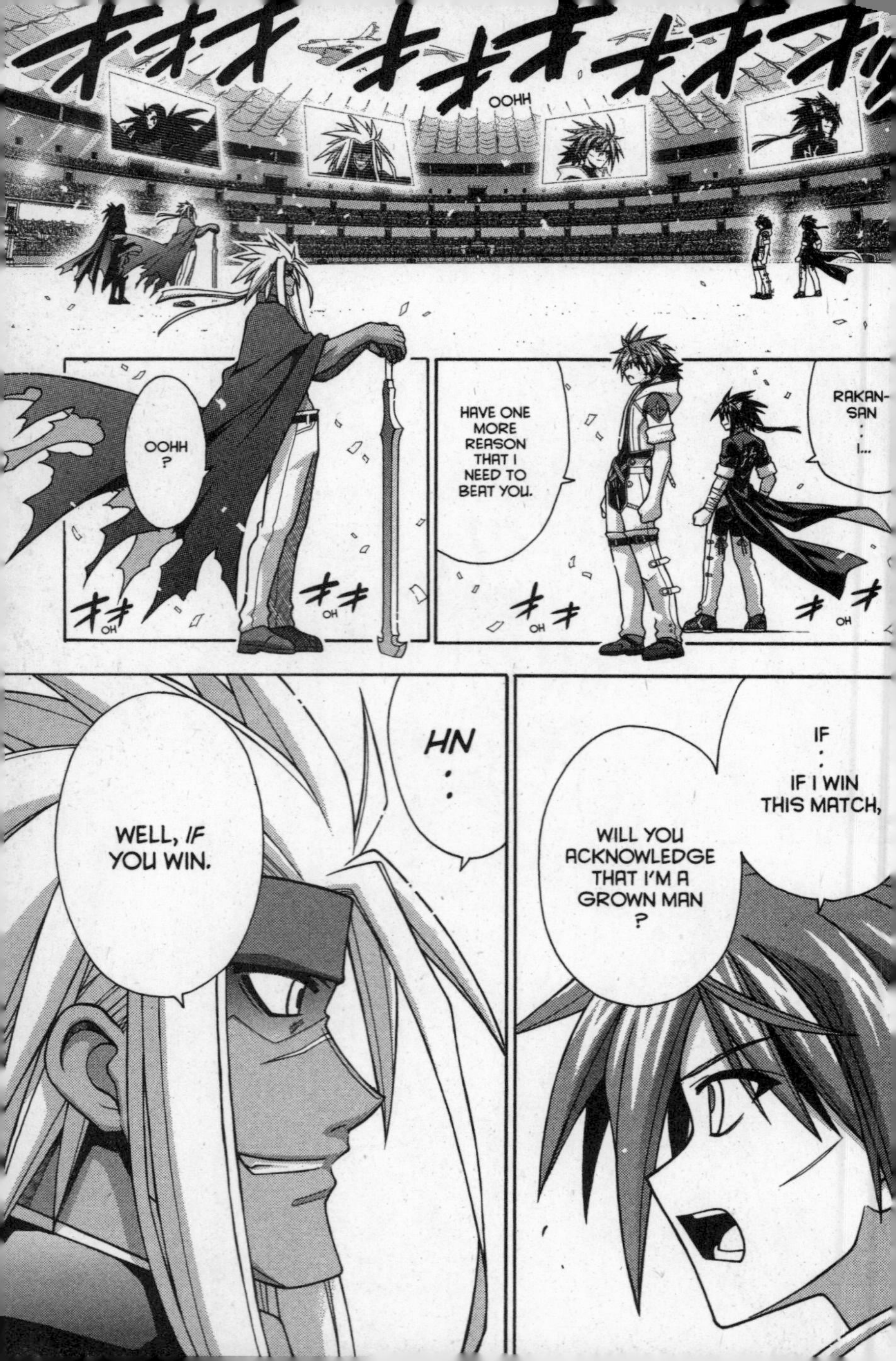
OOHH
RAKAN-SAN : : I...
HAVE ONE MORE REASON THAT I NEED TO BEAT YOU.
OH
OH
OOHH ?
OH
OH
IF : : IF I WIN THIS MATCH,
WILL YOU ACKNOWLEDGE THAT I'M A GROWN MAN ?
HN : :
WELL, *IF* YOU WIN.

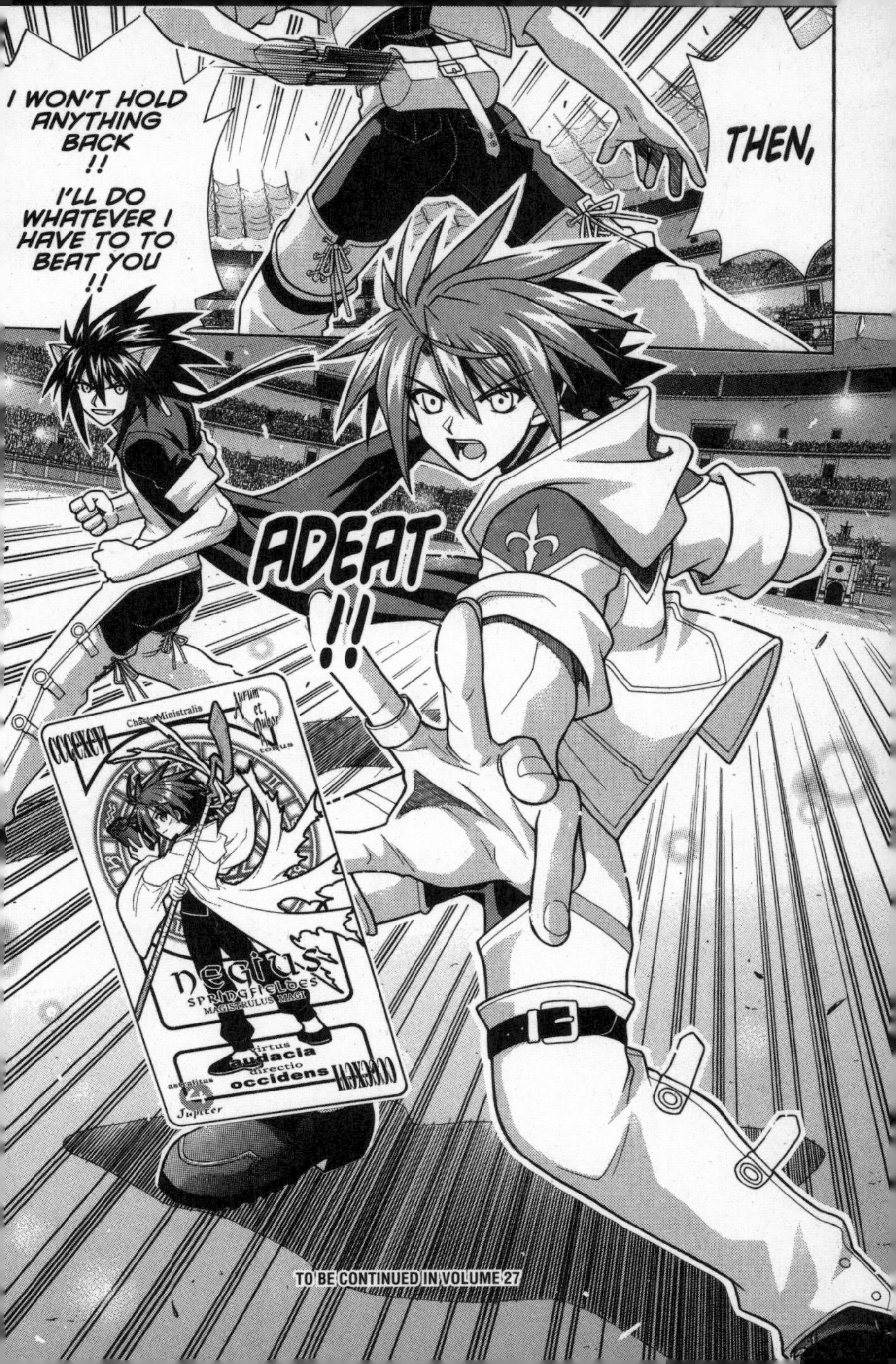
THEN,
I WON'T HOLD ANYTHING BACK !!
I'LL DO WHATEVER I HAVE TO TO BEAT YOU !!
ADEAT !!
Charta Ministralis
Aurum et Rubor
negius
SPRINGFIELDES
MAGISTRULUS MAGI
virtus
audacia
directio
occidens
astralitas
4
Jupiter
TO BE CONTINUED IN VOLUME 27

-STAFF-

Ken Akamatsu
Takashi Takemoto
Kenichi Nakamura
Masaki Ohyama
Keiichi Yamashita
Tohru Mitsuhashi
Yuichi Yoshida

Thanks to
Ran Ayanaga

NEGIMA! FAN ART CORNER

THANK YOU FOR ALWAYS SENDING PICTURES AND LETTERS. I ALWAYS HAVE A HARD TIME CHOOSING PICTURES, AND THIS TIME THE SELECTION WAS FIERCE. I REALLY AM FEELING THE POWER OF MIDDLE AND ELEMENTARY SCHOOLGIRLS ★ I GET THE FEELING THAT FATE AND NEGI SUBMISSIONS ARE GRADUALLY INCREASING, AND THERE'S LESS VARIATION ON THE FEMALE CHARACTERS. NOW THEN, LET'S TAKE A LOOK (^^)

TEXT BY MAX

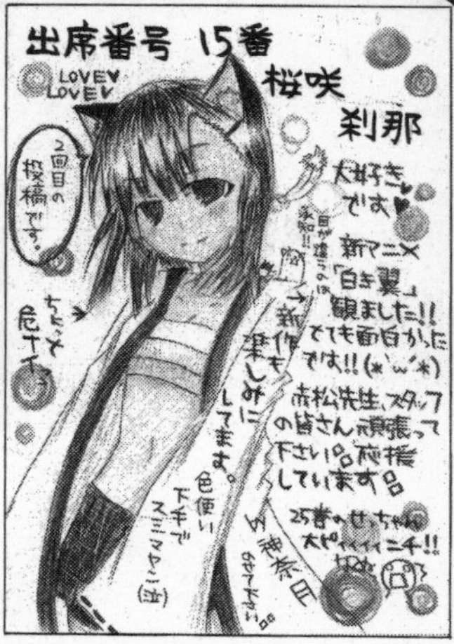
出席番号 15番
桜咲
刹那

I LIKE THE BANDAGE.

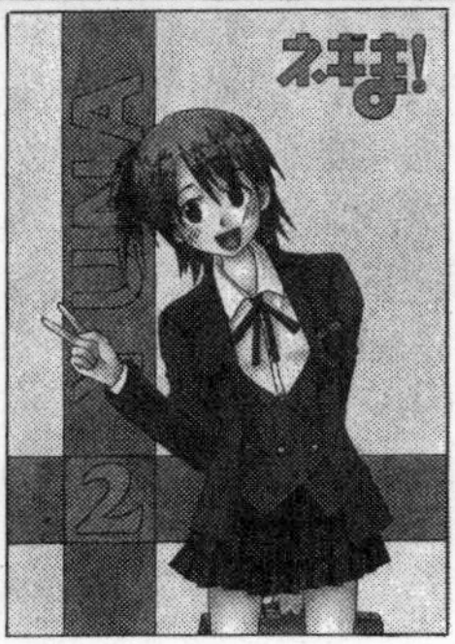
ネギま!

SHE LOOKS LIKE A PRETTY ORTHODOX SCHOOLGIRL.

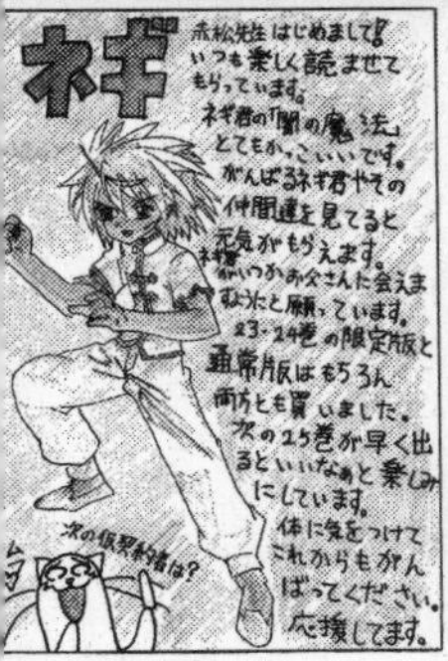
ネギ

IT'S A WHITE-COLORED NEGI.

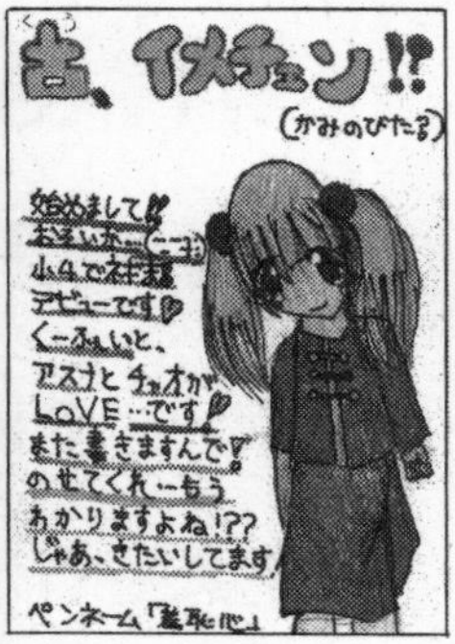

WHAT AN ADORABLE KŪ.

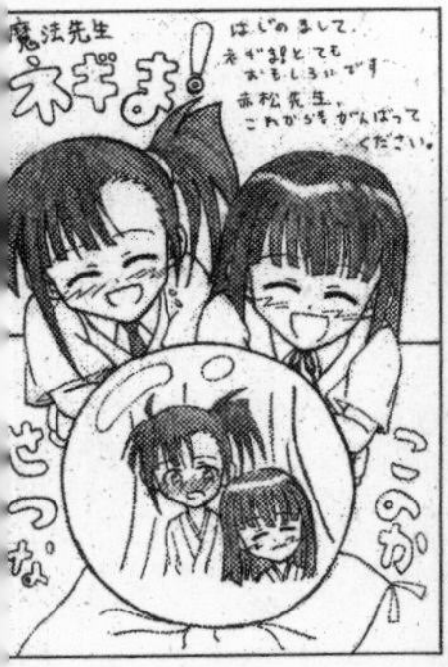
魔法先生
ネギま!

HEARTWARMING☆

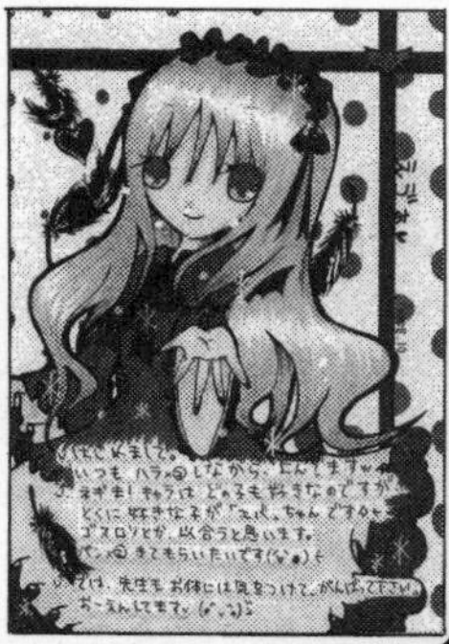

I GET A SENSE OF HER STYLE!

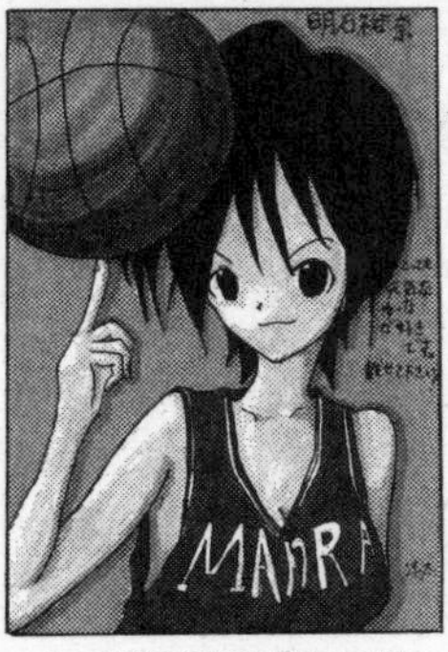
MAHORA

SHE'S COOL AND CUTE IN HER BASKETBALL UNIFORM.

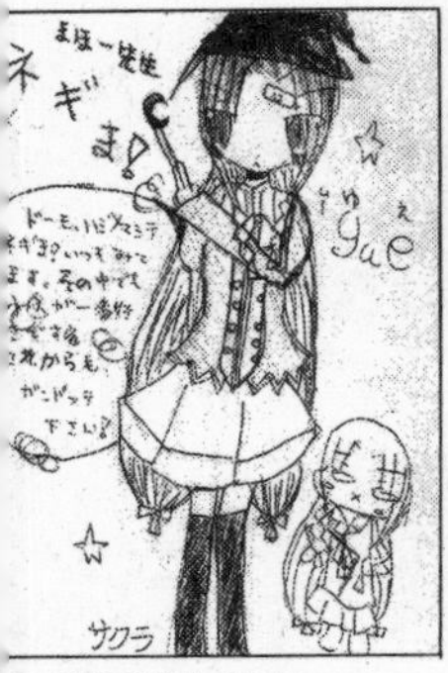

THE BAND-AID IS ADORABLE.

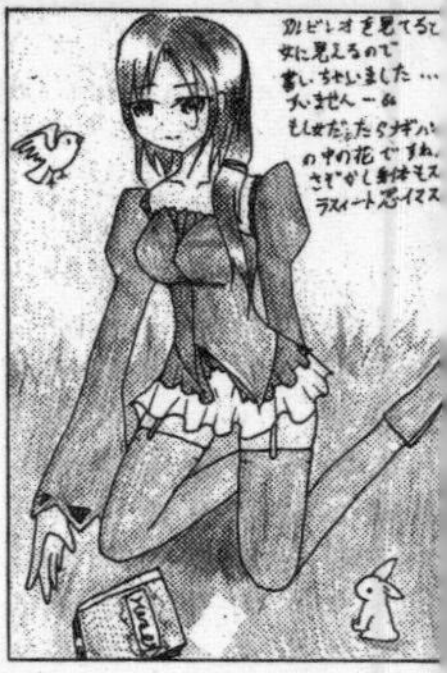

▲ A FEMALE KŪ:NEL. (LAUGH)

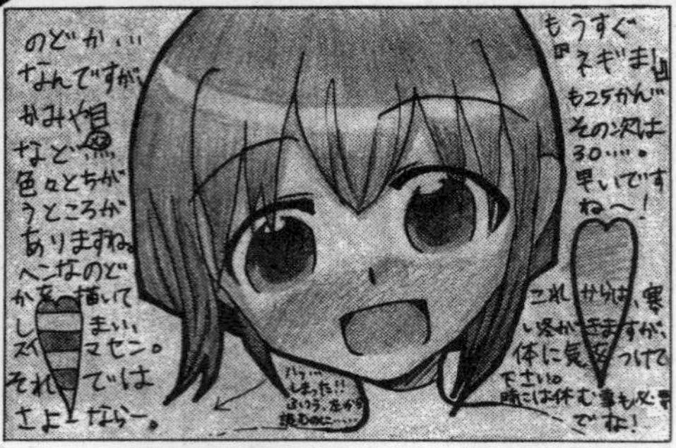
のどかいいなんですが、かみや目など色々とちがうところがありますね。
もうすぐ『ネギま!』も25かん その次は30…。早いですね〜!

▲ WHAT A BIG SMILE!

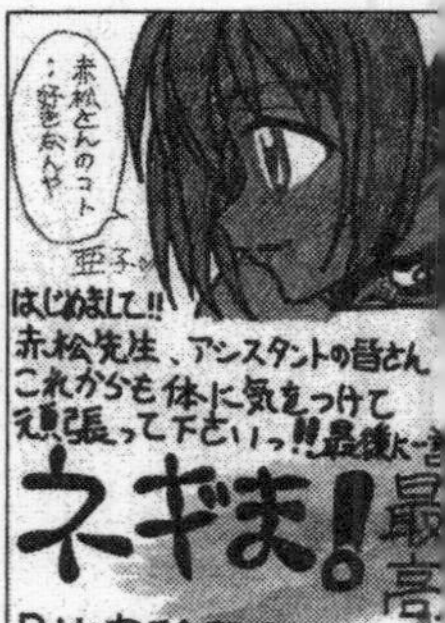
はじめまして!!
ネギま!最高
P.N:実験器具

▲ NICE DRAWING.

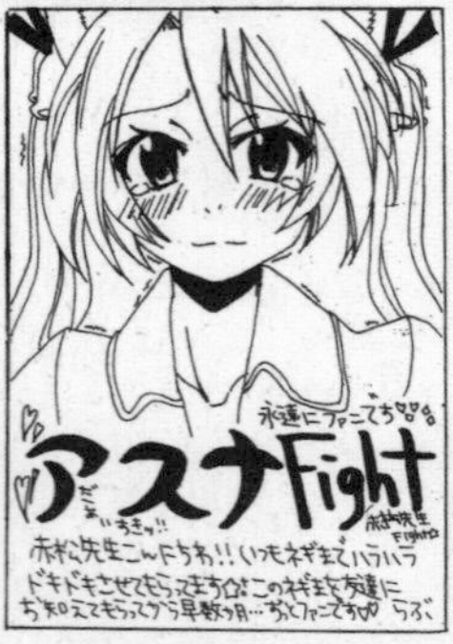
アスナFight

▲ HER FEELINGS ARE GOING TO OVERFLOW.

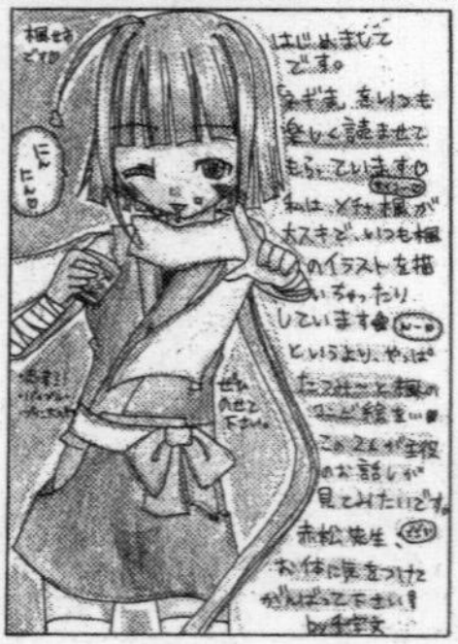

▶ KAEDE'S GOTTEN MORE POPULAR LATELY.

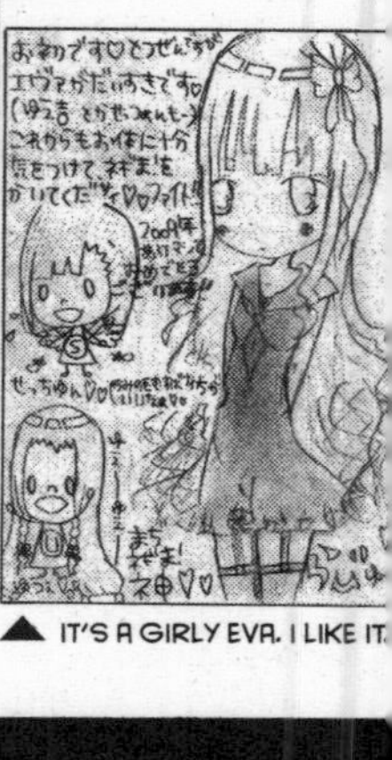

▲ IT'S A GIRLY EVA. I LIKE IT.

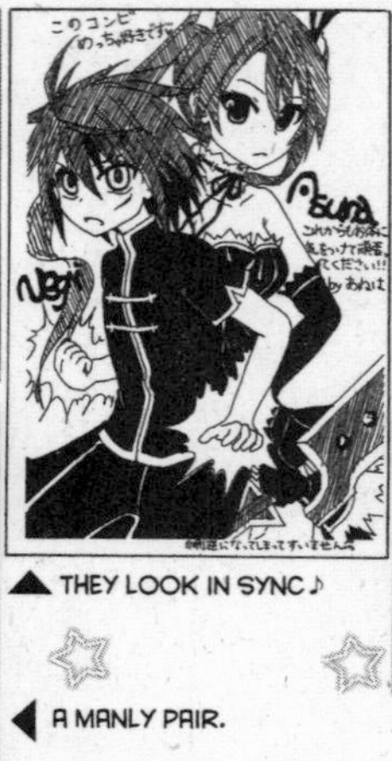
Asuna
Negi

▲ THEY LOOK IN SYNC♪

▼ IT HAS A NICE MOOD TO IT.

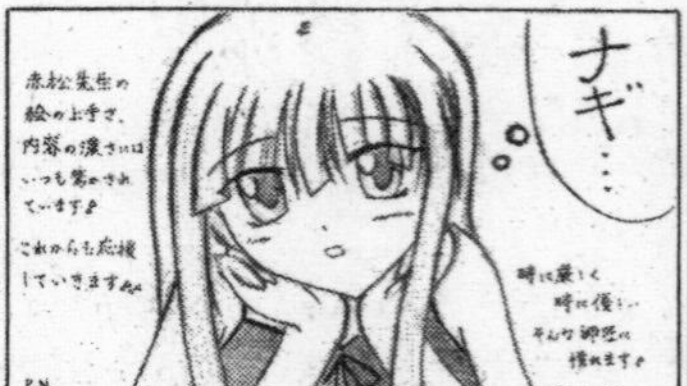
ナギ…

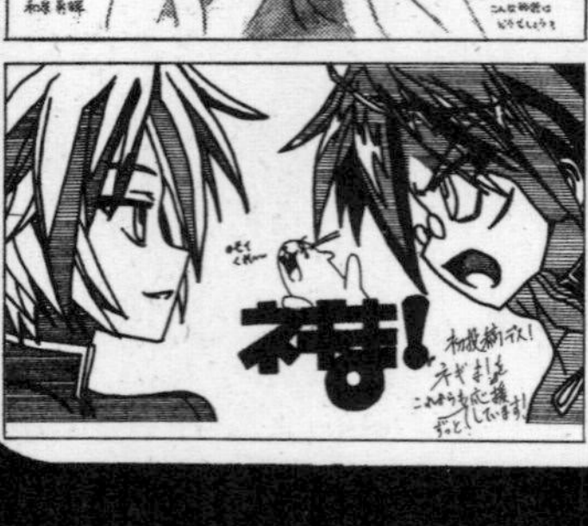
ネギま!

◀ A MANLY PAIR.

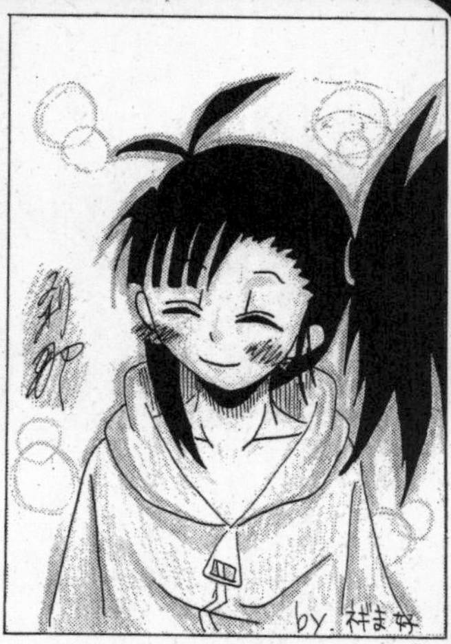
by. ネギま好

L-LIKE A BODHISATTVA, A BUDDHIST SAINT.

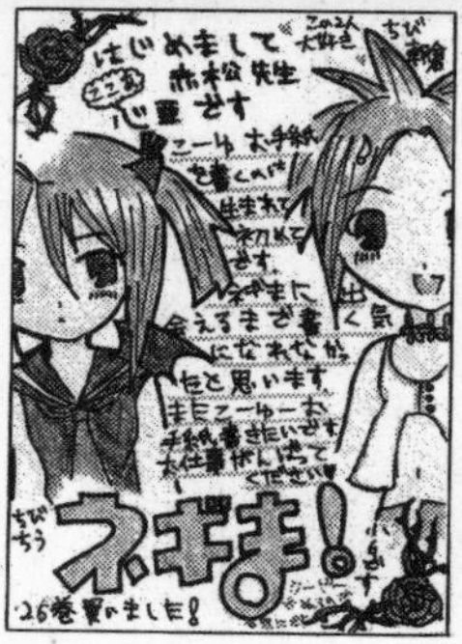
はじめまして
赤松先生
ネギま!
26巻買いました!

A TINY DUO.

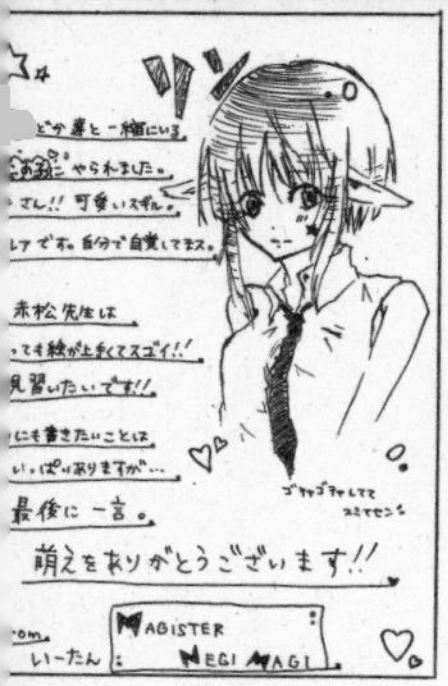
赤松先生は
見習いたいです!!
最後に一言。
萌えをありがとうございます!!
MAGISTER NEGI MAGI

IT'S TRUE; LYNN IS CUTE.

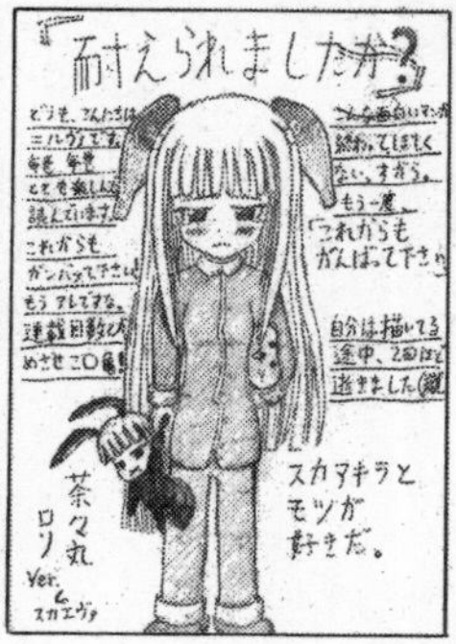
耐えられましたか?
これからも
がんばって下さい
スカヌキラと
モツが
好きだ。

HOW LOL.

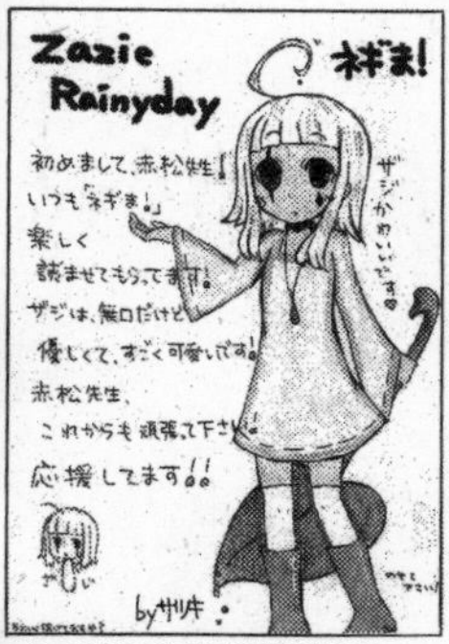
Zazie Rainyday
ネギま!
初めまして、赤松先生!
いつも「ネギま!」
楽しく
読ませてもらってます!
赤松先生、
これからも頑張って下さい
応援してます!!

THIS ZAZIE IS SOOOO CUUUTE☆

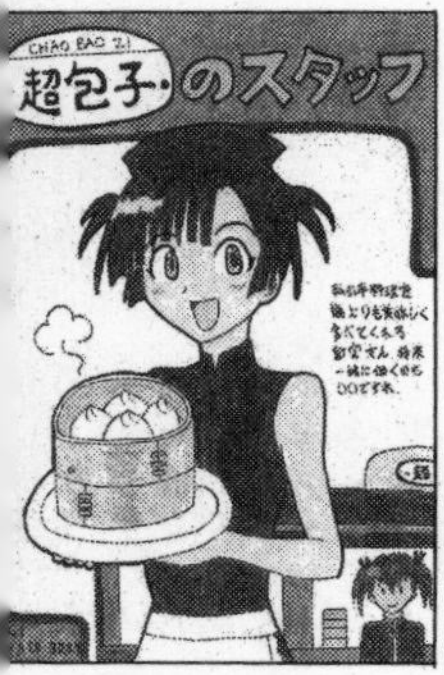
CHAO BAO ZI
超包子のスタッフ

LOOKS DELICIOUS☆

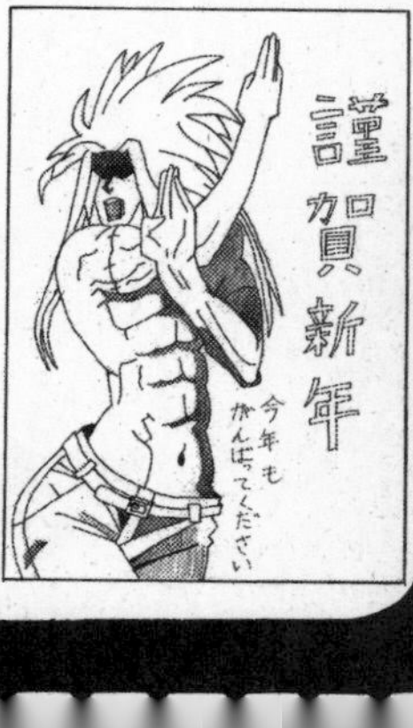
謹賀新年
今年も
がんばってください

THIS ONE'S GOOD.

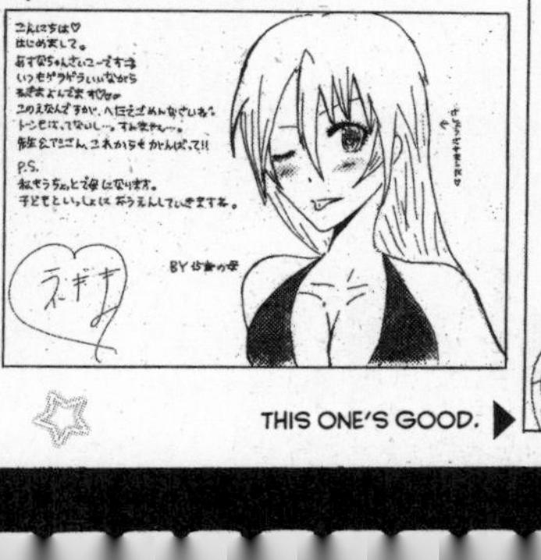
こんにちは♡
はじめまして。
P.S.

A SEXY♪ ASUNA (^^)

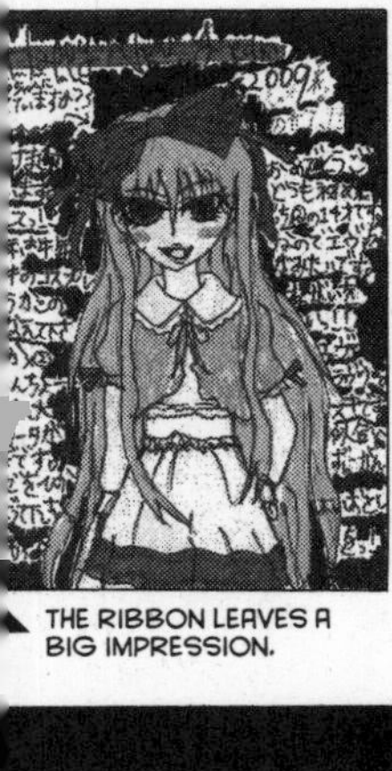
2009年

THE RIBBON LEAVES A BIG IMPRESSION.

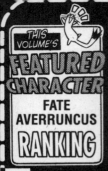

THIS VOLUME'S

FEATURED CHARACTER

FATE AVERRUNCUS RANKING

MAGISTER NEGI MAGI

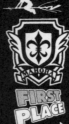

FIRST PLACE

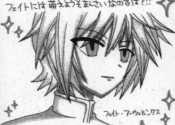

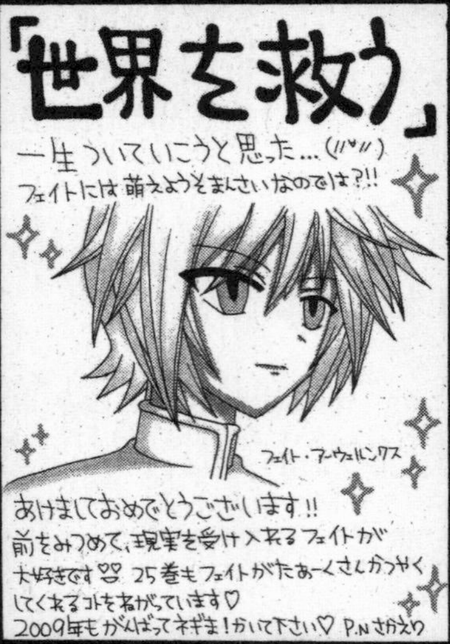

「世界を救う」
一生ついていこうと思った…(//▽//)
フェイトには萌えようそまんさいなのでは?!!
フェイト・アーウェルンクス
あけましておめでとうございます!!
前をみつめて、現実を受け入れるフェイトが大好きです♡ 25巻もフェイトがたあーくさんかつやくしてくれるコトを希がっています♡
2009年もがんばってネギま!かいて下さい♡ P.N さかえり

APPARENTLY THE FATE GIRLS (THOSE FIVE GIRLS) WANT TO FOLLOW HIM FOR THE REST OF THEIR LIVES, LIKE YOU DO. (LAUGH) HE SURE IS POPULAR (^^;)

(AKAMATSU)

SECOND PLACE

アーウェルンクス
By 雅歩
フェイト最強ーー★! 大人(?)フェイトもめちゃカッコイイです♡ 惚れましたww 私はフェイトを応援しますー(笑)
NEGIMA!

I BET AKIRA ISHIDA-SAN'S VOICE WOULD WORK EVEN BETTER FOR ADULT FATE!

THIRD PLACE

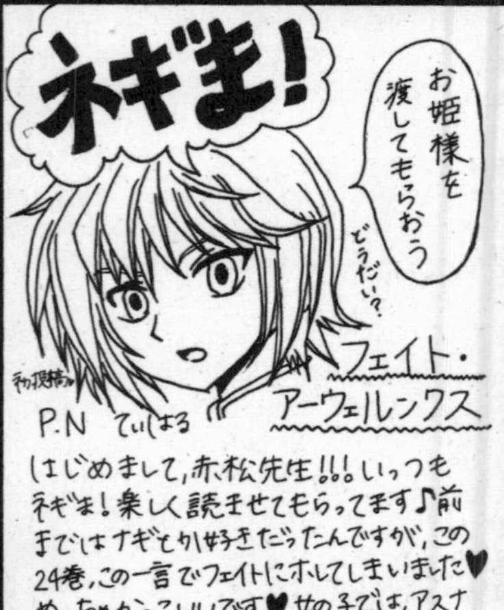

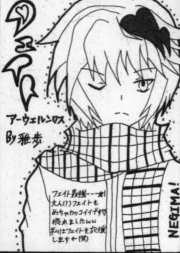

ネギま!
お姫様を渡してもらおう
どうだい?
フェイト・アーウェルンクス
初投稿
P.N ていはる
はじめまして、赤松先生!!! いつもネギま!楽しく読ませてもらってます♪ 前まではナギとかが好きだったんですが、この24巻、この一言でフェイトにホレてしまいました♥ めっちゃかっこいいです♥ 女の子では、アスナとかセツナ、このかが好きです! 本当、はやくアスナの過去が知りたいです!(次巻待ちどおしい…) では、お体に気をつけて。ずっと応援してます!!!

IF YOU LIKE THEM BOTH, THEN HOW ABOUT A FATE X NAGI PAIRING? (LAUGH) (HUH? WOULD IT BE NAGI X FATE?)

LEXICON NEGIMARIUM

[*Negima!* 232nd Period Lexicon Negimarium]

■ "Strongest Protection"
(kratistê aigis)
(ΚΡΑ΄ΤΙΣΤΗ ΄ ΑΙΓΙ΄Σ)

A spell that creates multiple wide-range magic circles equipped with extremely powerful anti-physical and anti-magical defense. It is extremely high-level magic, so the spell is incanted in Ancient Greek. The wind defense spell that Negi uses is derived from the defense magic with the *aigis* name used by Nagi's master Zecht. This is because it is believed that the true nature of *aigis* (αἰγίς, "aegis" in Latin and English) is a power that makes up storms and weather.

κράτιστη (kratistê) is the superlative feminine singular nominative case of the adjective κρατύ (kratu), meaning "strong." And—according to dictionaries such as Oxford's Liddell & Scott—it is the shield of the king of the gods, Zeus, as well as Athena, in Greek mythology. However, it is commonly accepted in modern studies of the classics that the *aigis* is not a shield. According to the legendary poet Homer (8C BC?), the *aigis* takes the following form:

"Meanwhile, Athena, daughter of *aigis*-bearing Zeus (...) placed the dreaded tasseled *aigis* about her shoulders. All around, the *aigis* was wrapped in fear, and in its center (...) was affixed the dreaded ill omen of the Gorgon's head, terrible to look upon, portent of the *aigis*-bearing Zeus." (The *Iliad*, 5.733-742)

Take note that Athena wrapped the aigis around her shoulders. The passage does not depict the equipping of a shield. The interpretation that the *aigis* is a shield comes from the depiction of the Gorgon's head being affixed to its center. For example, as written in Apollodorus' (1C BC) record, "[Perseus] (...) gave the Gorgon's head to Athena. Then (...) Athena placed the Gorgon's head in the center of the shield (αἰγίς)," (*Bibliotheca [Βιβλιοθήκη]*, 2,4,3), there was a myth in Ancient Greece in which the hero Perseus slays one of the three Gorgon sisters, the goddess Athena accepts her head, and places it on her shield. Based on this myth, one can logically come to the conclusion that the *aigis* is the shield with the Gorgon's head affixed onto it.

However, the Father of History, Herodotus (5C BC?), leaves the following record: "The Greeks used the dress of Libyan women as the basis for the clothing and *aigis* of the statue of Athena. This is determined because everything is fashioned in the same manner, excepting that Libyan women's clothing is made of leather, and their tassels are of leather cords and not of snakes. The name, too, is evidence that the attire of the Athena statue came from Libya. Libyan women wear over their clothes an *aigea*

(αἰγέα), or goatskin with the hair plucked, decorated with tassels, and dyed red. The Greeks took the name *aigis* from this *aigea*." (*The Histories*, 4.189)

Herodotus' linguistic theory here is mistaken. Nevertheless, his record of the Athena statue's attire was written at the time of its construction, and there is no room for doubt. Thus, the *aigis* is of course nothing like a shield, nor is it anything resembling armor.

The *aigis* is in the form of a cloak worn over one's clothing. Also, according to Herodotus' record, the *aigis* worn by the Athena statue had tassel decorations in the shape of snakes. This coincides with Homer's poem describing the *aigis* as being decorated by the Gorgon's head.

The reason such a cloak would be a priceless treasure in battle is that the *aigis* had the Gorgon's head affixed to it. Various archaeological research lends credence to this fact. For example, in a mosaic found at the Pompeii excavation site in Italy (now in the Naples National Archaeological Museum), the Gorgon's head was depicted on the breast of Alexander the Great at the Battle of Issus. From these evidences, we see that the Gorgon is no mere monster. The Gorgon is a guardian deity in a grotesque form. This is a commonality with the gargoyles of Europe and the *onigawara* of Japan, who ward off evil despite their monstrous appearances.

The name of the Gorgon slain by Perseus and offered to Athena is Medusa. The name Medusa (Μέδουσα) is the present participle active aspect of the feminine singular form of the verb μέδειν (medein, to protect) and means "protector." As the name suggests, the Gorgon's head placed on the *aigis* has the power of a protective charm. The basic-level superstitious practice of wearing a grotesque Gorgon as a protective charm came first, and it was from this practice that the statue of armed Athena came to be ornamented with a Gorgon. This begs the question: Why would a statue of Athena wear a Gorgon? The myth that Medusa had offended Athena and was changed into an ugly creature was born later, in answer to that question (e.g., *Metamorphoses* 4.791–804). Thus, Medusa would have had a terrifying appearance even before the myth was created. This is because if she were not grotesque, she could not serve as a guardian deity, or a "protector (Medusa)."

There is suspicion that Athena is associated with the *aigis* imbued with the Gorgon's magic, because of the popularity of the myth about Perseus slaying Medusa. However, the *aigis* originally belonged to Zeus. This is expressed in the epithets (ἐπίθετον) characteristic of Ancient Greek literary works. For example, Zeus is called "Zeus the *aigis*-bearing (αἰγίοχον, *aigiochon*), son of Kronos" (*The Iliad*, 2.375), and the epithet "*aigis*-bearing" is attached to Zeus, but never to Athena (Athena's epithets are "bright-eyed," etc.). Zeus' other epithets include "high-thundering" (ibid. 1.354), "cloud-gatherer" (ibid. 1.511), "lightning-wielder" (ibid. 1.580), and "loud-thundering" (ibid. 5.672), all fitting of a god who controls storms and weather. That being the case, we can guess that the epithet "*aigis*-bearing" also refers to phenomena relating to weather. The works of Aeschylus (525/524–456/455 BC), one of the three great Greek tragedians, provide the following:

"Indeed, the land nurtures a multitude of terrible things, of pains of fear. Both hands of the sea are filled with defiant beasts. The burning light hung

in the sky approaches. Those with wings, those who walk the earth, all tell of the blowing rage of the *aigis*" (*The Libation Bearers*, 585–593).

The "rage of the *aigis*" is described as "blowing" (ήνεμόεν). In other words, the rage of the *aigis* is a violent storm. Birds and other animals are all sensitive to changes in the weather. That is exactly why it is said that they can tell us of the rage of the *aigis*—the arrival of a storm. Thus, the "burning light hung in the sky" mentioned before would be flashes of lightning (though some interpret it as a falling star). Based on these examples, the *aigis* refers to something like the power of the weather, which takes the form of a storm when enraged. It is extremely appropriate that Zeus, the god of storms and weather, would have the epithet of "*aigis*-bearer."

That being the case, the Gorgon, who lends her magic to the *aigis*, would have a strong connection to the power of storms and weather. In *The Iliad*, cited above, the Gorgon's head is described as a "portent of Zeus." The Gorgon and Zeus are connected through the medium of the *aigis* symbol. We can also see this in the myth about Pegasus. "When Perseus cut off the head [of Medusa], from her neck (...) sprung the horse Pegasus. (...) And Pegasus leapt from the earth and flew to the immortal gods. He now carries the thunder and lightning to the wise Zeus and lives in Zeus' palace." (Hesiod's *Theogony*, 280–286)

According to Hesiod, Pegasus was born from the neck of the Gorgon, Medusa. And this Pegasus fulfills the duty of carrying Zeus' lightning. In fact, the word "pegasus" is said to come from "*pihassas*," a word from Luwian, one of the Indo-European Anatolian languages, meaning "lightning." Like the Zeus-*Aigis*-Gorgon formula, the Zeus-Pegasus-Gorgon formula, too, connects the Gorgon to Zeus.

[*Negima!* 234th Period Lexicon Negimarium]

■ Life-Stealing Signet

(signum biolegens)

The girl known as Shiori is awarded this item for her use by the power of the pactio with the white-haired boy. Through the sharing of a kiss with a human or humanoid life-form, it reconstructs the target's physical and mental characteristics inside the body and actions of the user.

Signum is Latin for "mark" or "symbol" (the origin of the English "sign"); "biolegens" is an adjective formed from a combination of the Ancient Greek βίος (bios), meaning "life," and the Latin *legere*, meaning "to read," and means "life-stealing." The word *legere* means "to read," but also means "to steal." This artifact steals the target's life (βίος) through a kiss.

[*Negima!* 236th Period Lexicon Negimarium]

■ "Water Spirit's Great Deluge"

(MAGNA CATARACTA)

Magic that produces a large quantity of water. It can quench the thirst of many living things. When generating water from a high place, the potential energy of the great mass will cause great destruction where the water lands, so use with care.

■ "Water Current Barrier"

(UNDANS PARIES AQUARIUS)

It is normal for a wizard to surround himself with a magical wall to protect himself from physical damage. That is why, in First Period, the blackboard eraser that fell on Negi's head floated in the air.

"Undans paries aquarius" means "wall of surging water" in Latin and is a barrier spell in the same category as "flans paries aerialis," which means "wall of blowing air." Both have enough defensive power to guard against the impact of a ten-ton truck. "Water Current Barrier" is also excellent against heat and dryness.

[*Negima!* 238th Period Lexicon Negimarium]

■ "Upon our pact, do my bidding, O Lord of the Heavens. Come forth, blazing bolts that overthrow Titans. Let hundreds and thousands combine; run forth, lightning. Thousand Lightning Bolts."

(To symbolaion diakonêtô moi basileu Ouraniônôn. Epigenêthêtô aithalous keraune os Titênas phtheirein. Êcatontakis kai kiliakis astrapsatô. KILIPL ASTRAPÊ)

Nagi used this superwide-range lightning annihilation magic back in *Negima!* volume 19, 169th Period. The spell is incanted in Ancient Greek. The full incantation appeared in the 238th Period, so it is now being listed here.

■ "Spread forth, extended aide magic circle. Capture targets one through ten. Lock on. Increase spirit pressure inside range to maximum. 3...2...critical pressure. Remove restraints. All lightning spirits, release full power."

(jactum extendentes circuli existant, captent objecta primum ad decimum. area constet. intus se premant spiritus ad pressuram criticalem. tribus...duobus...modo. capturam disjungens. omnes spiritus fulgurales fortissime emittam.)

A spell that generates a magic circle that expands and corrects the distance and effective range of magical abilities used in the physical world. In the story, Negi's Kilipl Astrapê (Thousand Lightning Bolts) was incomplete, so he demonstrated near-perfect results through the use of a support spell.

3-D BACKGROUNDS EXPLANATION CORNER

THIS TIME WE'RE CHANGING THE IDEA A BIT AND TALKING ABOUT THE PRACTICAL APPLICATIONS OF 3D CG.

LATELY, 3D BACKGROUNDS HAVE BEEN INCREASING LITTLE BY LITTLE, AND THIS TIME I WILL TALK ABOUT MAKING FINISHING TOUCHES WITH CG. I HAD BEEN CREATING LINE DRAWINGS FOR SOME OF THE *NEGIMA!* BACKGROUNDS WITH CG FOR SOME TIME NOW, BUT I HAD BEEN FINISHING THEM UP, AS ALWAYS, WITH THE OLD-FASHIONED, NON-DIGITAL TECHNIQUES OF SPREADING SCREENTONE ON THOSE LINE DRAWINGS. BUT WHEN THE BACKGROUNDS ARE MADE WITH 3D GRAPHICS, THEN SOMETIMES IT'S MORE CONVENIENT TO FINISH THEM UP WITH COMPUTER GRAPHICS, TOO, SO RECENTLY THE CG TOUCH-UPS HAVE BEEN GRADUALLY INCREASING. NOW I WOULD LIKE TO EXPLAIN THE TECHNIQUES FOR COMBINING THE 3D BACKGROUNDS WITH CG FINISHING TOUCHES.

- CASE 1: DROPPING SHADOWS -

I INTRODUCED THIS METHOD BEFORE, BUT THIS TIME, I WOULD LIKE TO GO THROUGH THE PROCESS STEP BY STEP. 3D GRAPHIC SOFTWARE HAS A FUNCTION THAT ALLOWS YOU TO SET A LIGHT SOURCE, THEN CALCULATES WHERE THE OBJECTS' SHADOWS WOULD FALL, AND WITH IT, WE CAN DROP SHADOWS ACCURATELY AND EASILY. NOW THEN, LET'S TAKE A LOOK AT THE PROCESS USING A SPECIFIC EXAMPLE.

• GRAVE KEEPER'S PALACE

SCENE NAME: DARK PALACE   POLYGON COUNT: 32,925

THE SCENE OF THE FINAL BATTLE BETWEEN NAGI'S PARTY AND THE BIG BOSS (MAGE OF THE BEGINNING). THE LINE DRAWING IS 3D, OF COURSE, BUT THERE WAS A NEED FOR REALISTIC SHADOWS, SO THEY WERE MADE IN 3D, TOO. I USED PHOTOSHOP FOR THE FINISHING TOUCHES, MAKING THEM CG AS WELL.

- STEP 1: CREATING THE LINE DRAWING -

FIRST, I CREATE THE LINES FOR THE 3D SECTIONS. THIS IS THE SAME AS ALWAYS.

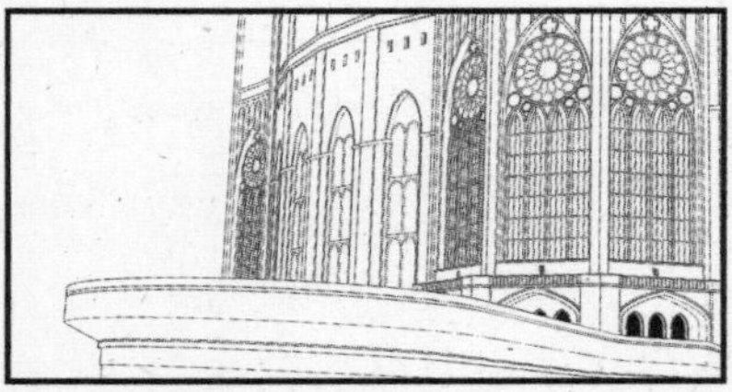

- STEP 2: CREATING THE SHADOW IMAGES -

NEXT, I MAKE THE IMAGE FOR THE SHADOWS SEPARATELY FROM THE LINE DRAWING. I DO MORE BRIGHTNESS ADJUSTING IN PHOTOSHOP, SO THIS IMAGE IS TEMPORARY.

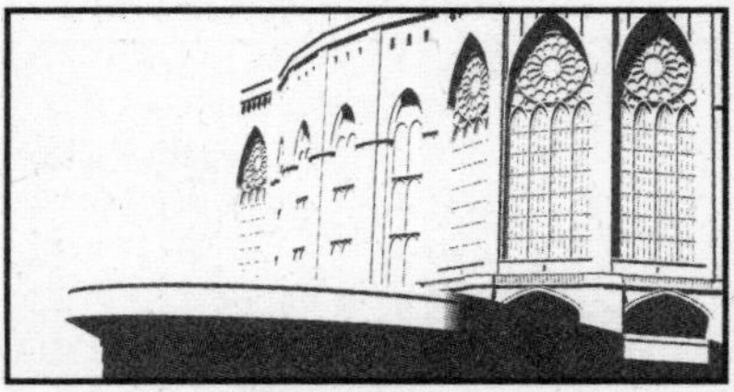

- STEP 3: ADJUSTING THE SHADOW BRIGHTNESS -

HERE, I MADE THE SHADOWS BLACK TO CREATE A SENSE OF TENSION. WHEN I COMBINE IT WITH THE LINE DRAWING AND HAND-DRAWN ELEMENTS, LIKE THE CHARACTERS, IT LOOKS LIKE THE PICTURE BELOW.

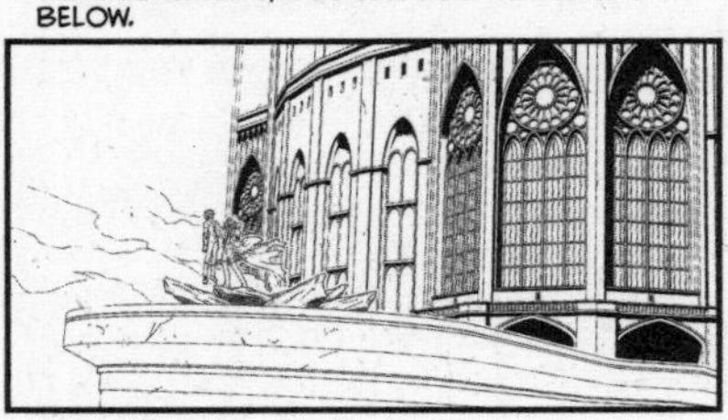

- STEP 4: FINISHING TOUCHES -

I TOUCH UP EVERYTHING ELSE. DROPPING THE SHADOWS IS A SNAP, SO ACTUALLY THIS IS WHERE THE REAL WORK STARTS (^_^;) BELOW IS THE FINISHED DRAWING. CHARACTERS WILL BE ADDED TO THE LOWER RIGHT.

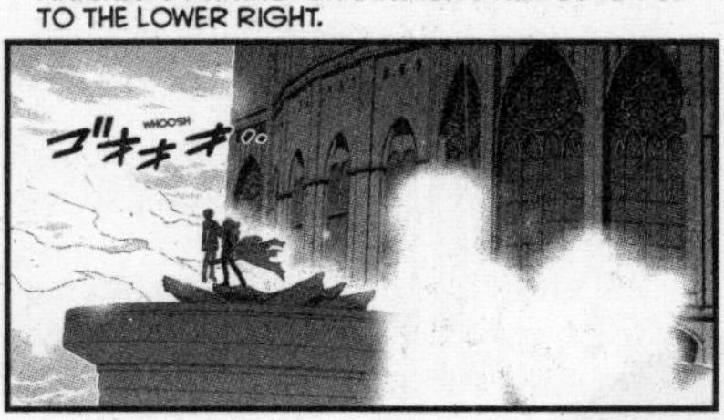
WHOOSH

- CASE 2: BACKGROUND REFLECTIONS -

3D CG SOFTWARE ALSO HAS A FUNCTION TO RE-CREATE THE PHENOMENON OF PICTURES REFLECTING OFF OF SURFACES SUCH AS WATER. THIS PHENOMENON IS VERY DIFFICULT TO REPRODUCE ACCURATELY BY HAND, BUT WITH 3D CG, IT'S SIMPLE. NOW THEN, I HAVE AN EXAMPLE REPRESENTING THE USE OF THAT TECHNIQUE, SO I WILL PROVIDE IT HERE.

• OSTIA'S BRICK BRIDGE

SCENE NAME: BRICK BRIDGE   POLYGON COUNT: 862,826

THIS IS THE PART OF OSTIA WHERE NEGI AND FATE HAVE THEIR STREET FIGHT IN VOLUME 25. I HAD A REQUEST TO MAKE THE WATER SURFACE IN THIS PANEL REALISTIC, SO I USED 3D CG TO RE-CREATE THE REFLECTION OF THE TOWN AND THE BRIDGE ON THE WATER.

- STEP 1: CREATING THE LINE DRAWING -

FIRST, I CREATE THE 3D LINE DRAWING. I MAKE ADJUSTMENTS USING PHOTOSHOP.

- STEP 2: CREATING THE REFLECTED IMAGE -

I CREATE A PICTURE TO BE USED FOR THE REFLECTION. SHADOWS ARE ADDED AS WELL. BUT THE WATER SURFACE IN THIS PICTURE IS TOO REAL, AND NOT VERY MANGA-LIKE, SO I ADJUST IT FROM HERE.

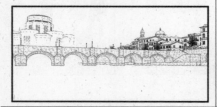

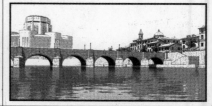

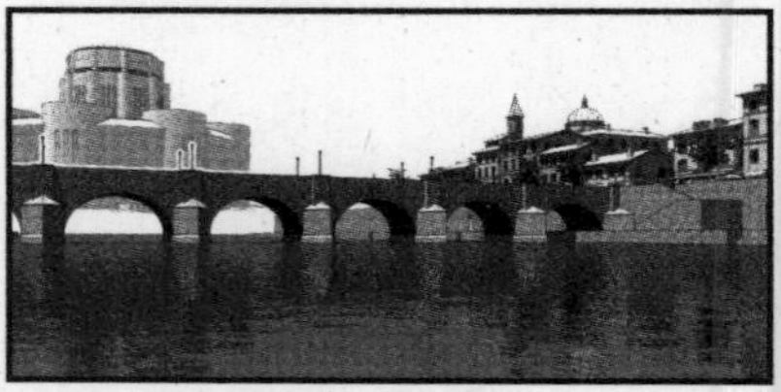

- STEP 3: CORRECTING COLOR TONE IN PHOTOSHOP -

I USE THE COLOR CORRECTION FUNCTION TO DECREASE THE NUMBER OF COLORS ON THE WATER'S SURFACE, SIMPLIFYING IT. BUT IT'S STILL REALISTIC, RIGHT? FROM HERE, I FIX IT BY HAND.

- STEP 4: ALTERING THE SHAPE -

I BLOT OUT THE PARTS WITH TOO MUCH DETAIL AND MAKE THEM MORE VAGUE. I STILL FEEL LIKE IT'S TOO REALISTIC, BUT THIS TIME WE'LL SAY IT'S GOOD ENOUGH...

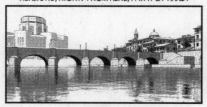

- STEP 5: TOUCHING UP THE WATER'S SURFACE -

I PUT THE CHARACTERS IN THE PICTURE AND ADD THEIR REFLECTIONS BY HAND. I ADD SOME MORE FLAVOR WITH DETAILS LIKE THE SHADOWS UNDER THE BRIDGE, THE RIPPLES, AND OTHER TONE-ERASING EFFECTS, AND THE WATER'S SURFACE IS COMPLETE.

- STEP 6: TOUCHING UP EVERYTHING ELSE -

I FINISH UP THE TOWN, THE SKY, AND EVERYTHING ELSE. I GET THE FEELING THEY DON'T QUITE BLEND WITH THE WATER, BUT WE'LL MAKE THAT OUR ASSIGNMENT FOR NEXT TIME (^_^;) AT ANY RATE, IT'S COMPLETE.

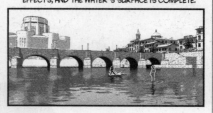

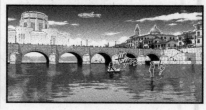

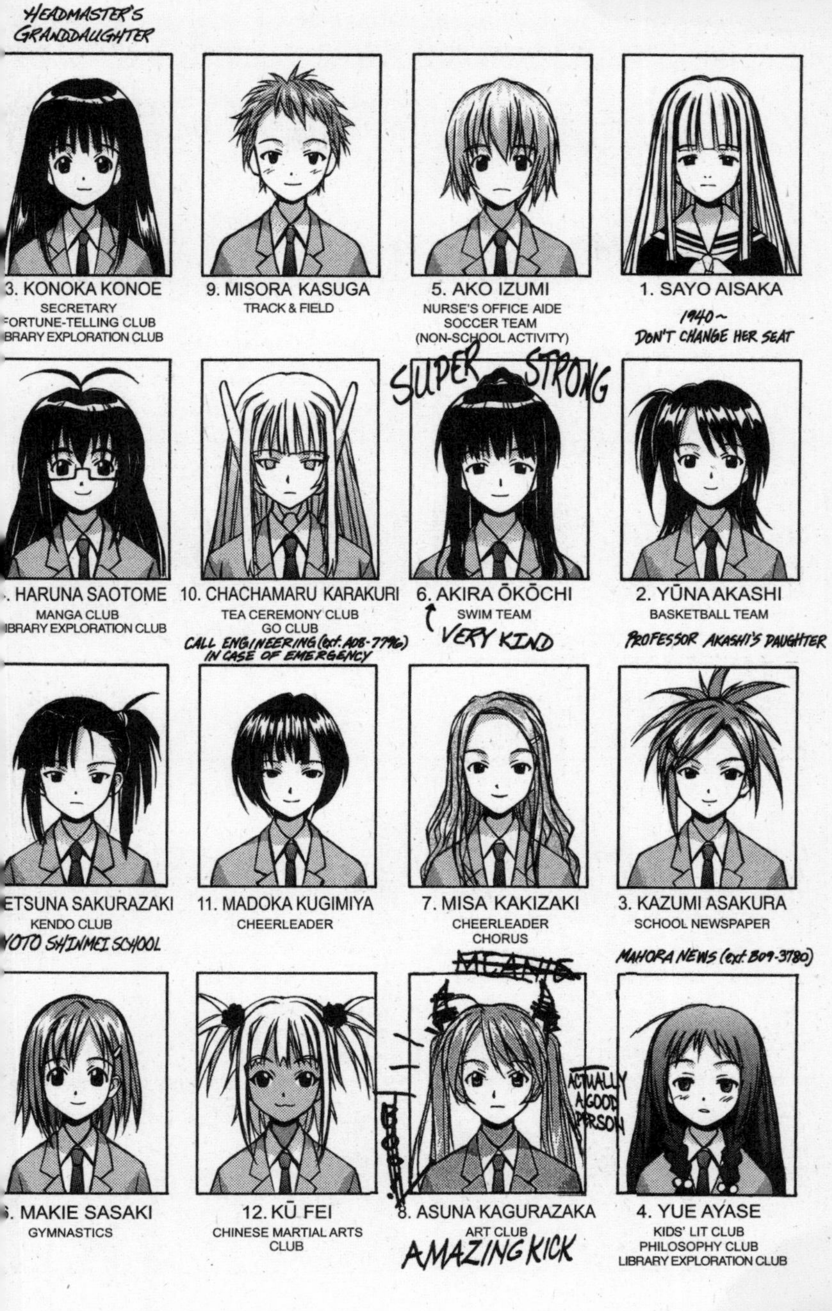
1. SAYO AISAKA
1940~
DON'T CHANGE HER SEAT
5. AKO IZUMI
NURSE'S OFFICE AIDE
SOCCER TEAM
(NON-SCHOOL ACTIVITY)
9. MISORA KASUGA
TRACK & FIELD
HEADMASTER'S GRANDDAUGHTER
3. KONOKA KONOE
SECRETARY
FORTUNE-TELLING CLUB
IBRARY EXPLORATION CLUB
2. YŪNA AKASHI
BASKETBALL TEAM
PROFESSOR AKASHI'S DAUGHTER
SUPER STRONG
6. AKIRA ŌKŌCHI
SWIM TEAM
VERY KIND
10. CHACHAMARU KARAKURI
TEA CEREMONY CLUB
GO CLUB
CALL ENGINEERING (ext. A08-7796) IN CASE OF EMERGENCY
. HARUNA SAOTOME
MANGA CLUB
IBRARY EXPLORATION CLUB
3. KAZUMI ASAKURA
SCHOOL NEWSPAPER
MAHORA NEWS (ext. 809-3780)
7. MISA KAKIZAKI
CHEERLEADER
CHORUS
11. MADOKA KUGIMIYA
CHEERLEADER
ETSUNA SAKURAZAKI
KENDO CLUB
YOTO SHINMEI SCHOOL
4. YUE AYASE
KIDS' LIT CLUB
PHILOSOPHY CLUB
LIBRARY EXPLORATION CLUB
~~MEANIE~~
ACTUALLY A GOOD PERSON
8. ASUNA KAGURAZAKA
ART CLUB
AMAZING KICK
12. KŪ FEI
CHINESE MARTIAL ARTS CLUB
. MAKIE SASAKI
GYMNASTICS

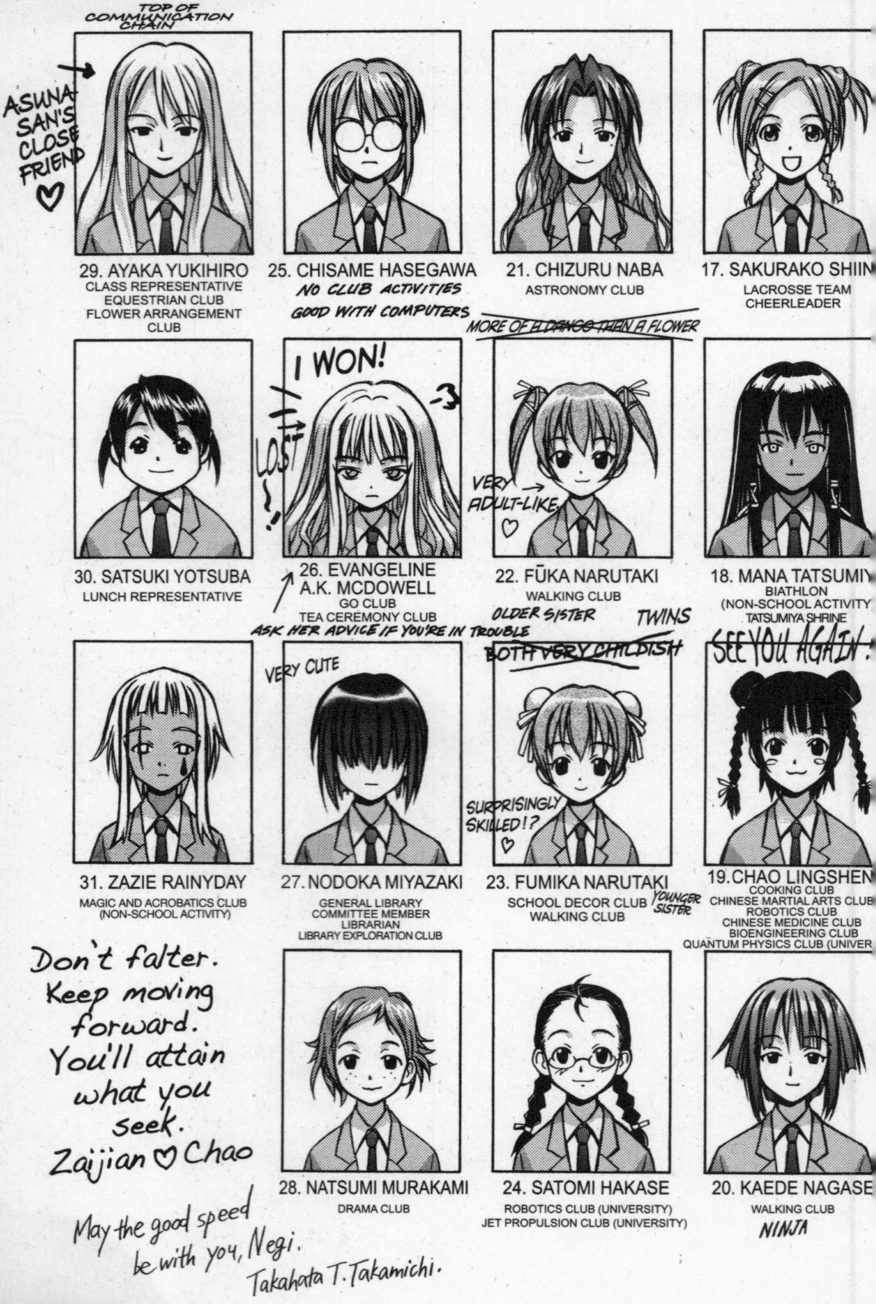

17. SAKURAKO SHIIN
LACROSSE TEAM
CHEERLEADER
21. CHIZURU NABA
ASTRONOMY CLUB
25. CHISAME HASEGAWA
NO CLUB ACTIVITIES
GOOD WITH COMPUTERS
TOP OF COMMUNICATION CHAIN
ASUNA-SAN'S CLOSE FRIEND ♡
29. AYAKA YUKIHIRO
CLASS REPRESENTATIVE
EQUESTRIAN CLUB
FLOWER ARRANGEMENT CLUB
MORE OF A DANGO THAN A FLOWER
18. MANA TATSUMIY
BIATHLON
(NON-SCHOOL ACTIVITY)
TATSUMIYA SHRINE
VERY ADULT-LIKE ♡
22. FŪKA NARUTAKI
WALKING CLUB
OLDER SISTER
I WON!
LOST
26. EVANGELINE A.K. MCDOWELL
GO CLUB
TEA CEREMONY CLUB
ASK HER ADVICE IF YOU'RE IN TROUBLE
30. SATSUKI YOTSUBA
LUNCH REPRESENTATIVE
TWINS
BOTH VERY CHILDISH
SEE YOU AGAIN!
19. CHAO LINGSHEN
COOKING CLUB
CHINESE MARTIAL ARTS CLUB
ROBOTICS CLUB
CHINESE MEDICINE CLUB
BIOENGINEERING CLUB
QUANTUM PHYSICS CLUB (UNIVER
SURPRISINGLY SKILLED!? ♡
23. FUMIKA NARUTAKI
SCHOOL DECOR CLUB
WALKING CLUB
YOUNGER SISTER
VERY CUTE
27. NODOKA MIYAZAKI
GENERAL LIBRARY COMMITTEE MEMBER
LIBRARIAN
LIBRARY EXPLORATION CLUB
31. ZAZIE RAINYDAY
MAGIC AND ACROBATICS CLUB
(NON-SCHOOL ACTIVITY)
20. KAEDE NAGASE
WALKING CLUB
NINJA
24. SATOMI HAKASE
ROBOTICS CLUB (UNIVERSITY)
JET PROPULSION CLUB (UNIVERSITY)
28. NATSUMI MURAKAMI
DRAMA CLUB
Don't falter. Keep moving forward. You'll attain what you seek. Zaijian ♡ Chao
May the good speed be with you, Negi. Takahata T. Takamichi.

魔法先生ネギま! MAGISTER NEGI MAGI

赤松 健 SHONEN MAGAZINE COMICS
KEN AKAMATSU

26

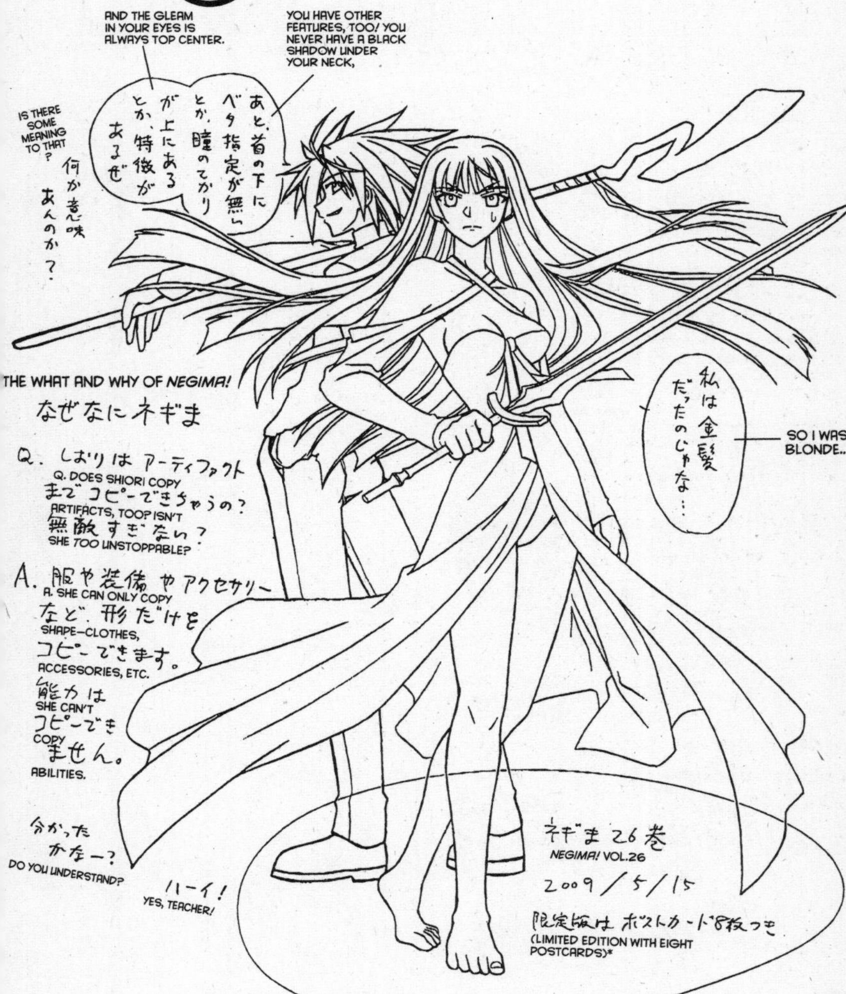
あと、首の下にベタ指定が無いとか、瞳のてかりが上にあるとか、特徴があるぜ
YOU HAVE OTHER FEATURES, TOO! YOU NEVER HAVE A BLACK SHADOW UNDER YOUR NECK,
AND THE GLEAM IN YOUR EYES IS ALWAYS TOP CENTER.
何か意味あんのか?
IS THERE SOME MEANING TO THAT?
私は金髪だったのじゃな…
SO I WAS BLONDE...
THE WHAT AND WHY OF NEGIMA!
なぜなにネギま
Q. しおりはアーティファクトまでコピーできちゃうの? 無敵すぎない?
Q. DOES SHIORI COPY ARTIFACTS, TOO? ISN'T SHE TOO UNSTOPPABLE?
A. 服や装備やアクセサリーなど、形だけをコピーできます。能力はコピーできません。
A. SHE CAN ONLY COPY SHAPE—CLOTHES, ACCESSORIES, ETC. SHE CAN'T COPY ABILITIES.
分かったかなー?
DO YOU UNDERSTAND?
ハーイ!
YES, TEACHER!
ネギま26巻
NEGIMA! VOL.26
2009/5/15
限定版はポストカード8枚つき
(LIMITED EDITION WITH EIGHT POSTCARDS)*

*LIMITED EDITION AVAILABLE ONLY IN JAPAN

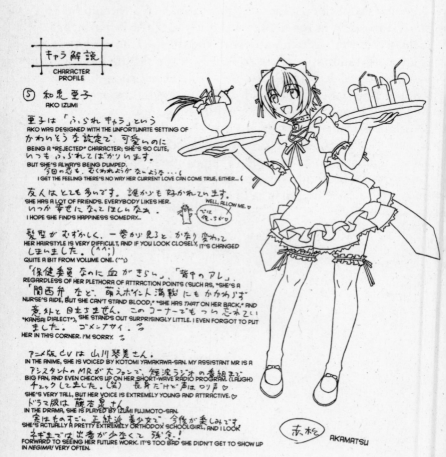

CHARACTER PROFILE

キャラ解説

⑤ 和泉 亜子
AKO IZUMI

亜子は「ふられキャラ」という
AKO WAS DESIGNED WITH THE UNFORTUNATE SETTING OF
かわいそうな設定で。可愛いのに
BEING A "REJECTED" CHARACTER; SHE'S SO CUTE,
いつもふられてばかりです。
BUT SHE'S ALWAYS BEING DUMPED.
「今回の恋も。むくわれようがないような…(
I GET THE FEELING THERE'S NO WAY HER CURRENT LOVE CAN COME TRUE, EITHER... (

友人はとても多いです。誰からも好かれています。
SHE HAS A LOT OF FRIENDS. EVERYBODY LIKES HER.
いつか幸せになってほしいなぁ。
I HOPE SHE FINDS HAPPINESS SOMEDAY...

WELL, ALLOW ME. ♡
ごは
使.すが♡

髪型がむずかしく。一巻から見るとかなり変わって
HER HAIRSTYLE IS VERY DIFFICULT, AND IF YOU LOOK CLOSELY, IT'S CHANGED
しまいました。(^^;)
QUITE A BIT FROM VOLUME ONE. (^^;)

「保健委員なのに血がきらい。「背中のアレ」
REGARDLESS OF HER PLETHORA OF ATTRACTION POINTS (SUCH AS, "SHE'S A
「関西弁」など。萌えポイント満載にもかかわらず
NURSE'S AIDE, BUT SHE CAN'T STAND BLOOD," "SHE HAS *THAT* ON HER BACK," AND
意外と目立ちません。このコーナーでもっい忘れてい
"KANSAI DIALECT"), SHE STANDS OUT SURPRISINGLY LITTLE. I EVEN FORGOT TO PUT
ました。ゴメンナサイ。♡
HER IN THIS CORNER. I'M SORRY. ♡

アニメ版CVは山川琴美さん。
IN THE ANIME, SHE IS VOICED BY KOTOMI YAMAKAWA-SAN. MY ASSISTANT MR IS A
アシスタントのMRが大ファンで。短波ラジオの番組まで
BIG FAN, AND EVEN CHECKS UP ON HER SHORT-WAVE RADIO PROGRAM. (LAUGH)
チェックしてました。(笑) 長身だけど声はロリ声♡
SHE'S VERY TALL, BUT HER VOICE IS EXTREMELY YOUNG AND ATTRACTIVE. ♡
ドラマ版は藤本泉さん。
IN THE DRAMA, SHE IS PLAYED BY IZUMI FUJIMOTO-SAN.
実はものすごい正統派美少女で。今後が楽しみです
SHE'S ACTUALLY A PRETTY EXTREMELY ORTHODOX SCHOOLGIRL. AND I LOOK
ネギまでは出番が少なくて残念。
FORWARD TO SEEING HER FUTURE WORK. IT'S TOO BAD SHE DIDN'T GET TO SHOW UP
IN *NEGIMA!* VERY OFTEN.

赤松 AKAMATSU

About the Creator

Negima! is only Ken Akamatsu's third manga, although he started working in the field in 1994 with *AI Ga Tomaranai* (released in the United States with the title *A.I. Love You*). Like all of Akamatsu's work to date, it was published in Kodansha's *Shonen Magazine*. *AI Ga Tomaranai* ran for five years before concluding in 1999. In 1998, however, Akamatsu began the work that would make him one of the most popular manga artists in Japan: *Love Hina*. *Love Hina* ran for four years, and before its conclusion in 2002, it would cause Akamatsu to be granted the prestigious Manga of the Year award from Kodansha, as well as going on to become one of the bestselling manga in the United States.

Translation Notes

Japanese is a tricky language for most Westerners, and translation is often more art than science. For your edification and reading pleasure, here are notes on some of the places where we could have gone in a different direction with our translation of the work, or where a Japanese cultural reference is used.

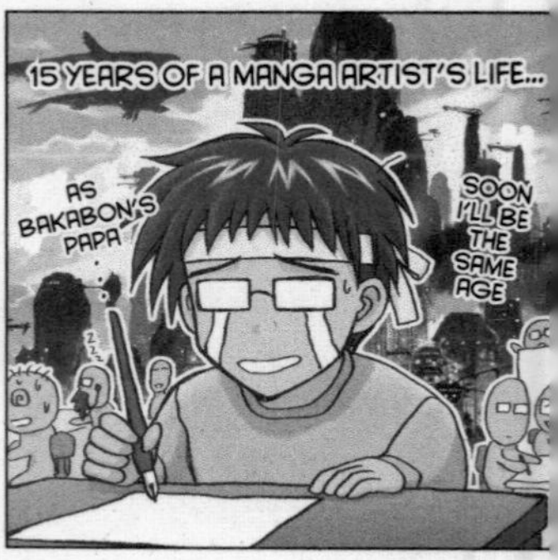
15 YEARS OF A MANGA ARTIST'S LIFE...
SOON I'LL BE THE SAME AGE
AS BAKABON'S PAPA

Bakabon's papa, page v

Bakabon is the main character of the anime *Tensai Bakabon* (*Genius Bakabon*). The main character is really his papa, who is forty-one years old.

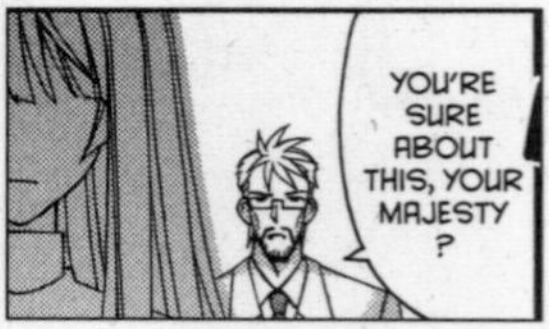
YOU'RE SURE ABOUT THIS, YOUR MAJESTY ?

Your Majesty, page 30

Until this point, everyone (except Nagi) called Arika "Your Highness," which is the proper form of address for a prince or princess. Now, Gateau addresses her as "Your Majesty," indicating that she is no longer a princess, but a queen.

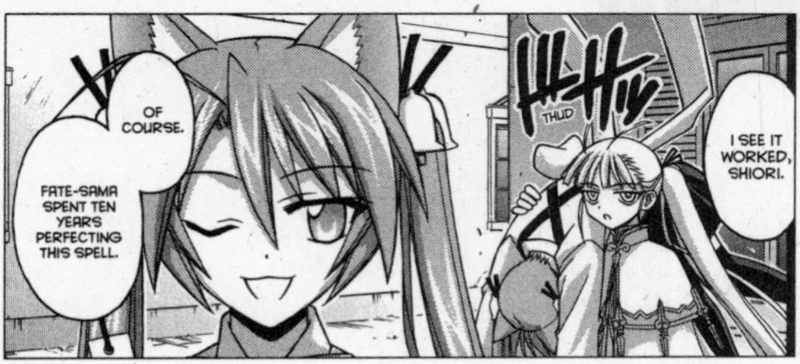
THUD
I SEE IT WORKED, SHIORI.
OF COURSE.
FATE-SAMA SPENT TEN YEAR'S PERFECTING THIS SPELL.

Homura and Shiori, page 41

As mentioned before, the name of each member of Fate's party has something to do with her artifact and/or magic power. *Homura* means "flame," and *shiori* means "bookmark."

I may be inexperienced, page 52

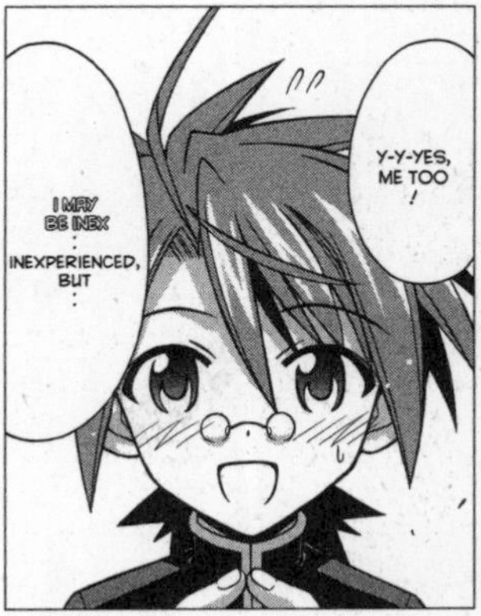
Y-Y-YES, ME TOO!
I MAY BE INEX ... INEXPERIENCED, BUT ...

What Negi says here is commonly said by newlyweds to their new spouse or their new in-laws as a sort of apology for not being perfect yet. Here, Negi is saying that he's not used to being a ninja's master, but there is a similarity.

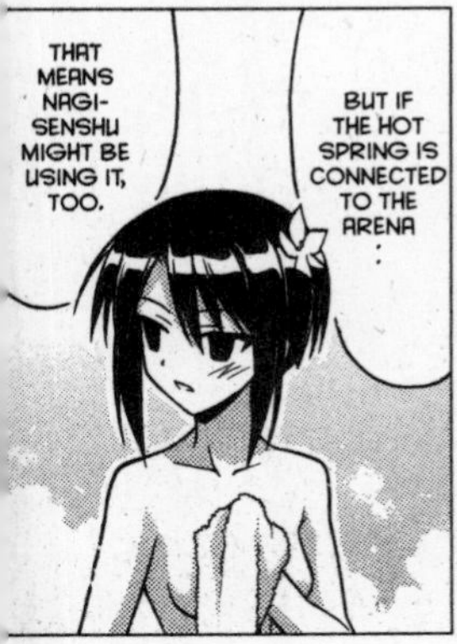
BUT IF THE HOT SPRING IS CONNECTED TO THE ARENA :
THAT MEANS NAGI-SENSHU MIGHT BE USING IT, TOO.

Senshu, page 66

Senshu is another title attached to people's names in order to show respect, like *sensei*. It is given to athletes, such as the fighters in this martial arts tournament. In the Magical World, they don't actually speak Japanese, so they are probably using their language's equivalent. Either way, it's a handy device for distinguishing "legendary hero Nagi" from "fighter in the tournament Nagi."

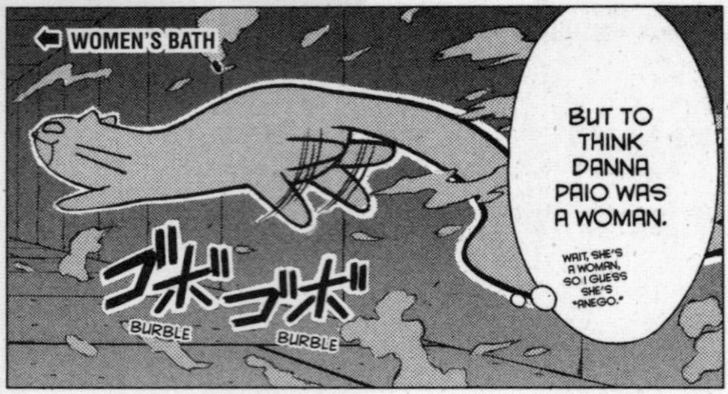
WOMEN'S BATH
BUT TO THINK DANNA PAIO WAS A WOMAN.
WAIT, SHE'S A WOMAN, SO I GUESS SHE'S "ANEGO."
ゴボゴボ
BURBLE
BURBLE

Danna and *anego*, page 71

Danna is a Japanese term of respect, roughly meaning "master." Chamo respects Paio Zi greatly as a kindred spirit, but since *danna* is used specifically for men, Chamo has to correct himself and use a female equivalent: *anego*.

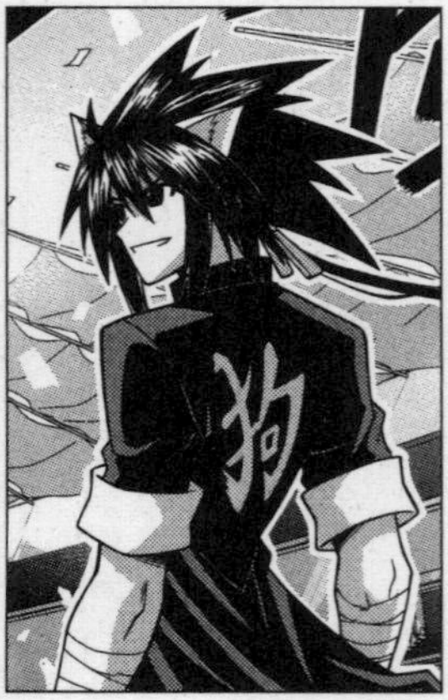

Kotarō's shirt, page 158

The Chinese character on the back of Kotarō's fancy new battle shirt means "dog," a fitting symbol for a dog boy like Kotarō.

Akira Ishida, page 167

As you may have figured out from the context, Akira Ishida is the voice actor who portrayed Fate in the *Negima!* anime, and he has come back to reprise the role in the new OADs coming out in Japan. He also happens to be the translators' very favorite Japanese voice actor.♡

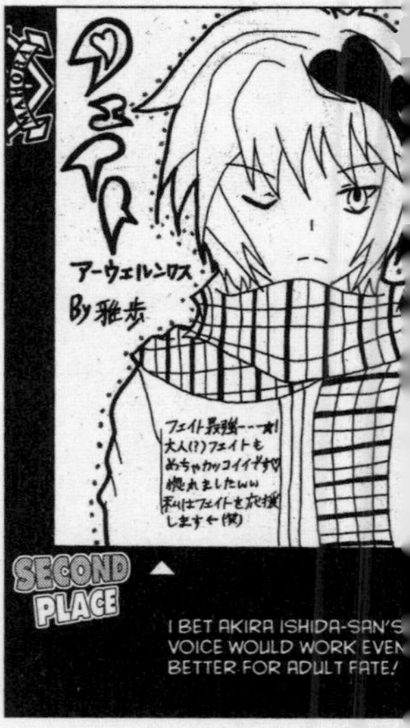
アーウェルンクス
By 雅歩
SECOND PLACE
I BET AKIRA ISHIDA-SAN'S VOICE WOULD WORK EVEN BETTER FOR ADULT FATE!

STORY BY KEN AKAMATSU
ART BY TAKUYA FUJIMA

BASED ON THE POPULAR ANIME!

Negi Springfield is only ten years old, but he's already a powerful wizard. After graduating from his magic school in England, the prodigy is given an unusual assignment: teach English at an all-girl school in Japan. Now Negi has to find a way to deal with his thirty-one totally gorgeous (and completely overaffectionate) students—without using magic! Based on the *Negima!* anime, this is a fresh take on the beloved *Negima!* story.

Available anywhere books or comics are sold!

S0-BOO-261

TOMARE!

[STOP!]

You're going the wrong way!

Manga is a completely different type of reading experience.

To start at the *beginning*, go to the *end*!

That's right! Authentic manga is read the traditional Japanese way—from right to left, exactly the *opposite* of how American books are read. It's easy to follow: Just go to the other end of the book, and read each page—and each panel—from right side to left side, starting at the top right. Now you're experiencing manga as it was meant to be.